# STUDIES IN CLASSICS

*Edited by*

## Dirk Obbink & Andrew Dyck

Oxford University/The University of California, Los Angeles

## A ROUTLEDGE SERIES

# STUDIES IN CLASSICS

DIRK OBBINK AND ANDREW DYCK, *General Editors*

# Simonides on the Persian Wars

## A Study of the Elegiac Verses
## of the "New Simonides"

Lawrence M. Kowerski

Routledge
New York & London

Published in 2005 by
Routledge
Taylor & Francis Group
270 Madison Avenue
New York, NY 10016

Published in Great Britain by
Routledge
Taylor & Francis Group
2 Park Square
Milton Park, Abingdon
Oxon, OX14 4RN

© 2005 by Taylor & Francis Group, LLC
Routledge is an imprint of Taylor & Francis Group.

Printed in the United States of America on acid-free paper.
10 9 8 7 6 5 4 3 2 1

International Standard Book Number-10: 0-415-97213-2 (Hardcover)
International Standard Book Number-13: 978-0-415-97213-0 (Hardcover)
Library of Congress Card Number 2005013702

### Library of Congress Cataloging-in-Publication Data

Kowerski, Lawrence M. (Lawrence Melvin), 1975–
    Simonides on the Persian Wars : a study of the elegiac verses of the "new Simonides" /
Lawrence M. Kowerski.
        p. cm. -- (Studies in classics)
    Includes bibliographical references (p.   ) and index.
    ISBN 0-415-97213-2 (acid-free paper)
    1. Simonides, ca. 556–467 B.C.--Criticism, Textual.   2. Greece--History--Persian Wars,
    500–449 B.C.--Literature and the wars.   3. Simonides, ca. 556–467 B.C.--Manuscripts.
    4. Simonides, ca. 556–467 B.C.--Authorship.   5. Elegiac poetry, Greek--Criticism,
    Textual.   6. Manuscripts, Greek (Papyri)   I. Title.   II. Studies in classics (Routledge
    (Firm))

PA4411.K69 2005
884'.01--dc22

2005013702

Taylor & Francis Group
is the Academic Division of T&F Informa plc.

Visit the Taylor & Francis Web site at
http://www.taylorandfrancis.com

and the Routledge Web site at
http://www.routledge-ny.com

*To Alison*

# Contents

# Abbreviations

The names of ancient authors and works are abbreviated according to the system used in Liddell-Scott-Jones, *A Greek-English Lexicon,* 9th ed., and Glare, *Oxford Latin Dictionary.*

The titles of journals and periodicals are abbreviated according to the conventions of *L'Année Philologique.*

Unless otherwise noted, all texts of ancient authors are cited according to the standard edition as found in the third edition of the *Oxford Classical Dictionary, A Greek-English Lexicon,* 9th ed., or *Oxford Latin Dictionary.*

| | |
|---|---|
| Adler | Adler, Ada, ed. 1928–1938. *Suidae Lexicon.* 5 vol. Stuttgart: Teubner. |
| *AP* | *Anthologia Palatina* |
| Beckby | Beckby, Hermann, ed. 1957–1958. *Anthologia Graeca.* 4 vol. Munich: Heimeran. |
| Bergk *PLG* 3$^4$ | Bergk, Theodor, ed. 1882. *Poetae Lyrici Graeci.* 4th ed. Vol. 3. Leipzig: Teubner. |
| Chantraine | Chantraine, Pierre. 1968–1980. *Dictionnaire étymologique de la langue grecque.* 4 vol. Paris: Klincksieck. |
| *CAF* | Kock, Theodor. 1880–1888. *Comicorum Atticorum Fragmenta.* 3 vol. Leipzig: Teubner. |
| *CAH* 5$^2$ | Lewis, D.M., *et. al.,* eds. 1992. *The Cambridge Ancient History.* Vol. 5. 2d ed. *The Fifth Century* B.C. Cambridge: Cambridge University Press |
| *CEG* | Hansen, Peter Allan, ed. 1983–1989. *Carmina Epigraphica Graeca.* 2 Vols. Berlin: Walter de Gruyter. |
| Diehl | Diehl, E., ed. 1949–1952. *Anthologia Lyrici Graeci.* 3d ed. Vol. 1. Leipzig: Teubner. |
| EM | Epigraphic Museum, Athens |
| FD | *Fouilles de Delphes.* Paris : De Boccard. |

FGE             Page, D. 1981. *Further Greek Epigrams*. Cambridge: Cambridge
                University Press.
FGrH            Jacoby, F. *et al.*, eds. 1923–. *Die Fragmente der griecheschen Histo-*
                *riker*. Berlin and Leiden: Weidmann and Brill.
Gentili-Prato   Gentili, Bruno, and Carlo Prato, ed. 1988–2002. *Poetarum Ele-*
                *giacorum: Testimonia et Fragmenta*. 2 vols. 2d ed. Vol. 1, Leipzig:
                Teubner; Vol. 2. Munich: Saur.
GHI             Tod, M. 1948–1951. *A Selection of Greek Historical Inscriptions;*
                Vol. 1, 2nd ed.; Vol. 2, 1st ed. Oxford: Clarendon Press.
GVI             Peek, Werner, ed. 1955. *Greek Verse Inscriptions*. Vol. 1. Berlin,
                1988 Reprint, Chicago: Ares.
IEG             West, M. L., ed. 1971–1972. *Iambi et Elegi Graeci*. 1st ed. 2
                Vols. Oxford: Oxford University Press.
IEG²            West, M. L., ed. 1989–1992. *Iambi et Elegi Graeci*. 2d ed. 2 Vols.
                Oxford: Oxford University Press.
IG              *Inscriptiones Graecae*
LSAG²           Jeffery, L. H. 1990. *The Local Scripts of Archaic Greece: A Study*
                *of the Origin of the Greek Alphabet and Its Development from the*
                *Eight to the Fifth Centuries B.C.* Rev. ed., with supplement by J.
                W. Johnston. Oxford: Clarendon Press.
LSJ             Liddell, H. G., R. Scott, and H. S. Jones, *Greek English Lexicon*,
                9th ed. Oxford: Clarendon Press.
M-L             Meiggs, Russell and David Lewis, eds. 1988. *A Selection of Greek*
                *Historical Inscriptions to the End of the Fifth Century B.C.* Oxford:
                Clarendon Press, 1975. Reprint, Oxford: Clarendon Press.
PCG             Kassel, R and C. Austin. 1983–. *Poetae Comici Graeci*. Berlin: De
                Gruyter.
PEG             Bernabé, Albert, ed. 1987. *Poetarum Epicorum Graecorum: Testi-*
                *monia et Fragmenta*. Leipzig: Teubner.
PMG             Page, D., ed. 1967. *Poetae Melici Graeci*. Oxford: Clarendon
                Press.
POxy            *Oxyrhynchus Papyri*. London : Published for the British Academy
                by the Egypt Exploration Society.
RE              Pauly-Wissowa, eds. 1893–1980. *Real-Encyclopädie der klassischen*
                *Altertumswissenschaft*. Stuttgart: Druckenmüller.
SEG             *Supplementum Epigraphicum Graeca*
SIG³            Dittenberger, Wilhelm. 1915–1924. *Sylloge Inscriptionum Grae-*
                *carum*. 3d ed. 4 vol. Ed. by Hiller von Gaertringen *et al.* Leipzig:
                Hirzelium.

| | |
|---|---|
| Smyth | Smyth, Herbert Weir. 1956. *A Greek Grammar.* Rev. by G. M. Messing. Cambridge, MA: Harvard University Press. |
| Snell-Maehler | Maehler, H. 1987–1989. *Pindari Carmina cum Fragmentis.* post B. Snell. 2 Vol. Leipzig: Teubner. |
| T | Testimonia |
| T . . . Campbell | Testimonia, Campbell, D. 1990–1993. *Greek Lyric.* 5 Vol. Loeb Classical Library. Cambridge, Mass.: Harvard University Press. |
| T . . . Gerber | Testimonia, Gerber, D. 1999. *Greek Elegiac Poetry: From the Seventh to the Fifth Centuries B.C.* Loeb Classical Library. Cambridge, Mass.: Harvard University Press. |
| W | West *IEG* |
| W$^2$ | West *IEG*$^2$ |
| Wendel | Wendel, Carl, ed. 1958. *Scholia in Apollonium Rhodium Vetera.* 2d ed. Berlin: Weidmann. |

# Series Editors' Foreword

*Studies in Classics* aims to bring high-quality work by emerging scholars to the attention of a wider audience. Emphasizing the study of classical literature and history, these volumes contribute to the theoretical understanding of human culture and society over time. This series offers an array of approaches to the study of Greek and Latin (including medieval and Neolatin), authors and their reception, canons, transmission of texts, ideas, religion, history of scholarship, narrative, and the nature of evidence.

While the focus is on Mediterranean cultures of the Greco-Roman era, perspectives from other areas, cultural backgrounds, and eras are included as important means to the reconstruction of fragmentary evidence and the exploration of models. The series reflects upon the role classical studies has played in humanistic endeavors from antiquity to the present, and explores select ways in which the discipline can bring both traditional scholarly tools and the experience of modernity to bear on questions and texts of enduring importance.

*Dirk Obbink, Oxford University*
*Andrew Dyck, The University of California, Los Angeles*

# Acknowledgments

The present study has gone through many stages. The idea originated in a course on Greek lyric poetry offered by Lowell Edmunds in the winter of 2000 at Rutgers, The State University of New Jersey. The seeds planted at this time would grow into a doctoral dissertation that was submitted to Rutgers in the summer of 2003. As is true for any academic endeavor, these seeds continued to grow. The pages the reader now has in hand are the product of this continued growth.

The completion of a dissertation is not a solitary effort, nor is the process of revision that creates a work suitable for a wider audience. The present work would not have been possible without the guidance and inspiration from many teachers, colleagues, and friends. Many a critical eye has been cast over parts or the entirety of this study at various points of its development. The influences of these readers will be found on every page. I would like to acknowledge the official readers of my dissertation, John Bodel (Brown University), David Sider (New York University) and Sarolta Takács (Rutgers University), who believed that the new fragments of Simonides were worthy of a second glance. I would also like to mention Thomas Figueira, whose comments on a part of an early draft of this project were extremely helpful. The comments of these scholars forced me to rethink some particularly tough issues and to reevaluate some of my more questionable positions at an early stage in this project. Special note must be given to the continued support by David Sider, who has been an invaluable resource and reader of this work as it has moved from a dissertation to its current form. Andy Dyck and Dirk Obbink, the editors of this series, as well as an anonymous reader provided thoughtful and detailed comments that were invaluable in the refinement of my ideas. While all factual, stylistic, and technical errors remain my own, it goes without saying that this project is better because of the insights of these scholars.

I also must thank Rutgers University for awarding me the Louis Bevier Fellowship which allowed the time and financial support needed to complete my dissertation. The revision of my dissertation was facilitated by the University of Cincinnati, where I spent a pleasant summer month as a Margot Tytus Fellow. In addition to the valuable resources of the Burnam Classics Library, this project benefited from the supportive conversations I had with Getzel Cohen, Kathryn Gutzwiller, and William Johnson during my stay at the University of Cincinnati.

I would like to also thank Michael Distefano who helped with the technical aspects concerning the digital images that facilitated much of this study. Much of the technical support that has allowed this project to appear in this final form came from the ICIT department at Hunter College. Without such help, this project would not have seen the light of day.

My greatest debt, however, is to my advisor and mentor, Lowell Edmunds. His belief that something new should be said about the "new Simonides" encouraged me to tackle these fragments. His perspicacity, careful criticism, meticulous editing and constant support have shaped this work in many ways. Much that may be considered useful in the following pages derived from on-going conversations with him. More importantly, my debt to Lowell extends well beyond this project. His teaching and encouragement of careful reading have been an inspiration. It is this inspiration that I hope is reflected in the following pages.

Finally, I come to my family and friends, whose continuous support has helped me in immeasurable ways. In particular, I mention Alison Distefano, my wife. Like all of those mentioned above, her careful criticism and insightful comments at every stage of this project have not only saved me from many mistakes but have also made me think more carefully about my own views on some of the tougher issues. Yet, more than anything, it has been her confidence in me that has furthered this project more than she knows.

# Introduction

*roges me quid aut quale sit deus, auctore utar Simonide, de quo cum quaesivisset*
*hoc idem tyrannus Hiero, deliberandi sibi unum diem postulavit; cum idem ex eo*
*postridie quaereret, biduum petivit; cum saepius duplicaret numerum dierum ad-*
*miransque Hiero requireret cur ita faceret, "quia quanto diutius considero" inquit*
*"tanto mihi res videtur obscurior"*

Cicero, *N. D.* 1.22.60

Should you ask me what god is or what kind of thing he is, I would use Simonides as an authority. When the tyrant Hiero had asked him this same thing,
he applied for one day for himself to deliberate. When, on the next day, Hiero
asked the same thing from him, he asked for two days. When he doubled the
number of days time and again and Heiro, in amazement, asked why he did
so, he replied, "Because the longer I deliberate, the more obscure the matter
seems to me."

Even before the publication of the new fragments of Simonides, this poet from Ceos
figured prominently in the ranks of the lyric nine. To the ancients his reputation
loomed large. It is as a poet for hire, a skinflint (κίμβιξ) according to Xenophanes,
with his mercenary muse that Simonides planted the poetics of the archaic period
firmly in the Classical age, along with the art of mnemonics. But the poetry was re-
spectable and Simonides, or *Melicertes* as he is nicknamed in the *Suda*, became a poet
of sweet, simple verses that above all evoked great pity. To modern critics, Simonides
is an innovator. Although the surviving fragments have given us only a glimpse of
the poet's corpus, they have justified his place in the history of early Greek poetry;
"Ibycus had himself formed a new combination of genres into a relatively cohesive
body of poetry . . . Anacreon had to some extent subverted tradition in irony, within
the poems; Simonides reworks the past with a larger ambition and wider scope."[1]
These judgments of G. O. Hutchinson reflect the importance assigned to Simonides
as a lyric poet. To be sure, in antiquity Simonides was also known as a composer of
elegies and was, in fact, famous as an epigrammatist. But too few elegiac fragments

survived and even fewer epigrams could be accepted as Simonidean for modern critics to make similar claims about the poet's work in these areas.

The papyrus fragments of elegiac verses given the name the "new Simonides" have gone a long way toward filling this gap in our knowledge. On many levels, these incomplete verses confirm the verdict given to Simonides' lyric compositions by showing the poet's interaction with and shaping of a poetic past. Importantly, these fragments also provide a tantalizing glimpse into Simonides' verses on the Persian Wars, about which our previous lack of knowledge was lamentable. So the "new Simonides" has promised to elucidate Simonidean elegy and to show us how elegy was used to commemorate the Persian Wars.

As Simonides would have told us, our good fortune must be tempered. It should be kept in mind that these glimpses into Simonides' elegies are far from complete. The "new Simonides" perhaps raises more questions than it answers about the elegies of Simonides and in particular his verses on the Persian Wars. The papyrus fragments are often not readily assignable to certain poems. Also, the text of the individual fragments is often not complete enough to discern what their content is. Furthermore, the surviving lyric verses of Simonides should keep us honest when confronting new fragments by revealing the difficulty of fitting the Cean poet into generic boundaries or recreating his verses within such limits. As I try to show, these caveats force us to rein in our zeal for this new evidence, but they do not diminish its importance.

## BACKGROUND

In 1992, P. J. Parsons published POxy 3965, thereby providing the *editio princeps* of the initial fragments of the "new Simonides."[2] The authorship of these fragments was determined through a series of overlaps with elegiac verses known to be by Simonides. POxy 3965 fr. 5 overlaps verses quoted by Plutarch and ascribed to Simonides (*de Herod. malign.* 872 D–E = frs. 15–16 W[2]); POxy 3965 fr. 26 overlaps verses quoted by Stobaeus also assigned to Simonides (4.34.28 = frs. 19–20 W[2]).[3] In addition, overlaps between POxy 3965 and POxy 2327, a set of papyri first edited by Edgar Lobel in 1954 but originally designated as *adespota*, further increased the number of new fragments that could be assigned to Simonides.[4] A reasonable conclusion is that these two groups of papyrus fragments represent copies of the same elegiac verses and poems. The "new Simonides," then, can be defined as the set of 81 fragments, which derive from POxy 2327, POxy 3965, the quotations that these new fragments overlap, and the possible *testimonia* for the poems represented by these fragments. It is in this form that the "new Simonides" was first published in its entirety by M. L. West in the second edition of his *Iambi et Elegi Graeci*, volume two.[5]

These new fragments are important for a variety of reasons. First, the acquisition of new verses of one of the major early lyric poets, whose work has not survived in any extensive way, provides a light in the darkness of archaic poetry. The position of Simonides as a poet who bridges both the archaic and the classical periods perhaps heightens interest in new verses by him for literary critics and historians alike.[6] But, this interest in these new verses is increased because Simonides is a poet whose reputation greatly surpasses the remnants of his literary output. He was known as the first poet for hire and became subsequently known for his avarice.[7] He is closely associated with the art of memory.[8] Simonides is also found in connection with prominent figures throughout Greece: the Pisistratids and Themistocles at Athens;[9] the Scopadae in Thessaly;[10] the Spartans and Pausanias, the Spartan leader at the battle of Plataea;[11] Gelon and Hieron in Sicily.[12] Simonides' ties to numerous locations in Greece are further attested by his epinicians.[13] His relations with other poets were also part of his reputation. He is reported to have quarreled with Timocreon and Pindar.[14] He may also have defeated Aeschylus in a contest involving the composition of elegiac verses on Marathon, a competition which is said to have resulted in Aeschylus' travel to Sicily.[15] This survey, by no means comprehensive, serves to demonstrate the large amount of attention Simonides generated as a literary figure in antiquity.

In terms of his poetry Simonides was known for his simplicity, sweetness and sadness, evaluations that are usually linked to his prominence as a poet of verses in lyric meters.[16] The more substantial remains of Simonides' lyric poetry, such as the Danaë fragment (543 *PMG*), the verses to Scopas quoted by Plato (542 *PMG*) and the fragment on the dead of Thermopylae (531 *PMG*), provide sufficient evidence to reveal how tantalizingly incomplete our knowledge of Simonides' lyric poetry is. Simonides was also known as an epigrammatist and at some point a collection of Simonidean epigrams, mostly spurious, was compiled.[17] While epigrams and lyric poems form the bulk of our knowledge of Simonides' poetic work, non-epigrammatic elegiac poems are also known to have been part of his corpus. It is for this part of the Simonidean corpus that the "new Simonides" is a most valuable piece of evidence. Before the publication of the "new Simonides," the first edition of West's *IEG* collected only 17 fragments of elegiac verse that could be reasonably assigned to Simonides. The identification of Simonides as the author of POxy 2327 and 3965 has increased this number of elegiac fragments more than fivefold.

While the "new Simonides" fills a large gap in our knowledge of Simonides' poetic output, the perceived content of these fragments is perhaps more important. Before the new fragments, Simonides was known to have composed three types of elegiac verses. First, there were the epigrams noted above. Second, there were verses assigned to a sympotic context because of their convivial content. Third, it was reported that Simonides composed elegies, as well as lyric poems, on the Persian Wars. It is these second two types of elegiac verses that the "new Simonides" has promised to elucidate.

In terms of verses on the Persian Wars, modern scholarship assumes that the "new Simonides" is evidence for three separate elegies on the Persian Wars: one on the battle of Artemisium, which the *Suda* lists as an elegy (= frs. 1–4 W$^2$); one on the battle of Salamis (= frs. 5–9 W$^2$), which the *Suda* lists as a lyric poem; and one on the battle of Plataea (=frs. 10–18 W$^2$), which was previously unknown. In terms of sympotic elegies, the "new Simonides" also includes fragments of an undetermined number of poems on themes suitable for performance at a symposium (= frs. 19–22, 27–33 W$^2$), of which thirteen verses were previously known from Stobaeus.

It is with the verses assigned to the poems on the Persian War that this survey is primarily concerned. Specifically, this study reconsiders the arrangement of the new fragments on the Persian Wars in an effort to provide a foundation for rethinking the interpretation of the poem(s) they represent. From this analysis, it will emerge that the current orthodoxy concerning the "new Simonides" raises as many questions as it answers about the poet's treatment of the Persian Wars. I shall argue that the "new Simonides" cannot be shown to represent separate poems on specific battles in the Persian Wars. I will suggest instead that the fragments must be confronted initially as part of an as-yet undetermined poem. While the emphasis here lies on the so-called historical fragments, such a reconsideration must also question the grounds on which all of the fragments of the "new Simonides" are separated from each other.

It is from this starting point that an interpretation of these fragments can best avoid the pitfalls that surround the study of incomplete texts and fragmentary verses. When poetic fragments are concerned, identification of content or the assignment of verses to certain contexts, genres, or specific poems is a slippery task that often involves slight-of-hand maneuvers and dangerous circular arguments to make a remotely plausible suggestion. The difficulty of this task is enhanced when knowledge of the works and even the genres to which the fragments belong is incomplete and confused, as is the case with Simonides' Persian War poems. The aim here, then, is to analyze the "new Simonides" by divorcing it from these problems as much as possible. The approach that best suits this aim is to attempt to define the content, context and genre of specific fragments by internal clues in the fragments rather than by a perceived association with a certain poem. It is hoped that by approaching the fragments in this way some of the confusion surrounding Simonides' work in particular and archaic elegy in general can be untangled.

## THE PROBLEM

The *Suda* entry on Simonides (Σ 439 Adler = 532, 536 PMG = *IEG*$^2$ 2, p. 114 = T1 Campbell) provides a convenient starting point for understanding the difficulties involved in reconstructing Simonides' Persian War poems from fragmentary evidence. The entry occupies a central place in modern scholarship on these poems because it provides a *testimonium* for what appear, at first glance, to be five works directly or indirectly pertaining to the Persian Wars: *The Kingship of Cambyses, The Kingship of Darius* and *The Sea-battle of Xerxes* in the Doric dialect, or lyric poems, an elegiac *The Sea-battle at Artemisium,* and a lyric *The Sea-battle at Salamis.* There are, however, real problems in this list, as we shall see when we examine the Greek text below. Still, by correcting certain details, scholars have used this list as a blueprint to assign various fragments to the specific poems mentioned in it. In what follows, the general nature of the *Suda* and its sources will be considered briefly in order to provide a background for understanding the difficulties present in the entry on Simonides. Then, the specific difficulties in the entry on Simonides will be addressed. Finally, the problems that these difficulties raise for assigning the fragments of the "new Simonides" to specific poems and for reconstructing Simonides' poems on the Persian Wars in general will be set out.

## The Suda *and Its Predecessors*

The *Suda* is the title given to a Byzantine encyclopedic work compiled in the tenth century CE.[18] It contains some 30,000 articles ranging from short lexical notes to longer historical entries on people, places, and concepts. Much of the information found in the *Suda* is invaluable because oftentimes it can be found nowhere else. Yet, the way in which the *Suda* was composed forces us to use it with caution. The *Suda* ultimately is a compilation of compilations because its information is drawn from earlier biographical and bibliographical lexica such as the *Onomatologos* of Hesychius of Miletus or extracts of works taken out of context, such as the *Excerpta* of Constantine VII "Porphyrogenitus" (b.905–d.959). Most, if not all, of the articles consist of information culled from such earlier lexica, biographies and bibliographies, compilations of extracts, and epitomes of compilations, rather than from direct consultation of the relevant ancient texts. It is unlikely, then, that the compiler or compilers of the *Suda* actually knew the poems of Simonides on the Persian Wars firsthand, even if they still would have had access to them.

This method of composition has allowed many avenues by which mistakes could enter into an entry in the *Suda*. Such mistakes could arise through omissions that are the very nature of excerpting, through inadequately following these sources, or through simple ignorance of the author's works. It is often difficult to pinpoint exactly when and how such mistakes made their way into the information that is found in the *Suda*. Many of the details had been compiled as early as the third century BCE at Alexandria and had passed through various sources before they reached the compilers of the *Suda*. It is also clear that these compilers further abbreviated the material available before it entered the *Suda*. For this reason, the best way to explain confused details in the *Suda* is to recognize and understand its sources. Unfortunately, such understanding is often difficult because massive works such as the *Suda* had supplanted many of these earlier works. Along with ancient works such as Simonides' poems on the Persian wars, the sources of the *Suda's* information for these poems are also lost save for their citation, often in abbreviated forms, in this larger compilation. Yet, scholars of the 19th and early 20th centuries produced much scholarship devoted to the *Quellenforschung* of lexical or encyclopedic works such as the *Suda*, the fruits of which research are still extremely valuable.

In her edition and subsequent article s.v. "Suidas" in *Pauly-Wissowa*, A. Adler provides a thorough elucidation of the sources of the *Suda*.[19] For the biographical and bibliographical information pertaining to ancient poets and prose authors, an epitome of the *Onomatologos* of Hesychius of Miletus, the lives of comic poets found in Athenaeus, Diogenes Laertius' work on the lives and thoughts of ancient philosophers, the biography of Apollonius and the lives of the Sophists by Philostratus, the life of Isidore by Damascius, the life of Proclus by Marinus, and a life of Pythagoras which is the same source used by Photius *Bibliothecae* 239 (Bekker 438–441) have been identified as the principal sources of the *Suda*.[20] As will be seen, much of the information in these works will have derived directly or indirectly from Alexandrian efforts such as the *Pinakes* of Callimachus.[21] The focus here allows this field to be narrowed even further. The most important of these for the lives and bibliographies of early poets is the epitome of the *Onomatologos* of Hesychius. It is most certainly the *Onomatologos* that is the source of the article on Simonides (Σ 439 Adler).

Hesychius of Miletus, or Hesychius *Illustrius,* was a historian and biographer during the sixth century CE who compiled a biographical lexicon of Greek authors.[22] Under the entry "Hesychios" (**H** 611 Adler), the *Suda* gives the name of this work as the "*Onomatologos* or lists of those renowned in learning." The entry also tells us that the *Suda* is an epitome of this work.[23] Except for these citations of this epitome the work is entirely lost.[24] Nevertheless, from such citations, the information included by Hesychius in his entries becomes clear. When the information was available, these entries include the following, usually in order: name of author, ethnicity, primary literary genre of an author, parents, children, teacher, pupils, period and area of activity, contemporaries, special aspects of the person's life, manner of death, and finally a list of works.[25] Other types of information might include nicknames with explanations for their origins, social class of parents, inventions made by the person, extent of a work and the dialect in which certain works were written.[26] It is generally accepted that the epitome of the *Onomatologos* listed authors alphabetically as the *Suda* does. It is not certain, however, whether Hesychius himself employed an alphabetical order, or listed authors primarily by class of writing, as earlier lists such as the *Pinakes* of Callimachus would have done.[27] This debate highlights an important aspect of our knowledge of the *Onomatologos*. While the format of entries in the *Suda* usually makes it clear which are derived from the *Onomatologos*, the extent of Hesychius' articles is no longer known. Often, the bibliographic record in the *Suda* will conclude with the phrases ἔγραφε πόλλα or καὶ ἄλλα. It is uncertain whether the Suda, the epitomator of Hesychius, or both shortened what may have been much fuller entries in the *Onomatologos*. Hesychius himself also may have included such phrases in abbreviating the fuller information of his sources.

R. Blum has suggested that Hesychius, unlike the *Suda*, actually conducted his own research.[28] The primary justification for this conclusion is the entry in the *Suda* for Damophilus (Δ 52), which derives from Hesychius. In this entry, the author states he has consulted libraries and found various works of Damophilus. While Blum's conclusion is reasonable, it is also possible that, like the *Suda*, Hesychius also has transferred this information directly from one of his sources.

Much in Hesychius' *Onomatologos* on the lives of lyric poets such as Simonides will have come from Dionysius "Musicus" of Halicarnassus. Dionysius "Musicus" is a shadowy figure from late antiquity. The *Suda* (Δ 1171 Adler) tells us that he lived under the reign of Hadrian (i.e. the first half of the second century CE) and that he composed three treatises on musical topics, hence the epithet "Musicus."[29] Among these works on music is a μουσικὴ ἱστορία, a work in 36 books, which is generally agreed to have been the principal source for Hesychius' lives of Greek poets.[30] The work, however, survives only through a few citations.[31] Photius cod. 161 (Bekker 103) tells us that Sopater, a fourth century CE writer who composed an ἐκλογαὶ διαφοροι, used a μουσικὴ ἱστορία written by a certain Rufus as a source. This work by Rufus is believed to have been an epitome of the work by Dionysius "Musicus," listed by the same heading μουσικὴ ἱστορία in the Suda.[32] From this link, then, a picture of what information was in Rufus' epitome emerges; therefore, we can tell what information Dionysius "Musicus" may have conveyed in his work. Photius tells us that Rufus included references to tragic, comic and lyric poets. Rufus also mentioned the origins, the family of authors and whether the authors were friends of kings. He told what a particular author invented and at what festivals the authors competed. It is also likely that the list of works, along with specific numbers of verses or books, which appear in the *Suda* articles that derive from Hesychius, can be traced back to Dionysius "Musicus."[33]

The type of material in the *Suda* that can be traced back to Dionysius "Musicus," in particular the indication of name, fatherland, parents, type of poetry written, age of poet, and the precise naming of songs, led A. Daub to conclude that the most reasonable source for this information is the *Pinakes* of Callimachus.[34] Callimachus of Cyrene, the prolific scholar and poet, who was active in Alexandria during the third century BCE, compiled lists, or *pinakes,* that formed a bibliography of Greek literature and ultimately detailed the collection of literature housed at the Museum in Alexandria. The *Suda* entry on Callimachus (K 227 Adler) tells us that Callimachus composed three sets of such lists: the *Pinakes,* which were "lists of all who had distinguished themselves in learning" in 120 books, a list of playwrights, arranged chronologically, and a list of glosses and writings of Democritus. It is the first of these that are a concern here because they are believed to be the ultimate source of much of the information that has come down to us in the *Suda* through Hesychius and Dionysius "Musicus."

The importance of the *Pinakes* is attested by the continued production of similar works, such as the works of Hermippus, the student of Callimachus, Diogenes Laertius, Dionysius "Musicus," Hesychius of Miletus, Photius' *Bibliotheca,* and the *Suda,* to name but a few. The *Pinakes* are the most cited of Callimachus' works.[35] From these citations, it is possible to reconstruct in part the type of information the *Pinakes* would have contained. Callimachus arranged the authors in the *Pinakes* according to type of writer; that is, philosophers, orators, historians, and so on, would be listed in their own *pinax*.[36] It is uncertain how the authors within a class were arranged (i.e. whether orators or philosophers were listed alphabetically as they would later come to be) or how the authors who wrote in more that one genre were handled.[37] It is generally agreed that some biographical details about each author would have been given, although the extent of this information is debated.[38] It seems likely that the biographical data given by Callimachus included details such as a patronym, birthplace, teachers and the students of the author, nicknames and how they were acquired.[39] Caution, however, is needed. Since none of the citations of the *Pinakes* is a direct quote, we do not know exactly how much biographical information was actually included.[40] It is not certain how much of this information would have been added by later Alexandrians, who are likely to have continued Callimachus' *Pinakes* or to have developed these efforts in separate biographical works, such as Hermippus the "Callimachean," or how much was mixed into the information Callimachus did provide by even later writers. As primarily a bibliographic record of the holdings of the Alexandrian library, the *Pinakes* would have contained lists of each author's work by title. It is not certain how these titles were arranged. Even more uncertain is how titles were assigned to works, especially the titles of lyric poems which, as far as we know, were not usually given titles by their authors.[41] Moreover, Callimachus not only provided titles, but he also gave the first line of a work and the number of lines that a work contained.[42]

In almost every case, it is impossible to determine with certainty whether the information Callimachus or his successors provided would have been found in Dionysius "Musicus," and so would have found its way into Hesychius' *Onomatologos,* and then, by way of the epitome of the *Onomatologos,* would have made it into the *Suda.* In tracing such information back to its source, it becomes apparent that there are too many unknowns and too many points at which the original information, say that of Callimachus or Hermippus, could have been added to, deleted, or simply misunderstood; therefore, it is difficult for us to know with certainty where a list such as the one in the *Suda's* entry on Simonides originated. Nevertheless, the *Pinakes* of Callimachus and the works of the next generation of Alexandrians were important and influential. So while we cannot be certain that the exact information derives from this fountainhead, it is reasonable to suggest that in form and in content these early Alexandrian works were the model for those later compilations that we can say with more certainty did provide the *Suda* with its information.

The preceding discussion has not been an attempt to provide a comprehensive overview of the history of the collection and transmission of information by early scholars from the Hellenistic period through the Byzantine era.[43] Rather, what I hope has emerged is that the type of information that often appears in the *Suda* has its origins in other works which may have been more, and sometimes less, systematic than the *Suda* in presenting details about people of note. By setting out the type of information that earlier bibliographic and biographic works would have transmitted and the various ways in which this information would have been handled before it reached the *Suda*, it is now possible to suggest some ways of explaining the difficulties that are present in the *Suda* entry on Simonides.

## *The* Suda *on Simonides*

It is worth repeating that that the *Suda* entry on Simonides (Σ 439 Adler= 532, 536 PMG = *IEG*² 2, p. 114 = T1 Campbell) is one of the key pieces of evidence used in reconstructing the Persian War poems. The value of the entry lies in the fact that it gives a list, albeit an incomplete and corrupt one, of these poems:

Σιμωνίδης, Λεωπρεποῦς, Ἰουλιήτης τῆς ἐν Κέῳ τῇ νήσῳ πόλεως, λυρικός, μετὰ Στησίχορον τοῖς χρόνοις· ὃς ἐπεκλήθη Μελικέρτης διὰ τὸ ἡδύ. καὶ τὴν μνημονικὴν δὲ τέχνην εὗρεν οὗτος· προσεξεῦρε δὲ καὶ τὰ μακρὰ τῶν στοιχείων καὶ διπλᾶ καὶ τῇ λύρᾳ τὸν τρίτον φθόγγον. γέγονε δ᾽ ἐπὶ τῆς πεντηκοστῆς ἕκτης ὀλυμπιάδος, οἱ δὲ ξβ΄ γεγράφασι. καὶ παρέτεινε μέχρι τῆς οη΄, βιοὺς ἔτη πθ΄, καὶ γέγραπται αὐτῷ Δωρίδι διαλέκτῳ ἡ Καμβύσου καὶ Δαρείου βασιλεία καὶ Ξέρξου ναυμαχία καὶ ἡ ἐπ᾽ Ἀρτεμισίῳ ναυμαχία δι᾽ ἐλεγείας, ἡ δ᾽ ἐν Σαλαμῖνι μελικῶς· θρῆνοι, ἐγκώμια, ἐπιγράμματα, παιᾶνες καὶ τραγῳδίαι καὶ ἄλλα.[44]

Simonides; son of Leoprepes; from Iulis, the city on the island of Ceos; a lyric poet; later in time than Stesichorus; he was called Melicertes because of his sweetness. He also discovered the mnemonic art; and in addition he discovered long vowels, double consonants, and the third note on the lyre. He was born in the 56th Olympiad, but some write the 62nd. He lived until the 78th, having lived 89 years. He wrote in the Doric dialect *The Kingship of Cambyses* and *Darius* and *The Sea-battle of Xerxes,* and *The Sea-battle at Artemisium* in elegiacs, and *The Sea-battle at Salamis* in lyric meter; he wrote dirges, encomia, epigrams, paeans, tragedies, and other works.

Taking the *Suda* at face value, we can conclude that Simonides composed five poems directly or indirectly pertaining to the Persian Wars: *The Kingship of Cambyses* and *The Kingship of Darius* and *The Sea-battle of Xerxes* in the Doric dialect, that is, lyric poems, an elegiac *The Sea-battle at Artemisium,* and a lyric *The Sea-battle at Salamis.* Although modern scholarship has not accepted the existence of all of these poems, it is still against the backdrop of this list that Simonides poems on the Persian Wars are reconstructed. There are, however, three large difficulties that force us to approach the *Suda* with more caution than is generally used.

The first difficulty, which has been noted by all scholars who have confronted Simonides since the 19th century, is the mention of ἡ Καμβύσου καὶ Δαρείου βασιλεία καὶ Ξέρξου ναυμαχία, presumably as titles of poems. There is no record of these poems and it is unlikely that they ever were composed by Simonides. The problem was observed already by Bergk in *Poetae Lyrici Graeci* and by Bernhardy in his edition of the *Suda.* The resolution proposed by both was to read these words not as titles but as an indication of the Simonides' period of activity or life-span.[45] The dates of Simonides' life are disputed and the result is that chronological arguments are often shaky when it comes to him. Yet, the traditionally accepted dates of his life, 556–468 BCE, and the alternative for his birth, 532 BCE, allow for the suggestion that the *Suda* records an indication of time that is relevant to Simonides' life;[46] the words, ἡ Καμβύσου καὶ Δαρείου βασιλεία will refer roughly to Simonides early life and Ξέρξου ναυμαχία will be an approximation of the later part of his life.[47] To accept this conclusion, however, it must be assumed that the Greek of the *Suda* is corrupt. In the *IEG²,* M. L. West follows this thinking and offers an attempt at explaining what has dropped out of the *Suda.* He proposes that the source of the *Suda* may have recorded the periods in which Simonides composed certain works in certain meters. He also provides a possible text (*exempli gratia*) for the words that the *Suda*'s source may have contained: γέγραφε δὲ Δωρίδι διαλέκτῳ, κατὰ τὴν Καμβύσου καὶ Δαρείου βασιλείαν, καὶ κατὰ τὴν Ξέρξου τὰς ναυμαχίας τήν τε ἐπ' Ἀρτεμισίῳ δι' ἐλεγείας τήν τ' ἐν Σαλαμῖνι μελικῶς. For West, then, Simonides composed in the Doric dialect κατὰ τὴν Καμβύσου καὶ Δαρείου βασιλείαν ("at the time of the kingship of Cambyses and Darius"), and κατὰ Ξέρξου ναυμαχίαν ("at the time of the sea-battle of Xerxes") he composed the sea-battle poems, namely the elegiac *Sea-battle at Artemisium* and the melic *Sea-battle at Salamis.* Thus, West suggests that the references are to the periods in which Simonides composed certain poems (the Persian War poems at the time of the sea-battle of Xerxes) and in certain meters (in the Doric dialect, at the time of the kingship of Cambyses and Darius).

Some difficulties, however, remain. First, it is not entirely clear how the original compilers of this list, either Callimachus or others who followed him, would have known the dates of Simonides' compositions or if they would have arranged his works in this way. To be sure, the poems on the Persian Wars can be put into chronological order by subject matter, but an exact time of composition cannot be gained for Simonides' other compositions. In fact, it is only possible to arrange Simonides' poems on the Persian Wars chronologically by time of composition if the original composition followed closely on the events these poems depicted. At least some of Simonides' verses on the Persian Wars seem to have been composed at a time near to the particular battles that they describe.[48] It may be that Simonides was regularly commissioned to compose such poems soon after an event and so a particular poem could be dated. For the Persian War poems, at least, this connection to an event, and moreover a time, may have become the feature that was used to arrange these works in a larger list or an edition of Simonides' works.[49]

Problems still remain, however, for Simonides' lyric compositions, for which a date of composition may have been more difficult for the Alexandrian scholars to ascertain. There may be some evidence for arranging poetic works chronologically in lists of works by a particular author. In particular, it appears to have been natural for Attic drama to be listed chronologically. Chronological records of Attic drama, or the *Didaskalia,* have survived in a fragmentary inscription that goes back to the fifth century BCE, although it was probably compiled sometime after 288 BCE.[50] This emphasis on chronology in a list of drama may have made its way into to later lists of author's works. A particular example is available in a list of plays by Aristophanes, first edited by F. Novati in 1879.[51] This list provides an alphabetically arranged catalogue, conveniently called the "Novati Index." In the same year, Wilamowitz observed that titles beginning with the same letter are further arranged chronologically.[52] Within this alphabetical arrangement of Aristophanes' works there appears to be the remnants of a chronological arrangement as well. This observation has suggested that this list, which is traced back to the *Pinakes* of Callimachus, represents an alphabetization of what originally was a chronological arrangement of an author's works in the library at Alexandria. In such an arrangement, groups of works, such as trilogies and tetralogies, would be kept together, while in an alphabetical arrangement they would be separated.[53] We cannot be certain, however, that the chronological arrangement in the Novati Index observed by Wilamowitz goes back to an Alexandrian list that was so arranged; therefore, the Novati Index is not an exact parallel for identifying chronology as the defining feature of lists of works by poets who composed other types of poetry. Moreover, it seems that chronology was not a factor in arranging many of Simonides' compositions. His epinicians appear to have been grouped by athletic event and further differentiated by the laudandus of the poem.[54] His *threnoi* and *encomia* may also have been differentiated by addressee.[55] Strabo mentions a dithyramb by Simonides entitled the *Memnon* in a collection he calls the *Deliaca,* or "(Dithyrambs) composed in Delos."[56] It appears, then, that the dithyrambs of Simonides were arranged by original location of performance.[57] Simonides' lyric compositions not on the Persian Wars do not seem to have been arranged chronologically in an Alexandrian edition. It would seem to follow that an emphasis on chronology of composition would not be found in a list of Simonides' works that perhaps derives from the efforts of Alexandrian scholars. Nevertheless, it should be remembered that the categorization of many of Simonides' compositions remains unknown to us; therefore, we do not known how these compositions were included in either an Alexandrian edition of Simonides' works or how they would have been included in a catalogue of these works. It must stand that such emphasis on the chronology of Simonides' works in the *Suda* remains speculative.

Another difficulty with the solution proposed by Bergk and followed by West is that the dating of literary compositions according to meter within an author's lifetime seems to be anomalous to the entry on Simonides. To be sure, authors could be dated by the works which they produced. The Ambrosian *vita Pindari* (= *post* Simon. fr. 4 W²) dates Simonides and Pindar in relation to each other by referring to their literary works.[58] But this dating is not the same as that proposed by Bergk and West as corrections to the *Suda*. The arrangement of an author's works according to the time period in which he or she composed in a specific meter remains an anomaly.

While for many reasons, the solution of either Bergk or West has seemed to make satisfactory sense of problems in the *Suda,* both highlight the difficulty of obtaining accurate information from this entry on Simonides. If, however, it is accepted that the *Suda* includes a confused reference to the time periods in which Simonides was active in certain meters, West's thinking, with some modifications, can be pushed a bit further. In particular, it is possible that the *Suda* includes references to three periods of time. That is, perhaps ἡ Καμβύσου καὶ Δαρείου βασιλεία καὶ Ξέρξου ναυμαχία indicate three distinct periods of time instead of the two proposed by West. If this suggestion is accepted, then, compositions that would fit into each period must be found. In fact, Simonides is credited with compositions that can be divided chronologically by the periods of the kingships of Cambyses, Darius, and Xerxes. West's *exempli gratia* provides for the compositions during the reign of Xerxes. These are the sea-battle poems on Artemisium and Salamis. The *vita Aeschyli* 8, however, records a composition that would fit well in the kingship of Darius. The *vita* tells us that, in one version of the story, Aeschylus went to the court of Hieron because he was defeated by Simonides in a contest for an *elegeion* for those who died at Marathon (ἐν τῷ εἰς τοὺς ἐν Μαραθῶνι τεθνηκότας ἐλεγείῳ).[59] It is not clear whether the word *elegeion* here means an elegy or an epigram. Both meanings are possible.[60] If we accept the story that the verses in question were performed in a public competition, it is more likely that Aeschylus and Simonides had composed elegiac poems and not simply short epigrams.[61] Yet, given Simonides' special connection with epigrams, particularly those on the Persian Wars, and the particular importance of the battle of Marathon, especially in the eyes of the Athenians, we should not wonder that an elegiac epigram would be assigned such importance that it could be listed among Simonides' other verses on the Persian Wars as a separate work. So, whether the *vita* refers to an elegy or an epigram is not of issue here. Nevertheless, the possible existence of verses on Marathon in some elegiac form provides an intriguing suggestion for how to explain part of the difficulty in the *Suda*. If we assume the existence of such elegiac verses, it is possible that at some point one of the *Suda*'s sources mentioned this composition. Following this line of thinking, we can modify West's suggested text and propose that following <κατὰ> Δαρείου βασιλεία some reference was made to a composition on Marathon perhaps as τὸν τῷ εἰς τοὺς ἐν Μαραθῶνι τεθνηκότας ἐλεγεῖον or the like.

But, then, what about the Δωρίδι διαλέκτῳ ἡ Καμβύσου . . . βασιλεία? As was noted above, the arrangement of Simonides' lyric compositions not on the Persian Wars by meter and time of composition raises serious questions. It should be remembered, however, that the *Suda* notes that Simonides' fame was primarily for his "sweetness" as a lyric poet and this estimation is confirmed by other ancient sources.[62] The loss of most of Simonides' poetry does not allow us to make any definitive claims on this score. Although we know so little about many of Simonides' lyric poems and their relation to an original performance, it is constructive to hazard a few guesses concerning which poems might be categorized by this heading in the *Suda*. If we believe the *testimonia* of the pseudo-Plato *Hipparchus* 228C (Anacr. T 6 Campbell) and the *Athenaion Politeia* 18.1 (Simon. T 10 Campbell), Simonides was summoned to Athens during the reign of Hipparchus (between 527–514 BCE). Since the reign of Cambyses ends with his death in 522 BCE, it is possible to construe one of Simonides' lyric compositions from this period as missing from the *Suda* entry following ἡ Καμβύσου . . . ᾿βασιλεία.[63] If any composition from this period was linked with an historical event, it is possible that it too, as the later Persian War poems may have been, was placed in a chronological list. It might also be suggested that the poems by Simonides for the Thessalian Scopadae (i.e. fr. 542 *PMG*) or Echecralidias (fr. 529 *PMG*) fit into this category. Yet, as was noted above, Simonides' *threnos* which he composed for one of the Echecratidae would likely have been arranged in another way.[64] Moreover, the dating of these rulers and Simonides' connection with them is far too uncertain.[65] Any of the other numerous lyric poems for which we have fragments but no certain context such as the Danaë poem quoted by Dionysius of Halicarnassus (Simon. fr. 543 *PMG* = *Comp.* 26) may also fit into this period. Unfortunately, we simply do not know enough about such compositions to know how they would have been arranged in an edition or a list of works.

Admittedly, the above suggestions are speculative and, in fact, they are built on supplements of a corrupt text. However, the conclusion that should be underscored is that it is possible that the *Suda* perhaps omits more than is currently allowed.

Furthermore, it should be seen that it is possible to square the information in the *Suda* with the type of information its sources would have provided. The presence of dialects and the reference to exact works is consistent with the type of information that Heyschius provided, to whom this entry is generally assigned. Dionysius "Musicus" may also have provided this information, as is seen in Photius cod. 161 (Bekker 103). In fact, Callimachus or one of his successors may be the source of the *Suda*'s information. It is sufficient to note that the list in the entry on Simonides potentially shares features with other bibliographic lists compiled by the *Suda*'s sources. By understanding the way in which these sources presented information, it then becomes possible to make suggestions, such as the ones made above, about what type of information is hidden behind the confusion in the *Suda*'s reference to the kingship of Cambyses and Darius. Yet, with these suggestions in mind, it must be admitted that the *Suda* entry is a malleable starting point for identifying various works by Simonides to which fragments without attribution to specific poems can be assigned.

The second bit of confusion, which has also been observed by all scholars working with Simonides' Persian War poems, involves the metrical descriptions given by the *Suda* to *The Sea-battle at Artemisium* and *The Sea-battle at Salamis*. In the *Suda*, these are said to be an elegy and a lyric poem respectively. Priscian, the fifth/sixth-century CE grammarian, however, quotes a poem on Artemisium by Simonides as a lyric poem under the same heading as is found in the *Suda* (fr. 532 *PMG:* ἐπ' 'Αρτεμισίῳ ναυμαχίᾳ).[66] It was generally assumed that the *Suda* and Priscian refer to the same poem, but they give different meters to this poem. Since Priscian quotes Simonides, it was believed that he preserves the correct meter. To make sense of this discrepancy, Bergk suggested that the compilers of the *Suda* had transposed the meters of these poems. With this in mind, he suggested that the *Suda* entry should be read as saying that Simonides composed a *lyric* poem on Artemisium and an *elegy* on Salamis.[67] At the time, this solution seemed to make reasonable sense out of the available evidence. The only clear reference to the Salamis poem outside the *Suda* is the Ambrosian *vita Pindari (post* fr. W²), which is of no help because it does not quote the poem nor does it mention the poem's meter.[68]

Before the publication of the "new Simonides," the transposition of meters suggested by Bergk was generally accepted.[69] The "new Simonides," however, has raised another possibility; namely, that Priscian and the *Suda* refer to two separate compositions by Simonides on Artemisium, one elegiac and one lyric. In particular, P. Parsons suggests that fr. 3 W² (=POxy 3965 fr. 20) from the "new Simonides" represents an elegiac fragment of a poem that details the battle at Artemisium.[70] If this suggestion is correct, the simplest solution, then, is to take the different references in the *Suda* and Priscian as *testimonia* for two separate poems. In this way, it is concluded that Simonides composed two poems on Artemisium, one elegiac and one lyric, and also an elegy on Salamis.

This conclusion has been generally accepted, as the words of M.L. West in *IEG*[2] volume two show: "*nunc autem videmus Simonidem ambo proelia elegiis celebravisse.*"[71] Yet, problems remain in the *Suda*.[72] In fact, this solution introduces a new difficulty concerning the reference to the poem on Artemisium. Namely, if Priscian is correct in his citation of a lyric poem on Artemisium, then the *Suda* omits a title of one of Simonides' poems on the Persian Wars. Such an omission is not surprising given the nature of the *Suda*'s acquisition of information. The work may have fallen out in the abridgement of information by the *Suda* or by one of its sources. The *Suda* also fails to list Simonides' verses on those who died at Thermopylae (fr. 531 *PMG*) as well as the recently discovered verses on the battle of Plataea, to which we shall return. The *Suda* will often conclude its bibliographic list with the inclusive phrase καὶ ἄλλα as a standard way to abbreviate what may have been a fuller list in his source. It is possible that Simonides' lyric composition on Artemisium as well as these other compositions on the Persian Wars fall under this inclusive heading.

Another explanation of this omission may come from the absence of a coherent practice of titling early poems. The practice of titling works, especially early lyric and elegiac composition, was not as consistent as we perhaps wish it had been. Herodotus refers to poems in the epic cycle by title, but his references to the works of lyric and elegiac poets are much more general.[73] For these compositions, he uses various phrases: for verses by Sappho, ἐν μέλεϊ (2.135); for ones by Alcaeus, ἐν ἰάμβῳ τριμέτρῳ (1.12); for a poem by Solon, ἐν ἔπεσι (5.113.2). For fifth-century drama, titles were attached to plays presumably by the authors, but even these could come to have alternative titles.[74] A lyric or elegiac poet such as Simonides, however, probably did not give a title to his compositions. Such titles may have arisen through a later association between a poem and its subject matter or some other feature of the work.[75] In short, Simonides' composition(s) may have been called ἡ ἐπ' 'Αρτεμισίῳ ναυμαχία because that is exactly what the subject matter of these verses was. Even then titles were not always certain for older texts as the existence of alternative titles shows.[76] Titles for older works or works that did not have one may also have been acquired during the Hellenistic period when the Alexandrian library was catalogued.[77] Yet, for lyric and elegiac poets titles may not have been solidified even by these scholars. The conclusion must be that titles for early works in antiquity were fluid.[78] The apparent reference by Priscian and the *Suda* to two different poems in different meters under the same heading ἡ ἐπ' 'Αρτεμισίῳ ναυμαχία is not surprising, nor is the confusion that may have resulted for later collectors of information on the works of Simonides. If Simonides did compose two poems in different meters on the battle of Artemisium, it is not difficult to see how confusion would have come about concerning them in the absence of a consistent method of assigning works titles. The *Suda*'s apparent omission may have resulted from such confusion.

The possible omission of the lyric poem on Artemisium in the *Suda* entry, however, underscores the third larger difficulty in the *Suda*. This difficulty, which has not been observed by modern scholars, is the omission the so-called "Plataea poem" from its list of Persian War poems. In addition to providing evidence for an elegy on Artemisium, the "new Simonides" is believed to provide many fragments of a poem that appears to be concerned with the battle of Plataea (frs. 10–18 $W^2$). Although there is no external confirmation of a "Plataea poem," it has been assumed that the *Suda* also omits this poem from its list. As has been observed, the omission of a work in a *Suda* entry is not striking by itself. Many works or types of works may not have made their way into the *Suda*. We have *testimonia* for various other works or types of poetry written by Simonides that the *Suda* does not include in its list. A scholiast on *Odyssey* 6.164 (= 537 *PMG*) refers to a work entitled *Prayers*.[79] Strabo 15.3.2 (= 539 *PMG*) mentions that Simonides composed a dithyramb entitled *Memnon* and says that it was in a collection called the *Deliaca*.[80] A scholiast on Apollonius Rhodius (= 540 *PMG*) refers to a collection of *Miscellaneous Works,* which contained verses by Simonides.[81] Our dearth of evidence for any of these other works or classes of poetry keeps us from assessing if the *Suda* omitted them or they simply were not legitimate works by Simonides. If the *Suda* did omit such works, they likely are to fall under the catch-all phrase καὶ ἄλλα. The absence of the verses on the dead at Thermopylae and the possible lyric composition on Artemisium in the *Suda*'s list has already been noted. The same possibility exists for the "Plataea poem." It is also possible that this poem is simply lost from the more specific list of Persian War poems earlier in the *Suda* entry, as we suggested above for the possible verses on the battle of Marathon. Yet, the omission of the "Plataea poem," the poem on the decisive battle of the Persian Wars, from a list that includes references to other Persian War poems is more striking. Given the difficulties noted above, however, it is possible that such a poem fell out of the *Suda*'s source at some earlier time or even was ignored by those compiling the *Suda* itself.

Nevertheless, the omission of the so-called "Plataea poem," coupled with the other difficulties noted above, brings to the foreground the precarious position that the *Suda* holds as a fundamental building block for the reconstruction of Simonides' poems. While the *Suda* has offered modern scholars a blueprint with which Simonides' compositions on the Persian Wars can be reconstructed, this blueprint itself is extremely fragmentary, and worse yet, is perhaps an inexact copy of what once had existed. The very nature of the *Suda* and the specific problems concerning the entry on Simonides underscore the fact that the *Suda* may not be the best starting point for assigning fragments of poems to specific works. Again, we are reminded that our knowledge of Simonides' poetic works on the Persian Wars is at best incomplete and at worst simply wrong.

## The "New Simonides:" The Problem in Modern Scholarship

Despite these problems in squaring the evidence of the *Suda* with the fragments of Simonides and the external witnesses to his poems on the Persian Wars, modern scholarship has accepted the following initial assumptions: 1) The "new Simonides" provides pieces of an elegy on Artemisium and so is proof that two compositions on Artemisium, one a lyric poem and one an elegy, once existed; 2) The "new Simonides" may provide pieces of a "Salamis elegy." The verdict on this poem, however, is still unclear. 3) The "new Simonides" provides evidence for a previously unattested "Plataea elegy." Yet, I hope that the foregoing discussion of the *Suda* has shown that these assumptions are far from certain.

From these initial assumptions about Simonides' poems on Persian Wars, most scholarly attention has turned toward the "Plataea elegy" and fr. 11 W[2], which provides at least 40 consecutive, albeit incomplete, verses. The overarching concern in the approaches to the so-called "Plataea elegy" has been to untangle the various ways in which it is representative of elegiac poems on historical topics. The elegiac poems on Artemisium and Salamis presumably would have been similar types of poems, but the "Plataea poem" garners more attention because of the number of verses that seem to belong to it. Along these lines, issues of content, performance context, and genre have come to the forefront of the discussion. A starting point for most discussions of the "Plataea poem" has been the assumption that it represents the elegiac sub-genre, narrative elegy, which was first defined by E. L. Bowie less than ten years before the publication of the "new Simonides."[82] The larger implications of the identification of these verses as part of a so-called "narrative elegy" have received the most scrutiny.

Two primary lines of discussion have arisen in applying Bowie's important findings to the "new Simonides." First, a key element in Bowie's hypothesis is that narrative elegy would likely have been performed in a competitive setting at a public festival.[83] In terms of the "Plataea elegy," various attempts have been made to situate these verses in such a context. For Antonio Aloni, a performance at the consecration of the tumuli at Plataea (Hdt. 9.85) of a poem commissioned by the Spartans or their leader, Pausanias, provides a suitable context of the poem. The occasion, then, explains the mix of praise and mourning found in fr. 11 W[2].[84] For Albert Schachter and P.-J. Shaw as well, the elegy represented by fr. 11 W[2] has a Spartan/Pausanias bias. Schachter places the initial performance at the supposed tomb of Achilles at the entrance of the Hellespont.[85] For P.-J. Shaw, the Isthmian Games provide a plausible context.[86] In contrast to these views, Deborah Boedeker argues that a more panhellenic emphasis exists in the poem, while she also maintains that the poem was performed in some type of public setting.[87] C. Bearzot has offered another provocative suggestion. For her, the poem could have been commissioned by Themistocles and performed at Delphi in an effort to obscure the Thessalians' Medism.[88] G. Huxley also has tentatively suggested that this poem had a similar emphasis on the Thessalians. He proposes a performance context at a Thetideion near Pharsalus.[89] Consensus on the specifics has not been reached and probably cannot be until more evidence arises. Furthermore, it is also not agreed that the poem represented by fr. 11 $W^2$ is to be defined generically through public performance. Ian Rutherford, Dirk Obbink, and David Sider have insightfully proposed that the so-called "sympotic fragments" of the "new Simonides" (frs. 19–22 $W^2$) may well find a place in the poem represented by fr. 11 $W^2$.[90] Yet, the underlying assumption in each of these attempts is that the poem represented by fr. 11 $W^2$ is a "Plataea elegy" and that this understanding will be helpful in identifying the context for the poem's performance.

Second, in terms of the content of Bowie's narrative elegy, efforts have been made to show a relation between Simonides and both epic poetry and the prose of Herodotus. Both Simon Hornblower and Deborah Boedeker have done much to illuminate the affinities and divergences from Herodotus in Simonides' poem. For both, Simonides' narrative provides a part of a literary continuum that moves from the conventions of epic narrative concerned with the past to historiography proper.[91] In terms of epic, Eva Stehle and Jenny Strauss Clay argue that fr. 11 $W^2$ demonstrates a conscious break on the part of Simonides from an epic predecessor. For them, Simonides, in making this break, is able to create heroes out of contemporary fighters.[92]

All of these studies provide valuable insights into how the "new Simonides" can be fit into literary history as a narrative elegy in relation to other types of poetry or prose. Yet, the fundamental assumption of each of these arguments is that the "new Simonides" represents a "Plataea elegy" and that this poem is to be reconstructed as a narrative. Given our incomplete knowledge of Simonides' Persian War poems, to say nothing at this point of early elegy in general, the questions raised by Obbink, Rutherford, and Sider concerning the genre of poem represented by fr. 11 $W^2$ deserve a bit more attention. Observations about the relation of fr. 11 $W^2$ to other types of archaic poetry are made by Dirk Obbink, who suggests that these fragments exploit prooimial features that are epic in form and lyric in function. For Obbink, fr. 11 $W^2$ involves a crossing of genres, such as would be expected from a Hellenistic poet.[93] Although Obbink also initially assumes that the fragment is a narrative elegy on Plataea, he points to some important implications of his study. He suggests that there is nothing in the new fragments or our knowledge of Simonides' works that would prohibit the inclusion of the new fragments designated as sympotic in the same poem as fr. 11 $W^2$. Ian Rutherford and David Sider make similar claims. Rutherford allows the possibility that the "Plataea elegy" contained a *sphragis* in which some of the sympotic fragments of the "new Simonides" could be placed.[94] Sider also allows for the possibility that the supposedly sympotic fragments, frs. 19–20 $W^2$, may be related to fr. 11 $W^2$.[95] In each of these views, then, the assumptions that fr. 11 $W^2$ is a narrative elegy on the battle of Plataea are directly or indirectly brought into question. While these views do not go so far as to dissociate the so called "Plataea elegy" from the form, content, and genre implied by the understanding that fr. 11 W² represents a narrative elegy, the possibilities they bring forward do remind us that our understanding of Simonides' poems on the Persian Wars is far from what we would wish it to be.

## HYPOTHETICAL FRAMEWORK

This state of evidence may, in fact, be masking more intrinsic problems with our knowledge of Simonides' works on the Persian Wars. It is plausible that the *Suda* and other *testimonia* hide the original scope and content of these works. The confusion in our knowledge of these works is then enhanced by the attempts to divide the new fragments into three separate works on Artemisium, Salamis and Plataea. This study is an attempt to elucidate the evidence offered by the "new Simonides" for the larger context to which these fragments belong. This evidence will be sought in the fragments themselves rather than in their division into battle poems. Following the implication of the suggestions of Rutherford, Obbink, and Sider, I will exploit the initial premise that at the outset these new fragments must be considered as part of an as yet undetermined poem or poem(s). This premise suggests that it is plausible to consider a hypothetical framework for reconstructing part of the "new Simonides" which explores the possibility that these fragments represent a poem that is broader in scope than the reference to a poem on Plataea, Artemisium or Salamis allows. This framework is attractive because it would help to explain the general confusion and silences in the *Suda* and other witnesses for Simonides' works on the Persian Wars. In this way, it may be reasonable to explain the mention in the *Suda* of *The Sea-battle of Xerxes*, *The Sea-battle at Artemisium* and *The Sea-battle at Salamis* as references to topics treated by Simonides or, more specifically, to sections within other poems. [96]

## PLAN OF STUDY

The aim of the present study is to explore the feasibility of approaching the "new Simonides" as a collection of fragments that represents a poem whose commemoration of the Persian Wars goes beyond the depiction of a single battle. The study will proceed in three chapters. The first will develop the premise that the fragments of the "new Simonides" do not provide certain evidence for individual elegies on Artemisium, Salamis or Plataea. Rather, it will be suggested that from the outset the fragments should be considered as part of an as yet undetermined poem or poems. First it will be considered what evidence there is for each of these elegies outside the "new Simonides." A papyrological analysis will then be used to consider what internal evidence exists for the assignment of each fragment to a particular poem.

Chapter Two confronts the content of these fragments. The initial assumption is that content must be divorced from genre before the reconstruction of these fragments begins. The focus will be primarily on fr. 11 $W^2$ because it is the longest and most complete of the new fragments. The chapter proceeds in two parts. First, the verses of fr. 11 $W^2$ will be set against a backdrop of other contemporary and near-contemporary commemorations of the Persian Wars to develop an idea of how we might expect its content to look. It will be shown that a panhellenic and multi-battle perspective of the Persian Wars is reflected in commemorations of the Persian Wars that appear following the battle of Plataea. After situating these verses in this framework, the second part of the chapter will take a closer look at the role of Achilles in fr. 11 $W^2$. The appearance of Achilles in fr. 11 $W^2$ will be used to determine to what this fragment falls in line with other commemorations of the Persian Wars. Through Achilles' presence in fr. 11 $W^2$, I will ultimately aim to connect this fragment with others from this same papyrus and attempt to gain a clearer sense of the larger composition in which the hero functions as a paradigm.

Finally, Chapter Three will turn to consider issues of genre. The aim will be to situate Simonides' verses on the Persian Wars within the broader category of elegy by identifying internal features in the remains of these verses. By nature, these verses on the greatest Greek victory are verses of praise; however, it is not immediately obvious how archaic elegy is linked with such praise. By building on the findings in Chapters One and Two, this search for generic features in verses on the Persian Wars will illuminate not only how these fragments fit into the genre of elegy, but also why this type of verse best suits a commemoration of the victory that saved all of Greece from the day of slavery.

Chapter One

# Too Many Fragments, Too Few Poems?
## Models for Combining the Fragments of the "New Simonides"

"The business of him that republishes an ancient book is, to correct what is corrupt, and to explain what is obscure."

Samuel Johnson

*Proposal of Printing the Dramatic Works of William Shakespeare, 1756*

## 1.1 INTRODUCTION

Following a practice of most recent writers on Simonides, I offer an initial word on the importance of the "new Simonides." The publication of the "new Simonides" has shed much light on what before was lamentable darkness. For most, one of the many intriguing aspects of these fragments is their apparent testimony for two types of elegy about which little was previously known, public elegy on historical subjects and sympotic elegy on erotic themes. In this chapter, the primary concern will be to consider what evidence these new fragments offer for the first of these types of elegy. Specifically, the aim is to determine what internal evidence for poems on the Persian Wars by Simonides exists within these fragments.

The current orthodoxy is that the "new Simonides" represents three separate elegies, one on the battle of Artemisium, one on the battle of Salamis, and one on the battle of Plataea. I suggest, however, that this orthodoxy is not beyond doubt. As will be seen, the confusion in the *testimonia* for the works of Simonides makes it difficult to assign any fragment to a particular poem unless its context is cited explicitly. In fact, as I propose, the evidence within these fragments does not confirm this division into separate poems. This analysis, then, will reevaluate the assignment of these fragments to specific poems and reconsider how the fragments relate to one another. The data for this study will be drawn primarily from the papyrological evidence as it is represented in the publication of POxy 2327 by Edgar Lobel, the publication of POxy 3965 by P.J. Parsons, the electronic images of POxy 3965, and the images of POxy 2327 published by Lobel in his *editio princeps* and in Boedeker-Sider.[1] This evidence will be compared with three texts of the "new Simonides," the one printed by M. L. West, which is the standard edition of the elegies by Simonides, the one published by David Sider, and the one most recently published by Gentili and Prato. This investigation will result in a critique of these editions, as well as the commentary on the "new Simonides" by Ian Rutherford, which is published with Sider's text.[2]

To begin, it is important to note that other arrangements of these fragments are possible. One such arrangement assumes that the "new Simonides" may represent a single elegy with references to the battles at Artemisium, Salamis, and Plataea. This model has some received attention in current scholarship, but has been overshadowed by the interest in the so-called "Plataea poem" (frs. 10–18 W[2]). Such a model, however, merits closer consideration. This model is particularly engaging because it untangles some of the confusion that arises from the separation of the "new Simonides" into three separate elegies on three separate battles in the Persian Wars. With this model in mind, the following chapter will evaluate the accepted arrangement of the fragments. There will be two overarching goals. First, the validity of the current division into three separate elegies on the Persian Wars will be assessed. Second, the viability of the model that posits a single elegy will be examined. It will be argued that this model is a viable and attractive way of explaining the confusion that surrounds Simonides' elegiac works on the Persian Wars. The conclusions concerning the arrangement of these fragments will form the foundation for the subsequent analyses of their subject-matter and content.

## 1.2 THE ARTEMISIUM POEM

### A. *The Evidence*

Priscian and the *Suda* are the only witnesses for an "Artemisium Poem" by Simonides. Priscian directly quotes this poem as *The Sea-battle at Artemisium* (ἐπ' ᾽Αρτερμισίωι ναυμαχίαι):

> Simonides et Alcman in iambico teste Heliodoro non solum in fine ponunt spondeum sed etiam in aliis locis. Simonides in ἐπ' ᾽Αρτερμισίωι ναυμαχίαι in dimetro catalectico: (a) ἐβόμβησεν θαλάσσας, in secundo loco spondeum posuit. ἀντιστρέφει δὲ αὐτῶι· (b) ἀποτρέπουσι κῆρας. Alcman autem . . . quarto loco spondeum posuit . . . teste Heliodoro qui ait Simonidem hoc frequenter facere.

["As Heliodorus testifies, Simonides and Alcman, in iambic verse, place a spondee not only at the end but also in other positions. Simonides in *Sea-battle at Artemisium* in a catalectic dimeter placed a spondee in the second position: a) 'sea's . . . roared.' The antistrophe to this is: b) 'they turn away the goddesses of death.' Alcman, however, . . . placed a spondee in the fourth position, as Heliodorus, who says Simonides does this often, testifies."][3]

According to Priscian's evaluation, the meter of Simonides' *Sea-battle at Artemisium* is catalectic dimeter, a lyric meter. The *Suda* mentions Simonides' *The Sea-battle at Artemisium* (ἡ ἐπ' 'Αρτεμισίῳ ναυμαχία), but calls it an elegy: γέγραπται . . . ἡ ἐπ' 'Αρτεμισίῳ ναυμαχία, δι' ἐλεγείας· ἡ δ' ἐν Σαλαμῖνι μελικῶς· ("He wrote *The Sea-battle at Artemisium* in elegiacs. *The Sea-battle Salamis* was in lyrics.").[4] From Priscian and the *Suda* there are two possible conclusions. First, this evidence alone suggests that there were two poems, one lyric and one elegiac, on Artemisium. Second, it is possible that Priscian and the *Suda* have the same poem in mind but that the *Suda* is mistaken concerning the meter of the poem. That both refer to a poem on the battle of Artemisium by the same name might suggest that the second possibility is correct, but there is simply not enough evidence to be sure.[5] No other *testimonia* or citations can be attributed certainly to any Artemisium poem, so it is impossible from these two witnesses to decide which conclusion is correct.[6] Nevertheless, the existence of at least one poem known as *The Sea-battle at Artemisium* is accepted because of these two witnesses and, more particularly, because Priscian quotes the poem.

A scholium on Apollonius Rhodius (1.211–15c Wendel) may also be evidence for an "Artemisium poem." Under the lemma Ζήτης καὶ Κάλαϊς, the scholiast refers to "The Naumachia" by Simonides:

τὴν δὲ 'Ωρείθυιαν Σιμωνίδης ἀπὸ Βριλησσοῦ φησιν ἁρπαγεῖσαν ἐπὶ τὴν Σαρπηδονίαν πέτραν τῆς Θρᾴκης ἐνεχθῆναι . . . ἡ δὲ 'Ωρείθυια 'Ερεχθέως θυγάτηρ, ἣν ἐξ 'Αττικῆς ἁρπάσας ὁ Βορέας ἤγαγεν εἰς Θρᾴκην, κἀκεῖσε συνελθὼν ἔτεκε Ζήτην καὶ Καλαϊν, ὡς Σιμωνίδης ἐν τῇ Ναυμαχίᾳ.

["Simonides says that this Oreithyia, being carried off from Brilessus, was taken to the Sarpedonian rock of Thrace . . . Oreithyia was the daughter of Erechtheus, whom Boreas, after he seized her from Attica, took to Thrace, and there, having intercourse with her, fathered Zetes and Kalaïs, as Simonides says in 'The Naumachia.'"][7]

According to the scholiast, Simonides' poem mentioned the abduction of Oreithyia, daughter of Erechtheus, by Boreas and the offspring of this rape, Zetes and Kalaïs. Although the battle that is the subject of "The Naumachia" is not specified, the poem has been connected to Herodotus' account of the battle of Artemisium (7.189). Herodotus records the belief that Boreas, the mythical γαμβρός ("son-in-law") of the early Athenian king, Erechtheus, aided Athens at Artemisium by destroying the Persian ships in a series of storms. The historian does not refer to a poem by Simonides, but the prominence of Boreas in both sources has led to the association between *The Sea-battle at Artemisium* and "The Naumachia."[8]

To be sure, these connections between the "The Naumachia" in the scholiast and Herodotus' depiction of the battle at Artemisium are powerful. Yet, it still must be admitted that they are far from certain because we know so little about Simonides' compositions on the sea-battles in the Persian Wars. Herodotus' mention of the Boreads in the context of the sea-battle at Artemisium does not guarantee that Simonides also mentioned them in a similar context. There would have been opportunity for him to refer to the Boreads in other compositions such as the one on Salamis. Herodotus explicitly and Plutarch implicitly tell us that the west winds were a factor at the battle of Salamis; Aeschylus too mentions the affect of the winds on the Persian survivors who were fleeing from Salamis.[9] Admittedly Zetes and Kalaïs are the sons of Boreas, the north wind; however, Herodotus and Plutarch also tell us that before the battle of Salamis, the Athenians made prayers to the gods. Herodotus tells us that after an earthquake at sunrise, the Athenians offered prayers to all of the gods and then summoned the sons of Aeacus from Salamis and Aegina (8.64.2). Plutarch tells us that before the battle, Themistocles offered sacrifices to the gods (*Them.* 13.2). Neither text is very explicit about the identity of the gods to whom the Athenians prayed. Nevertheless, it is possible that the Athenians included the winds in this general mention of the gods, especially since they were about to embark on another sea-battle. If the help of the Boreads was understood to have been crucial to the victory at Artemisium, it seems reasonable to think that their help would have been sought again for Salamis. It may be in such a context that Simonides mentioned the Boreads. Another possibility is that he mentioned them in the Salamis poem in such a way that looked back to the events at Artemisium. This speculation does not get us very far. The point to stress, however, is that since we do not know the scope or the details of content for either of these sea-battle poems, it is difficult to say with certainty in which composition Simonides' mentioned the Boreads.

Herodotus, then, does not confirm that the scholiast has Simonides' composition on Artemisium in mind. Moreover, even if the association were confirmed, questions about the Artemisium poem remain. Namely, to which composition do we assign this reference? The one mentioned by the *Suda* or the one mentioned by Priscian? These questions cannot be answered with the available evidence. The value of the scholiast's reference for defining Simonides' poem on Artemisium, or any other sea-battle poem, must be considered cautiously. There is simply not enough evidence in these three texts to tell us anything certain about Simonides' verses on the battle of Artemisium.

There are two other possible witnesses for Simonides' verses on Artemisium, both of dubious value. First, another scholium to Apollonius Rhodius refers to a mention of the island Skiathos by Simonides (=fr. 1 W² = 635 PMG = Schol. Ap. Rhod. 1.583–4a Wendel): ἡ παραθαλασσία. νῆσος γὰρ ἡ Σκίαθος ἐγγὺς Εὐβοίας, ἧς καὶ Σιμωνίδης μέμνηται ("(Skiathos) beside the sea. For Skiathos is an island near Euboea, which Simonides also mentions").[10] The reference is understood to be to the "Artemisium poem" because the island is also mentioned by Herodotus in his account of Artemisium.[11] The scholiast, however, does not provide the context in which Simonides mentioned Skiathos; therefore, the scholiast need not be understood as referring to a poem on the battle of Artemisium.[12] Even if this reference is assumed to be to an "Artemisium poem" by Simonides, the scholiast provides no clue about the form or the content of the composition in which Skiathos was mentioned. The reference could come from either a lyric poem or an elegy. The scholiast, then, does not resolve the problems surrounding the evidence in Priscian and the *Suda*, nor does it link "The Naumachia" with a composition on Artemisium. It must be concluded that the scholiast does not provide evidence for *The Sea-battle at Artemisium* in any meter.

Two references by Himerius, the rhetorician of the fourth century CE, to Simonides in relation to a poetic depiction of the wind are the second possible witnesses for the "Artemisium poem:"

λύσει δὲ τῆς νεὼς ᾠδὴ τὰ πείσματα, ἣν ἱερὸς προσᾴδουσιν Ἀθηναῖοι χορός, καλοῦντες ἐπὶ τὸ σκάφος τὸν ἄνεμον παρεῖναί τε αὐτὸν καὶ τῇ θεωρίδι συμπέτεσθαι. ὁ δὲ ἐπιγνοὺς οἶμαι τὴν οἰκείαν ᾠδήν, ἣν Σιμωνίδης αὐτῷ προσῇσε †μετὰ τὴν θάλατταν†, ἀκολουθεῖ μὲν εὐθὺς τοῖς μέλεσι, πολὺς δὲ πνεύσας κατὰ πρύμνης οὔριος ἐλαύνει τὴν ὁλκάδα τῷ πνεύματι.

["An ode will loosen the cables of the ship, the ode, which the Athenians in a holy chorus sing, when they call the wind to the boat both for it to be present itself and to fly with the sacred ship. No doubt, the wind, recognizing its own song, which Simonides sang to it after the sea, straightway is guided by the lyric song, and blowing much upon the stern favorably drives the ship with its blast."]

νῦν γὰρ ποιητικῶς ἐθέλων καλέσαι τὸν ἄνεμον, εἶτα οὐκ ἔχων ποιητικὴν ἀφεῖναι φωνήν, ἐκ τῆς οἰκείας μούσης προσειπεῖν ἐθέλω τὸν ἄνεμον ... ἁπαλὸς δ' ὑπὲρ κυμάτων χεόμενος πορφυρᾶ σχίζει περὶ τὴν πρῷραν τὰ κύματα.

["For now, wishing to call the wind poetically, and yet not being able to utter a poetic sound, I wish to address the wind according to my own muse ... the gentle (wind), being poured over the waves, divides the dark waves around the prow."][13]

Himerius' reference to the ship concerns the procession of the *Panathenaea*. The orator's words draw a connection between a Simonidean depiction of the wind and this procession. This connection could suggest that Himerius has a lyric poem by Simonides in mind that would have been sung during this procession.[14] The passages, however, do not demand this conclusion. As Rutherford rightly points out, Himerius' speech is linked with the *Panathenaea*, but Simonides' poem need not be.[15] Furthermore, the mention of the winds and a ship by Himerius in relation to the *Panathenaea* need not connect Simonides' image with a sea-battle poem. To be sure, Simonides mentioned the winds in other compositions. Another work that describes the wind is fr. 543 *PMG*, which concerns the plight of Danaë.[16] Furthermore, references to the wind may be lost in the gaps that permeate our knowledge of Simonides' works. Himerius only shows, then, that Simonides mentioned a wind. He does not, however, provide the specific context or the meter of the composition in which Simonides mentioned the wind.

The connection between the battle of Artemisium and Himerius' reference to Simonides is also obscured by the difficult text. These passages are corrupt at the very points that seem to refer to a sea-battle poem by Simonides.[17] The biggest problem lies in the phrase μετὰ τὴν θάλατταν. The phrase translates literally as "after the sea," but it is generally interpreted to mean "after the sea-battle" or the like.[18] This interpretation suggests that Himerius refers to a poem on a sea-battle in which the winds played a role. Wilamowitz connected these passages with Simonides' *The Sea-battle at Artemisium* by noting the conspicuous presence of Boreas in Herodotus' account.[19] This interpretation, however, presupposes that Himerius evokes an image from a sea-battle poem. The hypothesis remains speculative because the text simply refers to the wind and the sea. Furthermore, even if the emendations that make Himerius refer to a sea-battle are accepted, it is still not certain that the orator is adducing *The Sea-battle at Artemisium*. In fact, Bowra has suggested that Himerius has Simonides' *The Sea-battle at Salamis* in mind.[20] Bowra's suggestion rests on the presence of the wind in the accounts of the battle by Aeschylus, Herodotus, and Plutarch. Aeschylus has the Persian survivors fleeing Salamis with a favorable breeze (*Pers.* 481: κατ' οὖρον). Herodotus tells us that the west wind (ἄνεμος ζέφυρος) drove the wreckage from the battle to the Attic shores called Colias (8.96.2). Plutarch give the wind a more active role in the battle by stating that Themistocles waited until a fresh breeze came from the sea (τὸ πνεῦμα λαμπρὸν ἐκ πελάγους) before he turned his triremes against the Barbarians. This wind was helpful to the Greeks and disastrous for the Persians (*Them.* 14.2). Plutarch's description of the wind as λαμπρός and its mild impact on the Greek fleet suggests that he has the west wind in mind here, as Herodotus explicitly does in his account. In objection to Bowra, A. Podlecki has pointed out that the following bit in the speech of Himerius refers to the rape of Oreithyia.[21] Podlecki is probably correct in noting that these words of Himerius at this point refer to the Boreads, but it is not certain how these words relate to the indirect reference to Simonides in the preceding sentence. There is a lacuna which separates the reference to "the gentle (wind), being poured over the waves, divides the dark waves around the prow" and the words which allude to the rape of Oreithyia. [22] The text of Himerius at this point does seem to have some image or poem of Simonides' in mind in which the winds, in particular the Boreads, played a role. Still, this observation does not lead to the conclusion that the poem which Himerius has in mind is the Artemisium poem unless the link between "The Naumachia" and Herodotus' account of Artemisium is accepted. As we have seen, this link is not certain. The conclusion must be that it is uncertain to what composition by Simonides Himerius is referring.

The context for the image in Himerius remains obscure. Himerius is certainly adducing a poetic image. Whether the image is to be sought in a lyric poem or an elegy, or whether it comes from a poem that describes a sea-battle or from some other context cannot be determined. In fact, Simonides may have used an image of the wind in a variety of situations. It is possible that Simonides was famous for his depiction of the wind because he described it well not only once but many times. The verses on the battle of Artemisium, Salamis, or the Danaë fragment (543 *PMG*) are compositions that mention or may have mentioned the winds. Himerius, then, offers no evidence for a poem concerning any sea-battle.

None of this evidence resolves the difficulties in reconciling the quotation in Priscian with the *testimonium* of the *Suda*. The direct quote in Priscian makes it likely that Simonides composed a lyric poem on the battle of Artemisium. The lack of an elegiac fragment on Artemisium in the above evidence does not rule out an elegiac composition. As it stands, the *Suda* mentions an elegy on Artemisium and a lyric poem on Salamis. With the evidence above, Bergk's suggestion that the meters in the *Suda* have been transposed is reasonable.[23] This solution, however, is not entirely necessary. Even if we consider only the evidence presented above, it is just as reasonable that Simonides composed an elegy on Artemisium in addition to his lyric poem on this battle mentioned by Priscian. The lack of an elegiac quotation in the above evidence can be explained as an accident of transmission. It is only possible to conclude that there is evidence for a lyric ἐπ' Ἀρτεμισίῳ ναυμαχία. The existence of an elegiac treatment of Artemisium recorded by the *Suda* remains a possibility, but no other clear evidence for such a poem exists.

## B. The "New Simonides"
## Fr. 3 W2 (=POxy 3965 fr. 20) [see Figure 1]

The "new Simonides" has seemed to provide the missing piece of evidence for Simonides' elegiac composition on Artemisium. It is suggested by Parsons, who is followed by West, that fr. 3 W[2] (=POxy 3965 fr. 20), an elegiac fragment, is related to "The

| PARSONS | WEST |
|---|---|
| POxy 3965 fr. 20 | Fr. 3 W² |
| (a)  ] . [ | .                ]ǫ[ |
|    ] . εριωι[ | .                ]ιεριωι[ |
|    . . . [] . ν· | .                ]ν· ἀνδρ .[ |
|    ]ν· . . . . [ | ἀθανάτων] ἰότητι· τ[ |
|    ] . στοτι·τ[ | 5      Ζήτην καὶ] Κάλαϊ[ν |
| 5  ]κάλα . [ | .                ]σελθει[κ[ |
| (b)  ] . [ ] . . . . [] . [ | . . . . . ]ι ἐξ ἐρέβεος κ[ |
|         o | .                ]ι δῶρο[ν |
|    ] . ἐξερεβευσκ[ | .                ]εων δ[ |
|    ] . δωρο[ | 10·    ]αφοισι θ[ |
|    ]εωνδ[ |   ]ιητ᾽ ἠϋ[κόμοιο] κόρ[ης |
| 10  ] . φοισιθ[] [(c)  (d) | θάλ]ασσαν ὑ[πὸ] τ[ρ]υγός· α[ |
|    ] . ητ . ϋ[ . . . . ]κορ[ |   ἀγλαφόφημον ἁλός[ |
|    ][ασσαν . [ . . ] . [ . ]ν .[]c·α[ |   ]ωυ· τίνα δ .[ . ] . λωπ[ |
|    ] .´ φ[] . μοναλ . . [ | 15 ·    ]ωτεχ[            ]ενον[ |
|    ]ωυ· τίνα . . [ . . ] . []λω . [ |   ] . . [ |
|        ·ωι[ | |
| 15  ] . τε .[           ]ενον[ | |
|    ] . . [ | |

Figure 1.

Naumachia" mentioned in the scholium to Apollonius Rhodius.[24] This fragment consists of four separate scraps joined by both sense and fibers.[25] The presence of a sheet join in these fragments and three supplements serve as the basis for the connection to "The Naumachia." First, the letters ]ΚΑΛΑ . [ are found at fr. 3.5 W² (=POxy 3965 fr. 20.5). A dot over the uncertain letter before the break in the papyrus might be a diaeresis. Parsons supplements the line to read Ζήτην καὶ] Κάλαϊ[ν.[26] As a result, the fragment contains the names Zetes and Kalaïs, whom the scholiast places in "The Naumachia" of Simonides. Second, at fr. 3.11 W² (=POxy 3965 fr. 20.11) the papyrus reads, ] . η . ϋ[ . . . . . ]κορ[. West supplements the text as, ]ιητ᾽ ἠϋ[κόμοιο] κόρ[ης and suggests that the "fair-haired maiden" is Oreithyia, the mother of Zetes and Kalaïs, who is also mentioned by the scholiast to Apollonius.[27] Third, the papyrus reads ] [ ]ασσαν . [ . . ] . [ . ]ν . []c· α[ at fr. 3.12 W² (=POxy 3965 fr. 20.12). This line is reconstructed as: θάλ]ασσαν ὑ[πὸ] τ[ρ]υγός· α[ .[28] West suggests that this phrase refers to the bottom or sediment (τρύξ) of the sea being stirred up by the Boreads.[29] Through the sense obtained by these suppositions, he is able to connect the fragment to "The Naumachia." Further support for this interpretation is found in Parsons' observation of a sheet-join that might be in the same place as a join found in fr. 4 W² (= POxy 3965 fr. 12).[30] This join, which potentially places both fragments in the same poem, is important because fr. 4 W² appears to be concerned with nautical matters, as will be discussed below. The linking of fr. 3 W² to another fragment with nautical content adds weight to the interpretation that it contains details that pertain to one of the sea-battle poems.

These points have led to three conclusions. First, these verses, which possibly mention Zetes, Kalaïs, Oreithyia and the disturbance of the sea, belong in the "The Naumachia" referred to by the scholium to Apollonius Rhodius. Second, this fragment, when considered in the light of Herodotus 7.189, confirms that the "The Naumachia" is *The Sea-battle at Artemisium* listed in the *Suda*. Third, since POxy 3965 most likely contains only elegiac verses, it appears that there was in fact an elegiac *The Sea-battle at Artemisium*.[31] This interpretation of fr. 3 W$^2$ suggests that the list in the *Suda* is correct in its reference to an elegiac *The Sea-battle at Artemisium* and allows the conclusion that two poems on Artemisium, one lyric and one elegy, existed.

These conclusions, however, are not as certain as they may seem. First, the supplement that places Oreithyia in fr. 3.11 W$^2$ (=POxy 3965 fr. 20.11) only refers to her after Zetes and Kalaïs are placed in fr. 3.5 W$^2$ (=POxy 3965 fr. 20.5). Without Zetes and Kalaïs, the reference could be to any maiden. The fragmentary nature of the line also does not allow us to be certain that a maiden is even mentioned. In this line, the ink, printed by Parson as ]κ, appears in West's text without any sub-linear dot. Furthermore, while Parson's reading of this ink seems correct, it must be admitted that ]ς is also a possible reading. Second, the supplement in fr. 3.11 W$^2$ (=POxy 3965 fr. 20.11) concerning the sediment of the sea, no matter how certain it is believed to be, only belongs in *The Sea-battle at Artemisium* if the two other supplements are accepted. It must be admitted that if this reading is accepted, the presence of fragments that presumably depict symposia in the "new Simonides" allows other contexts to be imagined for the word related to τρύξ.[32] Yet, the reading of the ink here is also unclear. Where West prints τ[ρ]υγός, the papyrus images show that the τ and γ could both be π.[33] The most solid evidence, then, for assuming that this fragment represents an elegy on Artemisium mentioned by the *Suda* is the presence of Zetes and Kalaïs in fr. 3.5 W$^2$.

The letters that provide this supplement in fr. 3.5 W$^2$ are difficult to read. The iota in the name Kalaïs may only be a partial letter and the marks for diaeresis that ultimately lead to the supplement are unclear.[34] Furthermore, the support given to this supplement by Herodotus, the scholiast to Apollonius Rhodius, and the *Suda* is dubious. The glue that binds these bits of evidence depends on the assumption that "The Naumachia" is the same poem as *The Sea-battle at Artemisium*. Without fr. 3 W$^2$, the only link between "The Naumachia" and *The Sea-battle at Artemisium* in any meter is the narrative of Herodotus, which does not mention any poem by Simonides. As we have seen, before the publication of the "new Simonides," it could still be doubted that "The Naumachia" was Simonides' poem on Artemisium. It was even more uncertain that if the "The Naumachia" is this poem, it is an elegy. So the evidence of Herodotus is not particularly useful. It is only the discovery of fr. 3 W$^2$ that seems to confirm that "The Naumachia" is *The Sea-battle at Artemisium* and that this poem is an elegy. The reasoning behind this conclusion, however, is circular.

That is, Herodotus' account is assumed to provide the link between the *Sea-battle at Artemisium* and "The Naumachia;" this assumption in turn allows for the supplement in fr. 3 $W^2$, which confirms the link between Herodotus, "The Naumachia" and the *Sea-battle at Artemisium* mentioned by the *Suda*. The evidence that the supplement confirms is the same evidence that is used to provide the supplement. The result is that the supplement is of very little value for identifying an elegy on the battle of Artemisium.

Two conclusions about the "Artemisium poem" and fr. $3W^2$ must be reconsidered. First, it is still not certain that an elegy on Artemisium existed. Fr. $3W^2$ is the only direct evidence for this conclusion. The removal of West's supplement leaves only the *Suda* as a witness for such an elegy. Without the supplements in fr. $3W^2$, it must be concluded that the elegiac *The Sea-battle at Artemisium* mentioned by the *Suda* is not certainly attested elsewhere. Second, the relation between *The Sea-battle at Artemisium* and "The Naumachia" has no real basis without fr. $3W^2$. Since the supplement in fr. $3W^2$ that provides this link is problematic, it is difficult to conclude that this fragment proves that the scholiast to Apollonius and the *Suda* are referring to the same poem. We still must conclude that no clear evidence for an "Artemisium elegy" exists as it is currently reconstructed from the "new Simonides." This conclusion casts doubt on West's assertion, which reflects the current orthodoxy, that the "new material . . . provides apparent confirmation of the statement in the *Suda* that there was an elegiac poem dealing with the battle of Artemisium."[35] Without this supplement, the "new material" provides no such "confirmation." There is, then, no compelling reason to view fr. $3W^2$ as representing an elegy on the battle of Artemisium.

*Frs. 2 and 4 $W^2$ (=POxy 3965 frs. 13 and 12) [see Figure 2]*

The doubts concerning fr. 3 $W^2$ force a reconsideration of frs. 2 and 4 $W^2$, which are also assigned to *The Sea-battle at Artemisium*. Neither of these fragments necessarily comes from a poem on a sea-battle, though fr. 2 $W^2$ (=POxy 3965 fr. 13) might belong in a battle context. The letters at line fr. 2.2 $W^2$, ]εμαχ[ , seem to refer to a battle, but hardly specify which one. In addition, the papyrus reads ]εχει, [at fr. 2.6 $W^2$. Parsons notes a mark at line level before the break in the papyrus.[36] West suggests χειμ[ερι- as a possible supplement, but does not explain the suggestion.[37] It can be assumed that this suggestion derives from Herodotus 7.188–89, which emphasizes the winter storm (χείμων) that crippled the Persian fleet at Artemisium.[38] Taken together, line 2, with a possible word for battle, and line 6, with the possible mention of a winter storm, suggest that the fragment belongs to a poem on the battle of Artemisium. The suggestion in line 6, however, necessary to make this connection, is based on unclear paleographic evidence and is cautiously confined by West to his *apparatus criticus*.[39] Even if West's cautious supplement is accepted, other contexts

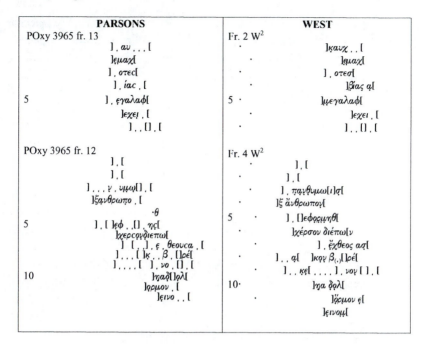

| PARSONS | WEST |
|---|---|
| POxy 3965 fr. 13 | Fr. 2 W² |
| ] . αυ . . . [ | ]καυχ . . [ |
| ]εμαχ[ | ]εμαχ[ |
| ] . οτεσ[ | ] . οτεσ[ |
| ] . ιας . [ | ]βίας α[ |
| 5   ] . εγαλαφ[ | 5 ·   ]μεγαλαφ[ |
| ]εχει . [ | ]εχει . [ |
| ] . . [] . [ | ] . . [] . [ |
| | |
| POxy 3965 fr. 12 | Fr. 4 W² |
| ] . [ | ] . [ |
| ] . [ | ] . [ |
| ] . . . ν . υμω[] . [ | ] . πανθυμω[ι]σ[ |
| ]ξανθρωπο . [ | ]ξ ἄνθρωπο[ν |
| ·θ | |
| 5   ] . [ ]εφ . [] . ησ[ | 5 ·   ] . []εφορμηθ[ |
| ]χερσονδιεπω[ | ]χέρσον διέπω[ν |
| ] [ . ] . ε . θεουσα . [ | ] . ἔχθεος ασ[ |
| ] . . . [ ]κ . . β . []ρε[ | ] . . α[ ]κον β . , []ρε[ |
| ] . . . . [ ] . νο . [] . [ | ] . . κε[ . . . . ] . νον [ ] . [ |
| 10   ]ηαδ[]ολ[ | 10 ·   ]ηα δ̣ολ[ |
| ]ορμον . [ | ]ὅρμον ε[ |
| ]εινο . . [ | ]εινομ[ |

Figure 2.

in the Persian Wars would be suitable for the reference to a winter storm. Aeschylus *Persians* mentions a winter storm that afflicted the Persian survivors who fled from the defeat at Salamis (496: χειμών' ἄωρον). Herodotus also mentions a storm that had destroyed Xerxes bridges that had led him to Greece, thereby slowing his retreat home after Salamis (8.117.1: χειμῶνος). At most, then, the fragment can be tentatively placed in a battle context. Further specificity cannot be gained. The fragment alone offers no clear evidence that it should be placed in an elegy on Artemisium.

As was noted above, Parsons suggests that fr. 4 W² (=POxy 3965 fr. 12) might be in the same column as fr. 3 W² (=POxy 3965 fr. 20). Parsons prints fr. 4.4 W² (=POxy 3965 fr. 12.4) as ]ξανθρωπο . [ and indicates a sheet join at π. He further suggests that this sheet join is in the second foot of the hexameter and corresponds to the alignment of a sheet join at fr. 3.4 W² (=POxy 3965 fr. 20.4). [40] Supplements are used to bolster this connection. West tentatively suggests Θρήι]ξ ἄνθρωπος as a possible reading for fr. 4.4 W² and finds a reference to Scyllias, the Skionian diver who appears in Herodotus' narrative of Artemisium (8.8). He also suggests νύ]ξ or πέρι]ξ or the like.[41] Each of these supplements are uncertain. At fr. 4.6 W² (=POxy 3965 fr. 12.6), χέρσον, "dry land," appears. The context provided by the letters διεπω[ in line 6 and ]ορμον in line 11 suggest that the fragment represents a sea-battle. Finally, at fr. 4.8 W² (=POxy 3965 fr. 12.8) ] . [ ] κ . β . [ ]ρε[ is printed by Parsons. He notes that Boreas would fit the sense taken from fr. 3 W², but that the marks following the β suggest a letter other than o. Taken together, these bits of evidence are used to connect this fragment to fr. 3 W². In this way, the fragment becomes more proof of an elegy on the battle of Artemisium. None of the suggested readings, however, is solid evidence either for connection to fr. 3 W² in terms of content or for an Artemisium poem in general. The presence of the Skionian diver can only be posited if this fragment belongs to an elegy on Artemisium. Furthermore, the presence of Boreas in this passage is uncertain on paleographic grounds. Finally, while the mention of dry land and the surrounding context may be suggestive of a sea-battle, it is not certain which one is being described. The suggestion that the sea-battle is the one at Artemisium is based on sense that is derived from fr. 3 W², where the mention of the Boreads and Oreithyia is highly conjectural and is based on a circular argument. Finally, the connection between the fragments through page-joins might seem the most probable evidence for connecting the fragments in an Artemisium elegy. Yet, for this reasoning to stand, fr. 3 W² must be from an Artemisium poem and this poem must have been long enough to fill two columns on the papyrus. The doubts about fr. 3 W² have been put forward and, more importantly, we do not know the length of any composition represented by the "new Simonides." Even with the combined evidence in these two fragments, there is still no clear evidence that these verses belong in the same poem or that either represents an Artemisium elegy. The only definite facts are the fragment mentions dry land, probably in a sea-battle context, and either follows or precedes fr. 3 W².

It must stand that frs. 2 and 4 W² provide few details about the poem to which each belongs; therefore, they offer no clear evidence for an "Artemisium poem" or any other poem.

### C. Conclusion

Our only evidence for a poem that could be called *The Sea-battle at Artemisium* comes from Priscian and the *Suda*. The possible mention of a title by Priscian suggests that he is quoting from a poem of considerable length that was mainly focused on the battle of Artemisium. The quotation shows that this poem was in a lyric meter. The evidence for an elegy on the same topic also called *The Sea-battle at Artemisium* reduces to the *Suda*. While it is possible that the *Suda* refers to a poem by Simonides also known as *The Sea-battle at Artemisium* which was in the elegiac meter, the existence of this composition cannot be confirmed. The only other possible evidence for this poem comes from supplements in frs. 2, 3, and 4 W². All of these supplements derive from an attempt to support the evidence of the *Suda*, but none does so with any certainty. Taking these points into consideration, it should be concluded that we have no decisive evidence for an Artemisium elegy to support the *Suda*'s claim. It is only his own supplements that allow West to conclude, "[t]he testimony to a melic poem on the same theme (PMG 533) looks unassailable, so we must accept that there were two compositions in different genres on the same subject."[42] This conclusion has gone a long way toward becoming scholarly orthodoxy as the recent comments of G. O. Hutchinson, in *Greek Lyric Poetry: A Commentary on Selected Larger Pieces,* show. For Hutchinson, this idea of two Artemisium poems is certain and becomes the basis for his evaluation of Simonides' innovation.[43] To be sure, Simonides composed both elegies and lyric poems, but it still cannot be shown that he composed two Artemisium poems in different meters.

The evidence, then, attests one lyric poem on the battle of Artemisium. This conclusion need not rule out the possibility that Simonides mentioned Artemisium in some elegiac context and that it is these verses to which the *Suda* refers. There does remain, however, considerable doubt that Simonides composed a separate elegy solely on Artemisium that is represented in the "new Simonides."

## 1.3 THE SALAMIS POEM

### A. Evidence

A similar reevaluation is necessary for the poem by Simonides called *The Sea-battle at Salamis* because the *Suda* links its existence and form with *The Sea-battle at Artemisium.* No quotations of this poem survive.[44] Three witnesses exist: the *Suda* already mentioned, the Ambrosian *Vita Pindari* i.2.21 Drachmann (= 536 *PMG* note), and Plutarch *Them.* 15.4 (=fr. 5 W²). [45] These witnesses, however, offer little concrete evidence about Simonides' poem on Salamis.

The *Suda* records that Simonides wrote a lyric poem entitled *The Sea-battle at Salamis* (ἡ . . . ἐν Σαλαμῖνι μελικῶς). This entry appears to provide a title and the meter of this poem. As stated above, before the "new Simonides," this poem was thought to be an elegy because of an assumed transposition of meters in the *Suda.*[46] The assignment of fr. 3 W² to *The Sea-battle at Artemisium* complicates this conclusion. It forces the assumption that the *Suda* correctly records the meters of these two poems and also omits a lyric poem on Artemisium, which Priscian quotes. So, one problem is solved by the introduction of another. My conclusion, however, that there is only evidence for a lyric "Artemisium poem" by Simonides, still suggests that a transposition of meters in the *Suda* may be necessary and that the Salamis poem may have been an elegy. The broader confusion in the *Suda,* however, makes any conclusions about the poems of Simonides on these sea-battles difficult. It must remain that the *Suda* alone is not a solid witness for the form of the "Salamis poem."

The *Vita Pindari Ambros.* i.2.21 Drachmann (=536 *PMG* [note] = *IEG²* 2: 116, following fr. 4 W² = T7 Campbell) is another witness for this poem:

ἐπέβαλλε δὲ τοῖς χρόνοις Σιμωνίδη νεώτερος πρεσβυτέρῳ. τῶν γοῦν
αὐτῶν μέμνηνται ἀμφότεροι πράξεων· καὶ γὰρ Σιμωνίδης τὴν ἐν
Σαλαμῖνι ναυμαχίαν γέγραφε, καὶ Πίνδαρος μέμνηται τῆς Κάδμου
βασιλείας.

["(Pindar), being younger, overlapped in time with Simonides, being older. At
any rate, both mentioned the same actions; for, in fact, Simonides described the
sea-battle at Salamis, and Pindar mentions the kingship of Cadmus."]

The *vita* wants to show that Simonides and Pindar were contemporaries by stating
that both composed works relevant to the Persian Wars.[47] The reference to τὴν ἐν
Σαλαμῖνι ναυμαχίαν in the *vita* appears to confirm the work listed by the *Suda*
under a similar heading. *Prima facie,* it would seem that these two testimonia provide
a title for a "Salamis poem" by Simonides.

Yet, since it is likely that neither the *Suda* nor the *vita Pindari* actually consulted Simonides' poem, this conclusion is not certain.[48] The relevant questions to
ask here are, do the references in the *Suda* and the *vita* suggest the primary subject
of a poem which became solidified into a title? Or do these witnesses simply refer to
a subject on which Simonides' composed? The *vita* reports that Pindar "mentioned"
(μέμνηται) the kingship of Cadmus, and so provides a subject on which Pindar
composed verses. By analogy, it would seem that the *vita* also provides a subject on
which Simonides composed verses. The reference to verses on Salamis in the *Suda*
described by a similar heading, however, allows the possibility that a title may be
recorded here. In fact, the *vita* also shifts verbs and says that Simonides γέγραφε
("wrote") *The Sea-battle at Salamis.*[49] This shift in verbs, however, does not guarantee
a title in the *vita* or even the primary subject of a poem. A most famous comparison
can be found in the opening lines of Thucydides, ξυνέγραψε τὸν πόλεμον τῶν
Πελοποννησίων καὶ ᾿Αθηναίων ("(Thucydides, the Athenian,) has written about
the war between the Peloponnesians and the Athenians.")[50] This compound referring to the act of composing on a subject also appears in Plato. In a list of examples at
*Gorgias* 518B5–6, Plato refers to a Mithaecus as ὁ τὴν ὀψοποιίαν συγγεγραφὼς
τὴν Σικελικήν, "the one who composed on Sicilian cookery." Again, at *Leges* 858
D, Plato refers to those who compose and record their counsels concerning life with
this verb: ὅσοι ... τὴν αὐτῶν εἰς μνήνην ξυμβουλὴν περὶ βίου κατέθεντο
συγγράψαντες. The compound of γράφω here introduces the subject-matter,
rather than the title. The word γράφω, not a compound form, is used similarly at
[Theophrastus] *de Signis* 1, σημεῖα ὑδάτων καὶ πνευμάτων καὶ χειμώνων καὶ
εὐδιῶν ὧδε ἐγράψαμεν ("We thus described the signs of rains, winds, storms, and
things in fair weather").[51] Here, γράφω is used to introduce not a title, but rather
the subject matter of the work that will follow. This subject matter has then become
the title of the work in the manuscripts.[52] [Theophrastus] thus provides a parallel for

the introduction of subject-matter with a form of the word γράφω. In this way, it is possible to understand that the *vita* and the *Suda* refer not to the title of a poem but to its subject matter.

The question still remains, how does this reference to subject matter reflect the larger composition as a whole? For Thucydides, the subject matter provided in the opening sentence may be more exact than that given by his predecessor Herodotus, but it still admits further specification. A similar observation can be made concerning the passages in Plato, which refer to the subject matter of works in a general way. The passage in [Theophrastus] may list more specifically the topics covered in the treatise which takes its name from the first line, but the larger structure of the work is not evident from this description. It cannot be determined from these words if *de Signis* described any other phenomena or why these phenomena were described. In fact, such a full description seems to be unusual. Later bibliographers and biographers, such as Hesychius would qualify titles that might not be immediately obvious, but the practice does not appear to be consistent.[53] Moreover, these are prose works and it is difficult to imagine titles that would fully explain every aspect of the work.[54] Turning to poetry, a similar pattern can be observed in the appearance of titles for Attic drama and in particular the titles of Old Comedy. A comic play was given a title later after its chorus. It is fair to say that a comic chorus need not reflect the subject matter of the play.[55] Aristophanes' *Frogs* and *Knights,* to which Aristophanes himself refers by these headings, provide a parallel as plays with titles that appear to reflect the play's subject matter only slightly.[56] With only these titles, it would be difficult to determine what the exact content of these plays had been.

To return to Simonides, it is possible that the reference to *The Sea-battle at Salamis* reflects the content in a similar way.[57] As we have seen, the *Suda* probably culled this reference from an earlier compilation and thus is unlikely to have actually consulted Simonides' work on Artemisium. In fact, such consultation would be contrary to the nature of the *Suda.*[58] The *vita* contained in the Ambrosian manuscript, which dates to the 12th century CE, most likely was composed in a similar way.[59] So these sources can be said simply to repeat the information of their sources. Whether this information in the *Suda* derives simply from Hesychius of Miletus or ultimately goes back to the Alexandrian bibliographers, it is possible that this heading was assigned to a composition to verses pertaining to the battle of Salamis or a composition which was largely concerned with this battle.[60] Still, this heading does not limit the content of the poem to this battle. It only tells us that at some point someone saw the primary focus as being the battle of Salamis. In this way, even if the *Suda* and the *vita Pindari* refer to what had become a title of a work by Simonides on Salamis, we have no way of determining how this title reflects the content of this larger composition. One plausible conclusion is that we can only go as far as to say that the *vita* and the *Suda* provide us with a theme on which Simonides composed verses. The definition of the context in which this theme appeared remains unknown. By approaching the *vita* and the *Suda* in this way, it can be said that neither provide concrete evidence about Simonides' treatment of the battle of Salamis other than that Simonides composed verses on this battle.

The third witness for a "Salamis poem" is Plutarch *Them.* 15.4 (=fr. 5 W²). In his description of the victory at Salamis, Plutarch cites Simonides:

> οἱ δ᾽ ἄλλοι τοῖς βαρβάροις ἐξισούμενοι τὸ πλῆθος ἐν στενῷ κατὰ μέρος προσφερομένους καὶ περιπίπτοντας ἀλλήλοις ἐτρέψαντο μέχρι δείλης ἀντισχόντας, ὥσπερ εἴρηκε Σιμωνίδης, τὴν καλὴν ἐκείνην καὶ περιβόητον ἀράμενοι νίκην, ἧς οὔθ᾽ Ἕλλησιν οὔτε βαρβάροις ἐνάλιον ἔργον εἴργασται λαμπρότερον.

> ["The other (Greeks), being equal in number to the barbarians in the strait, routed them, who attacked in turn with detachments and collided into each other, although they held out until the late afternoon, and as Simonides said, they (the Greeks) gained that fine and much-talked-of victory, than which neither by Greeks nor Barbarians has there been a more illustrious deed done on the sea."]

It is generally assumed that Plutarch is referring to the poem called *The Sea-battle at Salamis* by the *Suda* and the *vita* because he is narrating the victory of this battle. Unfortunately, it is not clear whether the biographer is paraphrasing or quoting Simonides. Bergk, Page, West, and Campbell do not indicate which words belong to Simonides, and, thereby, suggest that the poet is being paraphrased.[61] The phrase preceding the mention of Simonides, μέχρι δείλης ἀντισχόντας, metrically would fit in an elegiac couplet. The words following the mention of Simonides, τὴν καλὴν ἐκείνην καὶ περιβόητον ἀράμενοι νίκην, are not elegiac. In fact, it is possible that the words περιβόητον ἀράμενοι νίκην constitute a lyric phrase. The adjective περιβόητος is found in a lyric context at Sophocles *Oedipus Tyrannus* 193.[62] The adjective, however, is not strictly poetic and is found in prose works as well.[63] Nevertheless, all such attempts to pinpoint the words of Simonides are speculative. It cannot be discerned whether the biographer is paraphrasing or quoting the poet. As a result, no evidence is gained about the form of the poem to which Plutarch refers. It can be further noted that Plutarch does not mention a specific poem. It is only assumed that these words come from a "Salamis poem" because Plutarch is recounting the battle. It is just as likely, however, that the verses that Plutarch has in mind come from a mention of the battle of Salamis in a larger context. So, the evidence in Plutarch does not allow for a definitive conclusion about Simonides' "Salamis poem." At most, what can be gained from Plutarch is that Simonides mentioned the battle of Salamis.

These three witnesses provide little evidence for *The Sea-battle at Salamis* by Simonides. On the surface, it appears that Plutarch has the poem in mind that is mentioned by the *Suda* and the *vita Pindari*. The meter of this poem cannot be discerned with certainty. The *Suda* records it as lyric, but the problems in this entry allow some doubt. The other witnesses do not clarify this confusion. At most, then, each of these witnesses only informs us that that Simonides mentioned the battle of Salamis in some poetic context.[64]

## B. The "New Simonides"

In addition to the testimonia discussed above, West includes two of the new fragments, POxy 2327 fr. 31 coll. i and ii, as part of the "Salamis Poem." These columns are divided respectively into frs. 6 and 7 W².[65] West later rightly withdrew this ascription.[66] Neither of these fragments can be securely placed in this or any poem.

*Frs. 6 and 7 W² (=POxy 2327 fr. 31 coll. i and ii) [see Figure 3]*

Fr. 6 W² (=POxy 2327 fr. 31 col. i) consists of two letters of text, ]ης, in line 5 and marginalia in lines 1–4. The letters that can be read of these marginalia provides little sense. Nothing in the fragment reasonably places it in any particular poem. The only basis for assigning the fragment to a "Salamis poem" is its proximity to fr. 7 W² (POxy 2327 fr. 31 col. ii). This placement, however, can only be accepted with reservations because two adjacent columns need not represent the same poem.[67]

| LOBEL | | WEST | |
|---|---|---|---|
| POxy 2327 fr. 31 | | Fr. 6 W² | |
| Col. i | col.ii | | |
| | | · | ]. |
| ]. λ[ | | · | ] |
| ] .[ | | · | ] |
| ]π^ω μα .[ | | · | ] |
| ]κη.) | [ . ]ω . . . [ | 5 · | ]ης |
| 5 ]ης | ∩ προντοβραl | | |
| ] | X πειθωνταl | Fr. 7 W² | |
| ] | ωсυποсαλ[ | . ]ω . . . [ | |
| | ]· παισινμηl | ∩ προντοβραl | |
| | ] φρυξl | X πειθωνταl | |
| 10 | ] φοινικωl | ὡς ὑπὸ σάλ[πιγγος | |
| | ] ηλθl | 5 παισὶν μηl | |
| | | Φρυξὶ ⊓ε | |
| | | Φοινίκω[ν | |
| | | ἠλθl | |

Figure 3.

Fr. 7 W$^2$ (= POxy 2327 fr. 31col. ii, lines 4–11) is more reasonably assigned to a "Salamis poem." In fact, before the ascription of POxy 2327 to Simonides, Lobel speculated that this fragment was composed by Simonides.[68] First, Lobel noted that the hand of POxy 2327 is the same hand as that of a group of lyric fragments (POxy 2430), already ascribed to Simonides. Second, he saw a possible reference to a sea-battle. This mention presumably lies in πọντοβọα[ (fr. 7.2 W$^2$) but Lobel is not explicit on this point. The meaning of this partial word, however, is uncertain.[69] Nevertheless, these observations allowed him to suggest tentatively that these fragments could be placed plausibly in a poem on Artemisium or Salamis. In addition, Lobel suggested cάλ[πιγγος ("war-trumpet") as a supplement in line 4. The "war-trumpet" establishes a parallel with Aeschylus' *Persians* 395 and, thus, provides further evidence for the ascription of the fragment to a "Salamis poem."[70] To these points can be added the appearance of the Phrygians and the Phoenicians in line fr. 7.6–7 W$^2$ (= POxy 2327 fr. 31 col. ii line 9–10).[71] It is also conjectured that fr. 7.5 W$^2$ (παισὶν μη) refers to the children of the Medes.[72]

It must be noted that the reading πọντοβọα[ is not certain. The ink for πọ is almost completely missing from the papyrus. Furthermore, even if this reading is accepted, it simply suggests that fr. 7 W$^2$ belongs to a description of a sea-battle. The specific sea-battle cannot be determined. In fact, none of the supplements of this fragment offers a satisfactory link to a poem on the battle of Salamis. The closest link lies in the conjecture cάλ[πιγγος ("war-trumpet"). Contexts other than Salamis are imaginable for the mention of a war-trumpet. In particular, Rutherford suggests an account of the battle of Mycale within the "Plataea poem" as appropriate for the mention of a war-trumpet.[73] A war-trumpet, however, might be imagined in the context of a poem on any battle in the Persian Wars. Furthermore, the references to the Phrygians and the Phoenicians also would fit into a description of any part of the Persian Wars. To be sure, the Phoenicians were specifically a seafaring people and in fact they were among the best in the Persian fleet.[74] Herodotus also depicts them as having a prominent role in the battle of Salamis.[75] There presence, then, would seem to suggest a sea-battle context, and more specifically, the battle of Salamis. On the other hand, the Phrygians are listed as part of the Persian army by Herodotus in his general catalogue of Persian forces.[76] They are also mentioned as contributing a small number of troops at the battle of Plataea.[77] The Phrygians would seem to suggest a poem on a land-battle, possibly Plataea. There is no way to determine which of the two figures are to be emphasized. The conclusion must be that the larger context in which Simonides mentioned the Phrygians and the Phoenicians cannot be determined without the other supplements in this fragment. In terms of the "Salamis" poem, then, even the cumulative evidence of these suggestions offers no reason to associate fr. 7 W$^2$ with Simonides' "Salamis poem." In fact, Parsons initially suggested that this fragment belonged in the "Artemisium poem."[78] The conclusion must be that there is no reason to link fr. 7 $W^2$ with a depiction of Salamis and, as a result, the placement of fr. 6 $W^2$ in such a poem is also to be doubted as well. So, these fragments cannot be used as evidence for Simonides' description of Salamis.

### C. Conclusion

The *Suda* and the *vita Pindari,* then, become our only evidence for Simonides' depiction of the battle of Salamis. The evidence in Plutarch (*Them.* 15.4) is too vague to connect the passage to a "Salamis poem" or to give definition to the context that the biographer has in mind. None of the fragments from the "new Simonides" discussed here can be shown to belong to any particular poem and so provide no evidence about their original context. From the *Suda* and the *vita,* it can be assumed that Simonides depicted the battle of Salamis in some poetic context. The only certain conclusion that arises from the *Suda* and the *vita Pindari* is that Simonides composed verses on the battle of Salamis and possibly that this depiction was of considerable length or was memorable. It must be admitted that the larger poetic context for these verses remains a mystery.

## 1.4 THE PLATAEA POEM

### A. Evidence

West has grouped nine fragments under the heading *De proelio Plataico,* of which seven come from the new papyri.[79] Outside of the "new Simonides," no explicit testimonia for such a poem exist.[80]

Before the publication of the new fragments, Plutarch provided evidence that Simonides composed verses that depicted the Corinthian contingent at the battle of Plataea. Plutarch *de Herod. malign.* 872D (=frs. 15–16 $W^2$), contains six elegiac lines by Simonides on the valor of the Corinthians at Plataea:

Ἀλλὰ Κορινθίους γε καὶ τάξιν ἣν ἐμάχοντο τοῖς βαρβάροις, καὶ τέλος ἡλίκον ὑπῆρξεν αὐτοῖς ἀπὸ τοῦ Πλαταιᾶσιν ἀγῶνος ἔξεστι Σιμωνίδου πυθέσθαι γράφοντος ἐν τούτοις·

μέσσοις δ' οἵ τ' Ἐφύρην πολυπίδακα ναιετάοντες,

παντοίης ἀρετῆς ἴδριες ἐν πολέμωι

οἵ τε πόλιν Γλαύκοιο Κορίνθιον ἄστυ νέμονται·

οἵ

— ∪ ∪ κάλλιστον μάρτυν ἔθεντο πόνων

χρυσοῦ τιμήεντος ἐν αἰθέρι· καί σφιν ἀέξει

αὐτῶν τ' εὐρεῖαν κληδόνα καὶ πατέρων.[81]

ταῦτα γὰρ οὐ χορὸν ἐν Κορίνθωι διδάσκων, οὐδ' ᾆσμα ποιῶν εἰς τὴν
πόλιν, ἄλλως δὲ τὰς πράξεις ἐκείνας ἐλεγεῖα γράφων ἱστόρηκεν

["But concerning the Corinthians, both the arrangement of the army they employed against the Barbarians and how great the outcome was for them from
the battle of Plataea, it is possible to learn from Simonides, who wrote in these
verses

> In the middle were those who live in Ephyre with many fountains, who are
> experienced in every excellence in war, and those who inhabit the city of
> Glaukos, the Corinthian town

who

> established for themselves as the finest witness, that of the esteemed gold in
> the sky, of their struggles; and this (deed) increases for them the far-reaching
> glory of them and their fathers.[82]

For he (Simonides) has recorded these things, not while leading a chorus in
Corinth, nor while composing a lyric song for the city, but otherwise when writing about these undertakings in elegiacs."]

Despite the focus on the battle of Plataea, these verses were not generally considered
to represent a "Plataea poem" before the publication of the "new Simonides."[83] In the
first edition of *IEG*, West designated them as *Incertum an ex epigrammatis*.[84]

It cannot be determined whether what Plutarch designates as ἐλεγεῖα represents a larger elegiac poem or an epigram.[85] Nevertheless, he does provide valuable
information about the poetic context of these verses. He explicitly says that the verses
were not composed for performance at Corinth (ταῦτα γὰρ οὐ χορὸν ἐν Κορίνθωι
διδάσκων), and that they were not composed specifically for the Corinthians (οὐδ'
ᾆσμα ποιῶν εἰς τὴν πόλιν). Plutarch's comments reveal that these verses belong in
a larger composition which in some way pertained to the battle of Plataea. This context was not specifically concerned with the Corinthians' role in this battle. Moreover,
this composition was not meant as praise of the Corinthians alone. Further specificity
about the larger context cannot be garnered from Plutarch.

### B The "New Simonides"
### POxy 3965 fr. 5 + Plu. de Herodot. malign. 872D [see Figure 4]

An overlap between the citation in Plutarch (fr. 16 W²) and POxy 3965 fr. 5 provides
further evidence for the composition to which these verses on Plataea belong.[86] This
overlap provides part of a verse following those quoted by Plutarch. More importantly, this overlap provides the possibility that some of the other fragments from this
papyrus also belong to this composition and will be helpful in defining it. Since POxy
3965 overlaps POxy 2327, this composition should be found in both papyri.[87]

| PARSONS | WEST |
|---|---|
| POxy 3965 fr. 5 | Fr. 16 W$^2$ (POxy 3965 fr. 5 + Plu. *de Herod. malign.* 872D) |
|  | οἳ |
| ] . αιθερ[ | — ⏑ ⏑ κάλλιστον μάρτυν ἔθεντο πόνων |
| ] . δ . . [ | χρυσοῦ τιμήεντος ἐ᾿ν αἰθέρ᾿ι· καί σφιν ἀέξει |
| ]πολψ[ | αὐτῶν τ᾿ εὐρεῖαν κλ᾿ηδόν᾿ι α καὶ πατέρων |
|  | ]πολψ[ |

Figure 4.

There are various ways of defining this composition from the evidence of the "new Simonides." The papyri might represent longer non-epigrammatic elegiac poems, one of which was about the battle of Plataea or at least contained a depiction of the battle. It is also possible that the papyri contained a collection of epigrams or shorter non-epigrammatic elegies that depicted events in the Persian Wars. The larger context of Plutarch's quote remains obscure and the specific content of the poem cannot be determined from this evidence alone. POxy 3965 fr. 5 is, then, only the first step for identifying the composition which frs. 15–16 W$^2$ represent.

## Fr. 11 W$^2$ and Frs. 15–16 W$^2$

It is a reasonable assumption that fr. 11 W$^2$ (=POxy 2327 frs. 5 + 6 + 27 col. i + POxy 3965 frs. 1 + 2) belongs to the same larger context as the verses quoted by Plutarch. Although fr. 11 W$^2$ does not overlap the text given by Plutarch and it is not physically linked to POxy 3965 fr. 5, these fragments can be connected because of their common content. Pausanias, the Spartan leader at Plataea, is certainly named at fr. 11.34 W$^2$ (=POxy 3965 fr. 2.13) and the Spartans plausibly can be read in fr. 11.25 W$^2$ (= POxy 3965 fr. 2.4), Tyndarids in fr. 11.30 W$^2$ (=POxy 3965 fr. 2.9), Menelaus, the Homeric Spartan king, in fr. 11.31 W$^2$ (=POxy 3965 fr. 2.10) and the Corinthians at fr. 11.35 W$^2$ (=POxy 3965 fr.2.14).[88] These names suggest that this fragment is concerned with the battle of Plataea. The current orthodoxy is that fr. 11 W$^2$ represents the opening or an early section of an elegy that focused on this battle and frs. 15–16 W$^2$ belong in the same poem. It is on the basis of this connection in terms of content that West then is able to link these fragments and to amass the nine elegiac fragments for a "Plataea poem" which I have mentioned.

## Fr. 11 W$^2$ (=POxy 2327 frs. 5+6+27 col. i + POxy 3965 frs. 1+2) [see Figures 5 and 6]

It was not until the publication of the "new Simonides" in 1992 that the verses quoted by Plutarch were taken to be part of a "Plataea poem" by Simonides. The

POxy 2327 fr. 5 (Lobel)
```
  ]...[.]..[
  ]ηπιτυνε ‖ μ̣[βηc[
  ]υλοτομοιδαμ[
4 ]πολλονδ̣ηπ̣ω̣c[
```

POxy 2327 fr. 6 (Lobel)
```
   ]ρcλαο . [
   ]οκλου . . [
  ] . μαccενε . [
  ]ωνοcχειρι[                 POxy 3965 fr. 1 (Parsons)
5 ]ψcαπ̣ [              ]ςεουϲ . [        ]ςτ[
  ] . παι . c . ι[      ] . αμουπαιcιχ[     ]ομ[
  ]ριοκα . [           ] . δ̣ρ . ιοκακοφρ[  ]c,ωϲ . . . [    POxy 2327 fr. 27 (Lobel)
  ] . ερ
  ]ομακ[              ] . θειηcαρμα . αθειλεδ . . [    col. i                col. ii
  ] . ςcαο . [      5 ]υπερcαντεcαοιδιμον[            ] . οντο[ ][
10  [ . ′]             ]ωω . αγέμάχοιδαναόι[           ]              [
                       ] . ατουκεχυταικλεοcα . [       ]εκητι  [
                       ]λοκαμωνδεξατοπιεριδ[          ]              [
                       ]θειην·καιεπωνυμονο . [     5 ]οιcιν[
                    10 ] . θεωνωκυμορουγενε . [      ] ·ηρω[              ]θεα[
                       ]υνυνχαιρεθεαcερικυ[         ]              [        ]ρεμ[
POxy 3965 fr.2         ] . λιουνηρεοc· αυταρεγ . [    ]              [        ]ηπτο[
(Parsons)              ]c' επικουρονεμοι . [         ]εμουcα   [              ]ετερη[
(a) ]θρωπω[             ] . ευχομενω[            10 ] ·περ α"                 ]κουφ[
  ] . καιτουδ[    15   ] . φρονακ[                  ] . δηc          θ[       ]ηπτολε[
  ] . ρηcϊνατιc[              ] . . . . . . . [       ]                τ . λ[  ]αρα[
  ]γ . οιcπαρτ[                                      ]αρ              οφραπομενμηδ[
5 ]α . υν [] . . [     (b)  ]ωͺ[                      ]          [    ] καιπερcων·δωρουδ[
  ] . ηcελαθ[          ]γουρανο . [             15  ] . c     [       ]παιcικαιηρακλεοϲ[
    ] . θρω . ω . [ ] . . αθανατο  [                 ]α" εν ανθρωπ[  ]δεπιεcπεδιου[
    ] . ωͺτανακα[  ]cαcτυλιπουντ[                    ]          [    ] . ωποιδεφ[ . ]υ[[ο]] . [
    ]ξηνοcπα . cιcυνιπποδαμοιc         [             ] [         ]ρεcτε[ . ] . ντ[
10 ] . cηρωcικα[ τ]ευρυβιηιμενελαω[
    ] . ωιηcηγεμονεcπ[ . ] . εοc Ν [
       ] . [ρ . ου . [] . [ ]γ' αριcτ[      (c)  ] . . [
    ] α . . παυcανιης
    ] . καιεπικλεαεργακοριν[ ]ρυ
15  ] . ανταλιδεωπελοποc []
       ] . ςουπολιν·ενθαπερ·ω [
       ] . υλαπερικτιονων   [
       ] . ςι . εποιθοτ̣ . . οιδ[]ςcυχ[
    ] . [] . τ . υπεδιου
20    ]δͺ . νοcεξε[         ]υτε . [
       ] . οcαν . . θε . [] . [
       ] . cδαμαcαν . [
       ] . . ειδομεν[
          ]νυμονα . [
```

Figure 5.

silence on the part of ancient commentators about such a poem may be an accident of transmission; as we have seen, such silence on the part of ancient commentators, bibliographers or biographers is not surprising. Even still, the conclusion that these fragments represent such a poem that otherwise has been lost in the cracks of a lacunose tradition warrants some reconsideration. Although sense may connect the quote in Plutarch with fr. 11 W$^2$ as verses on the battle of Plataea, an analysis of the new

| SIDER | WEST |
|---|---|
| Fr. 11 | Fr. 11 W² |

Figure 6.

fragment reveals that it does not provide sufficient evidence for a "Plataea poem" as it is currently construed in modern scholarship.

The bulk of fr. 11 W² is constructed from POxy 3965 frs. 1 and 2. There is no physical relation between these scraps, but Lobel proposed their arrangement in the same column because he believed POxy 3965 fr. 2.1 was the continuation of POxy 3965 fr. 1.14.[89] Parsons secures this arrangement by arguing persuasively that POxy 2327 fr. 27 col. i contains notes and line ends for verses in both of these fragments.[90] This arrangement is now accepted as the standard text (fr. 11.9–45 W²). POxy 3965, then, provides a substantial section of continuous verses.

The number of verses from this single poem in the new fragments is increased by an overlap between POxy 2327 fr. 6.5–9 and POxy 3965 fr. 1.1–5 (=fr. 11.5–13 W[2]).[91] This overlap provides four additional verses. The combination of these three fragments is certain. So, the new papyri provide 40 consecutive elegiac verses, none of which is complete. These verses are fr. 11.5–45 W[2].

West's placement of POxy 2327 fr. 5 as fr. 11.1–4 W[2] is less secure. Two circumstances allow this connection. First, POxy 2327 fr. 5, a column bottom, and POxy 2327 fr. 6, a column top, may have originally belonged in adjacent columns.[92] Second, POxy 2327 fr. 5 may pertain to the death of a hero. This sense is derived from the words πίτυν ("pine") and ὑλοτόμοι ("woodcutters"), which echo Homeric similes for the deaths of heroes on the battle-field.[93] This interpretation would accord well with West's suggested reconstruction of POxy 2327 fr. 6 as a depiction of a burial of a hero who died at the hands of Apollo (POxy 2327 fr. 6.3–4 = fr. 11.7–8 W[2]).[94] In this way, POxy 2327 fr. 5 (= fr. 11.1–4 W[2]) contains a simile that refers to the death of Achilles, who is then said to have been killed at the hands of Apollo in POxy 2327 fr. 6.3–4 (= fr. 11.7–8 W[2]). That the hero in these verses is Achilles appears to be confirmed by the invocation of the hero as the son of Thetis at fr. 11.19–20 W[2]. This reconstruction of the sense allows West to confirm the connection between POxy 2327 frs. 5 and 6 originally suggested by the potential physical link between the fragments.

This arrangement, however, is not without problems. As Parsons has pointed out, although the physical evidence might suggest this arrangement, there is no real connection between these fragments.[95] West's reconstruction of the content, then, is the only substantial reason for linking these fragments. The references to the death of a hero, however, offer other possible interpretations. Parsons suggests that these verses may refer to the death of Mardonius (Hdt. 9.63) or Masistius (Hdt. 9.22).[96] Even if the link between POxy 2327 fr. 5 and Achilles is accepted, it is conceivable that the fragment represents a column bottom that came later in the poem. If this is the case, the poem represented by fr. 11 W[2] will return to the death of Achilles in some other section.[97] Each of these suggestions still allows that this fragment belongs to the same poem as fr. 11 W[2]. Yet, the inconclusiveness of the link between these fragments also allows the possibility that POxy 2327 fr. 5 does not relate to the same poem as fr. 11.5–45 W[2]. These doubts underscore the precariousness of West's placement of POxy 2327 fr. 5 as fr. 11.1–4 W[2]. These lines can only be tentatively tied to fr. 11 W[2] and should be considered separately.

As it stands, fr. 11 W[2] only provides forty consecutive lines of a poem with any degree of certainty. The subject of these verses is perceived by most scholars to be the Spartans, Pausanias, their leader at Plataea, and events leading up to the battle itself. The details of this focus are interpreted variously, but the ultimate conclusion is that the content of this fragment confirms the existence a "Plataea poem." Yet, the prominence of the Spartan and Pausanias in these verses, even if they come from the opening of the poem, does not necessitate a similar focus throughout the poem.[98] Further consideration is needed to draw conclusions about the scope of the poem represented by fr. 11 W².

A closer look at fr. 11 W² reveals that the poem represented by this fragment should be construed as having a focus that is broader than the Spartans and the battle of Plataea. First, the Corinthians are a certain reading in fr. 11.35 W²; *prima facie*, fr. 11 W² was concerned with Sparta and her Peloponnesian allies. Such a judgment is appealing, especially in the light of a possible connection of fr. 11 W² and frs. 15–16 W². It can then be concluded that fr. 11 W² represents a poem that is more broadly concerned with the battle of Plataea and not simply a depiction of the Spartan role in this battle.

Further support for a broader focus comes in the possible mention of the Athenians in 11.41–42W² (=POxy 3965 fr. 2.21–22). The interpretation of these verses is highly debated and the terrible state of the text does not make conclusions easy:

]δι . νοcεξε[    ]ντε . [
] . . οcαν . . θε . [] . [

There are two main problems. First, the interpretation of the action in 11.41 W² is uncertain. It is generally agreed that this line should be supplemented to read Παν]δίονος ἐξε[λάσα]ντεϲ.[99] The interpretation of the verses supplemented in this way is difficult because it is not clear how the action denoted by ἐξε[λάσα]ντεϲ pertains to the battle of Plataea. This participle elsewhere is translated transitively as "driving *someone* out" or intransitively as "marching out." [100]

Modern scholars have usually chosen between these meanings in accordance with their overall interpretation of the poem. Those who want to see the Athenians in fr. 11.41–42 W² favor the intransitive translation. By translating the participle intransitively, these scholars introduce the movement of the Athenians from Salamis to Plataea. In this way, Simonides' composition is made to correspond to the narrative of Herodotus, in which the Athenians come from Salamis to join the army marching to Plataea.[101] Yet, the intransitive meaning of ἐξελάσαντεϲ does not really refer to the act of setting out across the sea.[102] To solve this difficulty, Parsons, who places the arrival of the Athenians at this point in the poem, has suggested the passive ἐξε[λαθέ]ντεϲ ("being driven out") as an alternative to the intransitive ἐξελάσαντεϲ. This suggestion attempts to bring the sense closer to the meaning, "the Athenians disembarked" from Salamis.[103] Yet, as a passive, ἐξε[λαθέ]ντεϲ will mean "to be driven out," a meaning that is not entirely consistent with Herodotus' depictions of the Athenians' movement from Salamis. As Rutherford correctly points out, this passive is still unusual because the Athenians left Salamis willingly.[104] It must be concluded that both the intransitive ἐξελάσαντες and passive ἐξε[λαθέ]ντες present difficulties for interpreting the text at this point.

Those who do not want the Athenians to appear in fr. 11 W$^2$ favor the transitive meaning of this participle, as West's interpretation of this line shows. He solves the problem by removing the Athenians altogether and translating ἐξε[λάσα]ντες transitively, as "driving *someone* out." For West, this line depicts the Greeks driving the Persians from the land of Pandion, that is Attica (Παν]δίονος).[105] This interpretation, however, contradicts the account of Plataea in Herodotus, where the Persians are not driven out of Attica, but they march out willingly to meet the Greek forces.[106] A. Schachter offers another solution that would allow the transitive meaning to stand. He suggests that the Pandion in these verses refers to the Megarian hero. In this way, the line refers to the Megarid, not Athens. For Schachter, the narrative in Herodotus 9.14–15 provides the parallel for his interpretation of Simonides' words. In Herodotus, the Persian leader, Mardonius, first marches toward Megara when he hears that an advance force of Lacedaemonians had arrived there. He then retreats and marches through Decelea when he learns of the meeting of the Greeks at the Isthmus.[107] Schachter observes that Pausanias, the periegete, records a Megarian tale about these Persian troops who entered the Megarid. Pausanias tells the story of a detachment of Mardonius' troops (specifically called Medes at 1.44.4) which became lost in the night by the will of Artemis. Unable to see if the enemy was in the vicinity, they shot all of their arrows into the ground. The result was that they were vulnerable to a Megarian attack the next day. The troops of Mardonius were slaughtered, and in Pausanias' day one could still see a rock with the arrows of the Medes still in it (1.40.2, 1.44.4). According to Schachter two conclusions arise from this parallel. First, ἐξε[λάσα]ντες refers to the Megarians driving the Persians out the Megarid, or the land of Pandion. Second, the πεδίον mentioned in the preceding verse (fr. 11.40 W$^2$) may be the plain on which this massacre took place. He suggests that the reference is to the Leukou/ Leukon plain in the Megarid.[108] These observations lead Schachter to conclude that these verses provide part of a narrative which focuses on the Spartan march to Plataea, with reference to Megara as the army passed by this city. Ultimately, in Schachter's view, these verses form a piece of Spartan propaganda.[109] In such propaganda, there appears to be no room for the Athenians to be mentioned.[110]

Schachter's hypothesis is intriguing, because it connects these verses (fr. 11.40–41 W$^2$) with the surrounding context. It should be noted that in fr. 11.37 W$^2$, Megara may have been mentioned periphrastically as the city of Nisus (N]ίσου πόλιν). These letters are generally interpreted as referring to a geographic point along the Spartan march to the Plataea. It is in this way that both Schachter and West construe this section of fr. 11 W$^2$. Yet, if it is accepted that these verses refer to the Megarian hero Pandion, other conclusions concerning the relation between this reference and the larger composition represented by fr. 11 W$^2$ are possible. In particular, Schachter's

reading of the Megarian Pandion in fr. 11 W$^2$ would allow that the possible reference to Megara in line 37 introduced a longer description of their heroic deed that
ran from fr.11.37–41 W$^2$.[111] Some caution, however, is needed. While it is plausible
to connect Herodotus' narrative and the story of the Persian slaughter at the hands
of the Megarians told by Pausanias, the link is not specifically made.[112] Herodotus
does not mention the event and the story could have been a later invention by the
Megarians. Furthermore, it is not certain that such a story would have a bearing on
Simonides' composition. The point to make here is that while Schachter's reading of
ἐξε[λάσα]ντες leads him to remove the Athenians, his interpretation of these verses
may not support the reconstruction of a Spartan-centered poem. Ultimately, it must
be concluded that this transitive translation of ἐξε[λάσα]ντες also has difficulties.

The surrounding context of this verse further complicates the issue. Any conclusions concerning 11.41 W$^2$ must also take into consideration the interpretation
of 11.42 W$^2$. The interpretation of this line directly involves the introduction of
Athenians. The difficulty stems from the initial letters of the verse. There are two possibilities for reading these incomplete letters. Parsons reads the letters as—οπ—and
suggests Κέκρ]οπος ἀντιθέου for fr. 11.42 W$^2$.[113] For Parsons, 11.41 W$^2$ introduces the Athenians as they set out from Salamis and fr. 11.42 W$^2$ retains the Athenians as its subject in the paraphrase, "of god-like Kekrops." On the other hand, West
read the letters as—τι—and suggests μάν]τιος ἀντιθέου for fr. 11.42 W$^2$.[114] So
West's interpretation follows his reading of 11.41 W$^2$. First, the Persians are driven
out of Attica and then, in the second verse, the Spartan seer, Teisamenos, makes his
first appearance as the "god-like seer."[115] In this way, this supplement removes the
Athenians entirely and forces the interpretation that the poem is focused on the
Spartans at Plataea.[116]

Opinion on the supplements is divided. On paleographic grounds, Rutherford
prefers West's supplement.[117] Obbink, using digital analysis, follows Parsons' reading.[118] My own inspection of the digital images provided by Obbink shows that
]⸳π is preferable to ]⸳τι. The problem of reading the mark to the left of the π
remains. Parsons has suggested ]ọ with caution, noting that such a reading is difficult
to reconcile with similar letters throughout the fragments.[119] Again, inspection of the
images of the papyri reveals that this mark seems less likely to represent an elongated
horizontal of a τ and even less likely to belong to ]ν, as would be needed for West's
reading. Although all conclusions on this point must remain tentative, the papyrological evidence does appear to favor Parsons' supplement.

Still, if Parsons' supplement is accepted, the question remains: what are the
Athenian's doing in these verses? G. Huxley has recently pointed out in his excellent
review of Boedeker and Sider's volume that "a mention of Kekrops does not entail a
reference to the Athenians moving from Salamis to Eleusis (Hdt. 9.19.2). Mardonios,
for example burned the city of Kekrops and led his troops from the land of Kekrops

into Boiotia."[120] To be sure, Huxley's astute observation is correct; nevertheless, a mention of Cecrops, even in a reference to Mardonius' actions concerning Athens, would still directly or indirectly introduce the Athenians or Athens into the poem. The state of the fragment does not allow us to be more specific. Even if one of Huxley's suggestions is accepted, it is still possible that the Athenians were introduced into the poem in some way. We simply do not know what the poet said about them or their city. If the Athenians themselves appeared, it is unknown what the poet said they did in these verses.

More weight is given to Parsons' supplement and the presence of the Athenians in fr. 11 W[2] by evidence outside that "new Simonides" which suggests that a commemoration of the victory over the Persians would mention Sparta, Athens, and Corinth. Herodotus reports that after the battle of Plataea, the Greeks set up three thank-offerings for their victory: one to Apollo at Delphi, one to Zeus at Olympia and one to Poseidon at the Isthmus (9.81). The Serpent Column, dedicated at Delphi, provides useful insight into the commemoration of this victory. The opening two coils of this column read:

| Coil | 1 | το[ίδε τὸν] |
| | | πόλεμον [ἐ-] |
| | | πολ[έ]μεον |
| Coil | 2 | Λακεδ[αιμόνιοι] |
| | | Ἀθαναῖο[ι] |
| | | Κορίνθιοι[121] |

["These men fought the war: the Lacedaemonians, the Athenians, the Corinthians . . ."]

Importantly, the first three names on the inscription are, in order, Spartans, Athenians, and Corinthians. A similar arrangement is recorded by Pausanias, the periegete (second century CE), for the dedication at Olympia (5.23.1–2):

εἰσὶ δὲ καὶ ἐγγεγραμμέναι κατὰ τοῦ βάθρου τὰ δεξιὰ αἱ μετασχοῦσαι πόλεις τοῦ ἔργου, Λακεδαιμόνιοι μὲν πρῶτοι, μετὰ δὲ αὐτοὺς Ἀθηναῖοι, τρίτοι δὲ γεγραμμένοι καὶ τέταρτοι Κορίνθιοί τε καὶ Σικυώνιοι

["The cities who took part in the effort (at Plataea) have been inscribed along the right of the pedestal: first there are the Lacedaemonians, after these the Athenians, and third the Corinthians and Sikyonians."]

Although the presence of the Athenians on these monuments does not guarantee Parsons' interpretation of fr. 11.41–42W[2], these inscriptions do reinforce the idea that the epigraphic commemorations of the victory in 479 BCE were panhellenic.[122] It remains a possibility that a poem commemorating the battle of Plataea also would also be panhellenic in its scope and praise. This suggestion is even more plausible in the light of the evidence for the Corinthians in fr. 11.35 $W^2$ and frs. 15–16 $W^2$.[123] With this possibility in mind, this inscriptional evidence provides an example of commemorations of the victory over the Persians that can be construed to support Parsons' reading at fr. 11.41–42 $W^2$.

Various observations follow from this proposed placement of the Athenians in fr. 11$W^2$ and the possible understanding that the fragment should be construed as having a panhellenic perspective. First, the appearance of Achilles in fr. 11 $W^2$, who is recalled in the prooimial hymn of fr. 11.1–20 $W^2$ is consistent with this panhellenic perspective.[124] Second, the inclusion of at least six verses that praise the Corinthians (frs. 15–16 $W^2$) in the same poem as fr. 11 $W^2$ suggests that this panhellenism extended beyond a simple reference to other cities in a poem that focused on the Lacedaemonians. Similar praise of the Athenians may have occurred either at their introduction in fr. 11 $W^2$ or later in a section of the poem that does not survive. Third, although the nature of this treatment of other cities cannot be determined from the extant fragments, it remains a possibility that this panhellenic representation included references to other battles in the Persian Wars. It should be reiterated that the length of this poem is unknown. Frs. 15 and 16 $W^2$ and the verses that certainly belong to fr. 11 $W^2$ provide only 47 lines. Furthermore, only six of these lines (frs. 15–16 $W^2$) are complete and only three (fr. 15 $W^2$) are without textual problems.

From the above considerations, it can be concluded that frs. 11, 15 and 16 $W^2$ cannot be said with any certainty to represent a separate poem on the battle of Plataea as it is construed in modern scholarship. The possibility that the poem represented by fr. 11 $W^2$ is panhellenic in perspective allows the further suggestion that the content of this poem is to be construed more broadly. It remains possible that a poem, in which it is reasonable to conclude that the three main figures in this battle are at least mentioned, also contained verses that praised the role of these figures in the Persian Wars as a whole. Such a conclusion may, in fact, explain the silence that surrounds a "Plataea poem" in ancient sources. The evidence in frs. 11, 15, and 16 $W^2$ can only be used to demonstrate that Simonides mentioned the battle of Plataea.

The other fragments associated by West with a "Plataea poem" do not provide more decisive support for a separate elegy on the battle of Plataea. In fact, the connection between these fragments and such a poem is often built upon the preconceived notion that the battle of Plataea is a subject that is represented by many of the verses in the "new Simonides."

### Fr. 10 $W^2$ (=POxy 3965 fr. 22) [see Figure 7]

West places fr. 10 $W^2$ before fr. 11 $W^2$ because both supposedly address Achilles. In fr. 10 $W^2$, this address arises from a conjecture in line 5.[125] The sense that arises from

| PARSONS | WEST |
|---|---|
| POxy 3965 fr.22 | Fr. 10 W² |
| ]υχ . [ | ]υχα[ |
| ] . προπατω[ | ..... (.) πατὴ]ρ προπάτω[ρ τε |
| ] . θωνην . [ | ......... .(.)] . θωνην α[ |
| ] . ωνυπερημ[ | ..... . μελε]τῶν ὑπὲρ ἡμ[ετέρων |
|   ·α· | |
| 5  ] . λιηcαγλαο . . [ | 5  κούρης εἰν]αλίης ἀγλαόφη[με πάϊ |
| ] . c[ | ....... .(.)]ηση[ |

Figure 7.

this proposed text fits well with the sense of fr. 11.1–20 W², which is interpreted as a hymn to Achilles. At 11.19–20 W², West conjectures another address to Achilles, with the supplement ἀλλὰ σὺ μὲ]ν νῦν χαῖρε, θεᾶς ἐρικυ[δέος υἱέ / κούρης εἰν]αλίου Νηρέος·[.[126] With these supplements, he creates, in effect, a prooimial hymn to Achilles that is ring-compositional.

It is not entirely clear, however, that the creation of ring-composition is sufficient basis for the proposed arrangement. No physical connection exists between these fragments and the paleographic evidence for West's conjecture in fr. 10 W² is uncertain. The marks that provides ]αλι (10.5) are difficult to read. There appears to be an additional mark between the λ and the ι. The ]α is also unclear. Furthermore, as Parsons points out, West's reading of η[ at the end of the line is not immediately obvious.[127] It must be concluded, then, that there is little certain text to guarantee the presence of Achilles in this fragment.[128] Even if the supplements are accepted, the proposed arrangement is not guaranteed. As Rutherford points out, these addresses could frame the entire poem.[129] Furthermore, this fragment can be envisaged as coming from another poem. If Achilles is in this fragment, it should be recalled that Simonides is said to have composed a poem in which Achilles married Medea on the Isle of the Blessed.[130] With these points in mind, West's supplements establish no clear relation between these fragments and fr. 10 W² provides no direct evidence for a "Plataea poem."

*Frs. 12 and 13 W² (=POxy 2327 frs. 30+18 and fr. 27 col. ii) [see Figure 8]*

Fr. 12 W² is a small fragment that consists of the two smaller scraps, POxy 2327 frs. 30 and fr. 18. These pieces of papyrus offer no clues about the context from which they are drawn. Lobel originally connected these scraps by matching their fibers, but he could not determine the distance between them.[131] So the unity of the pieces that make up fr. 12 W² is not certain. Furthermore, no physical connection exists between frs. 12 W² and fr. 11 W². The only link between fr. 12 W² and the "Plataea poem" is its perceived proximity to fr. 13 W² (=POxy 2327 fr. 27 col. ii). Lobel originally noted this proximity and he is followed by West, who suggests that frs. 12 and 13 belong to

| LOBEL | | WEST |
|---|---|---|
| POxy 2327 fr. 30      POxy 2327 fr. 18 | | Fr. 12 W² |
| ] . [ | | ] . [ |
| ] . ∈ρ . [ | | ]δ∈ρ . [ |
| ] . ∈κ . [     ]γτα | | ]τ∈κ . [     ]γτα |
| ] . [ | | ] . [ |
| | | |
| POxy 2327 fr. 27 col.ii | | Fr. 13 W² |
|        ]θ∈α[ | |        ]θ∈α[ |
|        ]ο∈μ[ | |        ]ο∈μ[ |
|        ]πτο[ | |        ]πτο[ |
|        ]∈τ∈ρη[ | |        ]∈τ∈ρη[ |
| 5       ]κουφ[ | | 5       ]κουφ[ |
|    θ[    ]πτολ∈[ | |    θ[    ]πτολ∈[μ |
|   τ . λ[   ]αρα[ | |   τα . [   ]αρα[ |
|  οφραπομ∈νμηδ[ | |   ὄφρ' ἀπὸ μὲν Μήδ[ων |
| ] καιπ∈ρcων·δωρουδ[ | |   καὶ Περσῶν, Δώρου δ[ὲ |
| 10 ]παιcικαιηρακλ∈ρc[ | | 10   παισὶ καὶ Ἡρακλέος [ |
|    ]δ∈πι∈cπ∈διου[ | |   οἱ] δ' ἐπεὶ ἐς πεδίον [ |
|  ] . ωποιδ∈φ[ . ]ν[ο] . [ | |   ∈ἱ]cωποι δ' ἔφ[α]ν∈γ[ |
|    ]ο∈cτ∈[ . ] . νγ[ | |   ]ο∈cτ∈[ . ]ονγ[ |

Figure 8.

the same column.[132] The reasons for this placement, however, are not expressed. The lack of content in fr. 12 W² frustrates the connection. Since nothing in this fragment is informative about its content, it must be concluded that there is little reason to connect it to fr. 11 W².

Fr. 13 W² (=POxy 2327 fr. 27 col. ii) has a more certain relation to fr. 11 W². This relation is based on the identification by Parsons that POxy 2327 fr. 27 col. i provides the line ends of POxy 3965 fr. 1.5–2.6 (= 11.13–27 W²).[133] There is no physical evidence for this connection, but it is made certain by three coincidences. First, the spacing of the lines in POxy 2327 fr. 27 col. i reveals that only the hexameters survive. These hexameter ends can be shown to correspond to the partial verses in POxy 3965 frs. 1 and 2. Second, the resulting hexameters provide an allusion to Homer in fr. 11.13 W² (=POxy 3965 fr. 1.5), the source for an allusion in Theocritus at fr. 11.17 W² (=POxy 3965 fr. 1.9), and the vocative required by sense in fr. 11.21 W² (POxy 3965 fr. 1.13). [134] Third, a possible relation exists between a marginal note in POxy 2327 fr. 27 col. i line 16 and POxy 3965 fr. 2.7 (=fr. 11.28 W²). The marginal note is: ]αν ∈ν ανθρωπ[ . The letters ] . θρω . ω . [   ] . . αθανατο [ ] appear at POxy 3965 fr. 2.7 (=fr. 11.28 W²). The connection hinges on the correspondence between two certain letters (θρ) and one uncertain letter (ω). Doubt may be cast on this connection because, as Parsons remarks, ἄνθρωπος is a common word.[135] Although none of these connections alone secures a relation between POxy 3965 fr. 1+2 and POxy 2327 fr. 27 col. i, taken together they make the connection almost certain. As a result, fr. 13 W$^2$, which is col. ii of POxy 2327 fr. 27, contains verses that closely follow those of fr. 11 W$^2$ in the lost scroll.

Although POxy 2327 fr. 27 col. ii can be shown to have been near to verses in fr. 11 W$^2$ in the lost scroll, it cannot be known for certain that both of these fragments represent the same poem. Such a conclusion depends on the length of the poem represented by fr. 11 W$^2$. A discussion of the poem's length will follow below, but here it is sufficient to note that the length of the poem is unknown and, as a result, it cannot be said that it filled these two columns on POxy 2327. The sense of these verses, however, provides a better link between these fragments. Fr. 13 W$^2$ mentions the Medes (8), Persians and maybe the sons of Doros (9) and Herakles (10). It appears, then, that fr. 13 W$^2$ contains verses that pertain to the Persian Wars. Lobel originally suggested that POxy 2327 fr. 27 col. ii (= fr. 13 W$^2$) might be verses pertaining to Plataea by Simonides.[136] After the discovery of POxy 3965, West connected this fragment with the descent of the Greeks into the Asopus plain before the battle of Plataea.[137] This interpretation would guarantee that frs. 11 and 13 W$^2$ both depict events in the battle of Plataea and would make it more certain that a large section of this poem, if not the whole poem, narrated events pertaining to the battle of Plataea. Still, it must be noted that the fragmentary nature of the text makes all of these conclusions tentative. Even if these verses belong in the same poem as fr. 11 W$^2$, it is still possible that they describe any point in the battle of Plataea or even in any other battle.[138] These verses can only be interpreted as a depiction of an event at Plataea if the existence of a "Plataea poem" is presupposed. Without this assumption, any context in the Persian Wars might also be understood here. A poet who supposedly composed many poems on the Persian Wars may have mentioned the Persians, Medes, and the sons of Doros and Herakles in other contexts. In fact, before the publication of the "new Simonides," Barigazzi suggested that this fragment belongs in a supposed elegy on the battle of Marathon mentioned in the Ambrosian *vita Aeschyli*.[139] It could also be suggested that these verses pertain in some way to Thermopylae.[140] The content may link fr. 13 W$^2$ to fr. 11 W$^2$ in terms of the Persian Wars, but fr. 13 W$^2$ cannot be shown with certainty to pertain to the battle of Plataea. As it stands, fr. 13 W$^2$ is evidence for a "Plataea poem" only if such a poem is being reconstructed. Fr. 13 W$^2$, then, offers no evidence about the content, form, or length of the poem represented by fr. 11 W$^2$. If the fragments belong in the same poem, it can be said that fr. 11 W$^2$ pertains to Plataea, while fr. 13 W$^2$ can only be placed in a general context of the Persian Wars.

The conclusion must be that frs. 12 and 13 W$^2$ do not certainly depict the battle of Plataea. While the possibility remains that their proximity to fr. 11 W$^2$ might place them in the same poem, these fragments do not confirm the continued focus on Plataea.

## Fr. 14W² (=POxy 3965 fr. 21) [see Figure 9]

There are two primary reasons to posit a connection between fr. 14 W² (= POxy 3965 fr. 21) and fr. 11 W². First, Parsons observes that POxy 3965 fr. 21 (= 14 W²) and POxy 3965 fr. 2 (= fr. 11.14–45 W²) both have sheet joins in approximately the same position. A sheet join is present at POxy 3965 fr. 21 (=fr. 14.7–9 W²) and thus runs through the fifth foot of the hexameter;[141] a sheet join is present in a similar position at POxy 3965 fr. 2.8–10 (= fr 11.29–31 W²).[142] On this basis, Parsons tentatively suggests that these fragments may belong in the same column. This physical evidence, however, does not provide sufficient foundation for a link between the two fragments.

The second reason for placing fr. 14W² in the "Plataea poem" is its content. The poor state of the fragment, however, makes reconstruction of the verses difficult. Parsons first suggested that the river in 14.3 W² fixed the context of the verses as a depiction of the first battle of Plataea above the Asopus River.[143] West has further suggested that this fragment more specifically contains the prophecy delivered by Teisamenos before the Greeks crossed the Asopus River and thus corresponds to Herodotus 9.36. A series of conjectures forms the basis for this interpretation. First, West reads λ]έγω at 14.3 W² as an introduction of direct speech. He then uses supposed references to the river, the advance of the army, a disaster, and everlasting memory in the subsequent words to suggest that this direct speech is the prophecy of Teisamenos.[144] West's text, however, which provides all of these readings, is deceptively complete.

| PARSONS | WEST |
|---|---|
| POxy 3965 fr. 21 | fr. 14W² |
| ].[]...[]....[ | ].[]...[]....[ |
| ] . δονβαλλομ . [ | ]ạδον βαλλομε[ν |
| ]εγωποτạμμου[] . . [ | λ]έγω ποταμ ́ο λạ[ |
|     ᵃ | ]ϙ́ψαι πρῶτα β[ι]η[ι |
| ] . ψạιπρωταβ[ł]η[ι | 5 δεινὸν ἁμαι]μάκετόν τε κακ[όν· μίμνουσι δ' ἔσεσθαι |
| 5 ]μακετ . ν . ε . α . [ | νίκην, ἧς μνή]μην ἤματα πάντ[α μενεῖν. |
| ]μηννηματαπαν . [ | ἐξ Ἀ]ϙϊ[η]ϛ ἐλάσει, νεύϛαντοϛ̣ |
| ] . . []ϛελαϛ[] . ινευ . ạντοι | ]νην ϛυμμạι[χ]ίην φιλέω[ν |
|     ᵃ˙˙γ̣ε | ] . νωι γὰρ [ύ]η[ὸ κ]ϙηπῖδα ǝ̃ |
| ]νηνϛυμμι . [ ] . ηϙφιλεωι | 10 ]εται[ . . . . . ₍₎ ]ϙρίην β[ |
| ] . νωιγạ . . [ ] . [ ]ϙηπειδạτ[ | ]ϙδε[ ]ει ποτεφ[ |
| 10 ] . τι . [    ] . ρıην . [ | ]πολω[ |
| ] . δε[    ]ειποτεφ[ | ]ωϛτ[ |
|     ]ηϙ . . . [ | ]   [ |
|     ]ϙϛτ[ | 15 ]λυωι[ |
|     ]   [ | ]ϙεκ[ |
| 15 ] . νωι[ | ]ηι[ |
| ]ϙε . [ | |
| ] . . [ | |

Figure 9.

Few of the points in his reconstruction have a solid basis in the surviving text. The ink of the letters ]ἐγω is unclear.[145] The letters πο- are the only certain letters of the word for river. Although Parsons is certain of a reading ποταμου or ποταμους, he also suggests ποτ᾽ ἀμους- as another possibility.[146] The initial movement of the army lies in the letters ] . ψαιπρωταβ[ ]η[ at fr. 14.4 W². Both Parsons and West supplement the end of the line to read: πρῶτα β[ι]η[σαμένοις and interpret these words as a reference to the initial attack forbidden by Teisamenos.[147] The text, however, is too incomplete to be certain of this supplement and the meaning of the verse remains uncertain. The interpretation that links this verse to the battle of Plataea only arises after it is assumed that the fragment represents the prophecy of Teisamenos. Furthermore, the papyrus at line 5 provides the letters ]μακετ . ν . ε . α . [ , which West prints as δεινὸν ἀμαι]μάκετόν τε κακ[όν· μίμνουσι δ᾽ ἔσεσθαι.[148] It should be observed that only the supplemented text refers to a disaster. Finally, at line 6, West prints νίκην, ἧς μνή]μην ἤματα πάντ[α μενεῖν, which provides a mention of everlasting memory. Again, this content is derived largely from supplements. Ultimately, West's interpretation of the verses as the prophecy of Teisamenos proves to be derived from his own conjectures. These conjectures arise from the initial assumption that the fragment may represent part of a "Plataea poem."[149]

It must be concluded, then, that fr. 14 W² provides no internal clues that it should be connected with fr. 11 W² or that it pertains to the battle of Plataea at all. The link between fr. 14 W² and fr. 11 W² arises from supplements. The supplement in each instance is provoked by the assumption that the fragment belongs to the "Plataea poem."

*Fr. 17W² (=POxy 3965 fr. 19) [see Figure 10]*

POxy 3965 fr.19 consists of two columns. Col. i is a single marginal note. Neither West, Sider, nor Gentili-Prato records these letters.[150] Col. ii consists of 24 line beginnings. These line beginnings give the text of fr. 17 W².[151] The perceived content is the only link to fr. 11 W². West reads the name Demeter (Δημητ[) in line 1 and observes that a delay (δηρόν) appears in line 5. In these words, he sees a parallel to Herodotus' account of the battle around the temple of Demeter Eleusinia (Hdt. 9.57–65).[152] West also correctly points out that little sense can be made of the fragment as a whole beyond these words.

Rutherford adds two points that seem to bolster West's interpretation.[153] First, he suggests that ῥυσιόν ("a reprisal") in line 7 might pertain to the punishment meted out to the Persians for their violation of the shrine of Demeter. This interpretation allows fr. 17.1–7 W² to contain a narrative of the battle proper and fr. 17.7–24W² would be concerned with the aftermath of the battle. Second, Rutherford proposes that φῆ can be read in lines 3 and 21. In these words, he sees the possibility of direct

| PARSONS | | WEST |
|---|---|---|
| POxy 3965 fr. 19 | | fr. 17 W² |
| col. i  col. ii | | |

| | PARSONS | WEST |
|---|---|---|
| | POxy 3965 fr. 19 | fr. 17 W² |
| | col. i   col. ii | |
| | ]        δ[] . μητ[ | Δημητ[ |
| | ]        χ[ ]ημα . [ | χ̣[ο]η̣μα δ[ |
| | ]        φ . []θεδ . [ | φῆ δὲ δυ[ |
| | ]        ἀγρετοϲ . [ | ἄγρετο ϲε[ |
| 5 | ]        δηρο̣ν[ | 5 δηρὸν [ |
| | ]        τουϲα[ | τοὺς α[ |
| | ]        ρυσιο̣ν[ | ῥύσιον [ |
| | ]        κάιμ[ | καί μ[ |
| | ]        . αιμ[ | και μ[ |
| 10 | ]        δ̣ . . . . [ | 10 δα̣ι . .[ |
| | ] .      . η̣ευμ . [ | θηευμη[ |
| | ]        . [ ]εουϲα[ | η [ . ]εου α[ |
| | ]        ο̣[ ]κιϲχε[ | ο[υ]κ̣ ἴσχε[ |
| | ]        αλλε . [ | ἀλλ᾽ ετε[ |
| 15 | ]        ηϲπαι[ | 15 ηϲπαι[ |
| | ]        φρεικωθ[ | φρικωθ[ |
| | ] . ακου  ϲπευδο̣ν[ | σπευδον[ |
| | ] .      ευλεκτ[ | ἐν λεκτ[ |
| | ]        ξεινου . [ | ξείνου δ[ |
| 20 | ]        ερχομε[ | 20 ερχομε[ |
| | ]        . η . ε . [ | φηδε . [ |
| | ·κ[] [ | χρ [ |
| | χ . [ | . ] . φ [ |
| | ] . . [ | αλλ[ |
| | ]αλλ[ | |

Figure 10.

speech.[154] A similar repetition of phrases, although one not referred to by Rutherford, can be read in καίμ[ε in lines 8 and 9, which also suggest direct speech.[155] The combination of these readings increases the possibility that direct speech is to be read in these verses. Rutherford tentatively proposes that a prophet is the speaker, but there is nothing within the fragment to support this hypothesis.[156] To be sure, direct speech is possible, but the speaker and the subject remain a mystery.

The placement of these line beginnings in the context of the battle of Plataea, then, hinges solely on West's initial conjecture that the fragment has a parallel in Herodotus. Yet, as we have seen, parallels in Herodotus are not always the best guide in confronting the "new Simonides." Moreover, these parallels are all supplied in the uncertain text because of a preconceived concept of the fragment's context. For fr. 17.1 W², Parsons prints as δ[ ] . μητ[, which reflects the difficult state of the fragment at this point. While West prints Δημητ[, his conjecture seems to be motivated largely by an attempt to situate the fragment in the so-called "Plataea poem."[157] This reading is in no way certain and the link it creates to the poem represented by fr. 11 W² is questionable. Furthermore, δηρόν, which West understands as a delay in the battle of Plataea, could also have other contexts. It would not be difficult to envisage this word in the context of the battle of Artemisium or even the battle of Salamis. It is really only when this word is considered in the light of the supplement in line 1 that it possibly refers to the battle of Plataea. So the initial reasons for West's placement are dubious and the fragment in fact has no concrete points of connection to a description of the battle of Plataea. Along these same lines, Rutherford's suggestions are also without a firm connection to the battle of Plataea. His suggestion that ῥυσιόν in line 7 refers to Plataea only does so if West's arrangement is accepted. The presence of direct speech also does not link the poem to the battle of Plataea. If the direct speech is accepted, it could possibly be a prayer for reprisal that occurred before any of the battles in the Persian Wars.[158] None of these conjectures satisfactorily demonstrates that fr. 17 W² is linked to fr. 11 W² or that it pertains to the battle of Plataea.

*Fr. 18W² (=POxy 3965 fr. 10) [see Figure 11]*

POxy 3965 fr. 10 (=fr. 18 W²) consists of seven incomplete lines that offer little clue about their sense. Correctly, West is cautious about his assignment of this fragment to the "Plataea poem."[159] Three partial words have suggested that the fragment belongs in the context of a battle. First, line 2 possibly contains the word for hope ( ]ελπιδ[). Second, the letters in line 4, μάχη[, suggest either the word for a battle or some compound including this word.[160] Third, Parsons also suggests that ] ₎ ἐκύδα[ιν-, from κυδαίνω, "to give honor to," is to be read in line 7.[161] The text, however, is difficult to read at this point. Only the letters] ₎ ₎ κυδ ₎ [ are clear. The first two partial words may place the fragment in a battle context. The conjecture in line 7 may confirm this context, but the reading is too uncertain. A more specific context cannot be suggested. So there is no real reason to link this fragment to fr. 11 W² or to an account of the battle of Plataea. Given the text that survives, any battle could provide the context for this fragment.[162] With the available evidence, there is no clear reason to link this fragment to fr. 11 W² or to an account of the battle of Plataea.

| PARSONS | WEST |
|---|---|
| POxy 3965 fr. 10 | fr. 18 W² |
| | ]ε̣[ |
| ]ε ₎ [ | ] ἐλπίδ[ |
| ]ελπιδ[ | ]υτ̣ι̣q̣[ |
| ]υτ ₎ ₎ [ | ]μμαχη[ |
| ] ₎ μαχη[ | 5   ]λ̣ων καλο[ |
| 5   ] ₎ ωγκα ₎ ο[ | ] οὐδεμε̣[ |
| ]ουδεμ ₎ [ | ] ₎ ἐκυδα̣[ιν |
| ] ₎ ₎ κυδ̣ ₎ [ | |

Figure 11.

## C. Conclusion

In sum, the evidence used to reconstruct a "Plataea poem" by Simonides is: 1) a quotation in Plutarch (= frs. 15–16 W$^2$); 2) the overlap between this quotation and POxy 3965 fr. 5W$^2$ that allows the assignment of fr. 11 W$^2$ to Simonides. This evidence, however, does not support the existence of a separate work solely depicting the battle of Plataea. Such a poem has no ancient witnesses. Since Plutarch does not specify the poetic context of his quote, he offers little help in reconstructing the larger context from which Simonides' verses on the Corinthians is drawn. The verses he quotes need only come from a poem that mentioned Plataea and not a "Plataea poem" in any of the forms imagined by modern scholarship. The combination of Plutarch and fr. 11 W$^2$ also fails to confirm the existence of a "Plataea poem." At most, Plutarch reveals that Simonides praised in detail the Corinthians' actions at Plataea. Fr. 11 W$^2$ also reveals that Simonides mentioned the Lacedaemonians prominently in this poem and that he also introduced the Corinthians and possibly the Athenians in subsequent verses. None of these observations, however, reveals that this poem should be construed narrowly to focus on Plataea. In fact, as has been shown, these fragments plausibly reflect a poem with a broader content.

The other fragments of the "new Simonides" also fail to support the existence of a "Plataea poem." In terms of papyrological evidence, the only verses of the new fragments that clearly belong to the same poem are fr. 11.5–45 W$^2$ (= POxy 3965 frs. 1 + 2 +POxy 2327 frs. 6 and 27 col. i). Fr. 11.1–4 W$^2$ (=POxy 2327 fr. 5) should stand as a separate fragment. Even if it is correct that these lines refer to the death of Achilles, their position in the poem represented by fr. 11 W$^2$ is uncertain. As was seen above, frs. 15–16 W$^2$ in terms of content are likely to belong to this poem as well. The link between the other fragments and fr. 11 W$^2$ mostly arises from supplements. These supplements are often suggested because of a preconceived belief that the fragments depict the battle of Plataea and that the hypothetical content of these fragments has parallels in Herodotus' narrative. None of these fragments, however, independently pertains to the battle of Plataea.

Fr. 13 W$^2$ (=POxy 2327 fr. 27 col. ii) can be said to follow the verses of fr. 11.45 W$^2$ closely because of its proximity to POxy 2327 fr. 27 col. i, which provides marginal notes and column ends for fr. 11 W$^2$. Yet the fragmentary nature of the poem obscures the exact relationship between frs. 11 and 13 W$^2$. In fact, these verses plausibly could belong to different poems. Conclusions on this point depend on the length of the poem represented by fr. 11 W$^2$. It is possible only to guess at the length of this poem.

As for the length, the evidence suggests that a section of at least 41 consecutive lines in the poem represented by fr. 11 W$^2$ depicted the events leading up to the battle of Plataea. The prooimial features in fr. 11 W$^2$ might suggest that these verses came early in the poem; however, the verses may represent an internal prooimion.[163] Either way, it would seem that this poem was of considerable length if by line forty a depiction of a battle or even the praise of the Corinthians' efforts at Plataea, quoted by Plutarch, has not occurred. Further certainty on the length is difficult because the length of a column in POxy 2327 and 3965 is unknown.[164] Of the scraps that constitute fr. 11 $W^2$, only POxy 2327 fr. 6 (= fr. 11.5–13 $W^2$) has a specific placement on a papyrus as a column-top.[165] The physical relation between frs. 11 (= POxy 3965 frs. 1 + 2 +POxy 2327 frs. 6 and 27 coll. i) and 13 $W^2$ (=POxy 2327 fr. 27 col. ii) suggests that a column on POxy 2327 held more that 27 lines.[166] POxy 2327 col. i runs from POxy 3965 fr. 1.5 to POxy 3965 fr. 2.7 (= fr. 11.13–28 $W^2$). POxy 2327 fr. 27 col. ii has two more lines than col. i. So col. i must have contained at least the same verses as POxy 3965 fr. 1.5–fr. 2.9 (= fr. 11.13–30 $W^2$). Since POxy 2327 fr. 6 is the top of this column, it can be assumed that this column would have contained at least 26 lines (=fr. 11.5–30 $W^2$). [167] Furthermore, it is certain that fr. 11.30 $W^2$ (= the final line of POxy 2327 fr. 27 col. i) would not have been the last line in the column. There are fifteen lines (fr. 11.31–45 $W^2$ = POxy 3965 fr. 2.10–24), which do not overlap fr. 13 $W^2$ (=POxy 2327 fr. 27 col. ii).[168] Therefore, POxy 2327 fr. 27 col. i must have contained some of these verses. So, it can be assumed that a column in POxy 2327 contained more than 26 lines. This evidence, however, is only useful for estimating the length of the poem represented by fr. 11 $W^2$ if fr. 13 $W^2$ and fr. 11 $W^2$ belong to the same poem. If the fragments do belong in the same poem, it would have contained more than 54 lines. This conclusion about the relation between these fragments cannot be made with any certainty.[169]

These figures must be taken cautiously. The only certain conclusion is that the poem represented by fr. 11 $W^2$ contained at least 41 lines (11.5–45 $W^2$) and that these lines pertain to the battle of Plataea. With the addition of the verses quoted by Plutarch, 47 verses survive that pertain to the battle of Plataea. It can be concluded that POxy 2327 and POxy 3965 contained an elegy by Simonides that mentioned the battle of Plataea and that at least 47 verses of this poem are relevant to this battle. The Spartans figure prominently in this section of the poem. The Corinthians and possibly the Athenians had a place in this section. The exact part given to each of these figures in the poem is unknown. The Corinthians were praised. Nothing further about the scope and the content of this poem can be determined with certainty from these fragments. Moreover, none of this evidence definitively points to the existence of a poem solely on the battle of Plataea.

## 1.5 GENERAL CONCLUSIONS

To conclude, the current scholarly orthodoxy that the "new Simonides" contains three separate elegies on the battles at Artemisium, Salamis, and Plataea is unsubstantiated.

Evidence for an "Artemisium elegy" is lacking in the new fragments. The quotation by Priscian of Simonides' *The Sea-battle at Artemisium* shows that lyric verses on Artemisium by Simonides existed. The reference in the *Suda* to an elegy on this topic can neither be confirmed nor denied. Evidence for a separate poem on Salamis is also lacking. The references to Simonides' treatment of Salamis by the *Suda* and the Ambrosian *vita Pindari* tell us only that Simonides mentioned the battle but give no clues about the larger composition to which this mention belongs. The current belief in a "Plataea elegy" as a poem that focused solely on this battle stands only as a modern construct that derives from the fragments of the "new Simonides."

These conclusions do not remove the possibility that the fragments of the "new Simonides" are related as part of the same poem or group of poems. Rather, they aim to highlight that the confusion which surrounds Simonides' compositions on the battles of the Persian Wars forces us to be cautious when assigning fragments to specific poems. As has been shown, this confusion is not explained satisfactorily by the current arrangement of the "new Simonides" into separate poems on individual battles. In fact, this arrangement multiplies the problems. The issue is further complicated by the enthusiasm for a "Plataea elegy," which in many respects has glossed over our incomplete knowledge of the Persian War elegies by Simonides. Since the modern understanding of this poem also has been shown to be unclear, it is fair to suggest that how Simonides' poetic works on the Persian Wars are approached must be reconsidered.

Some modern scholars have pointed to such reconsiderations. In an effort to sort out the confusion concerning the poems on Artemisium and Salamis, Rutherford suggests that the poems listed in the *Suda* might have been a single composition. Specifically, he points to "the possibility that this composition as a whole was called "(ἡ) Ξέρξου ναυμαχία and that it had two sections, one on Artemisium (in elegiacs?), one on Salamis (in lyrics?) and that Priscian misapplies to the whole of it the title of a part."[170] A suggestion similar to that of Rutherford, is provided by Obbink. While Obbink hesitantly accepts West's placement of the fragments from POxy 2327 and POxy 3965 in the sea-battle poems, he continues to posit that all of the remaining fragments from these papyri belong to a single elegy on Plataea.[171] That is, the fragments currently assigned to the sea-battle poems and those assigned to sympotic poems may very well belong to the same poem as fr. 11W[2]. While both of these suggestions allow Simonides' compositions on the Persian Wars to be construed more broadly, they still emphasize a model that consists of poems on a specifc battle or battles. Given the confusion that surrounds Simonides' poems on the Persian Wars, another alternative is to combine these hypotheses by emphasizing a larger composition on the Persian Wars that mentioned to some degree all of the battles under discussion.

A complication to this idea of a single poem on the Persian Wars in the new fragments is found in fr. 34 W[2] (=POxy 2327 fr. 7). A *coronis*, a mark that indicates a division between two poems, appears to the left of fr. 34.2 W². Obbink addresses this difficulty by pointing out that at most fr. 34 W² is proof that POxy 2327 contained two poems, one on Plataea and one not on Plataea. He then suggests that the poem not on Plataea may have been the "Salamis poem" listed in the *Suda*.[172] This final point is little more than an intriguing guess. Even if the poem that precedes the *coronis* is the one that survives in fr. 11 W², there is still no guarantee that it was a poem solely on Plataea. The possibility still remains that fr. 11 W² represents a poem that detailed more than the battle of Plataea.[173]

The existence of *testimonia* for separate poems on individual battles could be considered to argue against searching for a broadly defined single elegy in the "new Simonides." As we have seen the omission of the "Plataea poem" in the *Suda* is not entirely surprising. Yet, the difficulty of reconciling the *Suda* with evidence from outside the entry may betray a more fundamental problem. It is possible that the *Suda* records titles of two groups of poems: larger poems, such as the single elegy proposed here, and sections of poems, divided later, that narrated specific battles. In fact, as Rutherford points out, (ἡ) Ξέρξου ναυμαχία, in the *Suda*, might reflect a title or related subject matter of these larger poems. Parts of these or similar poems could have been referred to as *The Sea-battle at Artemisium* or *The Sea-battle at Salamis*.[174] The *Suda* would then represent two stages in the transmission of Simonides' poems. This process of cutting up elegies may not be so unusual given the existence of collections of passages even before the famous anthology, the Garland of Meleager.[175] It is also not difficult to imagine that at some point, sections of poems may have become confused with larger compositions on the Persian Wars. These possibilities are intriguing because they would enhance our understanding of Simonides' poetic innovations by allowing the existence of longer epic-like poem(s) on the Persian Wars that perhaps were broken into shorter narratives on specific battles. So the *Suda* entry and other *testimonia* for separate poems on individual battles need not exclude the possibility of a larger more inclusive elegy on the Persian Wars by Simonides.

What this possibility brings forward is that the approach to the "new Simonides" should not emphasize reconstructing the form, genre, themes, and content of a "Plataea poem" or any other poem on an individual battle for that matter. This current approach assumes that the poems on the Persian Wars are defined by battles and by cities. The new fragments simply do not bear out this interpretation. Rather, the "new Simonides" suggests that other models might better explain the confusion that surrounds these fragments. The models which need to be considered are: 1) The "new Simonides" represents an elegy mainly concerned with the battle of Plataea, but the content of this poem extended beyond this battle and the praise of the Spartans. This poem will have introduced descriptions of other battles as digressions from the main narrative on Plataea. In this way, the "new Simonides" will represent what could loosely be called a "Plataea poem." This poem, however, would have panhellenic undertones and would allow for other aspects of these Wars to be mentioned. 2) The "new Simonides" represents an elegy not focused specifically on the battle of Plataea. The main narrative of the poem will be the Persian Wars as a whole. Emphasis will shift from the Lacedaemonians to the exploits of other figures, such as the Athenians and the Corinthians, throughout these wars. In this way, the "new Simonides" will represent a panhellenic poem on the Persian Wars, in which Plataea was just one part. These models bring to the foreground an important possibility which is lost in the search for three elegies on separate battles in the "new Simonides;" namely that each fragment may be considered as part of an as yet undetermined poem. I suggest that it is from this starting point that the form, content and performance context of these fragments are best reconstructed.

# Chapter Two
# A Panhellenic Poem
# for a Panhellenic War
## The Subject Matter of the "New Simonides"

οἴμοι, καθ᾽ Ἑλλάδ᾽ ὡς κακῶς νομίζεται· ὅταν τροπαῖα πολεμίων στήσηι
στρατός, οὐ τῶν πονούντων τοὔργον ἡγοῦνται τόδε, ἀλλ᾽ ὁ στρατηγὸς
τὴν δόκησιν ἄρνυται, ὃς εἷς μετ᾽ ἄλλων μυρίων πάλλων δόρυ, οὐδὲν
πλέον δρῶν ἑνός, ἕξει πλείω λόγον.

Euripides Andromache 693–698

Alas, throughout Greece how perversely customs are observed. Whenever the
army sets up trophies over an enemy, they do not consider this as the effort of
those who do the work, but the general gains the credit—the man who, one
among countless others, shakes his spear, but doing no more than one, will receive more credit.

## 2.1 INTRODUCTION

Once the arrangement of the "new Simonides" into three battle poems has been
brought into question, it becomes necessary to consider these fragments as part of
an as yet undetermined poem or poems. From this starting point, the content of
the individual fragments can be determined without presupposing that each should
narrate events in any particular battle in the Persian Wars. This approach avoids the
circularity entailed by the initial assumption of three separate compositions and allows the fragments to speak for themselves. To determine the content represented
by the fragments of the "new Simonides," then, we should not be asking how each
fragment can be made to narrate a specific battle. Rather, more appropriate questions
to ask are: What is the content of each fragment? How can this content be shown to
relate to a larger composition?

This chapter will evaluate the content of the "new Simonides" in terms of individual fragments. In particular, the content of fr. 11 W², the most substantial of these fragments, will be examined. The larger concern will be to determine if fr. 11 W² represents the so-called "Plataea poem" as it is defined by its content in modern scholarship or if it represents a poem of which the content is to be more broadly defined. This analysis will provide a basis for approaching the other fragments in terms of their content and their relation to a larger composition.

## 2.2 THE PANHELLENIC CONTENT OF FR. 11 W²

In his comments on the "new Simonides," Ian Rutherford writes of the "Plataea poem" that "the most reasonable interpretation is that the narrative was concerned with only the battle of Plataea, although there is no independent attestation of a Simonidean poem on this theme."[1] This assessment brings to the foreground two assumptions that have been central to the reconstruction of the content of fr. 11 W². First, it is assumed that this fragment represents a poem that is to be reconstructed as a narrative along the lines of an epic or a historical account. Second, it is thought that this narrative details the battle of Plataea. Yet, the incomplete state of the fragment and our lack of comparative models for such a poem reveal the need to consider these assumptions cautiously.

### A. Elements of Content in Fr. 11 W²

Some details of the content can be ascertained in the incomplete verses of fr. 11 W². The phrases χαῖρε (fr. 11.19 W²) and αὐτὰρ ἐγὼ[ (fr. 11.20 W²) as well as the direct addresses to the Muse (fr. 11.21 W²) make it certain that the fragment begins with a prooimion. The subject of this prooimion appears to be the Trojan Wars: the "battle-leading Danaans" (ἀγέμαχοι Δαναοί[) can be understood as those who destroy (πέρσαντες) and who arrived at something famous in song (ἀοίδιμον [ ἵ]κοντο) (fr. 11.13–14 W²); ]νδροιο κακόφρ[ονο]ς may be interpreted as Paris (Alexandros) (fr. 11.11 W²) and ]ιάμου παισί may be the sons of Priam (fr. 11.10 W²). It should be kept in mind that without supplements the only certain reference to the Trojan War in these lines is the appearance of the Danaan leaders in fr. 11.14 W². Support for understanding this theme in these verses, however, comes in the possible mention of Homer in fr. 11.15–16 W². In line 15, it appears that (deathless?) renown is poured (]νατον κέχυται κλέος) and in line 16 someone is receiving something from the (violet-wreathed?) Pierian Muses (]λοκαμων δέξατο Πιεριδ[). A reasonable conclusion is that this renown is associated with the Danaan leaders (fr. 11.14 W²) and that the Homer is the one who is "pouring" it after he received something from the Pierian Muse. This interpretation becomes even more likely with the introduction of the "short-lived race (of heroes?)" in fr. 11.18 W² (]ιθεων ὠκύμορον γενή[). In such a context, ὠκύμορον is suggestive of the Homeric epithet of Achilles.[2] The presence of Achilles is further suggested by references in the genitive to a (famous?) goddess (fr. 11.19 W²: θεᾶς ἐρικυ[), Nereus (fr. 11.20 W²: Νηρέος), and a possible adjective pertaining to the sea (fr. 11.20 W² ]αλίου), all of which evoke Thetis, the mother of Achilles. The genitives imply that it is not Thetis who is being addressed, but her son. [3] The accumulation of these details allows for the reasonable conclusion that the content of these verses pertains to the Trojan War and the Homeric tradition.

This content can be further delineated. The possible address to Achilles (fr. 11.20 W²) suggests that these verses are a hymn to him. Certain details indicate that the hymn, in fact, depicts the death of Achilles at the hands of both Paris and Apollo (fr. 11.7–11 W²). The adjective ὠκύμορον, then, not only evokes Achilles but also is suggestive of the hero's fate of death at Troy.

This interpretation, however, is not free from problems. First, nothing in fr. 11.5–10 W², the supposed Trojan narrative, is certain enough to demonstrate that Achilles' death is the subject. There is the overcoming of someone (δ]αμασσεν) presumably at the hand of someone (Apollo?) (]ωνος χειρὶ [) at fr. 11.7–8 W²; also, as was noted, Paris (]νδροιο κακόφ[   ]ς) is possibly mentioned at fr. 11.11 W². Since in the epic tradition Achilles was killed by the arrow of Paris with the aid of Apollo, it has been suggested that these fragmentary words describe this death. This interpretation gains some support in the possible appearance at fr. 11.16 W² of Patroklos (]οκλου), whose death and funeral in the *Iliad* can be taken as prefiguring the death and funeral of Achilles.[4] If this thinking is correct, the subject of these verses is the death and funeral of Achilles.[5] The difficulty of this interpretation is that this death and funeral are provided entirely from supplements. First, none of these incomplete words alone, or even collectively, suggests that the verses pertain to Achilles' death and funeral unless we are trying to reconstruct a description of these events. Second, the papyrus scrap that provides fr. 11.1–4 W², which is interpreted as a description of Achilles' death, is not certainly connected to the rest of fr. 11 W².[6] To be sure, the reference to a pine (fr. 11.2 W²: πίτυν) and woodcutters (fr. 11.3 W²: ὑλοτόμοι) suggests that the verses pertain to the death of a hero in the epic tradition.[7] In a persuasive literary argument, A. Barchiesi has argued that these words in the "new Simonides" refer to such a death. He points out that Horace *Odes* 4.6.9–12, which describes the death of Achilles in terms of a pine tree being felled, is possibly modeled on fr. 11.1–4 W². His conclusion is that these verses pertain to the death of Achilles and West's arrangement of these fragments is acceptable.[8] Although Barchiesi's evaluation compellingly elucidates the content in fr. 11.1–4 W², it does not solidly position these verses as preceding the rest of fr. 11 W². The possibility remains that these verses come later in the poem, even if they refer to the death of Achilles.[9] Even with Barchiesi's astute observations, fr. 11.1–4 W² still must be considered as a separate fragment and its interpretation as part of the hymn to Achilles in fr. 11 W² must be taken cautiously.[10] These incomplete verses then do not help to determine whether the death of Achilles is the subject of this prooimion. Ultimately, none of these references, alone or collectively, provides certainty that the death and funeral of Achilles are narrated in the opening of fr. 11 W².

That these prooimial verses are a hymn to Achilles receives support from the transitional phrase χαῖρε . . . αὐτὰρ ἐγὼ[ (fr. 11.19–20 W²) and an address to the Muse as the poet's helper (fr. 11.21 W²: σ' ἐπίκουρον ἐμοί, π[      ]ε Μοῦσα). In terms of content, these verses introduce the Muse as the helper or ally of the performer and continue the reference to Homer in the preceding verses.[11] The text following the request is too incomplete to be helpful in determining the specifics of what help is sought from the Muse. Nevertheless, it is a plausible suggestion that Simonides is requesting aid in singing about his subject in the following poem.[12]

Thus far, the opening of fr. 11 W² can be shown to be a prooimial hymn to Achilles. In this hymn, the epic tradition of the Trojan War, Homer, and the fame of heroes is introduced. It remains uncertain whether these verses described the death and the funeral of Achilles.

Immediately following the prooimion, Sparta is mentioned in some way (fr. 11.25 W²: Σπάρτ[).[13] Words such as οὐρανομ[ήκ]ης (fr. 11.27 W²) and ἀθάνατο⟨ν⟩ (fr. 11.28 W²) suggest that Sparta or the Lacedaemonians are being praised, but the text is too incomplete to be certain about the details of this praise. The following verses refer to the departure from a city (Sparta?), as well as the Spartan Tyndaridai and Menelaus: (fr. 11.29–31 W²: ἄστυ λιποντ[ / ]Ζηνὸς παισὶ σὺν ἱπποδάμοις / ]ις ἥρωσι καὶ εὐρυβίηι Μενελάω[ / ]ρωιης ἡγεμόνες π [ ]λεος[; ". . . leaving a city . . . with the horse-taming sons of Zeus . . . (with) heroes and (with) mighty Menelaus . . . leaders. . . ."). This departure is the first hint that these non-prooimial verses are to be read as a narrative. It is posited that the subject of this supposed narrative is the battle of Plataea because Pausanias, the leader of the Lacedaemonians at this battle, is an unambiguous reading of the text at fr. 11.34 W² (Παυσανίας).

The content of fr. 11.35–45 W² is more difficult to reconstruct: The famous deeds of Corinth are mentioned (fr. 11.35 W²: ἐπικλέα ἔργα Κορίν[θ]ου); Pelops, the son of Tantalus, appears and suggests reference to the Peloponnesus or the Isthmus (fr. 11.36 W²: ]Ταντaλίδεω Πέλοπος);[14] less certain is a reference to Megara, the city of Nisus, (fr. 11.37 W² ]ισου πόλιν);[15] the Athenians may also appear in the problematic text of fr. 11.41–42 W².[16] The standard interpretation of these verses is that they depict the march of the Spartan army from Sparta to Plataea with reference to geographic positions and people along the way. The text, however, is too fragmentary for this conclusion. The only certainties are the mention of Corinth, either the Isthmus or the Peloponnesus, and Pausanias, the Spartan leader. Even if these verses contain geographic references, they need not represent the skeleton of a narrative. It simply is not certain that these lines represent a geographically informed narrative of a Spartan march to Plataea.

In sum, the content of fr. 11 W$^2$ can be said to have the following elements with some degree of certainty: There is a prooimion that focuses on Achilles, the Trojan War and the fame given to these heroes by Homer. The following verses contain references to Sparta, to divine figures associated with the Lacedaemonians, and to Pausanias, the Spartan leader. Some action, perhaps the leaving of a city, is mentioned. Corinth and the Isthmus or the Peloponnesus appear. More definitive conclusions cannot be derived from the text. The presence of the Lacedaemonians and Pausanias suggests that the fragment represents a poem that is concerned with the battle of Plataea. It cannot be proven, however, that these verses represent part of a narrative of this battle with this evidence.

## B. Content of Bowie's Narrative Elegy before the "New Simonides"

The concept that an elegy could be defined in part by its emphasis on narrative content was first proposed by E. L. Bowie. In an influential article that appeared six years before Parsons' *editio princeps* of POxy 3965, Bowie considered the evidence for the link between social context and content in archaic elegy.[17] The views set forth by Bowie stand as a reaction to M. L. West's earlier study of archaic elegy that accompanied the first edition of his *Iambi et Elegi Graeci*. To understand the implications of Bowie's conclusions, it is best to turn first to the proposals of West.

To define elegy as a class of poetry, West argues for eight typical contexts in which elegy would have been performed: 1) before a battle; 2) a military setting (i.e. a watch); 3) a symposium; 4) a *komos;* 5) a public meeting; 6) a place with a view of a fountain; 7) funerals; 8) an aulodic competition at a festival.[18] This identification of contexts for the performance of elegy is derived primarily from internal references in elegy to places such as a fountain or situations such as a military watch. West further addresses the characteristics of elegiac poetry by suggesting that in terms of the content which would have been performed in these contexts almost anything goes in elegy. He observes that any theme dealt with in poetry is suitable for elegy, but he concludes that straightforward mythical, erotic, or historical narrative as well as didactic themes and natural philosophy are not found in elegy.[19] For West, the narrative or historical elements found in verses such Mimnermus' *Smyrneis* and Simonides' *The Sea-battle of Salamis* are "are not to be imagined as containing narrative for its own sake" but may have had morals for the present or simply may have been comments on current events."[20] West does not, however, link any specific content with a particular occasion.

Bowie's article reacts to these positions on the context and content of elegy. First he finds that there would have been only three suitable contexts for the performance for most archaic elegies: the symposium, the *komos* which followed the symposium, and public aulodic competitions.[21] The performance of elegy in symposia is widely attested, whether it is considered the primary performance context as Bowie suggests or just one of many contexts as West proposes.[22] The case for performance during *komoi* is less clear, but the close connection, between the symposium and the *komos* may make the distinction unnecessary. It seems reasonable to understand that elegy performed at a symposium could also be performed during the revel which followed it; therefore, it is plausible to accept the mention of *komoi* in elegiac verses as references to the context of their performance.[23] The performance of elegy at public festivals also is firmly attested.[24] It is known from Plutarch (*Per.* 13.11) and the *Athenian Politeia* (60.1) that musical competitions were part of the Panathenaic festival. The pseudo-Plutarch *de musica* (1134A1) informs us that these competitions included elegies set to music and that originally *aulodoi* sung such elegies. At the Panathenaic festival, there were elegiac competitions and these were believed to have some basis in other early festivals. Pausanias quotes an earlier dedicatory inscription made by Echembrotus to commemorate his victory in singing μέλεα and ἐλέγους at the Pythian games of 586 BCE (Paus. 10.7.5–6 = *IEG²* 2: 62). It can be concluded that public festivals provided a context for the performance of elegy. All of the other contexts suggested by West simply derive from internal clues in our scanty remains of archaic elegy and, as Bowie shows, need hardly refer to an actual performance context.

Second, Bowie argues against West's assertion that elegy could not contain narrative for its own sake. He suggests that, in fact, an elegiac sub-genre, which he calls narrative elegy, thrived from the seventh century through the middle of the fifth century BCE although it has left little trace on our knowledge of the tradition of Greek literature.[25] From evidence for poems by Mimnermus, Tyrtaeus, Semonides, Panyassis, Simonides (on Salamis), and Ion of Chios, he defines narrative elegy in the following way. Narrative elegies focused on local histories with an emphasis on common achievement.[26] They combined past and recent history; they may also have incorporated myth.[27] The use of first person verbs in the fragment of Mimnermus and Tyrtaeus is suggestive of the narrative use of speeches.[28] Narrative elegies also appear to present events in a chronological way that is similar to the narrative structure found later in fifth-century Greek prose historiography.[29] Finally, he observes that these poems would have been of considerable length; therefore, they would have been suitable for performance at public competitions.[30] In this way, Bowie closely associates the content and the performance context of narrative elegy.

Bowie's study has done much to highlight the presence of historical subject-matter in elegy and to elucidate some defining features of the genre of elegy by linking this content with public performances. Yet, the conclusions concerning the existence of a category of elegy defined as narrative and its link to public performances can rightly be questioned.

First, in terms of narrative content, the poems that Bowie presents as evidence for narrative elegy have left only a shadowy mark in the transmission of Greek literature. None of the representatives of narrative elegy are well preserved and no elegy is ever qualified as narrative in antiquity.[31] Closer examination of the evidence reveals that there is room to doubt the existence of a separate class of poetry that would have been defined by its narrative content.

The best cases for narrative elegies on historical topics in the archaic period can be made from the *Smyrneis* of Mimnermus and the *Eunomia/Politeia* of Tyrtaeus. Mimnermus' *Smyrneis* survives only as a title and two verses in which direct speech is implied (fr. 13a W²).[32] To these remnants, we may add the comments of Pausanias, who tells us that Mimnermus mentions two generations of Muses in the prooimion of an elegiac poem on a battle between the Smyrneans and the Lydians under Gyges (Paus. 9.29.4 = fr. 13 W²). While Pausanias does not tell us that this prooimion belongs to the *Smyrneis,* the content he describes strongly suggests that he has this poem in mind. Bowie suggests tentatively that two other fragments may belong to this poem. First, fr. 14 W² contains a description of a fighter who routed the Lydian cavalry across the Hermos plain that the poet had heard from some elders. The quote is provided by Stobaeus (3.7.1), but it is not ascribed to the *Smyrneis.* The comparison of generations that is implied by the reference to the elders has suggested two possibilities. Either the fragment belongs to an exhortatory elegy, that is not the *Smyrneis,* or the fragment belongs to the *Smyrneis* and suggests that narrative elegies contained comparisons between the present and the past.[33] Since the fragment is not ascribed to a specific poem, the decision is difficult. In a later revisiting of the evidence for narrative elegy, Bowie rightly exercises caution concerning this fragment and leaves its ascription to the *Smyrneis* as only a possibility.[34] Second, a group of six verses concerning the founding of Colophon by the Smyrneans is quoted by Strabo as belonging to the *Nanno* of Mimnermus (fr. 9 W² = Str. 14.1.4). It is possible that the ascription by Strabo is wrong and that the fragment comes from the *Smyrneis.*[35] Yet, while this suggestion is plausible, we cannot determine if Strabo actually means the *Smyrneis* in this situation, especially since the nature of either the *Smyrneis* or the *Nanno* of Mimnermus is not really known to us.[36] Bowie admits with due caution that this fragment may not belong to a narrative elegy.[37] It must be concluded, then, that only frs. 13 and 13aW² appear to provide evidence for the *Smyrneis* of Mimnermus. These two bits of evidence have led to the conclusion that this poem had an epic title, contained an invocation of the Muses and a narrative that was long enough to introduce direct speech.[38]

Slightly more of the *Eunomia/Politeia* by Tyrtaeus is believed to be extant. Two different titles survive for verses by Tyrtaeus concerning Spartan history and their government: *Eunomia* appears twice and *Politeia* appears once. The similarity between the titles, however, allows that they refer to the same work.[39] Aristotle tells us that the poem dealt with conditions created by one of the Messenian Wars (*Pol.* 1306 b36–1307a2). So, the poem is believed to have had historical content. It is uncertain which fragments of Tyrtaeus come from this poem. Only Strabo actually quotes verses from it. These verses pertain to the Heraklid origins in the Peloponnesus (8.4.10=fr. 2 W²). Strabo's quotation is augmented by fragmentary verses from POxy 2824, thereby providing sixteen consecutive verses presumably from the same poem. West assigns another quotation to this poem although the verses are not explicitly attributed to the *Eunomia/Politeia*. This fragment pertains to the Delphic origins of the Spartan *Rhetra* (fr. 4 W²). Bowie has argued that frs. 5–7 W², which in some way pertain to Spartan history, may also belong to this poem.[40] It must be kept in mind, however, that none of these verses is explicitly said to be part of the *Eunomia/Politeia*. The parameters of the poem cannot safely be reconstructed from these verses. More-over, it is not certain that these verses, even if they belong to the *Eunomia/Politeia*, provide evidence for a narrative poem. Originally Bowie suggested that the historical details along with the presence of first person verbs would be suitable for a narrative elegy. In particular, he postulated that a first person subjunctive verb (πειθώμεθα) at fr. 2.10 W² occurred in a speech that was part of a narrative pertaining to the Spartan arrival in the Peloponnesus.[41] He has, however, recanted this supposition and observed that this subjunctive may just as easily show that these verses represent "an exhortatory poem which simply had bursts of narrative which were function-ally similar to narrative elements in speeches of characters in the *Iliad*."[42] Following Bowie's later thinking, it must be concluded that Tyrtaeus' elegiac verses may contain historical narrative, but it cannot be shown that these verses constitute a poem solely devoted to this narrative.

A third possible seventh-century example of a narrative elegy is a poem by Semonides of Amorgos known only by the title ἀρχαιολογία . . . τῶν Σαμιῶν men-tioned in one *Suda* entry (Σ 431 Adler = *IEG*² ii: 98–99). This poem may be the same as the ἐλεγείαν ἐν βιβλίοις β´ ("elegiac verses in two books") mentioned in another *Suda* entry (Σ 446 Adler = *IEG*² ii: 98).[43] The link, however, remains only a guess.[44] More importantly, even if this link is accepted, it is not certain that this poem represents a longer elegiac work or that it was narrative. No real evidence for such conclusions exists.

Mimnermus and Tyrtaeus, then, show us that elegiac poetry could contain nar-rative on both distant and contemporary events. Semonides' ἀρχαιολογία . . . τῶν Σαμιῶν is nothing more than a possible title and so adds nothing to the definition of a sub-genre of narrative elegy. Little else is known about the scope of such poems. It cannot be determined how, if at all, they differed from other elegiac poetry.

There are four possible later examples of narrative elegy.[45] Diogenes Laer-tius says of Xenophanes, a poet from late sixth and early fifth centuries, ποίησε καὶ Κολοφῶνος κτίσιν καὶ τὸν εἰς Ἐλέαν τῆς Ἰταλίας ἀποικισμόν, ἔπη δισχίλια (D. L. 9.20 = Xenoph. fr. A1 W²: "he composed both a foundation of Colophon and the colonization of Elea in Italy, two thousand verses"). The word ἔπη is vague and obscures the meter of the poem. The word is often used of hexameter poetry, but it can also refer to poetry in general.[46] To be sure, it can even be used as a general term for elegiac poetry.[47] Nevertheless, we simply cannot be certain whether the meter of these poems was the elegiac distich or the hexameter. Moreover, we do not know if the poem was narrative.[48] Xenophanes must be considered to be tenuous evidence for the category of narrative elegy.

The *Suda* credits Panyassis, a poet of the fifth century BCE, with a long historical poem titled Ἰωνικά on Codrus, the Athenian King, his son Neleus, and the colonization of Ionia (Π 248 Adler = Panyas. T 1 *PEG*). The *Suda*, however, says the poem was in 7000 pentameters. The usual assumption is that this poem was not in pentameters but in elegiacs.[49] Three fragments have been assigned to this poem, but none with any degree of certainty.[50] Bowie, on the assumption that Panyassis' Ἰωνικά was in elegiacs, considers this lengthy work as evidence that narrative elegy was a well established category of poetry by the mid-fifth century BCE.[51] There is, however, simply not enough evidence for such a conclusion. As it stands, the Ἰωνικά does not provide a good example of a lengthy narrative elegy. Even if the poem was an elegy and it contained narrative elements, it cannot be determined to what extent the historical narrative was the sole focus of the poem. Furthermore, the difficulties in the *Suda* concerning the meter of the poem may also cast doubt upon the length of this poem.[52] The conclusion that arises is that there are too many unknowns about the Ἰωνικά of Panyassis to show that it belonged to a class of narrative elegy.

Bowie is more cautious about his final two examples of narrative elegy. First there is Simonides' *The Sea-battle at Salamis,* mentioned by the Suda and generally believed to be an elegiac poem. Little else is known about this composition.[53] Yet, given the evidence available to Bowie at the time, Simonides' *The Sea-battle at Salamis* can be said to offer nothing more than evidence of a poem, possibly in elegiacs, that had contemporary history as its subject. Finally, Ion of Chios is said to have composed a work on the foundation of Chios (Schol. Ar. Pax. 825 = *IEG*² ii: 79). It is not certain, however, whether this work was poetic or prose. The only extant quote, fr. 19, is a difficult bit of prose, which Bowie originally reconstructed to be a hexameter.[54] Bowie later admits that this restoration must be a mistake.[55] The conclusion must be that Ion's *ktisis* of Ionia offers no evidence for the supposed class of narrative elegy.[56]

As it stands, then, the evidence for a sub-genre of elegy defined by its narrative content must be taken cautiously. None of the surviving examples of narrative elegy is in tact enough to determine the role played by narrative in the larger composition. The *Smyrneis* of Mimnermus may have contained narrative bits, but we cannot determine the role played by narrative in the larger structure of this work. The *Eunomia/Politeia* of Tyrtaeus also may have had bits of narrative, but these narrative sections may have been couched in a larger poem that was exhortatory. It is reasonable to wonder if Mimnermus' poem also would have been exhortatory. None of the other examples of narrative elegy provides us with sufficient information to conclude that it was a longer narrative of its subject matter. The most that can be concluded from the evidence for the works of Semonides, Xenophanes, Simonides, Panyassis and Ion of Chios, is that if these works were elegies they presented subject matter that was historical. We must conclude that verses on historical matters were suitable to elegy and to some extent so was narrative. Nevertheless, there is simply not evidence to conclude that elegies with narratives on historical subjects constituted a separate elegiac sub-genre.

In terms of performance context, Bowie has suggested that these narrative elegies would have been suitable for performance at public competitions. The link, however, between any specific content and the context of public performance of elegy is simply a guess. That elegy was performed competitively at the various festivals during the archaic and classical period is not in doubt. It is less certain, however, what distinguishing features elegy performed in this setting would have had. Bowie links this content and context on the grounds that narrative elegy and public competitions would make a natural pairing.[57] Yet, without the later narrative poems of Xenophanes, Panyassis and Ion, a key feature of Bowie's hypothesis is lost.[58] It is from these poems that narrative elegy can be understood as being too long for performance in symposia and suitable for performance at public festivals.[59] There is no clear evidence about the length of the *Smyrneis* of Mimnermus or the *Eunomia/Politeia* of Tyrtaeus and the difficulties surrounding the *Samian Archaeology* of Semonides make it unhelpful. It should also be remembered that there is no ancient evidence for an understanding of a sub-group of elegy that would have been particularly suited to historical narratives. There is no evidence that public performances of elegy demanded narrative poems on historical topics, or any other types of content, for that matter. It is just as likely that elegies with historical content and possibly narratives would have been suitable for performance in a sympotic context. Such a context has been suggested for Solon's *Salamis* and the fragments of Xenophanes tentatively assigned to a historical poem.[60] That Solon's poem acquired a title may reveal that historical subjects were appropriate in sympotic contexts. Furthermore, if Solon's poem was composed primarily for a sympotic context, it might also be suggested that the appearance of a title may not be an indicator that poems on historical topics were devoted primarily to lengthy narratives. It may be that titles such as *Smyrneis, Eunomia/Politeia, Samian Archaeology, Sea-battle at Salamis, Ionica* simply reveal that these verses pertain to historical events and for later commentators this content became a way of identifying these poems.[61] It does not follow, however, that such titles represent longer narrative poems that would be epic-like depictions of historical events suitable only for public performance.

With these points in mind, the evidence that existed for narrative elegy before the publication of the "new Simonides" should be questioned. In terms of reconstructing elegiac poems from our fragmentary remains, Bowie's hypothesized sub-genre raises another significant problem. Namely, by following Bowie's conclusions, scholars ultimately define poems that belong to this elegiac sub-genre by their content. Along this line of thinking, narrative content, then, becomes the primary criterion in reconstructing the fragments. Such is certainly the case for the fragments of the "new Simonides" that are placed in poems on the Persian Wars and fr. 11 W$^2$ in particular. Yet, the fragmentary nature of the "new Simonides" and our incomplete knowledge of the poetic category, narrative elegy, suggest that this approach is flawed. As it stands, this approach requires an intricate relation between content and genre in early Greek poetry. The problems with such an approach can be most clearly demonstrated in the wide range of topics that is found in our surviving corpus of early Greek elegy. For the modern scholar, this variety of themes creates difficulty for determining limits for the genre of elegy or even the sub-species of this genre. These problems force us to recall that, although modern scholars can identify certain content that might be suitable for certain types of poetry, content was not the primary distinguishing feature of poetic classifications in the archaic period. For example, it should be noted that historical subjects and narrative would have been at home in other types of poetry including epic, hymns, and lyric.[62] Historical content cannot be said to have been a defining feature of archaic elegy. The genre of a poem, then, provides few clues about the poem's content. Even if a poem is known to belong to a certain poetic category, it remains difficult to reconstruct the poem's content on the basis of this categorization; therefore, genre and content should be distinguished.

These observations become even more important when attempts are made to reconstruct a fragmentary work such as fr. 11 W$^2$ on the assumption that its content is determined by its membership in a certain genre. The need for caution is reinforced when the category to which a poem is assigned is uncertain, as is the case with narrative elegy. In terms of reconstructing the "new Simonides," it is a useful heuristic exercise, then, to distinguish between genre and content. Here, it is the content that is clear in fr. 11 W$^2$ that will be considered rather than how the fragment's supposed membership in a sub-genre provides guidelines for recreating the content.

## C. Content of Bowie's Narrative Elegy and Fr. 11 W$^2$

Although Bowie expresses doubts that fr. 11 W$^2$ represents the same type of narrative elegy as he finds in Mimnermus' *Smyrneis*, many scholars have concluded that the "new Simonides" shows that Bowie's predictions were close to the mark if not prophetic.[63] The generally accepted view is that the "new Simonides" confirms the existence of narrative elegies as a class of poetry.[64] At this point, then, it is appropriate to consider the extent to which this approach to the "new Simonides" is justified.

The prooimion, mythical exempla, and references to contemporary events in fr. 11 W² have led to the belief that this fragment represents a narrative elegy.[65] The result is that fr. 11 W² and many of the other new fragments are reconstructed as if a narrative of the battle of Plataea provides the main structural principle of the verses.[66] This approach is most clearly exemplified by West's reconstruction of these verses, which is based largely on Herodotus' narrative of the battle of Plataea. In reconstructing the "Plataea poem" in this way, West designates the poem as an "elegiac epyllion" with a narrative of the battle of Plataea that would correspond to a historical narrative that might be found in a prose work.[67] The circularity of this interpretation is apparent: the proposed sub-genre of narrative elegy is helpful for reconstructing the content of fr. 11 W² and the poem to which it belongs; the interpretation of the resulting poem as a narrative elegy confirms the definition of this sub-genre.

There are, however, few clearly narrative elements in either fr. 11 W² or any of the other fragments linked with the Plataea poem. The belief in a narrative ultimately arises from an interpretation of fr. 11.25–45 W². These lines, however, depict at most some action, possibly the leaving of a city, in the words ἄστυ λιπόντ[ at line 29. The incomplete state of the text complicates the matter because it is not entirely clear how to interpret this action. While this action is generally taken to represent the Spartans' initial march from Sparta, it is also possible that these words refer to some motion within the mythological reference of fr. 11.30–31 W². These words do not necessarily point to a narrative of the battle of Plataea. Moreover, the possible list of geographic locations that follows these verses is also dubious evidence for a narrative. The extent, content, and function of this list are, for the most part, unknown. It simply cannot be assumed that these places represent geographic points within a narrative of a Spartan march to Plataea unless such a narrative is being reconstructed. All other potentially narrative moments in the fragment are conjectural.[68]

Finally, it should also be noted that even if these verses are to be reconstructed to reflect a narrative in some way, there is no reason to suppose that the entire poem represented by this fragment was organized as a narrative. Narrative features could form an integral part of other types of poetry, such as epinicians, tragic choruses, hymns, and even elegies, while not providing the primary structure of the work.[69] Narrative may, then, be present in the verses, but it is not certain that it should form the criterion by which the poem to which the fragment belongs is to be reconstructed.

The conclusion must be that few indicators of narrative are present in fr. 11 W² and that the reconstruction of this fragment as an extended narrative derives from the initial assumption that the poem belongs in the sub-genre of narrative elegy.

## D. Content of Fr. 11 W² and the Spartans

If fr. 11 W² need not be a narrative, how then is its content to be reconstructed? I propose that the answer to this question lies in exploring the emphasis on Sparta and Plataea that has been perceived in fr. 11 W² and has been projected, in various ways, into the whole composition represented by this fragment. To examine this emphasis, it is necessary to consider how other commemorations and accounts presented the Persian Wars. The near contemporary inscriptional record and epigrams on the Persian Wars, as well as the later accounts in Aeschylus' *Persae* and Herodotus, will be used to provide a backdrop against which fr. 11 W² can be read. The primary concern will be to determine what these other accounts lead us to expect in terms of the content of fr. 11 W². From this approach, it can be determined to what extent clues in fr. 11 W² suggest that its content is in line with this expectation.

Most analyses of fr. 11 W² allow for some degree of panhellenism because it is assumed to represent a poem about a victory in which many Greek cities participated. The term panhellenic needs definition at this point. Throughout this study, I take the term to indicate a notion of community among Greek cities derived from a shared sense of Hellenic identity.[70] In terms of the Persian Wars, various battles might be considered to be panhellenic efforts because many cities joined together on behalf of a larger cause, namely the freedom of Greece. In terms of poetic representations of these battles, a poem might be said to be panhellenic because it emphasizes this notion of a combined Hellenic effort on behalf of Greece. In studies of the "new Simonides," it is debated whether the hints of panhellenism in fr. 11 W² indicate that the poem is concerned with a combined Greek effort or simply indicate that the Spartans were the leaders of this combined effort.

The arguments put forward by Antonio Aloni and Deborah Boedeker provide a framework within which the modern understanding of panhellenism in the fr. 11 W² can be approached. Aloni has argued that the "Plataea poem" was commissioned for a public performance by either Pausanias or the Spartans. In this view, the poem has a Spartan bias.[71] Aloni allows that the prooimion in fr. 11 W² had a panhellenic nature by concluding that in it Achilles represents all the Greeks who fought at Plataea.[72] As Aloni shows, this interpretation of Achilles fits well with an inscriptional record that reveals a pride not simply in civic identities, but in Hellenic unity.[73] Aloni's conclusion, however, is not that the poem follows this spirit of panhellenism, but that fr. 11 W², like the historical narratives in Herodotus, Diodorus, and Plutarch, attests to a disunity among Greek cities following Plataea. So, for Aloni, the panhellenism evident in the inscriptional recorded quickly gave way to "political ambiguity and tension." [74] It against this backdrop of political tensions that he reads the "new Simonides."

In contrast, Deborah Boedeker has suggested that the "new Simonides" is panhellenic, or rather "poly-hellenic," in perspective.[75] Like Aloni, Boedeker interprets

Achilles as a paradigm for the Greeks rather than any specific hero at Plataea.[76] Unlike Aloni, she suggests that the nature of Achilles as panhellenic paradigm is carried over into the rest of the poem. For Boedeker, "the Lacedaemonians are not alone at Simonides' Plataea."[77] In this view, the poem represented by fr. 11 $W^2$ is panhellenic in that it is a multi-*polis* presentation of Plataea rather than a Spartan-biased one. [78]

The arguments of Aloni and Boedeker define two poles between which the content of the new fragments can be considered. Both approach fr. 11 $W^2$ as a poem in some way concerned with the *Plataiomachoi*. Each, however, understands a different emphasis in the depiction of the *Plataiomachoi*. A closer inspection of the Spartan references in fr. 11 $W^2$, however, reveals that the emphasis allowed by both will admit modification.

An emphasis on the Spartans in fr. 11 $W^2$ is detected most directly in the mention of Sparta at 11.25 $W^2$ and the name Pausanias, the Spartan leader at Plataea, at fr. 11.34 $W^2$.[79] The appearance of Tyndaridai (fr. 11.30 $W^2$) and Menelaus (fr. 11.31 $W^2$), figures closely associated with Sparta, has reinforced this interpretation.[80] The reasoning is that, because this Spartan emphasis immediately follows the prooimion, the Spartans led by Pausanias must be the subject of the following composition. Yet it is not at all certain that fr. 11 $W^2$ represents the content of the whole composition to which it belongs. The predominant position of the Spartans in the fragment surely reflects that these verses emphasize their role at Plataea. But, since the length of the poem is unknown, it cannot be determined whether this emphasis continued in the verses that follow fr. 11 $W^2$. If the composition ran more than a hundred lines, as is generally believed, there is no way of determining from fr. 11 $W^2$ if the Spartans maintained a prominent position in the lost verses.[81] The same conclusion is valid if the composition to which fr. 11 $W^2$ belongs is conceived of as a relatively short poem. Moreover, it should also be noted that the Spartan prominence in these verses need not guarantee that the composition was simply focused on the battle of Plataea. Since we do not know what or how much followed the verses of fr. 11 $W^2$, we must be cautious in asserting that the composition focused on Sparta or even the battle of Plataea.

*Epigrammatic Record*[82]

The assumption that fr. 11 $W^2$ represents a poem that is biased toward Spartans and their role at Plataea, in fact, is at odds with contemporary epigrams on the Persian Wars. Five epigrams pertaining to the Persian Wars, the first four of which are also discussed by Aloni, reveal that, to a certain extent, an atmosphere of "political harmony" followed the battle of Plataea.[83]

First, Plutarch quotes an epigram from the altar of Zeus Eleutherios at Plataea:

τόνδε ποθ' "Ελληνες Νίκης κράτει, ἔργωι "Αρηος,
[εὐτόλμωι ψυχῆς λήματι πειθόμενοι,]
Πέρσας ἐξελάσαντες, ἐλευθέραι 'Ελλάδι κοινόν
ἱδρύσαντο Διὸς βωμὸν 'Ελευθερίου.[84]

["Once, the Greeks, [obeying the courageous resolution of their soul], having driven out the Persians by the power of Victory, by the work of Ares, set up this common altar of Zeus Eleutherios for a free Greece."]

The epigram is quoted by Plutarch to demonstrate that the victory at Plataea was a common one (κοινὸν γενέσθαι τὸ κατόρθωμα). It is unclear, however, whether Plutarch, who is defending his home city's honor, is correct that this epigram proves the disingenuousness of Herodotus' account, in which only the Lacedaemonians, Athenians, and Tegeans fought at Plataea (Hdt. 9.85). A plausible suggestion is that such an epigram, like the Serpent Column at Delphi discussed above, commemorates not just Plataea, but the Persian Wars in general.[85] Nothing in the epigram itself confirms either possibility. Nevertheless, the obvious emphasis, as Plutarch mentions, is on the Hellenic effort and not the achievements of any particular city. Further emphasis is also placed on combined effort by the dedication of the altar "for a free Greece." Whether in commemoration of Plataea or of the fight against the Persians in general, the epigram at the altar of Zeus Eleutherios memorializes a collective effort.

Next, there are two epigrams that can be interpreted as commemorations of the dead at Plataea. Pausanias, the periegete, mentions that elegiac verses of Simonides were to be found on the separate graves of the Lacedaemonians and the Athenians (9.25: ἐλεγεῖα ἐστι Σιμωνίδου γεγραμμένα ἐπ' αὐτοῖς). Pausanias does not record these verses nor do they survive *in situ*. The *Anthologia Palatina*, however, provides two possible candidates:

εἰ τὸ καλῶς θνήσκειν ἀρετῆς μέρος ἐστὶ μέγιστον,
    ἡμῖν ἐκ πάντων τοῦτ' ἀπένειμε Τύχη·
'Ελλάδι γὰρ σπεύδοντες ἐλευθερίην περιθεῖναι
    κείμεθ' ἀγηράντωι χρώμενοι εὐλογίηι.[86]

["If to die well is the greatest share of excellence, Fortune has assigned this to us out of all others; for we, striving to bestow freedom on Greece, lie here possessing ageless glory."]

ἄσβεστον κλέος οἵδε φίληι περὶ πατρίδι θέντες
    κυάνεον θανάτου ἀμφεβάλοντο νέφος·
οὐδὲ τεθνᾶσι θανόντες, ἐπεί σφ' 'Αρετὴ καθύπερθε
    κυδαίνουσ' ἀνάγει δώματος ἐξ 'Αίδεω.[87]

["Inextinguishable renown these men bestowed on their fatherland; they surrounded themselves in the dark cloud of death. Although they died, they are not yet dead, since their valor from above gives them glory and leads them up from the house of Hades."]

Although the sentiment of these epigrams seems to be suited to epitaphs for the dead at Plataea, their link to the elegiac verses mentioned by Pausanias is not certain. The first, Simon. *FGE* VIII, is included in the *Anthologia Palatina* and mentioned by a scholiast on Aristides (III 154–5 Dindorf), both of which say that it is an epitaph for those who died at Thermopylae. The *Anthologia Palatina* refers the second epigrams to the same men.[88] These inscriptions, however, do not seem to be from the five inscriptions known to have commemorated Thermopylae.[89] A solution to the problem was proposed by Bergk, who suggested that these verses from the *Anthologia Palatina* are actually those mentioned by Pausanias in reference to Plataea.[90] With broad claims such as Ἑλλάδι γὰρ σπεύδοντες ἐλευθερίην περιθεῖναι (VIII.3 *FGE*) and ἄσβεστον κλέος οἴδε φίληι περὶ πατρίδι θέντες (IX.1 *FGE*), it is likely that these epigrams do commemorate the Persian Wars.[91] Furthermore, the coincidence between two epigrams ascribed to Simonides that claim the establishment of "freedom" and "inextinguishable fame" and two inscriptions, also ascribed to Simonides, seen at Plataea by Pausanias that commemorate a battle which achieved these claims does suggest some link.[92] As Page also points out, there is nothing incompatible in the inscriptions with an early date.[93] The evidence for connecting Simon. VIII and IX *FGE* and the elegiac verses seen by Pausanias at Plataea is compelling.

It is conspicuous that these two epigrams reflect an emphasis on the common effort and victory rather than the efforts of any particular group on behalf of its own city. The epigrams refer to men struggling on behalf of Hellas (VIII.3) or their fatherland (XI.1). To be sure, Pausanias does mention separate tombs at Plataea, and it would seem likely that those who viewed these tombs would have been able to identify them with individual cities.[94] Yet, even if the epigrams would have been linked to a specific city, the overall emphasis in these verses is the benefit for all. The emphasis remains on the benefit received by the collective group which fought at Plataea rather than the freedom of any particular city achieved by its own fighters. In the light of the epigram quoted by Plutarch above, this emphasis can be said to point toward an atmosphere in which public commemorations emphasized the common effort and the common benefit of these efforts.

Fourth, Thucydides (1.132.2) records an epigram that the Spartan leader Pausanias had inscribed on the Serpent Column at Delphi (M-L 27 = *SIG*³ 31). The historian tells us that the verses were later erased by the Spartans:[95]

Ἑλλήνων ἀρχηγὸς ἐπεὶ στρατὸν ὤλεσε Μήδων,
Παυσανίας Φοίβωι μνῆμ' ἀνέθηκε τόδε. [96]

["When he destroyed the army of the Medes, the leader of the Greeks, Pausanias, set up this as a memorial to Phoibos."]

This inscription is curious in comparison with the other epigrams commemorating either Plataea or the Persian Wars because it is a personal dedication that claims credit for the victory over the Persians for one man.[97] The arrogance is clear.[98] It is interesting, however, that Pausanias' claim is to be the leader of *Hellas* rather than the leader of the Lacedaemonians; that is, Pausanias claims to be the leader of a broader group of victors. It is possible that the arrogance of the epigram, in fact, betrays a panhellenism that followed the Greek victory. Such an atmosphere is also evident in the response to the inscription. Thucydides says that the inscription was erased immediately and replaced by the list of names now found on the Serpent Column. This response is suggestive of the way a Greek city may have viewed the effort at Plataea or at least wanted to present a view of it on public commemorations.[99] It is possible, then, to understand from the epigram and the response to it recorded by Thucydides that public commemorations of the Persian Wars were expected to emphasize a panhellenic effort rather than the actions of any particular city.

This attitude is paralleled in another inscription, associated with the dedication at Delphi, which Diodorus Siculus, the first-century BCE historian, records:

Ἑλλάδος εὐρυχόρου σωτῆρες τόνδ' ἀνέθηκαν,
  δουλοσύνης στυγερᾶς ῥυσάμενοι πόλιας.[100]

["The saviors of spacious Greece set up this monument, after having protected their cities from hated slavery."]

No other source records this inscription and there is no evidence of it on the surviving Serpent Column.[101] Nevertheless, if Diodorus is correct concerning the connection of the inscription with the Serpent Column, the verses provide another example of a commemoration of the Persian Wars that represents the victory over the Persians as a common effort with a common benefit for all.[102]

In sum, these epigrams suggest that public commemorations of the victory over the Persians, both in dedications to a god and in memorials to the fallen combatants, subordinated the individual efforts to emphasize the larger Hellenic effort and its benefits for all of Greece. To return to Aloni's estimation, it is possible that this "political harmony" in these epigrams is "unusual" and that it is not found in fr. 11 W². Simonides' depiction, then, would be an early example of "political ambiguity and tension" that appears in later historical accounts.[103] In viewing fr. 11 W² as a representative of a "Plataea elegy" biased toward the Spartans, Aloni is justified in his conclusions. It is still not certain that an atmosphere of "political ambiguity and tension" would have provided the backdrop for Simonides' composition. I posit that these public commemorations argue against understanding an atmosphere of political tension as the backdrop for Simonides' composition. Moreover, the story of immediate tensions over power following the Persian defeat at Plataea may be a later view that was projected back onto earlier events to explain the relations between Athens and Sparta. For example, Diodorus Siculus (first century BCE), whose source for this information was likely to have been the Ephorus (fourth century BCE), provides the story of Spartan resentment of Athens at the loss of hegemony over the sea forces following the recall of Pausanias, the rejection of the Spartan Dorcis as the new leader of the fleet, and the initial steps toward the foundation of the Delian League (11.50). Thucydides, on the other hand, tells us that the Spartans were not distressed by the Athenian control of the continuing naval campaign against the Persians or by the formation of the Delian League (1.95.7).[104] The epigraphic and epigrammatic record discussed above seems to reflect the same atmosphere suggested by the words of Thucydides. To be sure, tensions do arise between Athens and Sparta in the years following the Persian Wars. It is not certain, however, that these tensions arose immediately following the battle of Plataea. In fact, the inscriptions and epigrams as well as Thucydides suggest the opposite; that is, rather than the "political ambiguity and tension" that Aloni emphasizes, the atmosphere following the battle of Plataea appears to have been, to some degree, one of political harmony.

Turning to Simonides' composition represented by fr. 11 W², the mention of Pausanias in a prominent position in the fragment suggests that this poem was composed at some point before his recall and subsequent disgrace at Sparta. Most likely the composition originally appeared within the year following the battle of Plataea and no later than a decade after the battle.[105] A reasonable conclusion is that Simonides' composition is to be set against a backdrop of some degree of political harmony rather than political tension. It is reasonable, then, to understand that Simonides' composition would reflect the emphasis evidenced in the epigrammatic record and underlying Thucydides. For this reason, I suggest that by underscoring political tensions in his interpretation of fr. 11 W², Aloni wrongly dissociates these verses from the atmosphere of panhellenic unity following the battle of Plataea found in these contemporary epigraphic commemorations.

If Simonides' composition appeared in such an atmosphere, a reasonable assumption is that this political harmony should be found at various levels in other depictions of the Persian Wars. By looking at other representations of the Persian Wars, this atmosphere of panhellenic unity following the battle of Plataea becomes more apparent.


*Aeschylus* Persae

The *Persae* of Aeschylus, first produced in 472 BCE, stands not only as our sole example of a historical drama, but also as our earliest extant non-epigrammatic poetical account of the Persian Wars.[106] As such, the performance of this tragedy is close in time to the poem represented by fr. 11 W², which itself must have been first performed shortly after 478 BCE and the battle of Plataea because the Spartan leader Pausanias did not remain in favor long after this date. The *Persae,* then, provides a valuable point of comparison for understanding an attitude toward the Persian Wars in the aftermath of these battles.

Importantly, this play provides a balance to the epigrammatic record discussed above because without a doubt it is Athenocentric. Athens is the primary concern of the queen throughout the play in general; her initial preoccupation in her early questions to the chorus is Athens (226–245); she says that Xerxes' invasion of Greece was requital for Darius' defeat at Marathon (472–479). Significantly, the queen explicitly links the Persian defeat at sea with their defeat on land: ναυτικὸς στρατὸς κακωθεὶς πεζὸν ὤλεσε στρατόν (728: "Once the navy was injured, the army was destroyed").[107] At the heart of the drama lies the lengthy narrative of the Persian defeat at Salamis, which stands as an Athenian victory (353–432, 447–471). Salamis becomes the crucial blow that repelled the Persians and the Athenians are the ones who delivered of this blow. Later in the play, the advice of Darius' ghost to the chorus is μέμνησθ᾽ ᾽Αθηνῶν ῾Ελλάδος τε (824: "Remember Athens and Greece").[108] The tragedy, then, offers an important single-city perspective on the Persian Wars from which we may evaluate the presentation in the "new Simonides."

This Athenocentrism is not surprising in a drama performed for a largely Athenian audience at the City Dionysia. For this reason, caution is needed in viewing this city-centered view as a general perspective on the Persian Wars. At most, the play shows that by 472 BCE there was an attempt in Athens to present the Persian Wars as an Athenian-led victory. Such an attempt must be seen as natural in a play performed for an Athenian audience, whose interests in 472 BCE would be linked to their role in the Delian League.[109] An expedient control on this perspective, however, can be sought in the conclusions drawn from the epigrams discussed above.

If the epigrams represent a panhellenic perspective, one could expect this attitude to appear at some level even in an Athenian account that attempts to claim credit for the overall victory. In fact, undertones of a panhellenic understanding of the victory over the Persians can be detected in the ambiguous use of ethnic descriptive adjectives throughout this Athenocentric play. Throughout the play, the Persians refer to Greeks by the ethnic terms "Ionian," "Doric," and "Dorian." The general interpretation of these terms is that they are employed so as to refer to all Greeks inclusively. When the queen mentions Xerxes' intentions for invading Greece, she says ᾽Ιαόνων γῆν οἴχεται πέρσαι θέλων (178: "He (Xerxes) set out, intending to destroy the land of the Ionians"). It is generally agreed that the reference here is to the Greeks in general and not specifically the Athenians.[110] There are four pieces of evidence to support this claim. First, a scholiast on Aristophanes *Acharnians* 104 reports that the barbarians called all Greeks "Ionians."[111] Second, at Herodotus 7.9, Mardonius refers to "the Ionians living in Europe," where he is seen as using the term

Ionian broadly of all Greeks.[112] Third, Herodotus claims that the Athenians disliked being called Ionian.[113] Finally, as Edith Hall points out, the Persepolis tablets, which refer to "high-ranking Greek aides" in Persia as *Yāuna*, confirm that "Ionian" on some level meant "Greek" in Persia. This inclusive meaning of the term "Ionian" is understood to continue throughout the *Persae*.[114] The descriptive term "Doric" is also believed to have an inclusive meaning. The term is used once by the queen to describe the conflict between Persia and Greece, which are metaphorically represented as two women, one in a Persian robe and the other in a Doric (Δωρικοῖσιν) one.[115] Finally, the adjective "Dorian" also occurs once in the play. In his comments on the battle of Plataea, the ghost of Darius prophesies that there will be much blood spilt at Plataea by the Dorian spear (Δωρίδος).[116] The general view in antiquity that the victory at Plataea was a Spartan one suggests that Darius specifically means by the Spartans' spears.[117] These interpretations suggest the following pattern: in the *Persae* the adjective "Dorian" has a specific point of reference, while the terms "Ionian" and "Doric" do not.

This pattern, however, is incongruous and invites a re-evaluation of how these terms are used in the play. It is not obvious that an Athenian audience would understand the term "Ionian" in an inclusive way. To be sure, there is evidence, particularly the passage of Herodotus just mentioned, that the Athenians knew that the Persians considered the Greeks collectively as Ionians. Yet, there is also evidence which suggests that to an Athenian audience the term "Ionian" would evoke their kinship with the Greeks in Ionia. At *Iliad* 13.685–9, the Ionians are equated with the Athenians.[118] In Solon fr. 4a W², Athens is the oldest land of Ionia (πρεσβυτάτην . . . γαῖαν ['Ι]αονης). Herodotus records Athens among the Ionian states (1.143.1–2). Thucydides remarks on the kinship between the Athenians and the Ionians in terms of their shared affection for effeminate dress in previous times (1.6.3–4). Finally, the Ionian *phylai* were a viable organizational system in Athens, at least until the reforms of Cleisthenes. The use of these *phylai* may have continued into the late fifth and early fourth century BCE.[119] It seems odd, then, that a predominantly Athenian audience of *Persae* would ignore entirely this association implied by the term "Ionian."[120] In fact, it is possible to show that in the play the term "Ionian" takes into account this association and implicitly means "Athenian."

This understanding of the term "Ionian" is made clear by looking at the stated motives for Xerxes' invasion of Greece. First, the motive given by the queen is to destroy the land of the Ionians: Ἰαόνων γῆν οἴχεται πέρσαι θέλων (178). Later, however, the queen suggests that the motive is vengeance for Marathon:

πικρὰν δὲ παῖς ἐμὸς τιμωρίαν
κλεινῶν 'Αθηνῶν ηὗρε, κοὐκ ἀπήρκεσαν
οὓς πρόσθε Μαραθὼν βαρβάρων ἀπώλεσεν·
(473–476)

["My son found his vengeance on famous Athens to be bitter, and those of the barbarians whom Marathon destroyed before were not enough for him."]

With these two passages in mind, the destruction of Ionian land becomes equated with revenge for the Persian defeat at Marathon. By presenting Xerxes' motives in this way, the play exploits an ambiguity in the term "Ionian" and shifts the focus of the Persian attack. The play presents the Persians as referring to the Greeks in general as "Ionians" and thereby, on the surface, portrays the Persian attack as one against all of Greece. In the ambiguity of the ethnic terminology, however, the play also invites the interpretation that this reference to "Ionians" is more particularly to the Athenians. In this ambiguity the emphasis of the Persian attack is subtly shifted to Athens while the pretext of an attack against Greece is maintained. This shift of focus can be seen as an attempt to mask a more panhellenic view of the Persian attack.

A reevaluation of the context for the term "Dorian" provides further insight into the play's presentation of the victory over the Persians. Broadhead remarks, "Plataea receives quite as much attention as can be expected . . . That the slaughter is attributed to the Dorian spear is in itself impressive."[121] To be sure, in Darius' words, the Persian disaster at Plataea is described as κακῶν ὕψιστ' (807) and one that will be retold to three generations by piles of corpses (815–817: θῖνες νεκρῶν δὲ καὶ τριτοσπόρῳ γονῇ / ἄφωνα σημανοῦσιν ὄμμασιν βροτῶν). On the surface, then, by attributing such a feat to the Dorian spear, the ghost of Darius gives credit for the final defeat of the Persians to the Spartans. But Darius' words at this point also closely link the Persian defeat with their destruction of altars and pilfering of temples. These actions surely had a poignant significance for Athenians in the theater of Dionysus following the Persian capture of the Acropolis. It is possible to see in this passage an attempt to shift the focus of the Persian attack to Athens. In the impressive moment of crediting the victory at Plataea to the Spartans, the *Persae* presents the victory as one on behalf of Athens. The Persian Wars are about the Athenians and particularly about what they gave up rather than the threat to all of Greece. In this way, then, the *Persae* can present Plataea as a reminder not simply of the Doric spear, but of Athens, first, and Greece, second, as the words of Darius make clear, τοιαῦθ' ὁρῶντες τῶνδε τἀπιτίμια / μέμνησθ' 'Αθηνῶν 'Ελλάδος τε (823–24: "Consider such things and the penalties for them and remember Athens and Greece"). So the *Persae* emphasizes the Athenians in what was construed as a larger effort in which other cities distinguished themselves against the Persians.

In sum, the ambiguity of the ethnic terms in the *Persae* perceived by modern scholars, in fact, shows an attempt to shift emphasis to Athens and to move attention away from the perspective of the Persian Wars as a larger effort. Such an attempt to shift the emphasis of the Persian attack to Athens as well as to highlight the Athenian suffering in these attacks is easily explained. The *Persae* was performed for a

predominantly Athenian audience and its presentation of events certainly would have
been geared toward this audience.[122] Moreover, such an attempt can be explained by
the Athenian involvement in leading the Delian League in the decade following Plataea.[123] The point that is made here, however, works with these possible explanations.
What emerges in this play is an attempt to override a view of the Persian Wars as a
panhellenic effort. I suggest that this attempt does not completely mask the view of
the Persian Wars as a panhellenic effort. Rather the undertones of the presentation of
the Persian Wars that are found in the epigrams discussed above remain, albeit under
the surface, in the *Persae.*

*Herodotus*

The prose narrative of Herodotus provides another early account of the Persian Wars,
but one that is more removed from the events it depicts than the *Persae* is. Still, like
the *Persae,* the narrative of Herodotus is a valuable point of comparison for the new
fragments of Simonides.

The claim to give glory to the great deeds of the Greeks and the Barbarians in
Herodotus' preface in many ways sets the tone for the work.[124] It establishes a broad
scope for the narrative that is further developed in the parallel that is drawn between
the Persian Wars and mythical events culminating in the Trojan Wars. The overall emphasis in the introduction, then, lies on the Greek effort, construed broadly, against
the Persians. Yet, this broad perspective is not the same as the panhellenic one noted
in the epigrams above. Rather, Herodotus shapes his narrative of the Persian Wars by
dividing it into a series of battles in which individual cities and their allies are assigned
the lion's share of credit for each victory. An obvious example of this approach is
found in the prelude to the battle of Artemisium. Here, Herodotus credits the defeat
of the Persians in general to Athens' decision to fight for the freedom of Greece.[125]
On a smaller scale, this approach to the Persian Wars is found in Herodotus' presentation of each battle. At Salamis, distinction is given first to the Aeginetans and second
to Athens (8.93). At Plataea, it is the Lacedaemonians who excelled, followed by the
Tegeans and the Athenians (9.71–73). Finally, at Mycale, the Athenians are named as
the most distinguished fighters (9.105). In this way, Herodotus presents the Persian
Wars as a multi-polis effort with an emphasis on the efforts of individual cities within
the collective Greek resistance.[126]

Such an approach to the Persian Wars is certainly to be expected in Herodotus given that he composed his work at a later date than both the *Persae* and the
"new Simonides."[127] To be sure, Herodotus at points seems to admit tendencies
toward an Athenocentric tradition concerning the Persian Wars that are similar to
those found in Aeschylus. Yet, underneath the focus on the actions of individual
cities, it is possible to identify a view that emphasizes the combined Greek effort
in Herodotus.

Such an understanding of the Persian Wars is observable in Herodotus' narrative of the events following the battle of Plataea. Herodotus records that the Lacedaemonians were the most distinguished at Plataea (Hdt 9.71–72), but he also remarks that no award of distinction was given after the battle (Hdt. 9.81). This observation follows the reference to the monuments set up at Delphi, Olympia, and at the Isthmus, which are known to be panhellenic in scope.[128] While Herodotus overtly presents Plataea as being a Spartan victory, the events following the battle reveal a broader view of the victory as one that was a common effort undertaken by the Greeks in general. All who fought at the battle were given equal credit for the outcome. A similar emphasis on the common effort is found in three events that follow of the battle of Salamis. First, the Greeks set up thank-offerings at the Isthmus, Sounium, Salamis, and Delphi. After the gifts were sent to Delphi, the Greeks, as a community (οἱ "Ελληνες . . . κοινῇ) consulted the god (Hdt. 8.121–122). Second, the Greeks unsuccessfully attempted to choose a man to whom they should award a prize of valor (ἀριστία). Rather, each man voted for himself first and Themistocles second (Hdt. 8.123). This inability to choose a distinguished fighter may reflect a more panhellenic outlook, perhaps showing that the Greeks in general distinguished themselves. Finally, Themistocles was honored in Lacedaemonia for his distinction at Salamis. While the story of Themistocles' visit to Sparta may be informed by some larger political interests, the point here need only be that the recognition of the Athenian by the Lacedaemonians hints at a larger understanding of the effort against the Persian. The recognition of Themistocles suggests a broader view of the battle on the part of the Lacedaemonians.[129]

In these episodes following the battles of Plataea and Salamis, then, it is possible to see in Herodotus hints of a view that these battles were understood as having been won by a collective effort. That is, Herodotus' emphasis on the efforts of individual cities may in fact be superimposed on a broader understanding of the Persian Wars as battles that were won by a collective Greek effort. Following this line of thinking, the assignment of credit for specific victories to individual cities by Herodotus could reflect a more discordant view of the Persian Wars that is not reflected in the epigrammatic record discussed above. This division of credit, however, does not completely overshadow the vestiges of the understanding of the Persian Wars as a panhellenic effort that seems to have followed the battle of Plataea.[130]

In sum, both the *Persae* of Aeschylus and the *Historiae* of Herodotus on the surface present the climate following the victory over the Persians as one marked by political strife. To an Athenian audience, Aeschylus depicts Persians who view Salamis as the decisive battle and Athens as the invincible foe. Likewise, struggles for credit in the various battles are pervasive in Herodotus' narrative. Beneath these perspectives of the Persian Wars as efforts undertaken by individuals and separate cities, however, there are hints that these wars were perceived as a common effort for a common goal. Aeschylus and Herodotus can be said implicitly to contain elements of a panhellenic perspective concerning the Persian Wars. This implicit panhellenic perspective fits well with the interpretation of an explicit panhellenic emphasis in the epigrammatic record.

It is against the backdrop of this panhellenic perspective on the Persian Wars that the "new Simonides" must be considered. More specifically, this backdrop forces a reevaluation of the conclusion that fr. 11 W² is to be read as part of poem that emphasized the Spartans alone. Such a reading divides the Spartans and Plataea from the larger effort in a way that, as I hope to have shown, is distinct from other contemporary commemorations of the Persian Wars in general and Plataea in particular.

*The "New Simonides"*

The questions to be asked then are: Is there evidence of a panhellenic perspective in fr. 11 W²? If so, what do the remains of this perspective tell us about the content of the composition to which these fragmentary verses belong? To be sure, fr. 11 W² contains a prooimion that is followed with ten lines devoted to the Spartans in some way. Although this prominent position has suggested a Spartan bias, I have suggested that such a conclusion is not an obvious one. Both Herodotus and Aeschylus give prominence to the Spartans most likely because they were the leaders of the Greek forces at Plataea. A similar emphasis is to be expected in a poem on either the Persian Wars or Plataea, even if the emphasis is on the Hellenic effort. Fr. 11 W² confirms this expectation. Yet, it is also uncertain whether the fragment is the opening of a poem or is an internal prooimion.[131] The prominence of the Spartans in fr. 11 W² may not reflect a prominence in the larger composition. Moreover, although the length of the poem is unknown, it remains uncertain that this prominence continued into the following verses. For these reasons, the position of the Spartans in fr. 11 W² must be approached cautiously when reconstructing the content of the lost poem. Other suggestions for how to view the Spartans' role in this fragment can be made when the presence of other Greeks in these incomplete verses is taken into account.

To begin considering these other suggestion, we must turn outside fr. 11 W². From other fragments certainly linked to the same composition, it is clear that Simonides' composition concerning Plataea mentioned other Greeks. Specifically, Plutarch quotes verses by Simonides to show that Herodotus wrongly maligns the Corinthians role at Plataea (*de Herod. malign.* 872D = Simon. frs. 15–16 W²).[132] Plutarch says that Simonides composed elegiac verses (ἐλεγεῖα) concerning "the Corinthians, both the arrangement of the army they employed against the Barbarians and how great the outcome was for them from the battle of Plataea." (Κορινθίους γε καὶ τάξιν ἣν ἐμάχοντο τοῖς βαρβάροις, καὶ τέλος ἡλίκον ὑπῆρξεν αὐτοῖς ἀπὸ τοῦ Πλαταιᾶσιν ἀγῶνος). The verses he quotes begin with the phrase "those in the middle" (μέσσοις δ' οἵ τ'). Plutarch concludes by explaining the unbiased nature of

Simonides' verses. He tells us that the poet "recorded these things not while leading a chorus in Corinth, nor while composing a lyric song for the city, but otherwise when writing about these undertakings in elegiacs" (ταῦτα γὰρ οὐ χορὸν ἐν Κορίνθωι διδάσκων, οὐδ' ᾆσμα ποιῶν εἰς τὴν πόλιν, ἄλλως δὲ τὰς πράξεις ἐκείνας ἐλεγεῖα γράφων ἱστόρηκεν). The verses quoted by Plutarch as well as his comments on them are valuable bits of evidence for reconstructing the larger composition to which frs. 11, 15, and 16 W$^2$ belong. First, Plutarch shows us that other Greeks besides the Spartans appeared in Simonides' composition concerned with the battle at Plataea. More importantly, these verses and Plutarch's comments on them provide a starting point for further defining the content of this larger composition.

The verses themselves suggest that Plutarch is quoting a section of Simonides' poem that in some way was a catalogue. Wolfgang Luppe has argued that the phrase μέσσοις δ' οἵ τ' is to be interpreted as referring to the Corinthians' position in the battle-line ("In the middle of the line were those . . .") rather than their position in the battle ("In the midst of the battle . . .").[133] Plutarch's comment that these verses show the battle formation of the Corinthians (τάξιν) supports such an interpretation. Support for the presence of a catalogue or catalogues in the composition to which these verses belong may be found in fr. 13 W$^2$, another fragment of the "new Simonides" linked, although with less certainty, to the so-called "Plataea poem." In particular, Deborah Boedeker reads fr. 13 W$^2$, which mentions the Medes, the Persians, Doros, and the sons of Herakles, as a catalogue, similar to the one found in Herodotus 9.31 and 46–48, where the Greek troops line up against the Persians.[134] It is possible, then, that the verses of the "new Simonides" linked with the battle of Plataea may represent some form of a catalogue.

At this point, it must be noted that there is the danger of a circular argument. Two conjectured catalogues do not prove that Simonides' composition on Plataea contained one or more catalogues. It does, however, raise the possibility that these verses are to be reconstructed in this way. As I will discuss below, in the light of what remains of fr. 11 W$^2$ such a possibility is a valid alternative to reading these fragmentary verses as a narrative. It is useful to consider to what extent these verses that may contain catalogues can inform our reconstruction of Simonides' composition represented by these fragments.

Plutarch's statements concerning these verses (Plu. *de Herodot. malig.* 42 = 872D) elucidate the nature of this catalogue identified by Boedeker in fr. 15–16 W$^2$. According to Plutarch, these verses show the arrangement of the Corinthian army and the favorable outcome that arose from their efforts. These comments as well as the verses themselves show that Simonides praised the Corinthians outright. The extent of this praise is uncertain, but it is likely that Plutarch's quote represents only part of it. Metrical problems in fr. 16.1 W$^2$ and grammatical difficulties in reading the two fragments as being consecutive sections of a poem have led to various attempts to expand the fragment. For example, Luppe posits two lacunae in the passages that total three and a half verses, thereby allowing for at least eight verses on the Corinthians.[135] Although it is impossible to verify Luppe's estimates, the point to emphasize is that Corinthians must have received more attention in the lost poem than they do in the surviving fragments.[136] If we are to read a catalogue in these verses, then, it is clear that it must have been more than a list of figures who fought along side the Spartans at Plataea.

Plutarch's comments also allow further definition of the larger composition in which this catalogue with its praise of the Corinthians appeared. He also says that the verses were not composed as part of a song for the city or for the purposes of producing a chorus at Corinth. It can be inferred that the verses were not composed specifically for the Corinthians. The implication is that the content of the poem which frs. 15 and 16 $W^2$ represent must be construed more broadly.[137] More specifically, the verses may praise the Corinthians but this praise was not the sole aim of the larger composition.

The connection of frs. 11, 15 and 16 $W^2$ supports Plutarch's comments that the Corinthians were not the sole focus of Simonides' poem.[138] These three fragments show us that Simonides mentioned both the Corinthians and the Spartans. This link, however, also has important implications for how we read the appearance of the Spartans in fr. 11 $W^2$. While these observations do not exclude the Spartans as the focus of this poem, the praise of the Corinthians and the number of verses over which this praise extends argues against this possibility. Just as we can infer from Plutarch that the composition to which frs. 11, 15 and 16 $W^2$ belong was not a poem solely in praise of the Corinthians, so it is likely that the Spartans also were not the sole focus of the poem.

So far, it can be concluded that frs. 11, 15 and 16 $W^2$ belong to a poem that praised more than one city. As has been suggested, it is possible that this praise was presented in the form of a catalogue. The verses quoted by Plutarch on the Corinthians represent part of such a catalogue with praise of one of the *Plataiomachoi*. The extent of the catalogue represented by these verses is unknown, but it must have been more than a simple list of figures who appeared at the battle of Plataea.

The question remains, to what extent does the identification of a catalogue and the praise of cities other than the Spartans in the composition to which fr. 11 $W^2$ belongs inform the way in which the content of this composition is to be reconstructed? I suggest that fr. 11 $W^2$ allows us to see more clearly that Simonides' composition may have been organized around the form of a catalogue. In particular, modern scholars usually interpret fr. 11.35–45 $W^2$ as a geographically informed description of the Spartan march to Plataea. The suggested narrative sequence is that, after the Lacedaemonians depart from Sparta (fr. 11.29 $W^2$), they pass Corinth and the Isthmus (fr. 11.35–36 $W^2$), Megara (fr. 11.37 $W^2$), and come to Eleusis (fr. 11.40

W²), where the Athenians may join them (fr. 11.41–42 W²).[139] The conclusions reached above concerning frs. 15–16 W² point us toward clues in fr. 11 W² which suggest that this perspective should be modified. The correspondence between the undeniable appearance of the Corinthians at fr. 11.35 W² and their praise in frs. 15–16 W² suggests a possible structure in the poem that is being reconstructed. That is, the figures mentioned in fr. 11.35–45 W² may be a catalogue of figures to which the composition will return in the subsequent verses.[140] By fleshing out this structural principle, it becomes possible to obtain a guideline for how we are to reconstruct the poem represented by fr. 11 W².

The identification of verses in praise of other figures that appear in fr. 11.35–45 W² would validate this structural principle and would be a useful tool for approaching the reconstruction of the poem represented by fr. 11 W². The second possible reference in this list is to Megara or the Megarians at fr. 11.37 W². The conjecture is initially derived from Herodotus, who says that the Spartans marched to Eleusis where they were joined by the Athenians (9.19.2). Parsons suggests that a periphrasis for Megara, a point between Sparta and Eleusis, would suitably fit for the letters in fr. 11.37 W² and conjectures N]ίσου πόλιν.[141] As Parsons notes, Herodotus does not mention Megara in the march from Sparta to Eleusis, but he does place the Megarians in the battle (9.28.6). Despite the divergence from Herodotus, the following conclusions are generally accepted. First, it is reasonable that the Spartans passed by Megara in their march to Plataea. Second, since Herodotus does place the Megarians at the battle of Plataea, the reference to the city as a landmark on this march would be suitable in fr. 11 W².

The fragmentary state of the verse prohibits us from concluding with certainty that these words are to be read as a periphrasis for the Megarians. Two bits of evidence outside fr. 11 W², however, help to secure this reading. First, Parsons' supplement finds support in the reference to Nisaea (ὀμφαλῶι . . . / . . . Νισαίων), the seaport of Megara, in the Megarian inscription for those who died in the Persian Wars, discussed below.[142] This coincidence, however, requires caution because the inscription could have provided the supplement. From the inscription alone, we might conclude that some connection existed between Megara's identity as the "city of Nisus" and its role in the Persian Wars.[143] Second, a similar reference is found at Theocritus *Idyll* 12.27, where the Nisaean Megarians are addressed as those who excel with the oars.[144] Two scholia on this verse inform us that Simonides, in fact, praised the Megarians and did so for their sea-faring capabilities.[145] So it is possible that Simonides praised Megara by a periphrasis such as the "city of Nisus." From these scholia a parallel arises for a description of Megara as the "city of Nisus" in the composition represented by fr. 11 W².

Closer consideration of the scholia on Theocritus, however, reveals that their information may have important implications for how the Megarians fit into a poem represented by fr. 11 W². The scholia do not mention the context of Simonides' praise of the Megarians. It is usually thought that such praise would have been found in Simonides' poem on Salamis.[146] Yet the coincidence between these scholia, the reference to Nisaea in the Megarian inscription on the Persian Wars, and the potential that fr. 11.37 W² is to be read as Ν]ί̣σου πόλιν is suggestive. With these coincidences in mind, fr. 11 W² becomes a possible candidate for the composition in which Simonides praised the Megarians. If this assumption is accepted, there are important consequences for how fr. 11 W² is to be interpreted. Since the scholia record that Simonides praised the Nisaean Megarians for their sea-faring ability, it becomes possible that fr. 11 W² represents a poem that not only mentioned their presence at Plataea but also praised their efforts at sea. Along this line of thinking, any of the fragments assigned to the two sea battle poems because of supposed reference to nautical matters conceivably could have a place in the poem represented by fr. 11 W².

In sum, the appearance of Megara as the "city of Nisus" in fr. 11.37 W², although not certain, is probable. The acceptance of this interpretation places the mention of Megara in the same poem that mentioned the battle of Plataea. Following the model established by the mention of Corinthians at fr. 11.35 W² and the praise of the Corinthians in frs. 15–16 W², it is possible that the Megarians were praised at some point in the verses following 11 W². By analogy with the praise of the Corinthians in frs. 15–16 W², the praise of the Megarians may have been quite extensive. Since Simonides is also known to have praised the Megarians for their seafaring in some composition, one possibility is that he did so in the poem represented by fr. 11 W². It is possible, then, that the poem represented by fr. 11 W² praised the seafaring ability of the Megarians. With these possibilities in mind, the mention of the "city of Nisus" in fr. 11 W² need not be construed as part of a narrative of the battle of Plataea. An alternative interpretation is to understand that the Megarians appear in fr. 11 W² as part of a list of cities that will be praised later in the poem in an expanded catalogue. This praise is most fully represented by frs. 15–16 W². In this way, the content of the poem represented by fragment fr. 11 W² becomes defined more broadly and can be seen as being in line with the other commemorations of the Persian Wars discussed above.

Next, there is the problematic appearance of Athens or the Athenians in fr. 11.41–42 W². There are two ways of interpreting the incomplete verses.[147] Parsons has suggested that fr. 11.41 W² mentions the arrival of the Athenians at Eleusis, represented by the Athenian hero Pandion(Παν]δίο̣νος ἐξε[λάσα]ντες).[148] He then understands a reference to Athens or the Athenians in fr. 11.42 W² with the periphrastic phrase Κέκρ]ο̣πος ἀντιθέο̣υ[;[149] however, as Parsons notes, taking ἐξε[λάσα]ντες as a description of the Athenians' arrival is problematic. Herodotus says that the Athenians sailed from Salamis to join the Spartans at Eleusis. So ἐξε[λάσα]ντες, meaning "driving out, banishing, or leading out an army" seems to introduce an action that is inconsistent with Herodotus' narrative.[150] The letters that begin fr. 11.42 W$^2$ (]ọπος ἀντιθέọυ[) also are far from certain. On the other hand, West suggests that in fr. 11.41 W$^2$, ἐξε[λάσα]ντες is transitive and refers to the Greeks driving the Persians from the land of Pandion.[151] He then reads fr. 11.42 W$^2$ as μάν]τ̣ιος ἀντιθέọυ[ and introduces the Spartan seer Teisamenos.[152] The debate cannot be resolved with the papyrological evidence at hand or the proposed parallel between Herodotus and fr. 11 W$^2$. Electronic images of POxy 3965 fr. 2 published by Obbink support Parsons' reading of fr. 11.42 W$^2$, ]ọπος ἀντιθέọυ[, but these letters do not guarantee the conjecture Κέκρ]ọπος ἀντιθέọυ[.[153] Moreover, as Huxley has pointed out, even with the reference to Kekrops, the Athenians need not appear in these lines. He suggests that the verses could refer to the movement of Mardonius' troops out of Athens, that is, the city of Kekrops.[154] Also, the problems with interpreting ἐξε[ ]ντες in fr. 11.42 W$^2$ have not been able to be solved through comparisons with what is known from Herodotus' narrative. Even the reference to Pandion must be considered cautiously because most of the word is a supplement.

Although the placement of the Athenians in fr. 11.41–42 W$^2$ has little papyrological support, the objections to understanding the Athenians here hinge largely on the difficulties inherent in finding parallels to the narrative of Herodotus. The evidence of the thank-offerings set up after Plataea at the Isthmus and the Serpent Column at Delphi, in which the Athenians figured prominently, and the possibility that fr. 11.35–45 W$^2$ is a list of cities make it reasonable to suggest that the Athenians appear here. If so, the assumption that other verses in the new fragments return to the Athenians is justified.

By looking at fragments outside of fr. 11 W$^2$, it is possible to identify other potential references to the Athenians in the "new Simonides." In particular, both Parsons and West offer readings that would allow fr. 14 W$^2$ to be connected with the Athenians. West reconstructs the main section of these difficult verses to contain the prophecy of Teisamenos before Plataea that Herodotus mentions at 9.36. He continues to guess at the details of the prophecy: someone (Ares?) will drive the Medes out of Asia (i.e. Ionia) with someone (Zeus?) approving (fr. 14.7 W$^2$), and someone (Ares?) favoring an alliance (fr. 14.8 W$^2$) and establishing (?) a foundation (under Delos?) (fr. 14.9–11 W$^2$).[155] These conjectured details lead West to posit that the foundation (κρηπίς) in fr. 14.9 W$^2$ refers to the Athenian-led Delian League, which after Plataea would strive to remove the Medes from Ionia.[156]

Parsons provides another possible interpretation of these verses. He posits that the possible first person pronoun at fr. 14.3 W$^2$ as well as the singular verb and a possible reading of συμμα[χ]ίην (alliance) at fr. 14.8 W$^2$ might refer to the "Oath of Plataea."[157] This oath was purportedly sworn by the Greeks before the battle of Plataea, whereby they vowed to act together in a specific way: they would bury their allies, they would not destroy the cities of Greeks who participated in the Persian

Wars, they would make some sort of tithe, and possibly they would not rebuild temples destroyed by the Persians.[158] The historicity of this oath was doubted as early as the fourth century BCE. Theopompus claims that the oath was concocted by the Athenians (*FGrH* 115 F 153).[159] Yet, despite the problems with authenticity, it can be concluded that there was an Athenian tradition concerning this oath that was current in the fourth century BCE. It is also possible that this tradition originated earlier. If Parsons' reading is accepted, the "new Simonides" will be an early reference to such an oath.

The incomplete nature of the fragment makes it difficult to choose between either of these interpretations with any certainty. The point, however, to emphasize here is that both understand the fragment as introducing content that pertains to the Athenians in some way. The possible appearance in the "new Simonides" of content that would evoke Athens is interesting given the pattern observed with the mention of the Corinthians in fr. 11 W² and the praise of them in frs. 15–16 W². Although, as was shown in Chapter One, fr. 14 W² cannot be linked to fr. 11 W² with any certainty, the possible presence of the Athenians in both might allow for a stronger case in placing the fragments in the same poem.[160] Fr. 11 W² would mention the Athenians in a list of cities and fr. 14 W² would contain verses that mention the Athenians elsewhere in the poem. If the Athenians are read in both fragments, another possible structural parallel between the list of cities in fr. 11 W² and other fragments in the "new Simonides" may be identifiable. So, while the details of the content of fr. 14 W² that is relevant to Athens' role cannot be ascertained with certainty, the possible presence of such content deserves closer consideration.

The possibility that this fragment may pertain to the Athenians receives support from a closer examination of the wording of the fragment. Of particular interest are the letters κ]ρηπῖδα in fr. 14.9 W². For West, the image refers to the foundation of the Athenian-led Delian league. The word κρηπίς appears in two other contexts in reference to the Athenians' role in the Persian Wars. These contexts are useful in showing that this image links fr. 14 W² to the Athenians. The word appears in Pindar fr. 77 as a metaphor for Athens' role in the Persian Wars. Plutarch quotes Pindar's words to show why the poet calls the Athenians Ἑλλάδος ἔρεισμα ("the mainstay of Greece"):

> ὅθι παῖδες Ἀθαναίων ἐβάλοντο φαεννάν
> κρηπῖδ' ἐλευθερίας[161]

["where the children of the Athenians laid the shining foundation of freedom."]

According to Plutarch, Pindar is referring to the Athenian effort at Artemisium, upon which foundation the Athenians used the victories at Salamis, Plataea and Mycale to establish freedom in Greece.[162] Without fuller knowledge of the larger context, it is difficult to grasp with certainty the exact details of these images. The images of Athens as a mainstay (ἔρεισμα) and of her actions as laying a foundation (χρηπῖδ᾽) are complementary. Both point toward Athens as establishing and supporting the freedom of Greece through her actions at Artemisium. In Pindar's praise, Athens' actions at Artemisium keep the Persians out of Greece and the city is a mainstay of Greece.[163] Moreover, these actions become the foundation on which the subsequent freedom of Greece is built. The images seem to emphasize the solidity of Athens and the role of her actions during the Persian Wars in establishing freedom of Greece. For Pindar, then, an appropriate image for praising Athens is to refer to the city's role in Artemisium as laying the "foundation of freedom." Plutarch extends this praise beyond Artemisium to include the Athenians' efforts at Salamis, Mycale and Plataea. Thus, by Plutarch's time (second century CE), and perhaps even in Pindar's time (fifth century BCE), the Athenians could be praised for their actions in the entirety of the Persian Wars as those who provided the foundation for the freedom of Greece.

The image of a foundation is also associated with Athens' actions in the Persian Wars at Aeschylus *Persae* 815 in Darius' prophesy of the Persian defeat:

τοιγὰρ κακῶς δράσαντες οὐκ ἐλάσσονα
πάσχουσι, τὰ δὲ μέλλουσι, κοὐδέπω κακῶν
κρηπὶς ὕπεστιν, ἀλλ᾽ ἔτ᾽ ἐκπιδύεται.
(813–815)

["Therefore, acting evilly, they suffer things not less malicious, and they are going to suffer, for not yet is the foundation of their troubles set under them, but still the evils still gush forth."]

There are problems with the text and interpretation of line 815. It is not entirely clear to what the foundation refers or how it is linked with the Persian troubles that will continue.[164] The image seems to be that the Persians have not reached the lower limit, or the foundation, of their troubles, with the battle of Salamis. This limit, then, could be the battle of Plataea, which is the subject of the words of Darius' ghost. This interpretation, however, is unsatisfactory in a play that stresses the importance of Salamis. The idea may be that the Persians have not reached the lower limit of their troubles because the Persians, like a fleet in trouble, are sinking into their troubles.[165] Along this line of thinking, the battle of Salamis deals a blow to the Persians that sends them spiraling to the limit of their troubles. It is possible that the imagery that seems to refer to the sinking of a ship would also bring to mind the actions of the Delian League in the years following the battle of Plataea which largely involved Athenian led naval efforts against the Persians. That is, Salamis was only the start of the Persian troubles on the sea. These troubles were continued not only with the battle of Plataea, but also with the efforts of the Delian League. In this way, the prominence of Salamis is not diminished, nor is the Athenian role in the destruction of the Persians.

While the interpretation of this image cannot be ascertained with certainty, the use of this image in a context that stresses the importance of Salamis invites a comparison with the verses of Plutarch, in which the Athenians are explicitly linked with the foundation of freedom in Greece through their actions in the Persian Wars. Although Pindar and Aeschylus have separate battles in mind, both poets present Athens, as somehow establishing a foundation or leading to a foundation. The point to emphasize here, however, is that in some way the actions of Athens in the Persian Wars are connected with the image of a foundation (κρηπὶς).

With these passages in mind, it becomes possible that κ]ρηπῖδα in fr. 14 W$^2$ introduces a similar image. If it does, a reasonable suggestion is that this image evokes the Athenians' role in the fight against the Persians. Furthermore, by reading some reference to the Athenians in fr. 14 W$^2$, it becomes possible to strengthen the fragment's link to fr. 11W$^2$. More specifically, potential references to Athens in frs. 11 and 14 W$^2$ would follow the pattern suggested for the reference to the Corinthians and possibly the Megarians in fr. 11 W$^2$, which were discussed above. The Athenians would be listed in fr. 11.41–42 W$^2$ and would be mentioned more fully in fr. 14 W$^2$ which would appear elsewhere in the poem. What emerges, then, is a potential structure for the poem represented by fr. 11 W$^2$; cities that are listed in this fragment appear in more detail elsewhere in the poem. It is possible that references to and praise of other cities is to be sought in the fragments of the "new Simonides" rather than elements of a narrative that is biased toward the Spartans.

To conclude, the epigraphic record explicitly reveals that, in the aftermath of the battle of Plataea, the Persian Wars were understood as a panhellenic victory. This perspective is also implicit in Aeschylus and Herodotus. The poem represented by fr. 11 W$^2$, which was likely to have been contemporary with the epigrammatic record, should be expected to be a similar representation of these Wars. The content of this poem, then, should not be reconstructed as a narrative that has a Spartan bias. Rather the poems are to be construed as being panhellenic in scope. Elements in the "new Simonides" suggest that, in fact, the poem represented by fr. 11 W$^2$ is to be reconstructed to meet these expectations.

### E. Content of Fr. 11 W² and Plataea

The discussion of the Megarians in fr. 11 W$^2$ not only brought forward a panhellenic perspective but it also revealed the possibility that the poem's content might extend beyond a depiction of the battle of Plataea.[166] The victory at Plataea was the conclusion of a struggle that consisted of three other battles, Thermopylae, Artemisium, and

Salamis and may have coincided with one more, the battle of Mycale. The Persian Wars, then, were a multi-battle effort as well as a panhellenic one. It is to the multi-battle aspect of the Persian Wars that we must now turn.[167]

The epigraphic record again provides clues about the perception of the Persian Wars as a multi-battle war in the aftermath of Plataea. The panhellenic perspective in these epigrams has been identified above in such phrases as Πέρσας ἐξελάσαντες, ἐλευθέρᾳ Ἑλλάδι κοινὸν / ἱδρύσαντο Διὸς βωμὸν Ἐλευθερίου (Simon. VIII *FGE*), Ἄσβεστον κλέος οἵδε φίλῃ περὶ πατρίδι θέντες (Simon. IX *FGE*) and Ἑλλάδος εὐρυχόρου σωτῆρες (Simon. XVIIb *FGE*). It has been shown that these epigrams linked to the battle of Plataea emphasize explicitly the common effort rather than the efforts of one particular city.[168] This panhellenic emphasis, however, also conveys a sense that something more than the victory at Plataea is being commemorated. It may be, then, that these epigrams convey not only a panhellenic perspective, but also are informed by a view of the wars as being a multi-battle effort.[169]

An inscription from Megara on a monument erected for those who had fallen in the Persian Wars offers an example of a commemoration that explicitly emphasizes the multi-battle aspect of these wars:

> Ἑλλάδι καὶ Μεγαρεῦσιν ἐλεύθερον ἆμαρ ἀέξειν
>     ἱέμενοι θανάτου μοῖραν ἐδεξάμεθα,
> τοὶ μὲν ὑπ' Εὐβοίαι καὶ Παλίωι, ἔνθα καλεῖται
>     ἁγνᾶς Ἀρτέμιδος τοξοφόρου τέμενος,
> τοὶ δ' ἐν ὄρει Μυκάλας, τοὶ δ' ἔμπροσθεν Σαλαμῖνος
>     ⟨           ⟩
> τοὶ δὲ καὶ ἐν πεδίωι Βοιωτίωι, οἵτινες ἔτλαν
>     χεῖρας ἐπ' ἀνθρώπους ἱππομάχους ἱέναι.
> ἀστοὶ δ' ἄμμι τόδε ⟨ξυνὸν⟩ γέρας ὀμφαλῶι ἀμφὶς
>     Νισαίων ἔπορον λαοδόκωι 'ν ἀγοράι. [170]

["Hastening to foster the day of freedom for Greece and the Megarians, we received the lot of death, some under Euboea and Pelion, where it is called the sacred precinct of holy bow-bearing Artemis, some under the mountain of Mycale, some before Salamis, ⟨ ⟩, even others on the Boeotian plain, those who dared to use their hands against cavalry. The citizens gave to us this ⟨common⟩ gift around the navel of Nisaea in the agora where people gather."]

The verses are accompanied by a preface which states that the inscription is a copy made by the high priest Helliados to replace one, composed by Simonides, which had been worn away by time. The copy is followed by a statement that the city has sacrificed bulls up to the present for these dead.[171] Pausanias, the periegete, mentions a tomb for those who died in the Persian Wars at Megara and, although he does not mention an inscription, it is likely that these verses accompanied this tomb. Page dates the copy of Helliados to no earlier than the fourth century CE, but adds that there is nothing incompatible with an original composition in the early fifth century BCE, despite the unusual length of the piece.[172]

As it stands, the inscription contains certain features that are in line with the panhellenic perspective found in the epigrams discussed above. First, while the inscription is explicitly in praise of Megarians, emphasis is placed on the contribution of the city to the panhellenic effort. The statement that these men died to "increase the day of freedom for Greece and the Megarians" suggests that the local contribution is to be understood as having an important impact that extended beyond Megara. The association of Megara with Greece in effect establishes Megara as part of a larger whole and shows that the city was partly responsible for the preservation of this whole. The prominence given to the Megarians in the inscription, then, does not detract from the idea that the inscription commemorates a panhellenic effort. The inscription can still be interpreted as following the pattern of the other Persian War epigrams discussed above.

Another important feature of this inscription is the emphasis on the entirety of the Persian Wars. The inscription is a list of battles in which the Megarians participated: Artemisium (3–4), Mycale and Salamis (5), and Plataea (7–8). The only major battle not included is Thermopylae, which is unsurprising because Herodotus does not place the Megarians at this battle (7.202). A pentameter is missing after line 5. It has been suggested that this missing verse may have contained a reference to Thermopylae.[173] The missing verse may have also mentioned military engagements that accompanied the Persian withdrawal from the Megarid before the battle of Plataea.[174] Whether Thermopylae or some other military engagement appeared in this verse, the inscription provides a clear example of a panhellenic and multi-battle perspective in a commemoration of the Persian Wars. If Page is correct concerning a possible early fifth-century date for the original composition, then, the inscription could be contemporary with the poem represented by fr. 11 W$^2$.

What arises in the Megarian inscription is a commemoration of the Persian Wars that is plausibly a contemporary to the composition of the "new Simonides" and that is both panhellenic and multi-battle in perspective. A parallel, then, exists that allows the poem represented by fr. 11 W$^2$ to be construed not only as a panhellenic commemoration but also as being multi-battle in scope. This possibility is intriguing for the reconstruction of the content of fr. 11 W$^2$ because it allows the suggestion that the fragment need not represent a "Plataea poem" as it is currently defined by modern scholarship. Rather, these verses could represent a Persian Wars poem with references not only to Plataea, but other battles as well.

### F. Content of Fr. 11 W$^2$ and Achilles

The analysis above has shown that two assumptions about the content of the poem represented by fr. 11 W$^2$ must be reconsidered. First, it cannot be accepted without argument that the poem represented by fr. 11 W$^2$ focused on the Spartans. Second, the belief that this poem focused solely on the battle of Plataea is not above doubt; other battles in the Persian Wars may have been mentioned in the lost or fragmentary verses of this poem. This broader understanding of this poem's content receives support from the emphasis on Achilles and the Homeric tradition in the prooimial verses of this fragment. By comparing the details in these fragmentary verses with the tradition of Achilles and his death, it can be shown that Achilles' presence in this prooimion leads us to expect that the larger composition to which fr. 11 W$^2$ belongs will emphasize the panhellenic effort either at Plataea or in the Persian Wars in general.

All approaches to the prooimial verses in fr. 11 W$^2$ assume that certain details are present. First, the prooimion is believed to mention the death of Achilles (fr. 11.1–4, 8 W$^2$) and possibly to depict the funeral of the hero (fr. 11.6–7 W$^2$).[175] Although the details concerning the funeral are uncertain, its mention here would be unsurprising because the funeral has an integral place in the tradition of Achilles' death. Moreover, the possible references to Apollo, the children of Priam, and Alexander (fr. 11.6–11 W$^2$) tie this depiction to the epic tradition of the Trojan War. A more specific link to the Homeric tradition is confirmed by the reference to Homer read in fr. 11.15–18 W$^2$. Finally, fr. 11.19–20 W$^2$ suggests that the prooimion is more specifically a hymn to Achilles, the son of Thetis, the daughter of Nereus.

In addition to assuming the presence of these details, it is usually understood that Achilles functions in some way as a paradigm for those who are commemorated in the verses that follow. The way in which these details reflect on the content of the poem has generally been viewed in two ways. On the one hand, Achilles is taken as a paradigm for an individual warrior. Parsons initially observed "a possible parallel between Achilles and Pausanias," who is mentioned at fr. 11.34 W$^2$.[176] This interpretation of Achilles is followed at length by P.-J. Shaw, who concludes, "[i]t is on account of Pausanias *as current leader of Hellas* that Achilles, the original leader of Hellas, is invoked in the proem of this elegy."[177] Another candidate is put forward by C. O. Pavese, who posits that Thermopylae played a role in the verses preceding fr. 11 W$^2$. Pavese suggests that Achilles is a model for Leonidas.[178] On the other hand, Achilles is understood as a paradigm for the larger group of *Plataiomachoi*. In response to Parsons, West observes that there is little similarity between the career of Achilles and that of Pausanias. He concludes that the hero is a paradigm for the Spartans under Pausanias.[179] A. Aloni argues for an even broader interpretation of Achilles in the prooimion. He suggests that Achilles represents all who are commemorated in the poem because the defeat of the Persians was brought about not by an individual but by a larger group.[180] For Aloni, however, this broadly construed paradigm ultimately admits a Spartan bias because he argues for a commission by the Spartans and/or Pausanias.[181] D. Boedeker, too, takes Achilles as a paradigm for a larger group. For her, the hero's "representative role for the Greeks at Troy (i.e. in the prooimion) supports the hypothesis that Achilles serves here as a paradigm for the collective Greeks at Plataea."[182] Unlike Aloni, however, Boedeker allows this understanding of Achilles to reflect on the content of the poem in so far as she argues for a poem that at least has a poly-hellenic perspective on Plataea.[183]

The fragmentary nature of the evidence for the so-called "Plataea poem" does not make the choice between these general alternatives easy. The basic distinction between them lies in the overall interpretation of the poem. On the one hand, the larger poem represented by fr. 11 W$^2$ is construed as commemorating a single city. On the other hand, it is understood as being a panhellenic poem that focused on a larger effort. Yet, even with this distinction, a key assumption of each of these interpretations is that Achilles functions as a paradigm in a composition that is to be understood as a "Plataea poem." Again, this assumption must be rethought. By understanding the content of Simonides' poem as having a broader scope, then, we must also reconsider how Achilles fits into the larger composition.

The questions that must be answered are: How does Achilles function as a paradigm in the literary tradition into which the "new Simonides" is placed? Does the "new Simonides" present Achilles in a similar way? Finally, what clues about the content of the larger poem are provided by Achilles' appearance as a paradigm in fr. 11 W$^2$? In the following sections, these questions will be answered by turning to the tradition of Achilles in Homer and later writers, where the hero's death functions in some way as a paradigm. It will be seen that, in fact, Achilles is not a paradigm that is specific to a particular city but has one that has relevance throughout Greece. As such, he functions as a paradigm that has panhellenic value. Moreover, it will be seen that in Greek literature and art, Achilles' death or his choice to die is usually paradigmatic. It will be suggested that the emphasis on Achilles' death in fr. 11 W$^2$ aligns the composition represented by this fragment with this tradition. Along this line of thinking, it will be proposed that the details pertaining to Achilles in fr. 11 W$^2$ are best understood as giving a panhellenic emphasis to the poem represented by this fragment.

*Homer*

The death of Achilles is an integral part of the archaic epic tradition. Although it is beyond its narrative scope, the death of Achilles is an ever-present theme in the *Iliad*. The *Iliad* alludes to the death of Achilles at the hand of Apollo (19.416–417 and 22.358–60) and the hero's funeral (23.91–92 and 243–449). Thetis emphasizes the hero's short life by addressing him as ὠκύμορος (1. 414–427), and as ὠκυμορώτατος ἄλλων (1.503–510). In fact, the presence of Thetis throughout the poem serves to bring forward the thought of Achilles' impending death in the epic.[184] Moreover, Achilles' lament for Patroklos foreshadows the mourning that will accompany his own death.[185] It has also been suggested that in the *Iliad* Achilles dies symbolically when Patroklos is killed by Hector.[186] In these ways, the *Iliad* allows its audience to focus on the death of Achilles, while it suppresses the narrative details of this death.

The death of Achilles does receive a proper narrative in the epic cycle. The epitome by Proclus informs us that the lost *Aithiopis* narrated the hero's death.[187] The *Aithiopis* told how Achilles died at the hands of Apollo and Paris. This poem, however, does not survive. The only extant account of Achilles' death and funeral that has come to us from archaic poetry is found in the so-called *deuteronekuia* at *Odyssey* 24.36–97.[188] From the *deuteronekuia*, it can be seen that in Homeric poetry Achilles stands as an exemplum.

In *Odyssey* 24, Agamemnon gives a lengthy narrative of Achilles' death to the shade of Achilles.[189] The emphasis in this narrative is the mourning for the slain Achilles. Thetis and the Nereids lament the hero (47–49); the Muses attend his funeral (60); he is buried with Patroklos and a tomb is heaped upon them at the Hellespont (71–84); finally, Thetis initiates funeral games for her son (85–92). It is the degree of mourning that justifies Agamemnon's initial addresses of Achilles as ὄλβιε Πηλέος υἱέ, θεοῖς ἐπιείκελ' ᾿Αχιλλεῦ (36: "O fortunate son of Peleus, one who resembles the gods, Achilles"). In this way, Agamemnon's narrative establishes Achilles as a paradigm. In particular, it is the honor that Achilles' received in his death that makes him an example of one who obtained renown (κλέος):

> μάλα γὰρ φίλος ἦσθα θεοῖσιν.
> ὣς σὺ μὲν οὐδὲ θανὼν ὄνομ' ὤλεσας, ἀλλά τοι αἰεὶ
> πάντας ἐπ' ἀνθρώπους κλέος ἔσσεται ἐσθλόν, ᾿Αχιλλεῦ·
> 24.92–94

["For you were especially dear to the gods. Thus, having died, you have not lost your name, but always you will have good renown among all men."]

Achilles is an example of one rewarded with renown (κλέος) because of his death; therefore, he is fortunate (ὄλβιος), unlike Agamemnon.

The paradigmatic role of Achilles that is emphasized in these verses is reinforced by Agamemnon's speech to Odysseus later in the *deuteronekuia*. In this speech, Agamemnon addresses Odysseus as ὄλβιε Λαέρταο πάϊ, πολυμήχαν' ᾿Οδυσσεῦ (193: "O fortunate son of Laërtes, much-contriving Odysseus").[190] This initial phrase echoes the one used by Agamemnon to address Achilles, earlier in the passage, and creates a parallel between Achilles and Odysseus. This parallel further establishes both heroes as contrasts for Agamemnon. Odysseus is compared with Agamemnon as an example of a man who is fortunate (ὄλβιος) because his wife remembered him. It is the renown (κλέος) that Penelope gains which makes Odysseus fortunate (ὄλβιος). Achilles is compared with Agamemnon as one who received renown (κλέος) because of the circumstances of his death. For this reason, Achilles is fortunate (ὄλβιος). It is on these two scores that Agamemnon establishes these heroes as models through contrast with himself.

In establishing Achilles as a paradigm, Agamemnon emphasizes the death of and mourning for Achilles. This emphasis recalls the larger focus on Achilles in the *Iliad*. Perhaps, a similar role for Achilles is to be read in the *Iliad*, where the hero's death is ever-present, although it is not directly narrated. In many ways, the *Iliad* presents Achilles as an example of aspects embodied by all Homeric heroes.[191] The focus on Achilles' death throughout the *Iliad*, in particular, his death symbolically presented through the death of Patroklos, emphasizes the mortality of Achilles. The point that seems to be made by this focus in the *Iliad* is that Achilles, like other heroes in the epic, is mortal and as such he dies. For Achilles in the *Iliad*, this death is the very thing that gives him his heroic status. The *Iliad*, then, too may be focusing on the death of Achilles as a paradigm. Nevertheless, it can be said that in the Homeric tradition of the *Odyssey* and perhaps the *Iliad*, Achilles stands as an example because of the honor he received from his death.

## The Homeric Tradition and the "New Simonides"

Direct references to the Homeric poetry in fr. 11 W² suggest that Simonides is drawing specifically on the tradition of Achilles' death. To be sure, all Greek poets are allowed to innovate in their employment of traditional themes and narratives. The apparent links to the Homeric tradition in this fragment need not mean that Simonides followed this tradition in detail. It must be admitted, however, that the fragmentary state of fr. 11 W² does not allow us to know where or if Simonides may have deviated from the epic tradition in the details or in the whole of his use of Achilles. Nevertheless, it can be said that the potential references to Achilles' death as well as the direct mention of the Homeric tradition suggest that Simonides is employing the hero's death in some way that is consistent with its use in epic.

The link between Simonides' verses and the Homeric tradition is seen in various details of fr. 11 W². First, at fr. 11.15 W² someone "pours renown" (κέχυται κλέος) and at fr. 11.16 W² the Homeric poet seems to be introduced into the poem.[192] Although the connection is not certain, it is generally assumed that it is the Homeric poet who is pouring renown. Second, in fr. 11.17–18 W², a series of words that evoke the Homeric heroes in general and Achilles in particular appears. The word ἐπώνυμον ("famous"?) occurs in fr. 11.17 W². The word is linked to fame in future generations (ὁπ[λοτέρ]οισιν). It is also generally assumed to modify the noun γενεή|ν in line fr. 11.18 W², which is further qualified by the adjective ὠκύμορον and the incomplete word ἡμ]ιθέων. It should, however, be noted that since the beginnings of lines 17 and 18 are missing, we cannot be certain that ἐπώνυμον modifies γενεή[ν. Nevertheless, the adjective ὠκύμορος in fr. 11.18 W² would seem to show definitively that the Homeric tradition of the death of Achilles is alluded to in the fragment.[193] The sense of fr. 11.15–18 W², then, seems to be Homer poured renown and in doing so "made famous to posterity the swift-fated race of the demigods." [194] Moreover, the adjective, ὠκύμορος, allows us to link this sense more particularly with a context that evokes Achilles and his death. It is also possible that the tomb of Achilles is evoked here. His tomb was built at the Hellespont precisely so that it would be visible to future generations.[195] Finally, the address to Achilles as the "son of Thetis" in fr. 11.19–20 W², which is the conclusion of the prooimion, confirms that in some way the preceding verses pertain particularly to Achilles. In general, it appears that Achilles is being evoked as a representative of the Greek heroes who fell at Troy.[196]

With these details in mind, it is possible to hazard a few conjectures that would extend the focus on the death of Achilles into other fragments of the "new Simonides." In particular, fr. 3 W², which is generally associated with the Artemisium elegy by Simonides may also contain verses that are pertinent to the death of Achilles. The difficulty of linking this fragment with the battle of Artemisium has already been noted.[197] At fr. 3.11 W², there is a possible reference to a "fair-haired maiden" in fr. 3.11 W² (West = ]ιητ' ἠΰ[κόμοιο] κόρ[ης; Parsons = ] , ητ , ΰ[ . . . . . ]κορ[). West suggests that this maiden is Oreithyia because he places the fragment in Simonides' "Artemisium poem." Rutherford, however, hypothesizes that this maiden could be a Nereid.[198] If read in this way, fr. 3.9 W² may also recall the Homeric narrative of Achilles' death where the Nereids mourn the death of Achilles.[199] The possible references to the sea (11–12) would then refer not to nautical details relevant to the battle of Artemisium, but to the funeral of Achilles. Further reference to this tradition may be found at fr. 3.13 W². West's edition reconstructs fr. 3.13 W² as: ἀγλαόφημον ἁλός. [ (Parsons =] , , 'φ[] , μοναλ , , []). In West's translation, ἀφγλαόφημον describes the Old Man in the Sea, Nereus: "[Old Man, b]right-famed [guardian] of the sea." [200] For West, the Old Man in the Sea further links the fragment to an Artemisium poem. This rare adjective, however, could also be used of the Muses, as is seen in an Orphic hymn. In this hymn, the adjective describes the Muses, children of Zeus and Mnemosyne.[201] This use of the adjective is interesting because in the Homeric tradition, not only the Nereids but also the Muses mourn Achilles (*Od.* 24.60).[202] It can also be noted that this adjective may appear in the incomplete fr. 10 W², which is generally assigned to the hymn to Achilles in the so-called "Plataea poem."[203] Too much stress should not be placed on either of these conjectures given the incomplete state of the fragment. Both suggestions, however, do highlight the difficulty of assigning the new fragments to a specific context. If these conjectures are close to the mark, the emphasis on Achilles must be extended beyond fragment 11 W². It must be kept in mind that the details of these verses are nothing more than a conjecture.

The point that should be noted is the potential, albeit tenuous, link to the tradition of Achilles death in fr. 3 W². 

In sum, the wording and sense of fr. 11 W² have suggested that these prooimial verses in the "new Simonides" in some way relate to the Homeric tradition and Achilles. As has been shown, in the Homeric tradition, Achilles, specifically his death, serves as a paradigm. Since the language in fr. 11 W² evokes this tradition and seems to point to the very idea of the shortness of life (ὠκύμορος) that is emphasized in the Homeric tradition concerning Achilles, it can be suggested that in this prooimion Simonides is also employing Achilles and his death as a paradigm for what is to follow in the rest of the poem.

### Achilles as Paradigm: Pausanias and Sparta or the Greeks in General

This relation between Homer and Simonides in terms of Achilles raises important questions. First, what does this correspondence between the epic tradition and the "new Simonides" reveal about how fr. 11 W² employs Achilles? Second, what can be suggested about how Achilles reflects on the content of the poem that follows?

Let us first consider how a Greek audience may have viewed the paradigm offered by Achilles in his death. It has been suggested that the presence of Achilles in these verses make them appropriate for performance in some context which Achilles was worshiped as a cult hero; therefore, it is necessary to begin with some observations on how Achilles as a cult hero may have been understood to have functioned in a poem such as fr. 11 W².[204] P.-J. Shaw has observed that as a cult hero, Achilles was associated with certain geographical areas. She finds that Achilles was worshiped at sites close to the water, that he was connected with Poseidon because both are mainly worshiped in Aeolian areas, that he was not usually worshiped in the traditionally Aiakid regions of Aegina, Salamis, Attica where he would be expected, and that he was associated with marginalized peoples.[205] By developing the relation between these features of Achilles, Shaw concludes that a Poseidonian context would be most suitable for the initial performance of the so-called "Plataea poem." Since she understands fr. 11 W² to be panhellenic on some level, she then suggests the Isthmian games as this context.[206] She continues to hypothesize that a parallel can be drawn between Achilles and Pausanias, both of whom are depicted as leaders of the Hellenes. First, Thucydides (1.3.2–3) calls the earliest Hellenes τοὺς μετ᾽ ᾽Αχιλλέως, literally "those with Achilles," or the companions of the hero. Second, Herodotus reports that the Pausanias dedicated a krater to Poseidon at Exampeaus (4.81.3). Athenaeus records the inscription that accompanied this krater in which the Spartan leader is identified as the "ruler of Hellas" (ἄρχων ῾Ελλάδος) (12.536 A = Simon. XXXIX *FGE*).[207] For Shaw, the parallel between these men as leaders of the Hellenes makes Achilles an appropriate image to represent Pausanias. According to the equation made by Shaw, Achilles is a paradigm for Pausanias, who is the "dominant influence on Simonides' composition."[208]

Focusing on Achilles as a ritual figure, Shaw emphasizes the epichoric associations of Achilles to provide a basis for interpreting the hero in fr.11 W[2]. To be sure, as a cult hero, as Shaw and others have shown, Achilles was worshipped in certain geographic areas throughout Greece.[209] Yet, even with his status as a cult figure, Achilles also has a certain panhellenic relevance. Significantly, Achilles appears as the subject of poetry that was performed at many other ritual occasions. In particular, Pindar *Paean* 6. 66–122, shows that Achilles' death was suitable content for a paean to be sung at a *Theoxenia*.[210] The prominence of Achilles' son, Neoptolemus at the Delphic *Theoxenia* suggests that Achilles was tangentially associated with this ritual.[211] Achilles also makes appearances in various dramas at the Athenian City Dionysia.[212] As Shaw herself suggests, it may be a combination of this epichoric significance and the panhellenic value of Achilles on which a leader such as Pausanias would capitalize following Plataea.[213]

The epichoric value of Achilles, then, is only one side of the coin. I suggest that the emphasis on the local in Shaw's argument is too prominent. As Gregory Nagy has argued, the *Iliad* is panhellenic.[214] Achilles as the central figure of this epic was made panhellenic by it, whatever he may have been before the tradition of the *Iliad*. The epic tradition elevates Achilles above these epichoric associations and does so by emphasizing the hero's death, the exact episode relevant to the "new Simonides."[215] In this way, Achilles obtains a certain universality that makes him relevant as a paradigm anywhere in Greece.

A comprehensive survey of the cities that might be associated with Achilles and people for whom Achilles' death might be an apt example could demonstrate this point. Such a survey is beyond the scope of this study.[216] Three particularly relevant examples from Athenian literature, however, serve to show that Achilles could function as an example in Athens as much as he could elsewhere. First, there is a skolion recorded by Athenaeus:

φίλταθ' 'Αρμόδι', οὔ τί πω τέθνηκας,
νήσοις δ' ἐν μακάρων σέ φασιν εἶναι,
ἵνα περ ποδώκης 'Αχιλεὺς
Τυδείδην τέ φασιν Διομήδεα.[217]

["Dearest Harmodius, certainly you have not died, rather they say that you are on islands of the blest, where Swift-footed Achilles is, and where they say Diomedes, the son of Tydeus, is."]

It is explicitly the death of Achilles, who has a continued existence on the Isle of the Blest, that provides a parallel for Harmodius. Like Achilles, Harmodius will gain immortality through his life on the Isle of the Blest.[218] Second, Achilles appears as an example for Plato in Socrates' defense in the *Apology*. Here, Socrates emphasizes Achilles' choice to fight Hector regardless of danger and death as justification for his own decision not to give up his way of life.[219] Third, Achilles, like so many other mythological figures, made appearances on the Athenian stage throughout the fifth century.[220] These references show that Achilles was readily available as an example in Athens as elsewhere. It is fair to say, then, that in the fifth century Achilles could be an example to any Greek. When the hero is understood in this way, he has a panhellenic significance rather than purely local one.

The emphasis placed by Shaw on the epichoric associations of Achilles should, then, be reconsidered. The relevance of Achilles in the fifth century throughout Greece, at places such as Delphi and Athens, as well as those places noted by Shaw, seems to suggest that Achilles had a particular panhellenic value as a mythological example. This value, I suggest, makes it difficult to pinpoint a particular place for which Achilles would have been more relevant than he was for others. The emphasis on Achilles' death in fr. 11 W², the very aspect of the hero which the epic tradition emphasizes, would seem to show that Simonides' verses are aligned more with the panhellenic epic tradition than with specific local ones. Although the incomplete verses of fr. 11 W² cannot allow us to be certain on this score, the focus on the Persian Wars in Simonides' poem also seems to support the view that Simonides' Achilles is not to be read with reference to a specific locality. The Persian Wars themselves were panhellenic in the threat they posed to Greece. It would seem that the Achilles of the panhellenic epic tradition would be the most suitable example for such a composition.

These conclusions receive some support from representations of Achilles in a context that explicitly links the Persian and the Trojan Wars. The panhellenic value of Achilles as a paradigm in a context that pertains to the Persian Wars is found in the *Nekyia* by Polygnotus, one of the paintings that originally adorned the Cnidian *Lesche* at Delphi. Pausanias, the periegete, describes two paintings by Polygnotus in the *Lesche* (10.25–31): on the East side was the *Iliupersis*, which depicted the fall of Troy; on the West side was the *Nekyia*, which depicted Odysseus' travel into the underworld. In the *Nekyia,* Achilles and Patroklos are prominent figures. The link between Patroklos and Achilles and their presence in the Underworld suggests that the death of Achilles is relevant here.[221] Although there are various interpretations of these lost paintings, there is a consensus that in some way they link the Persian Wars with the Trojan Wars.[222]

First, in reconstructing the painting from the words of Pausanias, Richard Kebric establishes Odysseus as the central figure of the *Nekyia.* From this stand point, he interprets the paintings in the light of the final defeat of the Persians at Eurymedon (c. 466 BCE).[223] He concludes, "The paintings . . . reflect a solid pro-Cimonian, pro-Thesean sentiment which was not accidental . . . while the *Lesche* may have been a thank-offering to Apollo by the Cnidians, it was also another of the number of monuments and buildings which celebrated Cimon's conclusion of the wars with Persia."[224] In this way, Kebric understands the monument as having an Athenian bias. In contrast, Mark D. Stansbury-O'Donnell understands the *Iliupersis* and the *Nekyia* as constituting one pictorial scheme in the *Lesche*. In this reconstruction, Achilles is established as a central figure of both paintings.[225] Citing difficulties in dating the *Lesche* as part of a Cimonian building program he concludes, "there remains sufficient ground for seeing in the *Nekyia* not anti-Thracian, pro-Doric, or pro-Athenian propaganda, but rather a more even-handed argument for the necessity of Greek unity and cooperation."[226] It is the prominence of Achilles and the juxtaposition of him with the other Trojan War heroes that Stansbury-O'Donnell uses to bolster this image of panhellenic unity. [227]

The point for us to emphasize in both of these interpretations, despite their differences, is that the Trojan War and the Homeric tradition are used in some way as a parallel for the struggle against the Persians.[228] Similar parallels can be found in other monuments in Athens. The "Eion epigram," a series of inscriptions on three herms that celebrated Cimon's victory over the Persians at Eion in 475 BCE, draws an explicit comparison between the Trojan and the Persian Wars.[229] Likewise, the painting on the *Stoa Poikile* juxtaposes the battle of Marathon, among other things, with various mythical battles including the Trojan War.[230] It can also be noted that such a parallel was not limited to public monuments. In fifth-century literature, the opening chapters of Herodotus, as we have seen above, present the Persian War as the latest iteration of the Trojan War (1.1–7). Although each of these examples is presumably later than the poem represented by fr. 11 $W^2$ and so may be influenced by a practice found in this poem, they still may reflect a tradition that understood the Trojan Wars as a suitable paradigmatic parallel for the Persian Wars. The *Nekyia* is particularly significant because it places Achilles in an early example of such a parallel.[231] Moreover, it provides an example of the hero as part of a program that in some way deals with the issue of panhellenism in the fifth century. If Kebric is correct, Achilles becomes part of a painting that may promote a Cimonian push for panhellenism that centers on Athenian interests as a necessary effort to rid Greece of Persians.[232] If Stansbury-O'Donnell is correct, Achilles becomes a more general symbol for this idea of Greek unity. So the *Nekyia* of Polygnotus not only reinforces the understanding of Achilles as an apt Hellenic example, but also reveals that as a paradigm the hero has a panhellenic significance. Furthermore, this understanding of Achilles comes in an artistic program that, like fr. 11 $W^2$, draws on parallels between the Trojan and the Persian Wars.

To sum up, what we have seen is that while Achilles may have had an association with specific cities and local cults, as a figure in myth and poetry he also had a certain universal paradigmatic value. This value is often seen in the particular example offered by Achilles in his death, which, as is certainly the case in the painting by Polygnotus, draws heavily on the Homeric tradition. It is fair to suggest that in fr. 11 W², which employs Achilles as a paradigm and in doing so presents his death in a way that draws on the epic tradition, Achilles is to be interpreted as a panhellenic figure rather than as a local one. It is also reasonable to conclude that this emphasis on the panhellenic value of Achilles shows that he may have been chosen as a paradigm for the larger panhellenic effort against the Persians. It seems likely that Achilles introduced a more universal quality into the poem represented by fr. 11 W². The point of Achilles in these verses seems not to be his usefulness as a paradigm for a particular city or person, but rather his panhellenic value as a paradigm for one who is fortunate because of the circumstances of his death.

## 2.3 GENERAL CONCLUSIONS

To conclude, the backdrop of the epigraphic commemorations of the Persian Wars suggests that we should expect fr. 11 W² to represent a poem that presents a panhellenic perspective on the Persian Wars. This expectation is supported by the existence of a similar implicit panhellenism in such accounts as Aeschylus' *Persae* and Herodotus. Analysis of fr. 11 W² reveals that the poem of which it is a part most likely met these expectations. In particular, the list of cities at fr. 11.35–45 W² can be shown to be echoed by verses in praise of these cities in fragments potentially linked to fr. 11 W². The presence of Achilles and the emphasis on his death in fr. 11 W² also supports this interpretation. The hero is best construed as providing the poem with a paradigm for a panhellenic group of fighters rather than for an individual or one city. The emphasis on reconstructing the content of fr. 11 W² in terms of a narrative centered on the actions of one city in one particular battle should be reconsidered. A possible alternative is to view the poem as having the structure of a catalogue, in which cities that are listed in fr. 11 W² would appear again in the poem where they would be praised at length.

The evidence of Herodotus, Aeschylus' *Persae* and the epigrammatic record has also suggested that we should expect fr. 11 W² to represent a poem with a multi-battle perspective. It should be stressed, however, that we cannot be certain about the specifics of how this multi-battle perspective was presented since we do not know how long Simonides' poem was. Nevertheless, this emphasis is found especially in commemorations connected with the battle of Plataea. Moreover, an inscription from Megara provides an actual multi-battle perspective in an epigraphic commemoration of the Persian Wars. This parallel is interesting because the Megarians, who may have appeared in fr. 11 W², were praised in some context by Simonides for their seafaring ability. One possibility is that fr. 11 W² represents a poetic context in which

Simonides praised the Megarians for their sea faring alongside the Spartans and Corinthians for their efforts at Plataea. Again, the emphasis seems to be on a larger effort, rather than the effort of a single city. The universality of Achilles as a paradigm also seems to support this larger scope in terms of content. So, against the backdrop of other commemorations and records of the Persian Wars and through the paradigm of Achilles it becomes possible to construe fr. 11 W$^2$ as representative of a poem with a panhellenic and multi-battle perspective.

Chapter Three

# To Praise, To Commemorate, To Mourn
## The "New Simonides" and Elegy

paulum quidlibet allocutionis
maestius lacrimis Simonideis
Cat. 38.7–8

Give me some small word of encouragement, sadder than the tears of
Simonides.

## 3.1 INTRODUCTION

In his *Pindar's Homer*, Gregory Nagy provides a succinct definition of genre: "occasion is genre."[1] A similar understanding of genre informs many recent studies of
archaic Greek poetry.[2] In general, these studies emphasize both the shared formal
features of a certain group of poetry as well as the creation of a common communi-
cative relationship between performer/poet and audience in the moment of performance.[3] In the archaic period, then, a poem in a certain form will have established a
relationship between performer/poet and audience. With this relationship will have
come certain expectations on the part of the audience that defined the genre of the
poem being performed.[4] In this way, it is believed that the performance context in
general and the particular occasion of this performance defined the genre of a poem
for an ancient audience. For modern scholars, the language appropriate to a given
social or ritual situation as well as features of the performance, such as movements
and self-conscious references to the act of performing implied in the poetic language,
are crucial for recapturing this method of classification inherent in early poetry.[5] So,
to understand the genre, attempts must be made to understand how an archaic poem
fits into its particular occasion. The form of a poem and the practical function of the

verses that is evidenced in the language of the verses as well as cultural evidence about the social context for such performances must be taken into account.

This link between performer/poet, audience and poem has been played a large role in recreating the verses on the Persian Wars in the "new Simonides." The thinking has been that these verses, particularly fr. 11 $W^2$ and those associated with it, belong to the class of poetry, narrative elegy, identified by E. L. Bowie in his influential article concerned with the social contexts for the performance of early elegy.[6] A primary reason for this placement is the belief that these verses would have originally been performed in a public context, such as Bowie has posited for other narrative elegies. This belief has given rise to many assumptions about how to reconstruct these poems. Specifically, it is assumed that certain formal features and aspects of content that Bowie associated with narrative elegy are to be found in the so-called "Plataea poem." This composition should have a prooimion. It should deal with the past as well as more recent events. Most importantly, it should be in the form of a narrative.[7] By identifying these features in these verses, modern scholars have been able to reconstruct this composition so that it fits the notion of a genre that would have certain formal feature dictated by its occasion of performance. In this way, genre, with its link between form and function, has become a key element in the debate on how to reconstruct these verses. The primary emphasis has been placed on recreating narrative content in these fragments. It should be kept in mind, however, that the "new Simonides" has become a key piece of evidence confirming that such publicly performed elegies would have these features.

The circularity of this approach to the "new Simonides" has already been observed.[8] Yet, even more fundamental problems arise from using the understanding that "genre is occasion" as a starting point for reconstructing the scope and details of any fragmentary work such as the "new Simonides." First, given that Simonides' fragments under discussion here pertain to the Persian Wars, the uniqueness of these events must be taken into consideration. This uniqueness suggests that a commemoration of it might have been anomalous. The initial occasion for such a commemoration certainly would have been.[9] Furthermore, any occasion, either public or private, for Simonides' verses on the Persian Wars remains a matter of speculation. No source tells us when, where, or for what purpose such compositions, either elegiac or lyric, were performed. The result is that it is difficult to identify an occasion for such poems and even more difficult to derive generic features from any potential occasion. As D. Obbink rightly observes concerning the new fragments, "any conclusions about the genre of the poem [i.e. the so-called "Plataea poem"] can only be tentative in light of the unsettled question of the original circumstances of composition."[10] Finally, the focus on the historical events seen in these new fragments also hinders our understanding of the poems genre because we lack any substantive comparanda. Insights are difficult to gain from other elegiac poems on historical events because such elegies have not survived, if they existed at all, or they have left a barely perceptible mark on the Greek literary tradition.

The focus on narrative elements as the defining generic criteria also presents problems for the reconstruction of the "new Simonides." It is generally assumed that these verses are to be construed in terms of a narrative of particular battles that were originally performed publicly. The preceding chapter, however, has cast doubt upon our ability to use narrative as a primary guide in reconstructing the fragments on the Persian Wars. Since narrative is seen as the defining generic feature of elegies that were publicly performed, this doubt precipitates a new consideration of the genre of these fragments on the Persian Wars. It can no longer be assumed that if these verses were originally performed in some public setting that they would have been in the form of a narrative; therefore, some other criteria for identifying the generic boundaries of these verses must be found.

In the discussion that follows, the focus will be shifted away from an emphasis on narrative elements. Our understanding of various classes or sub-genres is incomplete. In fact, such a rigid form of categorization most likely did not exist in the archaic period. In the discussion of fr. 11 $W^2$ that follows, affinities will be sought in the broader category of elegy.[11] The initial assumption is that these verses belong to the broader poetic category of elegy. It will be shown that Simonides' verses have features that are found in other elegies about which we know more than we do about narrative elegy. In this assumption, elegy is construed as broadly as possible to include not only longer poems in the elegiac meter but also epigrams which share this metrical scheme. Such an approach is justified because Simonides composed what we would consider elegy proper as well as epigrams. In fact, Simonides was well regarded for his skill as an epigrammatist, as the tradition of epigrams ascribed to him shows.[12] Moreover, it is not entirely certain that the distinctions made between epigram and elegy would have been as obvious to an archaic poet as they are in modern collections.[13] Following this line of thinking, then, genre is identified through shared features, both formal and functional, found in similar types of poetry. Other elegiac poetry represented by our fragmentary corpus should provide clues about the generic features of these new fragments of Simonides. Such an approach to genre becomes necessary when the context for verses cannot be determined or it must be deemed to be unique. Both cases apply to the verses on the Persian Wars in the "new Simonides." It is assumed, then, that to discuss the genre of the "new Simonides," internal features that link these verses to other elegiac poetry must be sought. Moreover, elegy in general, because of its metrical form, admits elements found in other types of poetry, in particular hexameter; therefore, it can function in similar ways to epic and hymns. Since the "new Simonides" in many ways seems to emphasize features that are suitable to epic and hymnic poetry, further insight can be gained by attempting to understand more clearly how the "new Simonides" appears to position itself in relation to other traditions and types of poetry.

First, a backdrop for considering the genre of these verses will be provided by looking at the genre of elegy as a whole. Second, the current opinions concerning the genre of the "new Simonides" will be discussed. Finally, features will be sought that link the fragments of the "new Simonides" to other elegiac verses. The aim will be to consider how these features link these new verses with elegy as a whole rather than using fr. 11 W$^2$ to define a sub-category of elegy. By identifying this poetic posture, I hope to illuminate not only the genre of the "new Simonides" but also to provide insight into the genre of elegy in general.

## 3.2 ELEGY AS GENRE

Elegy is a notoriously difficult class of poetry to define generically. The following is not an attempt to provide a comprehensive study of this genre. Useful studies of this nature already exist.[14] Rather, the goal is to provide a brief overview of the major ideas concerning this category of poetry and create a backdrop against which the genre of "new Simonides" can be evaluated. Three features are generally seen as defining elegy as a poetic genre: form, context, and content.

### A. Form

In modern collections, the primary unifying feature of archaic elegy is form. All elegiac poetry is in the elegiac meter, an epodic meter that consists of one dactylic hexameter followed by one pentameter or more appropriately two hemiepes.[15] The ancient terminology for elegiac poetry reveals that the use of meter to distinguish elegy from other types of poetry is not a uniquely modern concept. There are three terms that appear in our ancient sources: ἐλεγεῖον, ἐλεγεία, and ἔλεγος. The relation between each of these terms reveals that by the late fifth century BCE elegy was defined to some extent by its metrical form.[16]

Modern collections further qualify form as a classificatory principle by distinguishing between epigrams and elegy proper, as M. L. West makes clear in the first edition of his *Iambi et Elegi Graeci*.[17] Although early verse inscriptions were hexametric, by the mid-sixth century BCE the elegiac couplet had become the standard meter for epigrams that were intended to be written on stone.[18] In the Hellenistic period, the elegiac epigram came to enjoy a life of its own as a literary exercise, as is evident in collections such as the *Garlands* of Meleager and Philip.[19] Although epigrams share many features with other verses in the elegiac meter, they are generally distinguished from elegy on the basis of their mode of delivery and their function. Elegy was intended for some type of performance, either in public or in private. The poems seem to have had a variety of functions. Epigrams were intended to be written on an object or to be imitations of such verses in order to commemorate an event or the dead. These criteria, however, do not always allow for an easy distinction, as the heading under Simonides "*Incertum an ex Epigrammatis*" in West's *IEG²* 2 attests.[20] A particular problem arises in distinguishing these types of verses in terms of function. As will be discussed later, elegy and epigram may be seen as having similar functions. Both can commemorate, praise and mourn. The real distinction, then, is their medium of presentation. Epigrams would be intended to be printed on stone and elegy would be intended to be performed, either publicly or in private.

## B. Context: Symposia and Public Festival

The recourse to function as a classificatory principle brings to the foreground the idea that in the archaic period other features would have defined elegy. In particular, to an archaic audience, context would have given a poem its generic definition.

In Chapter 2, it was shown that elegies were suitable for performance in either a public setting, such as in a competition at a festival, or in a private setting, such as at a symposia.[21] The debate over the context in which specific elegiac verses were performed is far from settled. As was noted, M. L. West observed eight performance contexts for elegy by identifying internal references to geographic locations and real situations in our corpus of early elegy.[22] Arguing against West's classification of contexts, E. L. Bowie has proposed that elegy would have been performed in only three contexts: the symposium, the *komos* which followed the symposium, and public aulodic competitions. As has been noted, the available evidence for the performance of elegy appears to be in favor of Bowie's findings.[23] The conclusion that arises is that both a private context (symposia) and a public context (aulodic competitions at festivals) were available for the performance of archaic elegy. These contexts, however, were not unique to elegy. Other melic poetry, such as skolia, was equally at home in the symposia. Other types of poetry, such as epic, dithyramb, and drama, also were performed in competitions at public festivals. The feature that seems to distinguish elegy from other types of poetry performed at public festivals appears to have been the accompaniment of the *aulos*. It need not be the case, however, that musical accompaniment would have distinguished the genre of elegy as a whole, as is shown by our inability to link elegy performed in symposia conclusively to the *aulos*.[24] At some level the shared meter and the similarity of content that could appear in these publicly and privately performed elegies suggest that the verses performed in these contexts had common features. Context alone, then, is difficult to use as the primary distinguishing feature of the elegiac genre. There were multiple contexts for the performance of elegy and these contexts were not limited to this type of poetry.

Moreover, little is known about the details of performance of elegy in any of these contexts.

## C. Content

The multiplicity of performance contexts for elegy suggests that other features helped to define this genre. Modern scholars have generally used content to provide these features. In this way, sub-classes of elegy, such as amatory, exhortatory, and paraenetic, have been identified in terms of content that would have been suitable for performance in certain contexts. Yet, even the most perfunctory glance at our fragments reveals that poetry in elegiac verse was a suitable medium for a large variety of topics. This multiplicity of topics has been observed by West.[25] Bowie and others have observed that most of these topics were suitable for performance in symposia; even these topics, however, have been shown to be appropriate for performance in a public setting.[26] It should be noted that many of the subjects identified in elegy are also found in non-elegiac poetry, such as iambos or epinicia. Thus, content does little to provide viable limits by which elegiac sub-categories or the genre of elegy can be defined. Furthermore, the content of an elegy does not give definitive clues about the context in which this poetry was performed. Elegy remains a genre which dealt with various topics and, regardless of its content, would have been performed in a variety of contexts.

Nevertheless, two attempts to link the genre of elegy to a specific type of content performed in public merit further consideration in a discussion of Simonides' verses on the Persian Wars. Both attempts are relevant because they place elegiac verses in such a setting. The first, narrative elegy, is significant for the "new Simonides" not only because it defines a class of elegiac verses by a type of content that would be suitable for a specific context, but also because it has played a large role in shaping modern views on Simonides' poems on Persian Wars. The second, threnodic elegy, also places elegy in a public setting. Threnodic elegy is significant because of an ancient perception that elegy had some connection with or origin in laments.

### Narrative Elegy

Much has already been said here about narrative elegy in terms of the content of fr. 11 W[2].[27] As has been noted, it is not entirely certain that a class of elegy would be defined in terms of its narrative content. It bears repeating that while Bowie adduces much evidence to make his case about the existence of narrative elegy, he offers no support for his linking of this category with a performance in a public setting. The link exists only because the elegies he defines as narrative would seem to be suited for public performance. In his words, "If both the existence of this genre (i.e.

narrative elegy) and elegiac competitions at festivals are admitted, then they surely go together."[28]

In terms of defining elegy as a genre that is distinct from other types of poetry that would have been preformed publicly, however, it must be admitted that narrative was not unique to elegy. Narrative would have been at home in other types of poetry. In the first decade of the fifth century, Phrynichus seems to have incorporated historical narrative into his *Sack of Miletus*.[29] A narrative of the battle of Salamis appears in Aeschylus' *Persae*.[30] Later in the fifth-century, Timotheus incorporated the same subject into a lyric nome.[31] It has also been noted that Simonides may have dealt with this battle in a lyric poem, although it is not known if this treatment would have been narrative.[32] Pindar, too, incorporates references to the Persian Wars in his *Odes*.[33] To be sure, narrative elements that relate historical details could appear in most of the other genres of archaic poetry that are known to us.[34] Moreover, narrative content is not universally agreed to have limited elegy to a specific performance context. For example, Bowie himself finds that narrative elements in what may be fragments of Tyrtaeus' *Eunomia/Politeia* do not situate these verses in a public performance context.[35] There is no consensus that narrative content, and more particularly historical narrative, identified a specific context for the performance of elegy; therefore, narrative cannot be said to have defined elegy as a distinct genre.

## Threnodic Elegy

The belief that elegy originated as some type of threnodic poetry is prevalent in our ancient sources. Although this view of the origin of elegy is not currently accepted, numerous modern scholars have argued for some link between elegy and lament.[36] The link derives largely from a perceived kinship between the ancient terminology ἔλεγος and ἐλεγεῖον. The term ἐλεγεῖον appears in the late fifth century and refers to an elegiac distich or the elegiac meter in general.[37] The term ἔλεγος also appears in the late fifth century with the meaning "lament," and so seems to represent some type of threnodic poetry.[38] In this period, however, the relation between these terms is far from certain.[39] It is generally assumed that ἔλεγος is the noun from which the adjective ἐλεγεῖον is derived and that ἔλεγος refers to the genre and that ἐλεγεῖον refers to the meter of this genre.[40] From this understanding, both ancient and modern commentators have concluded that some sub-genre of elegy is to be defined as threnodic.

The problems with the link between lament and elegy are most clearly demonstrated by Pausanias' quotation of a dedicatory inscription of Echembrotus (10.7.6 =*IEG*² 2, 62). The verses commemorate Echembrotus' victory in singing μέλεα καὶ ἐλέγους at the Pythian games in 586 BCE.[41] Pausanias quotes the inscription to show that aulodic songs were halted at the second Pythian games because they were too melancholy (σκυθρωπότατα). He also reports that elegies were sung to an aulos (ἐλεγεῖα {θρῆνος} προσαιδόμενα τοῖς αυλοῖς).[42] Pausanias' comments have been understood to say that the ἔλεγοι sung by Echembrotus were mournful; there-fore, it has been suggested that early elegy would have been defined as lament or that a sub-category of elegy was originally defined by its mournful content.

This sub-group of elegy may be represented by Andromache's lament at Euripides *Andromache* 103–116, the only example of elegiac meter found in extant tragedy. D. L. Page has argued that this lament is representative of a lost Doric tradition of such elegiac threnody. He suggests that Clonas (ca. eighth century BCE), Sacadas (ca. sixth century BCE), and Echembrotas (ca. sixth century BCE) may have been early composers of this type of elegy, which is entirely lost from our knowledge of Greek literature.[43] Along the same line of thinking, M. L. West has identified funerals as a context in which ἔλεγοι would have been performed. Thus, West also understands that a sub-category of elegy is to be defined as poetry of lamentation.[44] For both of these scholars the dedicatory inscription of Echembrotus is a primary bit of evidence. The epigram itself, however, reveals only that early ἔλεγοι were in some way distinct from μέλεα.[45] It does not tell us anything about the nature of ἔλεγοι. The words of Pausanias only show us that ἔλεγοι were akin to ἐλεγεῖα and that ἐλεγεῖα were mournful in the second century CE. It does not follow that the ἐλέγοι of Echembrotus were a lament. Moreover, this evidence does not show that early elegy was the same as a lament or that poetry of lamentation in elegiac meter was a particular sub-category of elegy.[46] The epigram, then, provides no clear evidence for the Doric tradition of elegy of lamentation posited by D. L. Page.[47] The epigram also offers only tenuous support for West's claims concerning the performance of ἔλεγοι at funer-als or an "occasion of loss or bereavement."[48] The only other evidence West offers is that in the late fifth century BCE ἔλεγος could mean lament. On the fifth-century usage of ἔλεγος, Bowie has suggested that since the meaning of "sung lament" is no earlier than the late fifth century, elegy which was primarily mournful did not exist as a sub-category for archaic poets.[49] With this evidence, then, the link between elegy as a class of poetry and lamentation remains tenuous.[50]

Yet, if elegiac inscriptions are taken into account, the link between elegy and lament becomes more substantial. There are four funerary inscriptions that help to link elegiac verse with lament.[51] The first is an inscription from a grave stele found at Nikaia, dating to the mid sixth century BCE:

αὐτοκλείδο τόδε σêμα νέο π|ροσορôν ἀν|ιôμαι /
καὶ θα|νάτοι ΤαΥ[ . . ]αΝ [—c. 7–10—][52]

["Looking upon this burial mound of young Autokleidos I am grieved and to the dead man. . . ."]

This epigram is a pronouncement of grief in the first person by a speaker who is not identified as being the stele which bears the inscription or the person commemorated by the inscription. The epigram is a lament uttered by an anonymous viewer for Autokleidos. The fragmentary nature of the inscription makes identification of the meter difficult. The first line is a hexameter, but it is unclear if the second line is a pentameter.[53] As a result, it is not possible to determine if the epigram is an elegiac example of such an expression. Nevertheless, the anonymous first person address on this grave stele allows that such a perspective can be expected in other early funerary inscriptions.[54]

With this evidence in mind, anonymous first person addresses can be read in two other funerary epigrams. First, there is Simon. LXXV *FGE* (=fr. 91 W²)

> Σῆμα καταφθιμένοιο Μεγακλέος εὖτ' ἂν ἴδωμαι
> οἰκτίρω σε, τάλαν Καλλία, οἷ' ἔπαθες.

["Whenever I see the tomb of dead Megakles, I pity you, poor Kallias, what sort of things you have suffered."]

The primary objection to understanding this epigram as a funerary piece is the presence of the anonymous first-person narrator.[55] The inscription discussed above, however, shows that the first-person address is not a sufficient reason for denying that the verses have features of a sepulchral epigram. It is most likely that these verses are not an elegy, but are either a true epigram or an imitation of one. The expression of consolation for a third party raises some suspicions that the verses represent an inscribed epigram.[56] This additional perspective distinguishes these verses from the inscription above, which appears to be a lament for the one who has died. It is probably best to interpret the epigram with Gentili as a literary exercise, akin to a skolion, that would have been performed at a symposium.[57] A fair assessment, however, is that the epigram imitates a funerary inscription and does so with actual inscriptional features.

An inscription that is more clearly a lament is *CEG* 51 (=*IG* 1³ 1219), a funerary inscription from Attica:

> οἰκτίρο προσορô[ν] | παιδὸς τόδε σῆμα | θανόντος·
> Σμικύθ[ο] | hός τε φίλον ὄλεσε|ν ἔλπ·[58] ἀγαθέν[59]

["I feel pity looking upon this burial mound of the dead child, Smikuthos, how he destroyed the good hope of his family."]

The reading of οἰκτίρο, found on the stone, was initially doubted by Willemsen, who emended it to οἰκτίρο⟨ν⟩ and thereby removed the first person address.[60] The previous inscriptions, however, reveal that such a first person is not an anomaly and may be kept here. The epigram, then, contains another anonymous first person expression of grief in a funerary inscription that is in the elegiac meter. In this way, the inscription becomes an elegiac lament.

These three inscriptions show that an anonymous first-person address is, in fact, an acceptable feature in funerary epigrams and that this feature is attested by at least the late sixth century. At least two of these inscriptions, the first and the third, can be interpreted as laments for the dead with certainty. Nevertheless, of these two elegiac epigrams, only the third can be said to be an example of a lament that is in the elegiac meter.

Another elegiac example of a lament in a funerary inscription is found in an inscription from Ambrakia:[61]

> ἄνδρας [τ]ούσδ᾽ [ἐ]σλοὺς ὀλοφύρομαι, hoῖσι Πυραιβὸν ⫶
>   παῖδες ἐμετίσαντ᾽ α[ἰ]κισθέντα[62] φόνον, ⫶
> ἀνγε[λ]ίαν με⟨τ⟩ιόντες ἀπ᾽ εὐρυχόροι[ο ϙορίνθου]
>   [missing pentameter and hexameter]
> πατρίδ᾽ ἀν᾽ ἱμερτὰν πένθος ἔθαλλε τότε ⫶
> Τόδε δ᾽ ἀπ᾽ Ἀνπρακίας· Ναυσίστρατος, αὐτὰ παθόν τε[63]
>   Καλλίταν τ᾽ Ἀΐδα δῶμα μέλαν κατέχει ⫶
> κα⟨ε⟩ὶ μὰν Ἀραθθίονα κα⟨ε⟩ὶ Εὔξενον ἴστε, πολῖτα⟨ε⟩ι, ⫶
>   hος μετὰ τῶνδ᾽ ἀνδρὸν Κὰρ ἔκιχεν θανάτου. ⫶

["I lament these brave men for whom the children of Pyraiboi inflicted slaughter outrageously[64], going with an embassy from spacious Corinth ... then grief blossomed throughout their dear fatherland; and these two from Ambrakia: Nausistratos suffering these same things and the dark house of Hades confines Kallitas. And indeed know, citizens, how Ker of death overtook Aratthion and Euxenos among these men."]

The epigram belongs to a polyandrion and is dated to sometime after 550 BCE.[65] The word ὀλοφύρομαι clinches the case concerning the anonymous first-person address in early elegiac funerary inscriptions. Yet, it is not only the first-person address, ὀλοφύρομαι, that allows the inscription to be read as a lament. The mention of grief blossoming (πένθος ἔθαλλε) reinforces the interpretation that the inscription is concerned with mourning, rather than with consoling or with commemoration. It is fair then to understand this epigram as a lament. This epigram is important here because it provides an early funerary epigram that is a lament in the elegiac meter.

To conclude, the inscriptional and epigrammatic evidence above reveals that funerary inscriptions in the elegiac meter could in fact be laments in content and function. This conclusion cannot be pushed to make the claim that funerary epigrams, inscriptional or otherwise, represent an origin for elegy in general, or a subcategory of elegy. It also cannot be claimed that content suitable to a lament in some way provides boundaries to the genre of elegy or its sub-genres at any point in the archaic period. There are plenty of examples of inscriptional elegiac epigrams that are not poetry of lamentation. Yet, these examples do help to show that lamentation was suitable content for elegiac verses. In this way, a clearer link between elegy proper, as it was viewed by ancient commentators, and early epigrams arises in terms of lament.[66] It is reasonable, then, that that early elegy also may function in some way as a lament, as we will see.

## 3.3 THE CURRENT STATUS OF THE GENRE OF THE "NEW SIMONIDES"

It is against this backdrop that the genre of the "new Simonides" has been identified and the lost verses have been reconstructed. Fr. 11 $W^2$ has seemed to confirm Bowie's category, narrative elegy. Fragments with historical content have been identified and historical narratives have been reconstructed for separate elegies on the battle of Plataea, the battle of Artemisium, and possibly on the battle at Salamis. The primary assumption for the reconstruction of these poems is that they belong to the sub-genre of narrative elegy. It bears repeating, however, that this reason is circular. The sub-genre, narrative elegy, is hypothesized and believed to have certain features; the "new Simonides" confirms the existence of this sub-genre; the "new Simonides," then, is reconstructed to have the feature of this hypothetical sub-genre. On the assumption that these verses represent narrative elegies, the genre of these poems has been further defined by identifying either general performance contexts at a public festival or more specific occasions for performance. Such attempts have been made recently for the "Plataea poem," but were made for *The Sea-battle at Artemisium* well before Bowie's identification of the sub-genre, narrative elegy.[67]

These considerations of genre have separated the narrative fragments (frs. 1–18 $W^2$) from other supposedly non-narrative ones in both the new fragments and verses previously known to be by Simonides (frs. 19–33 $W^2$).[68] The reasoning is that the latter group is not demonstrably narrative, but is interpreted as having a reflective tone usually associated with elegy performed in symposia. In particular, these fragments are understood to contain reflections on youth, old age and the attainment of a life of excellence (frs 19, 20 and 21 $W^2$), erotic themes (fr. 21 $W^2$ possibly, and frs. 22, 27 and 33 $W^2$ more specifically), references to symposia in general (frs. 23 and 24 $W^2$), or they are explicitly assigned to a sympotic context (frs. 25 and 26 $W^2$are said to have been sung by Simonides at symposia).[69] It is such content, especially in the unidentified papyrus scraps, that has led to the assumption that these fragments belong in a sympotic context.

The "new Simonides," then, is divided into two distinct classes of elegy and, by this separation, the genre of the poems which individual fragments represent is determined. The divide between these categories is primarily established by a perceived link between elegiac content and context in which the performance of such verses is envisaged.[70]

## 3.4 NEW CONSIDERATIONS OF GENERIC FEATURES IN THE "NEW SIMONIDES"

The reconstruction of poems in terms of the sub-genres established by this division of the fragments is far from certain because it largely relies on some relation between content and context. As was observed above, content is not clearly an indication of the context in which an elegy was performed. There is no evidence that historical narrative was inappropriate for private performance. Likewise, no supposed sympotic content can be said to have barred a poem from being publicly performed. This observation is troubling for the current understanding and reconstruction of the poems of the "new Simonides." For Simonides' elegiac verses, the only certain context is the symposium. We know this because witnesses place certain elegiac verses of Simonides in this setting.[71] The conclusion that the Persian War poems have content that was suitable for a public performance is simply unconfirmed.

The exceptional nature of the Persian Wars further complicates this approach to classifying the elegiac fragments of the "new Simonides." Not only were these wars exceptional, but so were commemorations of them, as can be seen in monuments such as the Serpent Column at Delphi or the later "Eion poem" (Simon. XL *FGE*). It is a fair assumption that the poetic depictions represented by the "new Simonides" also were atypical. It seems likely that the original occasion, if not the general context, for the performance of such verses would have been unparalleled before the Persian Wars. Occasions in public settings certainly were present. Herodotus mentions the interment of the dead at Plataea (9.85).[72] Following the battle, there was a ceremony at Plataea honoring of Zeus Eleutherios as well as the dedication of an altar to this deity commemorating the victory at Plataea.[73] There is also possibly the *Eleutheria*, the yearly offering to the *Plataiomachoi*, with games being held every fourth year.[74] Such occasions certainly would have provided opportunities, unparalleled earlier, for the performance of a poem concerning the Persian Wars. Furthermore, even if any of the new fragments were performed publicly, it need not follow that these poems are representative of other elegies believed to have been performed publicly. It also does not follow that the verses in the "new Simonides" should be reconstructed according to features assumed to have existed in other publicly performed elegies.

The context and content of the verses in the "new Simonides," then, are difficult to use for determining the genre of any of the "new Simonides," especially for the verses on the Persian Wars. Too many gaps exist in our understanding of the features of these elegies. To determine how these fragments fit into the genre of elegy, then, internal clues must be sought and compared with other verses for which generic constraints are more certain. Only in this way will it be possible to see how these fragments can be positioned in relation to other elegiac and non-elegiac poetry. It is in this positioning that we can finally consider how these verses would have functioned in a performance context and we can begin to make pronouncements concerning the genre each may represent.

Similar attempts to identify the genre of the "new Simonides" have been made that have largely concerned fr. 11 W². Dirk Obbink has analyzed the hymnic features in this fragment and demonstrated that the prooimial verses appear to approximate the form of an epic prooimion and the function of a lyric one.[75] He concludes that the poem is an intriguing early example of genre crossing. Similarly, Eva Stehle has set fr. 11 W² in relation to Homeric poetry to show that Simonides adopts a Homeric stance as performer, but also separates his verses from this tradition by taking a position as a poet similar to that found in the verses of Tyrtaeus.[76] Both discussions are insightful explorations of the way Simonides establishes a relation between his verses and other early poetry in fr. 11 W². The initial premise of both, however, is that the genre of the fragments is narrative elegy. The result is that these studies emphasize how fr. 11 W² represents and defines this elegiac sub-genre.[77]

In removing the assumption of narrative as the primary guide in reconstruction, features of genre in the "new Simonides" can be sought and analyzed to determine what aspects would be suitable for public and/or sympotic performance. To this end, Homeric, hymnic, and epigrammatic elements in these fragments will be considered. The main focus will be on formal, lexical and thematic aspects. An initial focus on fr. 11 W² is necessary because, although extremely incomplete, it is the largest fragment that survives. This focus will then be expanded to consider other fragments in the "new Simonides."

## A. Xenophanes Fr. B1 W²

To begin, Xenophanes offers a prescriptive list of topics that would be suitable for sympotic performance.

> χρὴ δὲ πρῶτον μὲν θεὸν ὑμνεῖν εὔφρονας ἄνδρας
>    εὐφήμοις μύθοις καὶ καθαροῖσι λόγοις,
> σπείσαντάς τε καὶ εὐξαμένους τὰ δίκαια δύνασθαι
>    πρήσσειν· ταῦτα γὰρ ὦν ἐστι προχειρότερον,
> οὐχ ὕβρεις· πίνειν δ' ὁπόσον κεν ἔχων ἀφίκοιο
>    οἴκαδ' ἄνευ προπόλου μὴ πάνυ γηραλέος.
> ἀνδρῶν δ' αἰνεῖν τοῦτον ὃς ἐσθλὰ πιὼν ἀναφαίνει,
>    ὡς ἦι μνημοσύνη καὶ τόνος ἀμφ' ἀρετῆς,
> οὔ τι μάχας διέπειν Τιτήνων οὐδὲ Γιγάντων
>    οὐδὲ ⟨  ⟩ Κενταύρων, πλάσμα⟨τα⟩ τῶν προτέρων,
> ἢ στάσιας σφεδανάς· τοῖς οὐδὲν χρηστὸν ἔνεστιν·
>    θεῶν ⟨δὲ⟩ προμηθείην αἰὲν ἔχειν ἀγαθήν.
>                       fr. B1.13–24 W²

["First, men of good sense ought to sing of god with auspicious tales and pure words, making a drink-offering while praying to be able to accomplish just things; for, indeed, to pray for these things, not outrages, is more suitable; then, to drink however much, while holding which, you could walk homeward without an attendant, unless you are very old; then, to praise such a one of men who, after drinking, reveals good things, so that memory and exertion are for the sake of excellence; to relate in no way the battles of Titans nor of the Giants nor of the Centaurs, the fictions of the men who have come before, or violent factions; there is no usefulness in these things; but to have good forethought for the gods always."]

From Xenophanes, we learn what he considered suitable subject matter for performance at a symposium. It is suitable first to hymn the gods with auspicious stories and pure tales (13–14), to pray to be able to do what is just (15), to proclaim noble things, after drinking, and praise men who do so (19). Importantly, we also learn what subjects are deemed unsuitable for symposia. One should not be hubristic (17). It is not fitting to relate battles of the Titans, Giants, or Centaurs, the fictions of previous generations. So the subjects of epic are unsuitable. Finally, there should be no talk of civil strife (23). Although the line is problematic, the goal for Xenophanes is that memory and one's exertion be concerned with noble things (20).[78] Less problematic is line 23, where the goal is that the subjects at the symposium be χρηστός ("useful").

Similar sentiments are offered by Anacreon (eleg. fr. 2 W²), which follows Xenophanes' fragment in Athenaeus. Anacreon too forbids talk of violence and war, preferring erotic themes.

οὐ φιλέω, ὃς κρητῆρι παρὰ πλέωι οἰνοποτάζων
    νείκεα καὶ πόλεμον δακρυόεντα λέγει,
ἀλλ' ὅστις Μουσέων τε καὶ ἀγλαὰ δῶρ' Ἀφροδίτης
    συμμίσγων ἐρατῆς μνήσκεται εὐφροσύνης.

["I am not fond of him, who drinking wine beside a full bowl, talks of quarrels and tearful war, but whoever, mixing the shining gifts of the Muses and those of Aphrodite, calls to mind lovely good-cheer."]

In these verses, Anacreon is in agreement with Xenophanes. Subject matter that we associate with epic poetry is undesirable in sympotic poetry. The fact is, however, that such topics were the stuff of sympotic verses as the commentators point out by suggesting that both had the poems of Alcaeus (seventh century BCE) in mind.[79]

A quick glance at the extant corpus of early Greek elegy reveals that the subjects barred from the symposia are prevalent. Archilochus fr. 1 W² speaks of being the attendant of Mars; frs. 2, 4, and 5 W² also presume the speaker has either a real or fictional status as a warrior; fr. 3 W² speaks of military practices. The fragments of Callinus and Tyrtaeus both focus on military exhortations. Mythical examples, such as Xenophanes excludes from sympotic poetry, are also found in early elegy.

Mimnermus fr. 11 $W^2$ mentions the myth of Jason and the Argonauts; Aelian reports that Mimnermus mentioned Niobe, although how the poet employed this myth is unknown (fr. 19 $W^2$). Tyrtaeus fr. 12 $W^2$ is filled with mythical exempla. The contexts of these fragments, however, are unknown and it could be argued that they are further evidence for narrative elegy that is similar to epic. As for political strife in elegy, we have Solon frs. 1–3 $W^2$ (his *Salamis*); Solon frs. 4–13 $W^2$ are concerned with political advice and prescriptions. Also, any number of fragments from the *Theognidea* will show that civil strife was a topic of elegy and, importantly, that such topics were sung at symposia.[80] The case has also been made that the fragments of Archilochus, Callinus, Tyrtaeus and Solon were recited in this setting.[81] While this overview is far from complete, it does demonstrate that the subjects banned from symposia by Xenophanes and Anacreon are in fact topics found in elegies that may have been performed in symposia.

Wolfgang Rösler goes a bit further in his discussion of sympotic poetry. He suggests that "the memory of brave behavior in battle, either in external or civil strife, must have been a strong element of sympotic *mnēmosynē*."[82] Rösler's point is to show that *mnēmosynē* played an important function at symposia. For him, sympotic literature will admit not only reflective songs but also historical poetry as well. If this view is correct, topics such as those ruled out by Xenophanes and Anacreon would have had an integral place in the symposia.[83]

A significant point that has not received attention in modern scholarship is that the fragments of the "new Simonides" contain both types of themes discussed in the verses of Xenophanes and Anacreon. In particular, the lengthy hymnic opening of fr. 11 $W^2$ explicitly elaborates on epic themes that would have been classed with the πλάσμα⟨τα⟩ τῶν προτέρων by Xenophanes. Fr. 22 $W^2$ may also contain the more erotic content requested by Anacreon. Following the pattern above, then, not only the erotic verses of fr. 22 $W^2$ but also the Homeric content of fr. 11 $W^2$ might be expected to have appeared in a sympotic context. Of concern at this point, however, are the poems on the Persian Wars.[84] The question that arises is: Does the appearance of Homeric themes in fr. 11 $W^2$ provide any clues about the context in which this fragment may have been performed?

### B. Homeric Poetry

Fr. 11 $W^2$ certainly draws on Homeric themes and language.[85] For some, this evocation of Homer has a dual function. It not only links the verses with Homeric poetry but also disassociates them from this tradition on various levels.[86] Although there is disagreement about the degree of differentiation from Homeric practices in Simonides, it is accepted that fr. 11 $W^2$ is working with and perhaps reshaping Homeric themes for elegy.[87]

Elucidation of how Simonides is specifically employing the Homeric tradition may, in fact, be thwarted by the fragmentary nature of these verses. As was noted above, we simply do not know how Simonides employed the details of this tradition in fr. 11 W[2].[88] For the purpose of genre, however, there may not be a need for further elucidation at this point. The link between archaic hexameter and elegy is nothing strange. Metrically, the two poetic types share one common unit, and epic vocabulary would be suited for almost any position in the elegiac distich. Elegy also could quote Homer, as in Simon. fr. 19 W[2] or simply refer to a Homeric image, as in Mimner. 2.1 W[2].[89] Elegiac poets could also rework Homeric passages to fit the elegiac meter and in doing so they could shift the meaning of the original context. Such is the case in Tyrt. fr. 11.31–33 W[2].[90] Simon. fr. 20.14 W[2] also may mention Homer directly, but the reading of the papyrus is uncertain.[91] The drawing on and reworking of Homeric themes (1–15) along with the possible self-conscious reference to Homer (15–18) in fr. 11 W[2] appears to be an example of a natural reflex for elegy. The wealth of references to myth throughout the elegiac fragments of Simonides may also be considered part of this reflex.[92]

How, then, do Homeric elements in fr. 11 W[2] help to define the genre of the fragment? In terms of content, these elements simply show that Homeric themes were suitable in elegiac poetry. In terms of context, however, a hexameter fragment of Xenophanes may provide a clue that helps us to understand how Homeric themes worked in sympotic literature. Again describing what is appropriate to say at a symposium, the poet suggests:

τίς πόθεν εἰς ἀνδρῶν; πόσα τοι ἔτε' ἐστί, φέριστε;
πηλίκος ἦσθ', ὅθ' ὁ Μῆδος ἀφίκετο;
                              fr. 13.4–5 G–P (= 22 D.-K.)

["Who are you? From where among men do you come, my friend? How many years do you have? What age were you when the Mede came?"]

Although these verses are not entirely Homeric, the first verse employs Homeric formulae or elements of Homeric formulae. The first half of the verse (τίς πόθεν εἰς ἀνδρῶν;) occurs once in the *Iliad* and seven times in the Odyssey. In these occurrences it always appears at the beginning of a line.[93] Xenophanes, then, borrows a formulaic unit mostly found in the *Odyssey.* The second half of the verse (πόσα τοι ἔτε' ἐστί, φέριστε;) is not formulaic. The vocative, φέριστε, however, is rare in archaic hexameter, occurring five times in Homer and always after the feminine caesura.[94] Three of these occurrences are found in the formulaic question, τίς δὲ σύ ἐσσι φέριστε, which occurs only at the beginning of a line in the *Iliad.* The second half of Xenophanes' line, then, uses the formulaic vocative (φέριστε) but shifts it to the end of the verse. The interrogatory context further suggests that Xenophanes is recalling the formulaic phrase of the *Odyssey* (τίς δὲ σύ ἐσσι φέριστε), but again does not employ this formula. It seems that in these verses Xenophanes combines one Homeric formula with part of another. Xenophanes reworks Homer to create a line that becomes a saying suitable for performance at a symposium.

This fragment of Xenophanes, however, is hexametric, not elegiac. An example of sympotic elegy that can be seen to function in a similar way to the verses of Xenophanes just analyzed are the four short elegiac hymns that open the collection of *Theognidea*.[95] Two of these hymns are addressed to Apollo, one to Artemis, and one to the Muses and the Graces. These verses draw on the traditional form and language of hymnic poetry. All but the first contain some mythical narrative pertaining to the deity invoked, a feature that is common in Homeric Hymns. The hymn to Artemis (Thgn. 11–14), particularly, introduces the Trojan cycle by referring to the temple set up by Agamemnon before sailing to Troy. These verses show that elegiac verses can employ Homeric content as their subject. For the discussion here, it is more interesting, however, that these hymns can be linked with a sympotic context and also appear to rework epic diction in a manner similar to that seen in Xenophanes.

In the first hymn to Apollo the performer sings: ἀλλ' αἰεὶ πρῶτόν τε καὶ ὕστατον ἔν τε μέσοισιν / ἀείσω (Thgn. 3–4: But I will sing (about you, Apollo,) first last and in the middle). The phrase πρῶτόν τε καὶ ὕστατον is common in archaic hymnody, and has one parallel in Hesiod.[96] At Hesiod *Theogony* 33–34, the poet is commanded to sing first, last and always of the Muses: σφᾶς δ' αὐτὰς πρῶτόν τε καὶ ὕστατον αἰὲν ἀείδειν. Although the *Theognidea* borrows the formulaic phrase αἰεὶ πρῶτον τε καὶ ὕστατον, it enhances it with the words ἔν τε μέσοισιν, which are not found elsewhere in archaic literature with the formula αἰεὶ πρῶτον τε καὶ ὕστατον. The *Theognidea* also appears to echo a formulaic line used to introduce *aristeiai* in Homer: ἔνθα τίνα πρῶτον, τίνα ὕστατον ἐξενάριξαν ("Whom did he slay first, and whom did he slay last?").[97] Although the *Theognidea* is not employing the Homeric formula, the concepts and language in both phrases are similar enough to suggest a connection. In these elegiac verses, then, we find a traditional hymnic formula used with a meaning and function similar to its use in archaic poetry. The phrase in elegy, however, is enhanced with the addition of a new concept, the phrase *in the middle*.

The *Theognidea* provides, with a fair degree of certainty, an elegiac example of the employment of epic themes and Homeric language in verses that can be called sympotic. These verses also contain the reworking of epic diction and formulae that were found in the hexameter verses of Xenophanes considered above. It now can be observed that perhaps the appearance of Homeric content is not a distinctive feature of elegy. Rather, the distinctive feature of elegy seems to be the tendency to rework deliberately Homeric diction. Moreover, this tendency is an aspect of sympotic elegy. Noting that the example from the *Theognidea* comes from a hymn allows this observation to be related to the "new Simonides." In both Simonides and the *The-ognidea,* Homeric content appears in a prooimial hymn. It is to the hymnic features that we must now turn.

## C. Hymnic Poetry

Dirk Obbink insightfully analyzes the hymnic structure of fr. 11 W² and puts forward two important observations. First, concerning genre, he suggests that the hymnic features in fr. 11 W² represent a crossing of poetic genres: the prooimion has the form of a hexametric hymn, but the function of a lyric one because it relates the poem's praise to the figure of the poet.[98] Second, he finds that the Hellenistic compilers did not categorize Simonides' works according to *laudandus.* His conclusion concerning fr. 11 W² is that "it was the collective effort of heroic proportions that is praised in an elegy that contained a 'pocket-book epic' on the subject."[99] The implication of these findings is that the hymnic features lead on to an epic-like narrative. Inter-estingly, while Obbink construes fr. 11 W² as a narrative poem, he also views it as potentially connected with frs. 19–22 W², the so-called "sympotic fragments."[100] Although Obbink's view still suggests that a narrative of Plataea dictates the overall structure of the lost poem, his linking of the narrative fragments with the sympotic ones can be expanded. I will suggest that the transition from hymn into a narrative is not guaranteed by fr. 11 W² and, therefore, it is plausible to give weight to Obbink's suggestion that fr. 11 W² may be linked to the other sympotic fragments. In this way, I hope to further elucidate the connection between fr. 11 W² and what is understood about the genre of elegy in general.

Of course, certain features in hymnic poetry mark transitions into narratives. Such is certainly the case with the terms χαῖρε and αὐτὰρ ἐγώ. The Homeric Hymn to Apollo demonstrates the practice. At line 14, the singer bids farewell (χαῖρε) to Leto and marks the beginning of a transition to the hymn proper, which contains a narrative of Apollo's birth on Delos. At the end of the Delian section of the hymn, the singer again marks a transition with the verses: αὐτὰρ ἐγὼν οὐ λήξω ἑκηβόλον Ἀπόλλωνα / ὑμνέων ἀργυρότοξον ὃν ἠΰκομος τέκε Λητώ (177–78: "But I will not stop singing of far-shooting Apollo of the silver bow, whom fair-haired Leto bore"). With these verses, the singer moves into the Pythian section of the hymn with another invocation of Apollo followed by a narrative of how Apollo arrived at Pythia. Finally, the hymn closes with the verses Καὶ σὺ μὲν οὕτω χαῖρε Διὸς καὶ Λητοῦς υἱέ· / αὐτὰρ ἐγὼ καὶ σεῖο καὶ ἄλλης μνήσομ' ἀοιδῆς. (545–46: "And so farewell, son of Zeus and Leto; but I will remember you and another hymn."). These verses would presumably mark a transition to another hymn or even an epic narrative as seems clear from similar closing transitions in many of the other Homeric Hymns.[101]

From the use of this hymnic language at fr. 11.19–20 W² it would appear that the prooimion here is marking a transition similar to the ones in the Homeric Hymns. That is, the close of prooimion with a farewell (χαῖρε) to Achilles, and an invocation of the Muses (fr. 11.21 W²) seems to suggest that the transition (αὐτὰρ ἐγώ) marks a movement into an epic-like narrative.[102] Yet, it is not entirely clear that all hymns in general would lead into narrative poems.[103]

It has already been pointed out that the *Theognidea* opens with four hymns that are to be understood to have been performed in a sympotic setting. As they stand in the collection, these hymns function as a unit; the first two are addressed to Apollo, the third to Artemis, and the final to the Graces and the Muses. It is fair to say that they were performed in a way similar to that described by Athenaeus for Attic skolia.[104] In fact, our collection of Attic skolia contains many songs that appear to function similarly as hymns in lyric meters. Frs. 884–887 *PMG* are skolia addressed to deities that serve as hymnic poetry. In this group there occurs a song to Demeter and Persephone that approximates a hymn in its language:

> Πλούτου μητέρ' Ὀλυμπίαν ἀείδω
> Δήμητρα στεφανηφόροις ἐν ὥραις,
> σέ τε, παῖ Διός, Φερσεφόνη·
> χαίρετον, εὖ δὲ τάνδ' ἀμφέπετον πόλιν.[105]

["I sing of mother of Wealth, Olympian Demeter, at the time for wearing garlands, and you Persephone, child of Zeus. Farewell, you two. Look after this city well."]

The performer sings (ἀείδω) of divine subjects. Similar language is found at the opening of the Homeric Hymn to Apollo 19 (ὑμνήσω) and in the opening hymn of the *Theognidea* (4: ἀείσω). The skolion also bids farewell to its subjects with χαίρετον, the hymnic closing that allows for transition to another song or topic. This skolion, then, provides an example of a song which employs language that typically opens and closes a hymn and which can be placed certainly in a sympotic context.

From this skolion, it becomes possible to understand how we are to conceive of hymnic verses in a sympotic setting. First, this song offers another example of a sympotic song that reworks traditional features from other types of poetry. More importantly, this skolion provides some evidence for hymnic verses that close with a formula for transition but need not effect a movement into narrative verses. From the four opening hymns of the *Theognidea* and the collection of Attic skolia preserved by Athenaeus, it is clear that such hymnic songs could mark a transition to another hymnic song. We now must consider if it is possible to define further the type of verses that we might expect to follow such as a hymn in a sympotic setting. If so, in what ways does this expectation affect how we might understand what followed the hymnic features in fr. 11 W²?

The opening of the *Theognidea* suggests an answer to this question. The four prooimial hymns are followed by the *sphragis* of Theognis, in which the poet's name appears and marks the verses that follow as part of the larger collection of verses by "Theognis." Putting aside the issues of orality and writing that surround the interpretation of these verses, what concerns us here is the structure of the *sphragis* in relation to the verses that precede and follow it.[106] In particular, the opening hymns of the *Theognidea* are followed by an address to the named individual Cyrnus (19). These are then followed by a self-conscious reference to a poet (21–24) and pronouncements of advice (25–38). From the *Theognidea,* then, it is seen that sympotic hymns could provide an introduction to paraenetic verses, which, to judge from elegists such as Tyrtaeus, Callinus, and Solon, were suitable for sympotic performance.

This pattern is of some interest to the "new Simonides" because fr. 11 W² may have a similar structure as that seen with the *sphragis* of the Theognidea. It is certain that fr. 11 W² begins with a hymn (1–21). The hymn closes with a self-conscious reference to the poet (21: ἐμοί) and possibly a reference to the poetic art (23: ἔντυνο]ν καὶ τόνδ[ε μελ]ίφρονα κ[όσμον ἀο]ιδῆς). Too much of the text is lost to be certain of this last point. Finally, we have references to a named place, Sparta (25), a named individual, Pausanias (34), for certain. The pattern of the *Theognidea,* then, may also appear in fr. 11 W²: a hymn followed by references to names and the poetic art. Taking the parallel to the *Theognidea* further, these references need not occur in a narrative, but may also be found in verses that function in some other way. These verses by Simonides may be non-narrative and they may also be suitable for performance in a symposium.

This coincidence allows the possibility that structurally fr. 11 W² would fit in a sympotic context. The lacunae of fr. 11 W², however, frustrate our ability to find further details for the reconstruction of the verses that follow the hymn. As it stands, fr. 11 W² could contain paraenetic verses after the prooimial hymn as is the case in the *Theognidea;* however, it need not.

Tyrtaeus fr. 12 W² provides another parallel that helps to specify what could follow the hymn in Simonides' fr. 11 W²:

> οὔτ' ἂν μνησαίμην οὔτ' ἐν λόγωι ἄνδρα τιθείην
>     οὔτε ποδῶν ἀρετῆς οὔτε παλαιμοσύνης,
> οὐδ᾽ εἰ Κυκλώπων μὲν ἔχοι μέγεθός τε βίην τε,
>     νικώιη δὲ θέων Θρηΐκιον Βορέην,
> οὐδ᾽ εἰ Τιθωνοῖο φυὴν χαριέστερος εἴη,
>     πλουτοίη δὲ Μίδεω καὶ Κινύρεω μάλιον,
> οὐδ᾽ εἰ Τανταλίδεω Πέλοπος βασιλεύτερος εἴη,
>     γλῶσσαν δ᾽ Ἀδρήστου μειλιχόγηρυν ἔχοι,
> οὐδ᾽ εἰ πᾶσαν ἔχοι δόξαν πλὴν θούριδος ἀλκῆς·

οὐ γὰρ ἀνὴρ ἀγαθὸς γίνεται ἐν πολέμωι
εἰ μὴ τετλαίη μὲν ὁρῶν φόνον αἱματόεντα,
καὶ δηίων ὀρέγοιτ' ἐγγύθεν ἱστάμενος.

["I would not recall nor would I take account of a man neither for his prowess in running nor for his skill as a wrestler, not even if he should have the great size and strength of the Cyclopes, nor should he outstrip Thracian Boreas in running; not even if he should be more desirous in form than Tithonus, nor should he be more wealthy than Midas and Cinyras; not even if he should be more kingly than Pelops, son of Tantalus, nor should he have the soft-voiced tongue of Adrastus; not even if he should have repute in everything except in furious strength. For a man is not good in war, unless seeing bloody slaughter he could endure and standing near he could assail the enemy."]

The phrase Τανταλίδεω Πέλοπος at line 7 also appears at Simonides fr. 11.36 W². The only other archaic occurrence of the phrase is in the *Cypria* (15.4 *PEG*). The phrase in Tyrtaeus is revealing for our approach to the "new Simonides" because it occurs within a list of mythical exempla for attributes which the poet would value little in a man who is not good in war. It will be recalled that fr. 11 W² also has elements of a list. This list may be similar to one found in Tyrtaeus because of an emphasis on mythical figures: the Tyndaridai and Menelaus appear at 30–31; Pelops, son of Tantalus, appears in 36; as we have seen, Pandion is a plausible conjecture for line 41 as well as Kekrops for line 42. The similarities cannot be extended. Nevertheless, Tyrtaeus provides a plausible elegiac parallel for the type of verses that could appear after the hymn in fr. 11 W².

To conclude, the hymnic structure in fr. 11 W² can be paralleled in sympotic verses of Attic skolia and the *Theognidea*. Moreover, these sympotic hymns provide another example of songs for symposia that rework traditional features of other poetry. It is expected from epic and the Homeric hymns that prooimial hymns close with a transition into a narrative section of the poem. The Attic skolia and the *Theognidea* show that in symposia hymns can lead into other non-narrative songs. These sympotic examples provide alternatives for what could follow such hymns in place of narrative. These points do not mean that the poem represented by fr. 11 W² was performed at a symposium. They do, however, reveal a closer affinity between the verses usually divided into the categories of private and public elegy. They also allow that fragments usually associated with sympotic themes may in fact be linked to fr. 11 W². In this way, the line between types of elegy defined by specific context becomes blurred. Moreover, the suggestion of Obbink and others that fr. 11 W² could have been linked in some way with other so-called sympotic fragments of the "new Simonides" becomes more attractive. An understanding of the genre of fr. 11 W² arises that is in line with features exhibited by other elegiac verses.

## D. Lament

Having begun to develop an affinity between fr. 11 W$^2$ and elegiac verses whose context may have been sympotic, I now hope to show that fr. 11 W$^2$ may have further associations with other elegiac verses. My purpose will be to show that fr. 11 W$^2$ represents a poem that not only praises the heroes who defeated the Persians but also may have been a composition that had some features found in poetry of lamentation.[107] I contend that this hypothesis makes the most sense of Simonides' choice of elegiac meter for this poem commemorating the victory over the Persians and fits well with the affinities between fr. 11 W$^2$ and other elegies noted above.

The similarities between fr. 11 W$^2$ and other elegiac verses supposedly performed in sympotic contexts have shown that narrative need not be a defining aspect of the poem. As such, narrative need not be the generic feature that dictates the reconstruction of this poem. In this way, fr. 11 W$^2$ may be said to be more akin to other elegiac verses than has previously been allowed. As has also been seen, this view does not go far in defining generic boundaries within which fr. 11 W$^2$ can be reconstructed. The questions that must be answered now are: How can we use these affinities to define further the genre represented by fr. 11 W$^2$? How do these affinities help to identify a reasonable plan for reconstructing the poem?

Margaret Alexiou's study of ritual lament in the Greek tradition provides a convenient starting point for answering this question. The main goal of Alexiou's study is to identify some level of continuity in Greek laments from the earliest period to modern times. In elucidating this continuity, she proposes a theory that distinguishes the meanings of different terms used by ancient sources to define types of expressions of lamentation:

> While the *thrênos, góos,* and *kómmos* were based on a ritual act or cry of lamentation, preformed by women often to a musical accompaniment, the epigram, *élegos, epitáphios logos,* and *epikédeion* grew out of the social and literary activity of men, developing the elements of commemoration and praise, which had been present in the archaic *thrênos.*[108]

Alexiou observes that types of expressions of lamentation were separated from each other in terms of gender. Lament proper, or an expression of grief closely associated with the mourning by the individual relatives of the deceased, is preformed by females;[109] literary expressions of similar sentiments are linked with elements of praise and commemoration and associated with performances by males.[110]

For the purposes of this study, two conclusions that arise from this categorization are particularly relevant. First, Alexiou observes certain formal and thematic features in both of these categories of lament that are proposed in the quote above. In terms of form, she observes that ritual laments performed by female mourners that are represented in literature have a tripartite structure: the mourner addresses the dead person, the past is remembered or the future envisaged, and the dead person is addressed and lamented again.[111] According to Alexiou, this structural pattern is observable not only in early literary representations of ritual lament, but is also behind the stichomythia found in laments in tragedy as well as in the dialogue form of many early funerary epigrams that function as lamentations in some way.[112] In terms of themes, Alexiou also observes certain patterns in ritual laments; laments often open with initial statements of hesitation;[113] the past is often contrasted with the present;[114] the mourner and the deceased are often contrasted;[115] laments often contain statements of an unfulfilled wish;[116] praise of the deceased, which could also appear as a reproach, was common in laments.[117] To be sure, as Alexiou rightly points out, many of these features are found in both ritual laments and expressions of lamentation associated with male performances. These features may also appear in other types of poetry, such as hymns and encomia.[118] Some link, then, in terms of theme exists between these two categories. This link is seen as a development in genres associated with ancient lament. In the view of K. Derderian, elements that are dominant in female ritual laments, which work in a way that is contrary to the continuation of the memory of the dead, are suppressed by male expressions, such as epic, epigrams, and elegy, which emphasize the continued memory of the deceased.[119] Nevertheless, thematic and formal parallels remain.[120] The point made here is that the emphasis on certain shared formal and thematic features in lament in general allows us to search for these characteristics in other verses that may be concerned with lamentation. In this way, these features, which mark certain literary and popular expressions of grief as laments, become useful for identifying generic features in Greek literature.

The second point derived from Alexiou that is relevant to the present study is the link between mournful content and *élegos* in the expressions of lamentation assigned to "the social and literary activity of men." We have already observed the link between elegy and the mournful content of funerary inscriptions.[121] Alexiou's categorization, however, further develops this link. In particular, Alexiou emphasizes not only the link between elegy and mournful content, but also the link between such verses and commemoration and praise.[122] In particular, the praise and commemoration found in our surviving corpus of elegiac verses were suitable for a male expression of lamentation and can be viewed an extension of mournful expressions that are related to female oriented ritual laments. The lamentation in these expressions has become diminished in the elegy and epigrams that have survived, while commemoration and praise are emphasized.[123]

Following this line of thinking, then, it is possible that early elegiac verses, such as those on the Persian Wars found in the "new Simonides," could retain some features that Alexiou identifies in early expressions of lamentation. In what follows, it will be proposed that this link between elegy and lament is most useful for defining the generic boundaries of Simonides' verses on the Persian Wars. It will be observed that by accepting this link, specific elements in these verses associated with the Persian Wars can be shown to be in line with elements that Alexiou finds to be characteristic of Greek laments. By emphasizing this link, an attempt will be made to define more clearly how Simonides' verses fit into the generic boundaries of elegy.

The link between elegy and epigrams on the Persian Wars has been noted above. In particular, it has been observed that fr. 11 W$^2$ and epigrams commemorating the Persian War are similar in scope and perspective.[124] Both can be understood as presenting a panhellenic perspective in terms of content. This link, however, extends beyond content to the function of such elegiac verses. In this way, this link can be used to further define how the poem represented by fr. 11 W$^2$ fits into the poetic category of elegy. The epigrams on the Persian Wars perform the dual function of commemoration and praise. They stand as funerary commemorations of the dead either on tombs, cenotaphs or memorials. They also, by their very nature, serve as praise for these men.[125] This function is exemplified in the Megarian inscription for those who died in the Persian Wars.[126] The inscription commemorates those who died, notes their accomplishments and draws attention to its praise of the dead by noting that the memorial is a gift of honor (γέρας).[127] The same features are observable in epigrams associated with Plataea.[128] These epigrams commemorate the dead and, in doing so, praise those who "hastened to bestow freedom on Greece" and "bring renown (κλέος) to their fatherland." The inscriptions, then, can be understood to achieve the function set out by Alexiou for the category of epigram that she links with expressions of lamentation; namely, they praise and commemorate. Yet, there is no clear indication of lamentation in these verses, a point which Alexiou would explain by noting that praise and commemoration of the dead in this way are extensions of themes that were suitable to mournful expressions of lamentation.[129] Evidence for such expressions of lamentation has been seen in early funerary epigrams with their anonymous first person addresses and expressions of grief.[130]

The inscriptions and epigrams for those who fell in the Persian Wars seem to meet the criteria set out by Alexiou for literature linked with expressions of lamentation. Her categorization of elegy and epigram as included in literature of lamentation that emphasizes praise and commemoration receives some support from this evidence. Yet, another question arises: Is there any evidence of this function of praise and commemoration linked with lamentation in non-inscriptional or non-epigrammatic elegy? I suggest that the fragments of the "new Simonides" provide this evidence. It can be said that the function of fr. 11 W$^2$, which belongs to a poem concerned with the victory over the Persians, is both to commemorate and to praise those who made this victory possible. This function becomes clear in the relationship that these verses establish between themselves and Homeric poetry. In lines 13–17, the words ἀοίδιμον, κλέος, and ἐπώνυμον ὁπ[λοτέρ]οισιν[131] bring to mind what the heroes of the Homeric poetry gain from their place in this tradition. The word ἀθάνατο⟨ν⟩ at 11.28 W² refers not to Homer's subject but to Simonides' own. The appearance of this word makes it a reasonable conclusion that fr. 11 W² is concerned with functioning in a way similar to Homeric poetry. As Homer's verses bestow renown and fame on the heroes of the Trojan War through their function as praise and commemoration of their actions, so will Simonides' poetry have a similar function for the victors in the Persian Wars.[132] So, we have an example of non-inscriptional elegiac verses that function as praise and commemoration in a way similar that is similar to the function epigrams on the Persian Wars.

While the poem represented by fr. 11 W² both praises and commemorates the victors over the Persians, the fragment offers no clues that it lamented those who died defending Greece. It would be a fair assumption, however, that the dead are also praised along with living figures, such as Pausanias, in the poem represented by the fragment.[133] There is, then, some justification for searching for features of laments in the "new Simonides." The identification of the performance context of this poem as the funeral or burial of those who died at Plataea (Hdt. 9.85) would lend support to the hypothesis that these verses are to be seen as poetry of lamentation in some way. Unfortunately, the performance context of these verses is unknown.[134] Our ignorance concerning the performance context of these verses forces us to look for formal and thematic features of lament in these verses. Since the fragmentary nature of the verses of fr. 11 W² does not provide these features, it is necessary to look outside this fragment for such clues.

Simonides' reputation as a mournful poet is well documented in the ancient *testimonia*.[135] To be sure, this reputation would seem to have been earned from his *threnoi*, or laments that are in lyric meters.[136] Our fragments of Simonides' *threnoi*, scanty as they are, reveal a gnomic character with reflections on topics such as the shortness of life or death as an inevitable consequence of life.[137] Yet, such reflections are not limited to Simonides' lyric *threnoi*, as the "new Simonides" clearly shows. Simonides' lyric *threnoi*, then, may not provide the sole basis for this reputation. His elegiac verses may have also contributed to this appraisal of his poetry.[138]

In particular, frs. 19 and 20 W² offer content that is similar to that found in the *threnoi* of Simonides. The text of these fragments largely comes from Stobaeus, who quotes fr.19 W² and lines 5–12 of fr. 20 W². Stobaeus quotes these verses as consecutive lines from a single poem. The new papyrus, however, reveals that this view is incorrect. The new fragments, which overlap the concluding lines of Stobaeus' quotation (fr. 20.5–12), also provides bits of the four preceding lines, which do not overlap the opening lines offered by Stobaeus (fr. 19 W²). The new papyrus, then, shows that Stobaeus' quotation was in fact not a consecutive unit.[139] Yet, even with this difficulty in mind, these fragments help to identify gnomic sentiments akin to the poetic expression of lamentation found in Simonides' *threnoi*.

Fr. 19 W², after quoting Homer's simile on the generation of leaves, comments that few men hear these words and have hope for the future:

ἓν δὲ τὸ κάλλιστον Χῖος ἔειπεν ἀνήρ·
"οἵη περ φύλλων γενεή, τοίη δὲ καὶ ἀνδρῶν"
παῦροί μιν θνητῶν οὔασι δεξάμενοι
στέρνοις ἐγκατέθεντο· πάρεστι γὰρ ἐλπὶς ἑκάστωι
ἀνδρῶν, ἥ τε νέων στήθεσιν ἐμφύεται.

["The man from Chios said one best thing: "As is the generation of leaves, so is the generation of men." Few men hearing this, place it in their heart. For each man has hope which flourishes in the heart of the young."]

Likewise, fr. 20 W² contains reflections on the inability of humans to realize the shortness of life and their tendency to have hope in the future:

```
              ]ε̣ι̣θο[
                 ]ν̣τ[ . . . ] . [
              τυτ]θὸν ἐπὶ χρό[νον
    . . . . . .]ρλ[ . . . . . ]ω παρμενο̣[
5   θνητῶ̣ν δ' ὄ̣φρα τις̣ ἄνθος ἔχει̣ πολυήρατον ἥβης,
    κοῦφο̣ν ἔχω̣ι̣ν θυμ̣ὸν πόλλ' ἀτέλεσ̣ιτα νοεῖ·
    οὔ̣τε γὰρ ἐλπ̣ίδ' ἔχ̣ει γηρασέμεν ̣οὔτε θανεῖσθαι,
    οὐδ', ὑ̣γιὴς ὅτα̣ν ἦι, φ̣ροντίδ' ἔχει κ̣αμάτου.
    νή̣π̣ιοι, οἷς ταύ̣τηι̣ κεῖται νόος, ο̣ὐδὲ ἴσασιν
10  ὡς χρό̣νος ἔ̣σθ' ἥβη̣ς καὶ βιότοι' ὀλίγος
    θνη̣τοῖς. ἀλλὰ ̣σὺ̣ ταῦτα μαθὼν ̣βιότου ποτὶ τέρμα
    ψυχῆι τῶ̣ν̣ ἀγαθῶν τλῆθι χα̣ριζόμενος.
    . . . . . . . .(ω) ]φράζεο δὲ παλα[ιοτέρου λόγον ἀνδρός·
    ἢ λήθην] γλώσσης ἔκφυγ' Ὅμηρ[ος
15  κοὔ μιν] παν̣δαμά[τωρ αἱρεῖ χρόνος
    . . . . . .(ω) ]ω ψυδρῆις ε[
    . . . . . .(ω) ] ἐν θαλίηισι[
    . . .]ι̣ ἐϋστρέπτων [
    . . . . ]ων, ἔνθα καὶ [
    .        ] . . [
```

["As long as some mortal has the lovely bloom of youth, he plans many unful-filled things having a light heart. For he does not have the expectation that he will grow old nor that he will die. Nor when he is healthy does he have a care for sickness. Fools are they whose mind is in such a state. Nor do they know that the time of youth and life is short for mortals. But you, learning these things, endure to the end of life while enjoying the good things in your soul."][140]

Both fragments, then, contain expressions of the shortness of human life as well as the inability of human's to grasp this reality. Significantly, these expressions come not in lyric *threnoi*, but in elegiac verses.

Of course, the sentiments on the shortness of life and the belief in the inescapable fate of man in frs. 19 and 20 W² are also found in other elegiac poetry that is not linked with lament. For example, Mimnermus fr. 2 W² refers to the same Homeric simile of generations that is found in Simonides fr. 19 W². Yet, the point to emphasize here is that these sentiments found in frs. 19 and 20 W² can be compared with the *threnoi* proper of Simonides:

ἄνθρωπος ἐὼν μή ποτε φάσῃς ὅ τι γίνεται αὔριον,
μηδ' ἄνδρα ἰδὼν ὄλβιον ὅσσον χρόνον ἔσσεται·
ὠκεῖα γὰρ οὐδὲ τανυπτερύγου μυίας
οὕτως ἁ μετάστασις.

(521 *PMG*)

["Since you are a man, do not ever think what will happen tomorrow, nor, when you see a fortunate man, think how long he will be so. For not even is the death of a long-winged fly so swift."]

Again, the emphasis is on the shortness of life. The content of frs. 19 and 20 W², then, mirrors verses assigned to Simonides' threnodic poems in terms of content. It is possible that they also had a similar function, namely to be expressions of lamentation in some way.

While frs. 19 and 20 W² appear to have threnodic features, there is a more probable link to early elegiac poetry of lamentation in frs. 21 and 22 W². The text of both fragments is difficult; as they are printed by West and Sider, the fragments are the result of reasonable connections between various papyrus scraps made either by Lobel (fr. 21 W²) or Parsons (fr. 22 W²).[141] It must be kept in mind, however, that the joins which allow the creation of these fragments are often a result of the sense that is created rather than the product of physical links. Nevertheless, keeping in mind the textual difficulties and the general problems of interpretation, these fragments contain features that are consistent with the tone and form of poetry of lamentation.

Fr. 21 W² is generally interpreted as a depiction of sexual desire at a symposium, an interpretation that largely arises from the assignment of these verses to a category of sympotic elegy.[142] This interpretation, however, can be modified by observing that the fragmentary details in the lacunose text of this fragment are reminiscent of expression of lamentation as characterized by Alexiou:

]οὐδ' ὑπερ[
]..[....]μενος.
ο]ὐ δύναμαι, ψυχ[ή,] πεφυλαγμένος ε[ἶ]ναι ὁπηδός·
χρυσῶπιν δὲ Δίκ[ην ἄζ]ομαι ἀχνύμενος,
5    ἐ]ξ οὗ τὰ πρώτιστα νεο[τρεφέ]ων ἀπὸ μηρῶ[ν
ἡ]μετέρης εἶδον τέρμ[ατα πα]ιδεΐης,
κ]υά[ν]εον δ' ἐλεφαντίνεόν [τ' ἀνεμί]σγετο φέ[γγος,

. . . . . ] δ' ἐκ νιφάδων [ . . . . . . . . ., (.,) ἰ]δεῖν.
ἀλλ' αἰδ]ῶς ἤρυκε, νέου δ . [ . .] . ι [        ] ὕβριν
            ] ἐπέβη[                              ]νοι·
                                                 ]οφύλλοις
                    ← ? ἀκροπόλοις]
                                                 ]ι η ι

["I am not able, soul, to be a cautious attendant; but I [worship?] grieving Justice,
shining like gold from the moment when first from [newly-reared?] thighs I saw
the end of my [youth], when a [black] and a white [luster] were [mixed] . . . from
. . . snows . . . to see . . . [But shame] hindered, of youth . . . violence . . . [came
upon] . . . [with leaves?] . . . [on citadels]. . . ."][143]

In the first bit of intelligible text (3), a speaker in the first person admits the inability
to be an attendant. In the next line (4), another possible first person address (]ομαι)
occurs and is accompanied by the participle ἀχνύμενος ("grieving"). Finally, another
possible first person (εἶδον) appears in the next line (6). The repeated use of the first
person perspective is prominent in the fragment. This perspective is linked with the
expression of lamentation in the participle ἀχνύμενος ("grieving"). Moreover, the
object of these first person addresses is presumably the speaker's soul, which appears
in the vocative in line 3.[144] These features in this fragment are consistent with characteristics observed in Greek laments. The emphasis on the inability to do something
is reminiscent of fr. 19 W² and Simon. fr. 521 *PMG*, where the speaker also points
to human powerlessness to control the future. The gnomic expression of human inability and the first person perspective in a context of grieving also are suggestive of
characteristics identified by Alexiou in Greek lamentation.[145] Furthermore, the first
person speaker and the emphasis on grieving recall the funerary inscriptions discussed
above.[146] If the presence of the vocative ψυχ[ή,] is accepted, another characteristic of
expressions of lamentation arises. By looking at the laments for Hector in the *Iliad*,
Alexiou observes that such laments tend to have a tripartite structure, the first and
third parts of which are a direct address to the deceased.[147] The fragmentary state of
the papyrus prevents us from identifying such a structure in these verses. It is possible,
however, that this address comes from one such part of a lament. Even if this point
cannot be pressed too hard, the vocative ψυχ[ή,] does introduce a dichotomy between
first and second person perspectives. One possibility is that the second person perspective contrasts a mourner and someone, who is deceased or something which is lost.[148]
Again, the participle ἀχνύμενος supports a mournful context for this dichotomy.
The fragment also appears to be contrasting the past with the present of the speaker. In
line 5, the reading ἐ]ξ οὗ πρώτιστα ("from the moment when") suggests that a past
time is indicated, but the reading is not certain.[149] The aorist εἶδον (6) may also imply
a past time, but again need not do so. In line 8, however, the reference to youth and
hubris (νέου . . . ὕβριν) more solidly supports this contrast. As Alexiou has observed,

laments not only contrast a first person with a second person one, but they also can contrast a present time with a past one.[150] The contrast in Simonides' verses seems to be between some present time marked by grieving and a previous time marked by youth and hubris. These observations taken together make it possible to conclude that the fragment is concerned with the past, youth and some present condition, the inability to do something and grieving. While the various supplements in these verses result in different interpretations, there are features in this fragment that are consistent with ancient laments. In this way, these verses can be construed as being poetry of lamentation or at least having features consistent with expressions of lamentation.

A similar understanding of fr. 22 W² in terms of ancient expressions of lamentation is possible:

        ].οιο θαλάσσης
        ]ρουσα πόρον·
        ]μενος ἔνθα περανα[
        ]
5        ]οιμι κελευθο[
        ]ν κόσμ[ο]ν ἰοσ[τ]εφάνων
        ] ἕδος πολύδενδρον ἱκο[ίμην
        εσ[....] εὐαέα νῆσον, ἄγαλμα β[ίου·
        κα[ί κεν] Ἐχεκ[ρατί]δην ξανθότρ[ιχα
10       ὀφ[θαλμοῖσιν ἰδ]ὼν χεῖρα λάβοιμ[ι
        ὄφρα νέο[ν] χ[αρίε]ντος ἀπὸ χροὸς ἄν[θος
        λείβοι δ' ἐκ βλ[εφάρ]ων ἱμερόεντα [πόθον.
        καί κεν ἐγ[ὼ μετὰ πα]ιδὸς ἐν ἄνθε[σιν ἁβρὰ πάθοιμι
        κεκλιμένος, λευκὰς φαρκίδας ἐκτ[ὸς ἐλῶν
15       χαίτη[ισι]ν χαρίε[ντ]α νεοβλάστ[
        .[   ] εὐανθέα πλε[ξάμενος στέφανον·
        μο[....] δ' ἱμερόντα λιγὺν  .[
        ἀρτι[επέα] νωμῶν γλῶσσαν ἀ[πὸ στόματος
        [                ]
20       τῶνδε .[
        εὔπομπ [

["... of sea... passage... there... [journey]... arrangement of violet-crowned ... [I would come to] the thickly-wooded abode... fresh island, image [of life] ... [and]... fair-haired Eche[crati]das... [seeing with eyes]... I would take the hand... so that youthful [bloom] from [delightful] skin, while he would shed from [eyes] lovely [desire]... and I [with a youth]... in [flowers] [would enjoy a favorite slave]... reclining,... white wrinkles... [free from... taking], for hair a delightful... [weaving]... [spouting afresh ?] flowery [crown]... desirous... clear... plying a [ready of speech] tongue [from my mouth]...."]

Despite the difficulties in the lacunose texts, it is generally agreed that certain details appear in these verses. It is understood that these verses depict a journey to an island

(1–8), a meeting (9–10), an erotic interaction (?) that involves rejuvenation at a symposium (11–15), and a description of a symposium (15–21). A similar agreement has not yet been reached concerning the overall interpretation of these details. The views of Sarah Mace and Dimitrios Yatromanolakis show two poles of the debate.[151] For Mace, the fragment represents a homoerotic encomium which fuses elements traditionally associated with utopian and erotic poetry.[152] In contrast, Yatromanolakis understands the fragment as a lament composed by Simonides and sung by Dyseris for her son Antiochus.[153] The choice between these interpretations is not easy because there is simply not much text that survives. It is not entirely certain, however, that both of these interpretations exclude each other. Elements that Mace identifies as utopian, such as a wish to escape from something and the descriptions of a journey and a destination, would also be suitable in an expression of lamentation as it is characterized by Alexiou.[154] In this way, the differences in these two interpretations is reduced to specific details of who the speaker and addressee are and what is envisaged as the context for the performance of these verses. In general, however, the verses can be said to have elements that would allow them to be classified as a lament or at least grouped with other verses that have features that are consistent with laments.

As in fr. 21 W$^2$, this fragment has a first person perspective: ]οιμι appears in line 5; Parsons suggests ἱκο[ίμην in line 7;[155] he also reconstructs λάβοιμ[ι in line 10.[156] Although the final two examples are uncertain, the letters ]οιμι in line 5 inform us that this fragment has a first person perspective. Further support for the first person perspective might be gained by the reading of ε . [ in line 13. Lobel originally printed ἐπ[;[157] Parsons in reediting the fragment suggests ἐγ[ω;[158] Yatromanolakis, however, returns to Lobel's reading and suggests ἔπ[ειτα as a possibility.[159] Inspection of the papyrus reveals no easy solution; both readings are possible. More importantly, however, both readings are of interest because each creates features that have been seen in expressions of lamentation. On the one hand, Parson's reading would continue an emphasis on the first person. As has been noted, a first person perspective can be associated with lament especially in the contrast between a first person and second person perspective. A second person perspective may be found in line 9, where the name Echecratidas is a possible reading, a point which will be discussed in more detail later. On the other hand, Lobel's reading, if Yatromanolakis' supplement is correct, would provide a temporal reference. It has also been shown that such temporal references in contrasting a present and a past time are characteristic of ancient laments. Both suggestions, then, provide a feature that has been shown to be indicative of the content of laments.

The verbal forms ]οιμι (5) and λάβοι . [ (10) are also interesting because they represent optative forms.[160] Also, with the problems in the letters following the *epsilon* aside, line 13 reads καίκεν ε . [ . These letters imply that the optatives are to be read either as potential or conditional.[161] Yatromanolakis has suggested two possibilities for interpreting these optatives.[162] First, he suggests that ]οιμι (5) introduces a rhetorical question and allows that the other optatives are potential. These potential optatives then express wishes after a lost interrogative πῶς or τίς.[163] As Yatromanolakis observes, such questions would be suitable in a lament as a way of introducing some initial hesitation.[164] If the some of these optatives are taken as potential in the context of a wish, another element of lament is present.[165] Second, Yatromanolakis observes that the optatives may be part of a "future less vivid" conditional clause and, therefore, not wishful, but descriptive of a potential future. The poem might express a thought such as "If I should go, I would. . . ." The following lines would describe or narrate the journey. It is implicitly along this line of thinking that Mace understands these verses. She reads the speaker of the poem as expressing a wish for an escape through a journey to another place. More particularly, the wish, then, is for an escape from old age through a rejuvenation of youth. Simonides' verses describe a journey to a place where such a wish and the activities that come along with this rejuvenation are possible.[166] Yet, this suggestion could also be read as introducing into Simonides' verses a feature found in expressions of lamentation. A parallel may be found in Andromache's lament for Hector at *Iliad* 24.725–45. Alexiou suggests that these laments show a tripartite structure, containing an address to and a reproach of the dead, a narrative, and a renewed address and reproach.[167] In Andromache's lament, the narrative concerns the future of Hector's son.[168] It is possible that Simonides' verses contain a similar narrative concerned with a potential future. Again, the choice between these interpretations is not easy. The point to be emphasized here, however, is that one allows the verses to be read explicitly as a lament and the other allows the verses to have features that would also be suitable for a lament. Both interpretations allow for some connection to expressions of lamentation in fr. 22 W².

Some tentative conclusions can now be drawn about how to account for the features that are suitable for lament in frs. 21–22W². It is perhaps significant that the scraps that are reconstructed to provide frs. 21 and 22 W² represent two adjacent columns on the same papyrus; fr. 21 W² consists of POxy 2327 fr. 1 + fr. 2(a) col. i; fr. 22 W² consists of POxy 2327 fr. 3 and 4 + 2(a) col. ii, as well as POxy 3965 fr. 27. So POxy 2327 fr. 2 provides part of each fragment. Parsons argues for some connection between the fragments;[169] West places the verses in two separate poems;[170] Hunter, in an early article, Mace, and Yatromanolakis treat fr. 22 W² as a separate poem.[171] In a later article, Hunter identifies the common theme of aging and immortality in Simonides' frs. 19–22 W² and assumes some internal connection between the fragments. He does not, however, go so far as to claim these fragments belong to the same poem.[172] From the state of our evidence, it is impossible to determine on any grounds other than sense if these fragments belong to one poem or two. A safer conclusion, however, would be to suggest that these fragments contain verses with similar features. The usual assumption is that these verses share the distinction of representing the category of "sympotic elegy." Yet, as was discussed above, the context of symposia may not have been a valid way of defining particular elegies as distinct from others.[173] Even if such a categorization is accepted, however, it can be noted that both sets of verses contain elements that are suitable to laments. Following this line of thinking, if frs. 21 and 22 W² were not from the same poem, they can be said to represent a papyrus that grouped similar fragments together. Part of the classification system would seem to be defined by elegies with elements of laments. Further support for this understanding of how these papyrus scraps relate to each other is gained from frs. 19–20 W², which also have been shown to have some features suitable for lament.[174]

If it is correct to identify aspects of lament in frs. 19–22 W² and to view these aspects as providing the common feature that linked these verses on papyrus represented by the "new Simonides," the presence of fr. 11 W² on the same papyrus may be informative about how it fits with these other elegiac poems. The emphasis on praise and commemoration in fr. 11 W² has been noted. It has also been observed that Alexiou shows that praise and commemoration also would have been suitable in expressions of lamentation such as epigrams and *élegos*. Furthermore, it has been shown that fr. 11 W² has similarities to commemorative epigrams on the Persian Wars.[175] Yet, it is still unclear whether fr. 11 W² represents a poem that not only praised the Greek victors but in doing so may also have lamented those who died in the effort.[176]

There is certainly an emphasis on a first person perspective in fr. 11.20–21 W². This emphasis, however, is clearly associated with the prooimial hymn and it is best not to construe these as features of a lament.[177] It is also tempting to read ειδομεν[ at fr. 11.44 W² as a first person verb, but there is too little text to determine the sense. The contrast between first person perspective and those being mourned seen in ritual lament simply cannot be observed with certainty in fr. 11 W².

A possible link in terms of content between the so-called "sympotic fragments" provides some basis for understanding a relation between the poems represented by these fragments. It has been observed by Rutherford, Obbink and Sider that some or all of the "sympotic fragments" may belong to the same poem that is represented by fr. 11 W².[178] In the arguments of these scholars, the potential link exists in terms of content. The references to mortality and immortality as well as to the poetic tradition in both fr. 11 W² and the sympotic verses create a basis for seeing some relation between these fragments. A more solid link between these fragments, however, may be present.

As has been noted, D. Yatromanolakis argues that fr. 22 W² represents a lament sung by Dyseris, mother of Antiochus and wife of Echecratidas, a member of the Scopad family who ruled Thessaly.[179] The scholiast to Theocritus *Idyll* 16.36 and 44 tells us that Simonides composed at least one dirge for this family;[180] Aelius Aristides seems to imply that a dirge by Simonides was sung by Dyseris for her son

Antiochus.[181] The evidence, however, for understanding fr. 22 $W^2$ as this threnody is not above debate. The primary link exists in the possible appearance of the name Echecratidas in fr. 22 $W^2$. West prints κα[ίκεν] 'Εχεκ[ρατί]δην ξανθότρ[ιχα at fr. 22.9 $W^2$. Parsons originally speculated that Echecratidas may be read in the line, although the reading does not make it into any of his reconstructions of the text.[182] Two difficulties with this reading arise. First, it must be noted that about half of the letters that provide this name are supplements. The general acceptance of this supplement as well as the paucity of suitable alternatives does not make this observation an insurmountable problem. Yet, caution is still necessary. Second, by accepting the reading of Echecratidas in these verses, we must ask, who is the specific addressee of these verses? Most of the difficulty arises from our lack of knowledge concerning the Thessalian ruling families of this period.[183] Two figures with this name are known to us. The first Echecratidas was the father of Antiochus and the patron of Simonides. This is the Echecratidas mentioned by the Scholiast to Theocritus *Idyll* 16.36 and 44.[184] The second Echecratidas is mentioned by Thucydides as the father of an Orestes who was banished from Thessaly c. 457 BCE in a failed attempt to restore himself to the Thessalian throne.[185] In his historical study of Simonides, Molyneux notes that the second Echecratidas could be the son of Antiochus, who was the son of the first Echecratidas.[186] Yatromanolakis proposes that these verses of lamentation are addressed either to Echecratidas, the husband of Dyseris, or to Antiochus, the son of Dyseris. In the latter option, the form Echecratidas would be a reference to the dead Echecratidas himself in a lament for Antiochus.[187] S. Mace interprets the fragment as an erotic encomium for a third hypothetical Echecratidas, who would be the son of Antiochus and the grandson of Simonides' patron.[188] The choice between these options is not easy. The decision depends largely on the overall interpretation of the fragment as either a lament or a utopian fantasy as well as the uncertain chronology of these figures. In his review of the volume edited by Boedeker and Sider, G. Huxley removes the difficulty by suggesting that the Echecratidas of fr. 22$W^2$ is the father of Orestes and he is imagined as a youth in these verses.[189] Still, the point remains that the fragmentary nature of this fragment does not allow us to know with certainty which Echecratidas is mentioned or if this Echecratidas was the subject of the verses or was mentioned simply in reference to one of his relations, either Antiochus or a later Echecratidas.

Nevertheless, it can be assumed that some Echecratidas appeared in these verses. It is the appearance of this name that allows for a tentative connection between frs. 22 $W^2$ and the so-called "Plataea poem." Huxley has suggested that the letters ]χεκ[ in fr. 14.16 $W^2$ allows this fragment to be linked with fr. 22 $W^2$, where the name Echecratidas appears. In this way, he proposes that fr. 22 $W^2$ belongs to the same poem as fr. 14 $W^2$. More specifically, he suggests that these fragments belong in the so-called "Plataea poem" which is best represented by fr. 11 $W^2$. As a tentative hypothesis, he suggests that this poem had a Thessalian performance context, that the Echecratidas mentioned was the father of Orestes mentioned in Thucydides 1.111.1, and that the poem's goal was to "assist a Spartan rapprochement of the Thessalian dynasts" for their medizing in the Persian Wars.[190] This link is engaging, but it does not get us any closer to identifying elements of lament in the poem represented by fr. 11 W². The letters in fr. 14.16 W² may in fact connect this fragment to fr. 22 W², but the link to fr. 11 W² remains speculative. While Huxley's suggestion would nicely provide a link between verses in the "new Simonides" that have been shown to have features of lament and the verses on the Persian Wars, the evidence for this connection remains tenuous.

The potential link between frs. 14 and 22 W², however, does suggest that other fragments in the "new Simonides" may contain elements associated with lament. Fr. 10 W² is generally believed to provide a direct address to Achilles.[191] It has been seen that this fragment is linked with fr. 11 W² but its position in this relation is unclear. The address may have come close to fr. 11 W² in the lost composition or it may have come elsewhere in the poem, thereby representing a return to the hero. More to the point, however, is the fact that fr. 11 W² potentially contains a narrative of Achilles' death and fr. 10 W² can also be read as pertaining to Achilles. By construing fr. 10 W² as an address to Achilles that comes either before or after the verses on the hero's death, these verses can be understood to parallel the introductory or closing addresses that are found in the three laments for Hector in *Iliad* 24.[192] In each of these laments, Hector is placed in relation to other relatives, either his wife and son, or his other siblings. A similar comparison may be present in fr. 10.2 W²: ]ρ προπάτω[ρ. Achilles may be addressed here through some comparison with his ancestors.[193] The address in fr. 10 W², then, may provide a link to lament in two ways. It may introduce an address and it may draw a contrast between past and present. Both aspects were seen in frs. 19–20 W² of the "new Simonides" and were identified as features characteristic of laments. In this way, the hymn to Achilles may also represent a lament of the hero that draws on epic and hymnic features.

The contrast between past and present may also be present at the list at the end of fr. 11 W² and in the references to Δώρου and παισὶ καὶ Ἡρακλέος in fr. 13.9–10 W². In these verses, the use of references places and people in terms of myth draws a comparison between those who fought in the Persian Wars and earlier mythical figures. Such an emphasis is certainly present in fr. 15 W², where the Corinthians are mentioned in reference to their ancestry. But such references are not unique to lament, as we have seen, in the elegiac exhortations of Tyrtaeus.

More solid evidence, perhaps, can be found in fr. 14 W². At fr. 14.3 W², West prints, λ]έγω ποταμοῦ λα[. In this way, he creates a moment within a narrative of the battle of Plataea.[194] An alternative reading given by Parsons is: ]εγω ποτ' άμους.[195] Parsons' reading would allow the fragments to contain both a first person perspective as well as a temporal reference which may draw a contrast with a past time. This reading would work in a narrative, but it also would fit a context of mourning, in which the past is contrasted with the present.[196] The choice for a context of mourning gains further support from the reading that provides the verb ἐλάσει in fr. 14.7 W². Parsons' endorsement of this reading is cautious, and inspection of images of the papyrus shows that ἐλάσαι would work just as well for the traces.[197] This second form can be read either as an infinitive, an optative, or a future. If the form is optative, it could be read as a wish and so would provide another feature characteristic of a lament. Furthermore, if Huxley's link between this fragment and fr. 22 W² is accepted, this reading of lamentation in these verses would be supported.[198]

One final feature found in fr. 17 W² need only be mentioned briefly because little sense can be made of the 24 line-openings in this fragment. There does appear, however, to be some repetitions in these verses: φη δε δυ[ in line 3 and φηδε[ in line 21; κάι μ[ in line 8 and ϙαι μ[ in line 9. These verses have been interpreted by Rutherford as representing direct speech. Rutherford points to a parallel in Simon. LXXIV *FGE*, which begins φῆ ποτε.[199] The epigram acts as a narrative, providing the final words of someone. The relation between the sense of the epigram and fr. 17 W² remains obscure. It is sufficient to note, however, that repeated phrases and refrains were features of archaic laments.[200] The letter κάι μ[ in line 8 and ϙαι μ[ in line 9 also may introduce a first person perspective. So, even if Rutherford is correct to read direct speech here, it is still possible that these words belong to verses that are in some way an expression of a lamentation.

To conclude, it is difficult to find with certainty that the fr. 11 W² and the fragments associated with it represent a poem that could be called a lament. What has emerged, though, is that features that have been construed as historical or narrative, such as the presence of first person addresses, can be interpreted as features of a lament. This observation combined with the emphasis on praise and commemoration expected from a poem concerned with the Greek victory over the Persians allows for the possibility that fr. 11 W² represents verses that can be placed in the continuum established by Alexiou between ritual lament and later *elegos*. With this possibility in mind two conclusions can be considered.

First, it becomes possible that fr. 11 W² and the other fragments assigned to battles in the Persian Wars could be joined in the same poem with fragments currently designated as being sympotic in theme and context. This suggestion is also offered by Rutherford, Sider and Obbink in their individual appraisals of the "new Simonides." Here, however, it has been suggested that the poem that is to be reconstructed is the result of combining fragments that have features of laments or a potential function as a lament.

Second, it is possible that fr. 11 W² and the other fragments assigned to battles in the Persian Wars are not part of the same poem as the fragments designated as having sympotic themes; however, these fragments from the same papyrus are in fact grouped together because of a common element. The common element would not only be the meter of these verses or similar performance contexts. Rather, these verses would share a common feature in their relation to expressions of lamentation that were suitable to elegy. It has been noted that frs. 21–22 $W^2$ were close to each other on the lost scroll that provides the "new Simonides." POxy 2327 fr. 1 + 2(a) col. i (= fr. 19 $W^2$) form one column. POxy 2327 fr. 3 (=fr. 22.1–7 $W^2$) is the column bottom of this fragment. POxy 2327 fr. 2(a) col. ii + fr. 4 (=fr. 22.9–19 $W^2$) are in the adjacent column.[201] POxy 2327 fr. 4 is the top of this column. Lobel suggested, but recanted the idea, that POxy 2327 fr. 5 (= fr. 11.1–4 $W^2$) was the bottom of this column.[202] West has suggested that POxy 2327 fr. 5 (column bottom) preceded POxy 2327 fr. 6 (column top = fr. 11.5–13 $W^2$). As Parsons points out, the verses of fr. 11 $W^2$ may come soon after those of fr. 22 $W^2$ on POxy 2327.[203] The details of this relation cannot be pushed too far. Nevertheless, the possibility of this relation serves to show that the battle poems and the sympotic poems may have been closely associated in the lost scroll. Fr. 11 $W^2$ can be said to have been grouped in some way with other verses that had features of poetry of lamentation. If the sole principle of classification for this papyrus was not simply the metrical attributes or performance context of these verses, it might be concluded that fr. 11 $W^2$ was considered to be akin to the other verses on the papyrus as some sort of expression of lamentation.

Both conclusions are equally plausible. The point to emphasize, however, is that both allow the genre of fr. 11 $W^2$ to be defined in relation to other elegiac verses and, in particular, to other verses from the same papyrus.

## 3.5 GENERAL CONCLUSION

In terms of genre, it has been shown that the verses on the Persian Wars have much in common with other elegiac verses assigned to a sympotic context. I hope to have shown that the "new Simonides" represents verses on the Persian Wars that function in ways similar to other elegiac verses and that historical narrative should not be used as a primary guideline for reconstructing these verses. Other possible models for reconstruction have been located within limits of elegy. In particular, features of lamentation have been identified throughout the fragments of the "new Simonides" and it has been suggested that these features should be emphasized when defining the genre of the verses on the Persian Wars.

Antonio Aloni has suggested that the "new Simonidean elegy dedicated to the battle of Plataea seems to show that historical narrative elegy and threnody were not mutually exclusive. The historical narrative was used for largely threnodic purposes to mourn the dead of the battle and to glorify their memory."[204] I agree with Aloni's link between lament and the "new Simonides." I, however, put less emphasis on the inclusion of a historical narrative in these verses. Rather, like other elegy, the fragments on the Persian Wars may contain narrative moments, but it is some other generic feature that defines these verses as elegiac.

What fr. 11 $W^2$ offers us, then, is a glimpse not into narrative elegy, but a clue about how Simonides commemorated the victory over the Persians with elegy. In comparison with epigrams on the Persian Wars and other elegies that have similar features as fr. 11 $W^2$, it would seem that Simonides praised the victors over the Persians while at the same time he memorialized the dead. In doing so, he used elegy and appears to have exploited the genre for all it could do. Like Homeric poetry, he provides renown through praise and commemoration of heroes who have fought well. Like elegiac poetry, he reworked his Homeric model and provided renown for the dead through praise and commemoration that are the natural results of lamentation. It is perhaps because elegy could function in this way that it was chosen as the meter for this poem, which appears to be an anomaly in what has survived for us of Greek elegy.

# Toward a Conclusion

The preceding discussion has questioned the current arrangement and interpretation of the papyrus fragments going under the name the "new Simonides." The particular focus has been on the fragments that are presumed to belong to compositions pertaining to the Persian Wars. The premise underlying this study has been that our incomplete knowledge of Simonides' verses on the Persian Wars makes it difficult to assign any of the new fragments to a particular elegy concerned with battles in these wars. It has also been assumed that the appearance of verses presumably belonging to a hitherto unknown poem on the battle of Plataea highlights and increases this difficulty. With these assumptions in mind, I have aimed to show that the current orthodoxy concerning the arrangement of the new fragments into separate elegies on battles in the Persian Wars, one on Artemisium, one on Salamis and one on Plataea, must be reevaluated. Since our overall ignorance about Simonides' poetic works extends beyond his verses on the Persian War, I have suggested that this need for a reevaluation forces us to rethink many of the details that are believed to be present in all of these new fragments. It must be admitted that we know very little about any of the works by Simonides that have survived in a fragmentary state or have slipped through the cracks of transmission; therefore, the current views on the so-called "sympotic fragments" in the "new Simonides" have also been scrutinized. The conclusion that has arisen is the current assignment of these fragments to specific poems on the Persian Wars or on other topics is not supported by the new evidence itself.

The initial problem lies in understanding how the "new Simonides" fits with the other evidence for Simonides' works on the Persian Wars. Analysis of the "new Simonides" has revealed that there is very little evidence within these fragments with which we can confirm their division into three separate elegies on three separate battles in the Persian Wars. Furthermore, the "new Simonides" itself does not require that these fragments on historical topics be separated from others that are presumed to have sympotic themes. Such divisions arise from an attempt to make the "new Simonides" consistent with external *testimonia* for Simonides' compositions on the Persian Wars. It has been observed, however, that these *testimonia* are often cryptic and confused. Moreover, the elements in the new fragments that make them consistent with these external witnesses often are the result of supplements. These supplements aim at making the "new Simonides" conform to this tripartite division. The result of these supplements is that the evidence for dividing these fragments into separate poems is constructed to fit a preconceived notion of the works they should represent. We are again confronted, however, with the difficulty that the new fragments themselves give few clues about which compositions they represent. These observations force us to conclude that the external witnesses for Simonides' compositions on the Persian Wars are not the best guides for reconstructing these fragmentary verses and the works they may represent. To resolve these problems, I have suggested that all of the new fragments should be approached initially as if they belong to an as yet undetermined poem.

I have suggested that by removing this division, a clearer understanding of the content of these new fragments arises. The focus has been on the so-called "Plataea poem" because of the number of verses that are associated with this composition. Viewing these verses against a backdrop of inscriptions, epigrams, and other depictions of the Persian Wars has given rise to two conclusions in terms of the content of this composition. First, a panhellenic perspective is to be expected in the composition represented by fr. 11 $W^2$. This perspective would make these verses consistent with other commemorations and representations of the Persian Wars. More specifically, it has been suggested that these verses should be viewed as part of a composition that mentioned and praised the various cities which contributed to the Greek victory over the Persians. Second, the content of fr. 11 $W^2$ need not be limited by the view that these verses mentioned only the battle of Plataea. This fragment can also be construed to reflect a poem that was multi-battle in perspective. The implications of these conclusions are vast. By broadening the potential content of the poem represented by fr. 11 $W^2$, what is considered to be the "Plataea poem" may have been much more. Any fragment from the "new Simonides" may belong to this composition, not just those concerned with the battle of Plataea or even those overtly concerned with historical topics. Furthermore, the fragments need not be reconstructed to provide a narrative that focuses solely on this battle. Other reconstructions become possible, such as understanding the composition as being arranged around a catalogue that not only narrated events but also praised those who contributed to the victory over the Persians.

These observations concerning content have also forced a reconsideration of the genre represented by fr. 11 $W^2$. Broadening the scope of fr. 11 $W^2$ has called into doubt the understanding that this fragment represents the ill-attested sub-genre of narrative elegy. The placement of fr. 11 $W^2$ and those fragments associated with it in this sub-genre separates them from other elegiac verses about which we have more knowledge. I have shown that these new fragments have affinities with other types of elegy, such as early epigrams, which are verses associated with public commemorations, and elegiac verses typically associated with sympotic contexts. In terms of genre, I have suggested that the "new Simonides" can be viewed as having features that are consistent with these other types of elegy. To explore these affinities, I have emphasized the role of commemoration, praise and lamentation found in Greek elegy and, in particular, early epigrams. It has been suggested that early epigram functioned as commemoration and praise. Simonides' verses on the Persian Wars can also be viewed as having a similar function. This similarity, however, can be extended. Elegiac epigrams also served as expressions of lamentation. I have suggested that Simonides' verses on the Persian Wars would also function in this way. Simonides' verses would commemorate and praise those who fought the Persians as well as lament those who died in these battles. To this end, features of commemoration, praise and lament have been sought in the "new Simonides." By identifying such features in these fragments, the "new Simonides" has been aligned with other elegiac verses rather than distinguished from them. The conclusion that has arisen is that the features of commemoration, praise and lament may define the genre of Simonides' verses on the Persian Wars. Furthermore, it has been suggested that these features may have provided the link between the fragments on the papyrus represented by the "new Simonides." The poems that were originally found on this papyrus may have been grouped together because they shared these features that were suitable to expressions of lamentation. By viewing the "new Simonides" in this way, I hope to have shown that these new fragments not only provide valuable information about Simonides' verses on the Persian Wars, but also about the genre of elegy in general. Although the link may not be direct, the "new Simonides" may in fact provide a real connection between elegy proper and epigram along the lines of the function and the content of lament.

In the end, however, it must be admitted that any positive conclusions concerning the "new Simonides" will remain in dispute because of the fragmentary nature of the evidence. The conclusions proposed here are not an exception. Yet, I hope that the negative observations, primarily the dissolving of the division of these fragments into separate elegies and the dissociation of these verses from the category of narrative elegy, go some way toward laying the foundations for further studies of the "new Simonides." These conclusions in no way diminish the importance of these fragments. Rather, I hope that they invite further exploration of how these fragments are akin to other elegiac verses and how this kinship provides more pieces of the puzzle that is our corpus of archaic elegy. What should be certain is that the final chapter on the "new Simonides" has not been written.

# Appendix
## Persian War Epigrams

## A. MARATHON

1. Simon. XXI FGE. "The epitaph for the Athenians who fell at Marathon."[1]

   Ἑλλήνων προμαχοῦντες 'Αθηναῖοι Μαραθῶνι
   χρυσοφόρων Μήδων ἐστόρεσαν δύναμιν.[2]

   Sources:
   Lycurg. *in Leocr.* 108–9; Aristid. *Or.* 28.63 (Keil); schol. In Aristid. *Or.* 46.118, p. 289 Frommel; *Suda* s.v. Ποικίλη (Π 3079 Adler).

2. M-L 19; *SIG*³ 23b. "Athenian Thank-offering for Marathon: 490 B.C."

   'Αθεναῖοι τ[ὸ]ι 'Απόλλον[ῖ ἀπὸ Μέδ]ον ἀκ[ροθ]ίνα
   τῆς Μαραθ[ὸ]νι μ[άχες].[3]

   Sources:
   M-L: "On eight fragments of a long limestone base built against the front of the south wall of the Athenian Treasury at Delphi."

3. M-L 18; *IG* I³ 784; EM 6339; *SEG* 14.12; *CEG* 251. "Memorial of Kallimachos: 490 B.C."

   [Καλίμαχός μ' ἀν]έθεκεν 'Αφιδναῖο[ς] τἀθεναίαι:
   ἀν[γελον ἀθ]ανάτον ℎοὶ 'Ο[λύμπια δόματ'] ἔχοσιν,|
   [ . . . . 8 . . . . πολέ]μαρχο[ς] 'Αθεναίον τὸν ἀγὸνα:
   τὸν Μα[ραθον . . . ℎ]ελενονο[ . . . . . 11 . . . . . . :]
   παισὶν 'Αθεναίον μυ [ . . . . . . . . . . 21 . . . . . . . . . . ]⁴

   Sources:
   M-L: "Eight fragments of an ionic marble column found on the Acropolis."

4. Simon. V *FGE*. "Dedication of a statue of Pan by Miltiades."

τὸν τραγόπουν ἐμὲ Πᾶνα, τὸν ᾿Αρκάδα, τὸν κατὰ Μήδων,
τὸν μετ᾿ ᾿Αθηναίων στήσατο Μιλτιάδης.

Sources:
*A. Plan.* 232 [Simon.].

## B. THERMOPYLAE

5. Simon. XXII(a) *FGE;* 3 *GVI.* "Epigram(s) on men who fought at Thermopylae."

μυριάσιν ποτὲ τῇδε τριηκοσίαις ἐμάχοντο
ἐκ Πελοποννήσου χιλιάδες τέτορες.

Sources:
Hdt. 7.227–28; D. S. 11.33; Aristid. *Or.* 28.65 (II Keil); *A.P.* 7.248 [Simon.];
cf. Aristid. *Or.* 69.64 (II Keil).

6. Simon. XXII(b) *FGE;* 4 *GVI.* "Epigram(s) on men who fought at Thermopylae."

ὦ ξεῖν᾿, ἀγγέλλειν Λακεδαιμονίοις ὅτι τῇδε
κείμεθα, τοῖς κείνων πειθόμενοι νομίμοις.[5]

Sources:
Hdt. 7.227–228; Lycurg. *In Leocr.* 109; D. S. 11.33.2, Str. *Chr.* 9.4.16; *A.P.*
7.249 [Simon.]; *Suda* s.v. Λεωνίδης (Λ 272 Adler); Cic. *Tusc.* 1.101 ("dic,
hospes, Spartae nos te hic vidisse iacentes, / dum sanctis patriae legibus
obsequimur").

7. Simon. VI *FGE*. "Epitaph for Megistias."

μνῆμα τόδε κλεινοῖο Μεγιστία, ὅν ποτε Μῆδοι
Σπερχειὸν ποταμὸν κτεῖναν ἀμειψάμενοι,
μάντιος, ὅς τότε Κῆρας ἐπερχομένας σάφα εἰδώς
οὐκ ἔτλη Σπάρτης ἡγεμόνας προλιπεῖν.

Sources:
Hdt. 7.228.3; *A.P.* 7.677.

8. Simon. XXIII *FGE;* 6 *GVI.* "Epitaph on Locrians who fell at Thermopylae."

τούσδε ποθεῖ φθιμένους ὑπὲρ ῾Ελλάδος ἀντία Μήδων,
μητρόπολις Λοκρῶν εὐθυνόμων ᾿Οπόεις.

Sources:
Str. *Chr.* 9.4.2.

9. Philiadas I *FGE;* 5 *GVI.* "On the Thespians who fell at Thermopylae."

ἄνδρες θ' οἵ ποτ' ἔναιον ὑπὸ κροτάφοις Ἑλικῶνος,
λήματι τῶν αὐχεῖ Θεσπιὰς εὐρύχορος.

Sources:
Eust. *Il.* 266.11; St. Byz. s.v. θέσπεια.

10. Simon. VII *FGE.* "On men who died with Leonidas at Thermopylae."

εὐκλέας αἶα κέκευθε, Λεωνίδα, οἳ μετὰ σεῖο
  τῆιδ' ἔθανον, Σπάρτης εὐρυχόρου Βασιλεῦ,
πλείστων δὴ τόξων τε καὶ ὠκυπόδων σθένος ἵππων
  Μηδείων ἀνδρῶν δεξάμενοι πολέμωι.

Sources:
*A. P.* 7.301 [Simon.].

11. Simon. LXXXIII (a) and (b) *FGE*; 1173 *GVI.* "Lions sculptured on tombs" (Leonidas (?))

(a)
θηρῶν μὲν κάρτιστος ἐγώ, θνατῶν δ' ὃν ἐγὼ νῦν
  φρουρῶ τῶιδε τάφωι λάινος ἐμβεβαώς.
(b)
ἀλλ' εἰ μὴ θυμόν γε Λέων ἐμὸν οὔνομά τ' εἶχεν
  οὐκ ἂν ἐγὼ τύμβωι τῶιδ' ἐπέθηκα πόδας.

Sources:
(a) *A. P.* 7.344 [Simon.]
(b) *A. P.* 7.344b (post 7.350 scriptum) [Call.] or [τοῦ αὐτοῦ =Simon.][6]

# C. ARTEMISIUM

12. Simon XXIV *FGE.* "Dedication to Artemis"

παντοδαπῶν ἀνδρῶν γενεὰς Ἀσίας ἀπὸ χώρας
  παῖδες Ἀθηναίων τῶιδέ ποτ' ἐν πελάγει
ναυμαχίαι δαμάσαντες, ἐπεὶ στρατὸς ὤλετο Μήδων,
  σήματα ταῦτ' ἔθεσαν παρθένωι Ἀρτέμιδι.

Sources:
Plu. *Them.* 8.4; Plu. *de Herodot. malig.* 867 F.

## D. SALAMIS

13.  Simon. XI *FGE,* 7a *GVI*, M-L 24, *CEG* 131 (=vv. 1–4); *IG* I³ 1143, EM 22, *SEG* 10.404ᵃ (vv. 1–2). "Epitaph of the Corinthians who died at Salamis: 480 B.C." M L; "Epitaph for Corinthians who died in the battle of Salamis and were buried on the island." Page.

ὦ ξεῖν', εὔυδρόν ποκ' ἐναίομες ἄστυ Κορίνθου,
    νῦν δ' ἄμ' Αἴαντος νᾶσος ἔχει Σαλαμίς·
ἐνθάδε Φοινίσσας νᾶας καὶ Πέρσας ἑλόντες
    καὶ Μήδους ἱαρὰν Ἑλλάδα ῥυσάμεθα.⁷

Sources:
1–2: M-L: "Marble block found at Ambelaki on the island of Salamis."
1–4: Plu. *de Herodot. malig.* 870E; Favorin. (ps. D. Chr.) 37.18, II 21 Arnim.

14.  Simon. XII *FGE;* 8a *GVI;* 8 *GVI* (= vv. 1–2). "On a monument at the Isthmus commemorating Corinthians who fell in the Persian War of 480/479 B.C."

ἀκμᾶς ἑστακυῖαν ἐπὶ ξυροῦ Ἑλλάδα πᾶσαν
    ταῖς αὐτῶν ψυχαῖς κείμεθα ῥυσάμενοι
[δουλοσύνης· Πέρσαις δὲ περὶ φρεσὶ πήματα πάντα
    ἤψαμεν, ἀργαλέης μνήματα ναυμαχίης.
ὀστέα δ' ἡμὶν ἔχει Σαλαμίς, πατρὶς δὲ Κόρινθος
    ἀντ' εὐεργεσίης μνῆμ' ἐπέθηκε τόδε.]

Sources:
1–2: Plu. *de Herodot. malig.* 870C; *A. P.* 7.250 [Simon.]; schol. In Aristid. III 136.22 Dindorf (with Simon. XVIII *FGE,* see below).
1–6: schol. In Aristid. *Or.* 28.65, II 163 Keil.

15.  Simon. XIII *FGE.* "Dedication of weapons by Corinthian sailors after the battle of Salamis."

ταῦτ' ἀπὸ δυσμενέων Μήδων ναῦται Διοδώρου
    ὅπλ' ἀνέθεν Λατοῖ, μνάματα ναυμαχίας.

Sources:
Plu. *de Herodot. malig.* 870 F; *A. P.* 6.215 [τοῦ αὐτοῦ = Simon.]

16.  Simon. X *FGE.* "Epitaph for Adeimantos, commander of the Corinthians at the battle of Salamis."

οὗτος Ἀδειμάντου κείνου τάφος, ὃν δία πᾶσα
    Ἑλλὰς ἐλευθερίας ἀμφέθετο στέφανον.

Sources:
Plu. *de Herodot. malig.* 870 F; Favorin. (ps. D. Chr.) 37.19, II 21 Arnim; *A.P.* 7.347.

17. Simon. XIX(a) *FGE.* "On Democritus, a Naxian hero of the battle of Salamis."

Δημόκριτος τρίτος ἦρξε μάχης, ὅτε πὰρ Σαλαμῖνα
  Ἕλληνες Μήδοις σύμβαλον ἐν πελάγει·
πέντε δὲ νῆας ἕλεν δηίων, ἕκτην δ᾽ ὑπὸ χειρός
  ῥύσατο βαρβαρικῆς Δωρίδ᾽ ἁλισκομένην.

Sources:
Plu. *de Herodot. malig.* 869C

## E. AT PLATAEA

18. Simon. XV *FGE.* "Dedication of an altar to Zeus at Plataea."

τόνδε ποθ᾽ Ἕλληνες Νίκης κράτει, ἔργωι Ἄρηος,
  [εὐτόλμωι ψυχῆς λήματι πειθόμενοι,]
Πέρσας ἐξελάσαντες ἐλευθέραι Ἑλλάδι κοινόν
  ἱδρύσαντο Διὸς βωμὸν Ἐλευθερίου.

Sources:
Plu. *Arist.* 19.7; Plu. *de Herodot. malig.* 873 B; *A. P.* 6.50 [Simon.].

19. Simon. XXXIX *FGE.*[8] "Dedication by Pausanias."

μνᾶμ᾽ ἀρετᾶς ἀνέθηκε Ποσειδάωνι ἄνακτι
  Παυσανίας ἄρχων Ἑλλάδος εὐρυχόρου
πόντου ἐπ᾽ Εὐξείνου, Λακεδαιμόνιος γένος, υἱός
  Κλεομβρότου, ἀρχαίας Ἡρακλέος γενεᾶς.

Sources:
Ath. 12.536A.

## F. PERSIAN WARS IN GENERAL

20. M-L 27; *SIG*³ 31; *SEG* 14.412; *GHI* I² 19; *LSAG*² 104 no. 15. "Greek Thank offering for Victories in the Persian War: 479–8 B.C."

το[ίδε τὸν]
πόλεμον [ἐ]-
πολ[έ]μεον·

Λακεδ[αιμόνιοι]
'Αθαναῖο[ι]
Κορίνθιοι

Τεγεᾶ[ται]
Σικυόν[ιο]ι
Αἰγινᾶται

Μεγαρês
'Επιδαύριοι
'Ερχομένιοι

Φλειάσιοι
Τροζάνιοι
'Ερμιονês

Τιρύνθιοι
Πλαταιês
Θεσπιês

Μυκανês
Κεῖοι
Μάλιοι
Τένιοι

Νάξιοι
'Ερετριês
Χαλκιδês

Στυρês
ϝαλεῖοι
Ποτειδαιᾶται

Λευκάδιοι
ϝανακτοριês
Κύθνιοι
Σίφνιοι

'Αμπρακιôται
Λεπρεᾶται.

Sources:
"Engraved on the 'Serpent Column.'" The monument was set up at Delphi after Plataea (Hdt. 9.81) and currently stands in the Hippodrome in Istanbul.

21.  Simon. *FGE* XVII (a).[9] "Epigram(s) for a dedication at Delphi commemorating the end of the Persian Wars of 479 BC."

'Ελλάνων ἀρχαγός, ἐπεὶ στρατὸν ὤλεσε Μήδων,
    Παυσανίας Φοίβωι μνᾶμ' ἀνέθηκε τόδε.

Sources:

Th. 1.132.2; [D.] LIX (*in Neaeram* 97); Aristodem. 4.496 *FGrH;* Plu. *de Herodot. malig.* 873C; Apostol. 7.9d; *Suda* s.v. Παυσανίας (Π 820 Adler); *A.P.* 6.197 [Simon.]; Mentioned, but not quoted, by: Nep. *Paus.* 1; Paus. 3.8.2; Aristid. *Or.* 46.175, II 234 Dindorf.

22. Simon XVII (b). "Epigram(s) for a dedication at Delphi commemorating the end of the Persian Wars of 479 BC."

Ἑλλάδος εὐρυχόρου σωτῆρες τόνδ' ἀνέθηκαν,
δουλοσύνης στυγερᾶς ῥυσάμενοι πόλιας.

Sources:

D. S. 11.33.

23. Simon. XVI *FGE;* 9a *GVI; IG* VII 53; *SIG³* 13; 9 *GVI* (= *vv.* 1–2). "On a memorial in Megara for citizens fallen in the Persian Wars."

Ἑλλάδι καὶ Μεγαρεῦσιν ἐλεύθερον ἆμαρ ἀέξειν
ἱέμενοι θανάτου μοῖραν ἐδεξάμεθα,
τοὶ μὲν ὑπ' Εὐβοίαι καὶ Παλίωι, ἔνθα καλεῖται
ἁγνᾶς Ἀρτέμιδος τοξοφόρου τέμενος,
τοὶ δ' ἐν ὄρει Μυκάλας, τοὶ δ' ἔμπροσθεν Σαλαμῖνος
⟨                                                              ⟩
τοὶ δὲ καὶ ἐν πεδίωι Βοιωτίωι, οἵτινες ἔτλαν
χεῖρας ἐπ' ἀνθρώπους ἱππομάχους ἱέναι.
ἀστοὶ δ' ἄμμι τόδε ⟨ξυνὸν⟩ γέρας ὀμφαλῶι ἀμφίς
Νισαίων ἔπορον λαοδόκωι 'ν ἀγορᾶι.

Sources:

Dittenberger, *SIG³*: " perisse videatur." Page, *FGE* gives the scholarly history of the inscription.

24. Simon. XIV *FGE.* "Dedication by Corinthian women to Aphrodite."

αἵδ' ὑπὲρ Ἑλλάνων τε καὶ ἀγχεμάχων πολιατᾶν
ἔστασαν εὐχόμεναι Κύπριδι δαιμόνια.
οὐ γὰρ τοξοφόροισιν ἐβούλετο δῖ' Ἀφροδίτα
Μήδοις Ἑλλάνων ἀκρόπολιν προδόμεν.

Sources:

schol. in Pind. *Ol.* 13.32b; Plu. *de Herodot. malig.* 871A–B; Ath. 13.573C

25. Simon. XIX *FGE.* "Dedication by Athenian archers who fought in the Persian Wars."

τόξα τάδε πτολέμοιο πεπαυμένα δακρυόεντος
νηῶι, Ἀθηναίης κεῖται ὑπωρόφια,

πολλάκι δὴ στονόεντα κατὰ κλόνον ἐν δαῒ φωτῶν
Περσῶν ἱππομάχων αἵματι λουσάμενα.

Sources:

*A. P.* 6.2 [Simon.]

## G. INCERTA

26.   "Epigrams on Athenians Fallen in the Persian Wars."[10]

A. Simon. XX (a) and (b) *FGE;* M-L 26; *IG* I³ 503/504 (lapis A), Agora I, 303,
*SEG* 10.404, *CEG* 2.

(a) (Salamis ?)
ἀνδρῶν τῶνδ᾽ ἀρετῆ[ς ἔσται κλέ]ος ἄφθι[τον] αἰε ...
[. . . . . . . . . . .]ρ[      ]νέμωσι θεοί·
ἔσχον γὰρ πεζοί τε [καὶ] ὠκυπόρων ἐπὶ νηῶν
Ἑλλά[δα μ]ὴ πᾶσαν δούλιον ἦμαρ ἰδεῖν .

(b) (Marathon ?)
ἦν ἄρα τοῖσζ᾽ ἀδάμ[αντος ὑπερβιον ἦτορ,] ὅτ᾽ αἰχμήν
στῆσαν πρόσθε πυλῶν ἀν[
ἀγχίαλον πρῆσαι ρ[c. xix litt.                    ]
ἄστυ, βίαι Περσῶν κλινάμενο[ι προμάχους.

Source:

M-L: "Two fragments of a base." Both found in modern houses. Their original
position is unknown. See M-L 26 for the history of these verses and a bibliography. The remains of a fourth-century copy of the first epigram has been
identified. M-L 26 prints the text of this copy:

]ος ἄφθι[—]
]νέμωσι θεοί·
]ὠκυπόρων ἐπὶ νηῶν
]ον ἦμαρ ἰδεῖν

B. *IG* I³ 503/504 (lapis B); Agora I 6963A; *SEG* 13.34; *CEG* 3.

[– ∪∪– ∪∪– ∪∪–πε]ζοίτε καὶ |≡– ∪| – ∪∪– ∪∪– – ∪∪– ∪∪–
– ∪∪– ∪∪– ∪∪– ∪∪– ∪] ο νέσοι ||[– ∪∪– ∪∪– – ∪∪–έ]βαλον

Source:

A third fragment linked to *lapis A*. The text with bibliography is printed in *IG*
I³ under the heading, "lapis B *cum continuatione in lapide* C."

C. *IG* I³ 503/504 (lapis C); EM 6739.

ℎέρκος γὰρ προπάροιθεν ∪– ∪∪– ∪∪– ∪ˇ |ΤΕΣ ∪∪– ∪∪μεμ
Παλλάδος ℎιππο |∪– /

οὖθαρ δ' ἀπείρο πορτιτρόφο ἄκρον ἔχοντες ˅ | τοῖσιμ πανθαλὲς ὄλβος
ἐπιστέ |[φεται ]

Source:

The final letters (]βαλον) printed with *IG* I³ 503/504 *Lapis B* above are found on a fourth fragment (Lapis C). This fragment, the original position of which is unknown, was identified by Matthaiou 1986.

27. Simon. VIII *FGE;* 28 *GVI.* "Epitaph for men fallen in Battle" (Plataea or Persian Wars in General?)

εἰ τὸ καλῶς θνήισκεν ἀρετῆς μέρος ἐστὶ μέγιστον,
    ἡμῖν ἐκ πάντων τοῦτ' ἀπένειμε Τύχη·
Ἑλλάδι γὰρ σπεύδοντες ἐλευθερίην περιθεῖναι
    κείμεθ' ἀγηράντωι χρώμενοι εὐλογίηι.

Sources:
*A.P.* 7.253 [Simon.]; schol. In Aristid. III 154–5D.

28. Simon. IX *FGE.* "Epitaph for men fallen in Battle" (Plataea or Persian Wars in General?)

ἄσβεστον κλέος οἵδε φίληι περὶ πατρίδι θέντες
    κυάνεον θανάτου ἀμφεβάλοντο νέφος·
οὐδὲ τεθνᾶσι θανόντες, ἐπεί σφ' Ἀρετὴ καθύπερθε
    κυδαίνουσ' ἀνάγει δώματος ἐξ Ἀίδεω.

Sources:
*A.P.* 7.251 [Simon.].

29. Simon. XVIII *FGE.* "Epitaph for Athenians who fell in battle against the Persians."

παῖδες Ἀθηναίων Περσῶν στρατὸν ἐξολέσαντες
    ἤρκεσαν ἀργαλέην πατρίδι δουλοσύνην

Sources:
*A.P.* 7.257; schol. In Aristid. III 154 Dindorf; schol. In Aristid. III 136 Dindorf (Page: "perperam cum XII 1–2 supra coniunctum).

30. M-L 25; *SIG*³ 29; FD II (1953); *SEG* 36.5. "Dedication of the Athenian Portico at Delphi: (?) 479 B.C."

Ἀθεναῖοι ἀνέθεσαν τὲν στοὰν καὶ τὰ hόπλ[α κ]αὶ τἀκροτέρια hελόντες
τὸν πολε[μίο]ν.

Sources:

M-L: "On the highest of the three steps of the stylobate of the Athenian Portico at Delphi, built on the north side of the Sacred Way against the polygonal wall that supports the terrace of the temple of Apollo."

31. Simon. LIII *FGE;* 11 *GVI.* "Epitaph for men fallen in defense of Tegea." (Plataea?)

τῶνδε δι᾽ ἀνθρώπων ἀρετὰν οὐχ ἵκετο καπνός
    αἰθέρα δαιομένας εὐρυχόρου Τεγέας,
οἳ βούλοντο πόλιν μὲν ἐλευθερίαι τεθαλυῖαν
    παισὶ λιπεῖν, αὐτοὶ δ᾽ ἐν προμάχοισι θανεῖν.

Sources:
*A. P.* 7.512 [Simon.].

32. Simon. LIV *FGE.* "Epitaph for men fallen in defense of Tegea." (Plataea?)

εὐθυμάχων ἀνδρῶν μνησώμεθα, τῶν ὅδε τύμβος
    οἳ θάνον εὔμηλον ῥυόμενοι Τεγέαν,
αἰχμηταὶ πρὸ πόληος, ἵνα σφίσι μὴ καθέληται
    Ἑλλὰς ἀποφθιμένου κρατὸς ἐλευθερίαν.

Sources:
*A.P.* 7.442 [Simon.].

33. Aeschylus 1 *FGE;* 10 *GVI.* "Epitaph on men killed in battle near Mount Ossa."

κυανέη καὶ τούσδε μενεγχέας ὤλεσεν ἄνδρας
    Μοῖρα πολύρρηνον πατρίδα ῥυομένους.
ζωὸν δὲ φθιμένων πέλεται κλέος, οἵ ποτε γυίοις
    τλήμονες Ὀσσαίαν ἀμφιέσαντο κόνιν.

Sources:
*A.P* 7.255 [A.].

# Notes

## NOTES TO INTRODUCTION

1. Hutchinson 2001: 290–91.
2. Parsons 1992: 4–50.
3. For the view that Stobaeus 4.34.28 actually quotes verses by Semonides of Amorgos see Hubbard 2001: 226–231; however, contrast Sider 2001b: 276. I assume throughout that these verses are by Simonides, not Semonides.
4. Lobel 1954: 67–76. For the reediting of these fragments as *Adespota Elegiaca* 28–60 in the first edition of *IEG* 2, see West 1974: 167. Parsons 1992: 5 reports that Lobel had already noticed coincidences between POxy 2327 and 3965. The overlaps are: 1) POxy 3965 fr. 1 and POxy 2327 fr. 6 (= fr. 11 W²); 2) POxy 3965 fr. 27 and POxy 2327 frs. 3 and 2(a) col. ii and 4 (= fr. 22 W²). Parsons 1992: 29 adds a connection between POxy 3965 frs. 1 and 2 and POxy 2327 fr. 27 col. i. Although there are no physical overlaps between these fragments, he demonstrates persuasively that the latter contains the line ends of the former. See also Rutherford 2001a: 45.
5. All references to or quotations of the fragments of Simonides are from West's edition (= *IEG*² volume 2 = W²), unless otherwise noted. In this definition of the "new Simonides," I omit Simon. frs. 23–26 W², which West designates as "Convivalia," because they cannot be shown to have any relation to the new fragments. For similar reasons, this definition does not include Simon. frs.86–92 W², which West designates "Incertum an ex Epigrammatis." Sider 2001a: 13–27 only prints frs. 1–22 W² as the "new Simonides." Gentili-Prato 2002: 183–225 prints all of the fragments of the "new Simonides" that are found in West, but omits frs. 5 and 8 W² as well as all other testimonia included in West. Gentili-Prato also does not print frs. 25, 26 and 87–92W².
6. For the dates of Simonides, see Molyneux 1992: 307–345. Molyneux is reacting against Stella 1946: 1–24. The issue is whether Simonides' life can be dated to 556–468 BCE, which is traditionally accepted, or to 532–450 BCE, as Stella argues. For this study, either set of dates is acceptable.
7. T 3 (Call. fr. 222), T 21 (Call. fr. 64.1–14), T 22 (Ar. *Pax* 695–701 and Schol. ad loc.), T 23 (Athen. 14.656d–e), T 47d (Aris. *Rh.* 2.16 1391a); cf. Aris. *EN* 4.1.27 (1121a5–7) and Stob. 3.10.61. All tesimonia (T) in this note are cited from Campbell 1991.
8. T 1 (*Suda*, s.v. Σιμωνίδης Λεωπρεποῦς, Σ 439Adler) T 21 (Call. fr. 64.1–14), T 24 (Plin. *Nat.* 7.24–89), T 25 (Cic. *Fin.* 2.32.104), T 26 (Longin. *Rh.*718), 510 *PMG*

(Cic. *de Orat.* 2.86.351–3 and Quint. *Inst.* 11.21–11–16), fr. 89 W² (Aristid. *Or.* 28.59). All tesimonia (T) in this note are cited from Campbell 1991.

9.    Pisistratids: T 10 (*Ath. Pol.*18.1), 607 *PMG* (P. Berol. 3875), Simon. XXVI (a) and (b) *FGE;* see also Molyneux 1992: 65–79. Themistocles: T 12 (Plu. *Them.* 5.6) and T 27 (Plu. *Them.* 5.7); see also Molyneux 1992: 107–110, 154–55. All tesimonia (T) in this note are cited from Campbell 1991.

10.   T 13 (Theoc. *Idyll* 16.42–47), T 14 (Plu. *aud. poet.* 15c), 510 *PMG* (Cic. *de Orat.* 2.86.351–3 and Quint. *Inst.* 11.21–11–16), 521 *PMG* (Stob. 4.41.9), 528 *PMG* (Aristid. *Or.* 31.2 and schol. Theoc. *Idyll* 16.34), 529 *PMG* (schol. Theoc. *Idyll* 16.36), 542 *PMG* (Pl. *Prt.* 339a–346d); see also Molyneux 1992: 121–129. All *testimonia* (T) in this note are cited from Campbell 1991.

11.   T 17 (Pl. *Ep* 2.311a), 531 *PMG* (D.S. 11.11.6), Simon. XVII (a) and XXXIX *FGE,* Plu. *Cons. Apoll.* 105A and Ael. *VH* 9.41. All *testimonia* (T) in this note are cited from Campbell 1991.

12.   T 17 (Pl. *Ep.* 2.311a), T 18 (Paus. 1.2.3), T. 19 (Schol. Pindar *O.* 2.29d), X. *Hier.;* see also Molyneux 1992: 220–33. All *testimonia* (T) in this note are cited from Campbell 1991.

13.   511–519 *PMG.*

14.   Timocreon: T16 (D. L. 2.46); see also Molyneux 1992: 107–110. Pindar: T 20 (P. *O.* 2.86 and Schol. ad loc.) T 21 (Call. fr. 64.1–14) and T 45 (Schol. Pindar *N.* 4.60b); see also Molyneux 247–75. All *testimonia* (T) in this note are cited from Campbell 1991.

15.   T 15 (*Vit. Aeschyli*), Molyneux 1992: 151–52. All *testimonia* (T) in this note are cited from Campbell 1991.

16.   T 34 (Pl. *Prt.* 316d), T 35 (Pl. *R.* 335e), T 37 (*A.P.* 4.1.8), T 36 (Catul. 38.7–8), T 38 (Hor. *Carm.* 2.1.37–40), T 39 (D. H. *Comp.* 23), T 40 (D. H. *Imit.* 2.420), T 41 (Quint. *Inst.* 10.1.64), T 42 (*A.P.* 9.184.5), T 43 (*A.P.* 9.571). All testimonia (T) in this note are cited from Campbell 1991.

17.   The standard work on the epigrams of Simonides is still Boas 1905. On the history and origin of a *Sylloge Simonidea,* see particularly Boas 1905: 39–76. More recently, Page 1981: 120–123 has noted that the *Garland of Meleager* (ca. 100 BCE) is the earliest authority for a collection of epigrams ascribed to Simonides that circulated independently before it was incorporated in later anthologies. The exact form and nature of this collection of *Simonidea* is unknown. Page suggests two possibilities: A) an early collection of inscriptional epigrams to which later compositions were continually added with subsequent publications; B) Two separate collections, one which contained inscriptional epigrams and one which contained later literary exercises, both going under the name of Simonides. Page supports option "A." See also Cameron 1993: 1–2, 270, who claims that a "collection of *Simonidea* which contained much demonstrably later in date than Simonides appeared no earlier than the fourth century and more probably in the Hellenistic age." Cameron also rightly suggests that there may have been multiple collections of epigrams assigned to Simonides. The point to emphasize is that by the time of Meleager, Simonides was famous as an epigrammatist and can be said to represent a tradition to which early epigrams, some with more authority than others, would be assigned. The dissertation, "Kommentar zu den Simonideischen Versinschriften," completed in 2004 by Andrej Petrovic, appeared too late to be taken into account here. I thank David

Sider for bringing this dissertation to my attention before the final publication of this book.

18. The standard edition of the *Suda* is Adler 1928–1938. The standard starting points for discussions about the *Suda* are the introduction to Adler's edition and her article *RE* s.v. "Suidas." For the title, see Dölger 1936. For title and date see Adler *RE* s.v. "Suidas:" 674–675; Lemerle 1985: 344–45; Wilson 1996: 145–47.

19. Adler 1928–1938, v.1: XVI–XXII and *RE* s.v. "Suidas:" 685–714, which contains early and essential bibliography. Before Alder, Daub 1880: 401–490 and Flach 1882: XLVIII–LXVII contain useful information and bibliography.

20. Importantly, where the sources for an entry are clear, Adler notes them in the margins of her text.

21. See "Introduction: The Problem" at n. 34 ff. All cross-references to discussions within this study will be made by chapter number, heading/subheading name, and note numbers on the pages where the discussion can be found. Such references will serve as an approximation of the pages to which the reader is referred.

22. Photius 69 (Bekker p. 34) lists three works by Hesychius of Miletus. 1) A universal history in six books from the founding of the Assyrian Empire to the Emperor Anastasius. A fragment of this work survives under the title *Patria Konstantinoupoleos* (=*FGrH* 390); 2) the *Onomatologos;* 3) A history concerned with the reign of Justin I, which is lost. The *Suda* (H 611 Adler) only lists the first two of these.

23. ἔγραψεν Ὀνοματολόγον ἢ πίνακα τῶν ἐν παιδείᾳ ὀνομαστῶν οὗ ἐπιτομή ἐστι τοῦτο τὸ βιβλίον. ("He wrote *Onomatologos* or a list of those renowned in learning, of which this book is an epitome.") It is debated whether this means that the *Suda* used an epitome of the *Onomatologos* or that the *Suda* itself is an epitome of the *Onomatologos*. For the debate, see Schultz *RE* s.v. "Hesychios" [10]: 1323–1325. It is possible that Hesychius included a reference to himself in his own list. Yet, two bits of information in the entry have suggested that the *Suda* is actually incorporating an entry of an epitome of the *Onomatologos*. First, the explanation of the title as "a list of those renowned in learning" has seemed out of place in Hesychius' original work. It is unlikely that Hesychius would have to gloss his own title. Yet, the title of the *Pinakes* of Callimachus as recorded by the *Suda* is similar. See "Introduction: The problem" after n.34. Second, later in the entry, the *Suda* tells us that Hesychius does not mention any of the Church Fathers. This leads to the statement that Hesychius himself was not a Christian. This information is also unlikely to have been included by Hesychius himself. It cannot be determined whether such a statement originates with the compilers of the *Suda* or an earlier epitomator of Hesychius. Since it is generally assumed that *Suda* has taken information from the *Onomatologos* either completely or with further abridgement, the conclusion has been that this information was added by an earlier epitome of Hesychius. In this way, the *Suda* itself becomes an even more abbreviated version of this epitome. See Blum 1991: 203. It cannot be ruled out, however, that the compilers of the *Suda* may have added this information. So the *Suda* may remain an epitome of Hesychius. If an earlier epitome existed, its date is unknown. Flach 1882: XIV suggests the seventh century CE by allowing that the ecclesiastical lives which made their way into the *Suda* were inserted at that point into the epitome. Adler *RE* s.v. "Suidas": 707 dates it to the mid-ninth century CE. See also Blum 1991: 203 who does not believe that the epitomator added the material on the Church Fathers and rightly doubts that we can find a date for the epitome.

24. The standard collection of these citations is Flach 1882.

25. Adler *RE* s.v. "Suidas:" 707.

26. Blum 1991: 206–207. For good examples of the type of material found in *Suda* entries derived from Hesychius, see K 227 Adler (Callimachus), Σ 439 Adler (Simonides), and Θ 199 Adler (Theophrastus).

27. Blum 1991: 208–210 argues that the *Onomatologos* was alphabetically arranged. Flach 1882 presents his collection of citations of Hesychius as if the work had been arranged alphabetically. Daub 1880: 405–410 proposes that the work was arranged by class of author (i.e. Poets, Philosophers, Orators, etc.). See Schultz *RE* s.v. "Hesychios" [10]: 1328 and Spoerri *Der kleine Pauly* s.v. "Hesychios" [4]: 1122. On the arrangement of the *Pinakes* of Callimachus, see "Introduction: The Problem" at nn. 36–42.

28. Blum 1991: 203 n. 136.

29. For Dionysius "Musicus" see Cohn *RE* s.v. "Dionysios" [142]: 986–991 and Montanari *Der neue Pauly* s.v. "Dionysios" [20] 638–639. It is not certain if this Dionysius "Musicus" is the same person as Aelius Dionysius of Halicarnassus (Cohn *RE* s.v. "Dionysos" [142]: 987–991 and Montanari *Der neue Pauly* s.v. "Dionysios" [21]: 639). Flach 1882: XLVIII–L lists Duris the Samian, Hermippus the Callimachean, Nicander the Alexandrian and a certain Crates as other possible early sources of Hesychius.

30. Meineke 1839 v. 1: 16–18; Schneider 1870 v.2: 29–33 and v.5: 1; Wachsmuth 1867: 145–149. Daub 1880: 418–421 sets out the pertinent details nicely. See also Flach 1882: LVII–LIX.

31. See Cohn *RE* s.v. "Dionysos" [142]: 986 for a list of places where this work is cited.

32. Schneider 1870 v.2: 29–30; Wachsmuth 1867: 146; Daub 1880: 411.

33. Daub 1880: 411 is certain that the lists in the *Suda's* entries for poets derive from Dionysius "Musicus" via Hesychius. The reasons are not entirely clear. It seems that his argument is circular. That is, Dionysius "Musicus" can be shown to be a source of information in the *Suda* (via Hesychius); therefore, since the *Suda* entries that derive from Hesychius often have lists, albeit abbreviated ones, Dionysius "Musicus," the source for Hesychius, must also have included lists. For a slightly more solid argument, the *vita* of Aeschylus provides a bit of evidence. In the manuscript tradition, the plays of Aeschylus are accompanied by a *vita* and a catalogue of Aeschylus' work. The text of the life in various manuscripts is often corrupt or confused and the catalogue is only preserved in two of the manuscripts. See Wilamowitz 1914: 3–8. In two manuscripts (V and M), the *vita* clearly contains the phrase ἐκ τῆς μουσικῆς ἱστορίας. In others, this conclusion to the *vita* is corrupt. It is generally agreed that this phrase refers to the work by Dionysius "Musicus;" however, it is not certain how much of the text that precedes or follows this phrase is to be considered a citation from Dionysius. See Scherer 1886: 39–40. If the entry derives entirely from Dionysius, as Blum 1991: 175 n. 156 assumes, then, we may have two bits of evidence to prove that Dionysius "Musicus" included lists in his work. At the close of the *vita* we are told about the proper arrangement of the author's name in relation to a literary work in a list. For epic poems, the name of the author precedes the title of his work, and for dramatic poets, the author's name follows the title of the work. Moreover, the two manuscripts that clearly contain this phrase (M and V) are also the ones that preserve the catalogue of works by Aeschylus. See Wilamowitz 1914: 6 and 7 (*app. crit.*). If all or parts of the *vita* go back to Dionysius "Musicus," this catalogue may also go back to him as well,

although it most likely originates with Callimachus or his Alexandrian successors. For the texts of the life and catalogue see Wilamowitz, ibid.; Murray 1955: 370–372 and 102 (under the hypothesis of *Prometheus Bound.*); Page 1972: 331–335.

34. Daub 1880: 419–421. Before Daub, Nietzsche 1867: 200 observed that this information was likely to have derived from a pinagrapher. Cf. Blum: 1991: 202–203: "Such a comprehensive lexicon of authors (i.e. the *Onomatologos* of Hesychius) had not been compiled since the days of the *Pinakes* of Kallimachos. Hesychios probably did not have access to those anymore. His *Onomatologos* was based mainly on later compilations whose material was indeed partially derived from the *Pinakes* of Kallimachos." Blum's book on the make-up and influence of Callimachus' lost catalogue is a useful introduction to the issues of early bibliography.

35. Blum 1991: 150. See particularly n. 176 for a list of places where citations to the work are collected. The standard text is Pfeiffer 1949 v.1: frs. 429–453.

36. Call. frs. 430–432 mentions a *pinax* or list of Orators; frs. 431, 438, and 442 imply one of Philosophers; fr. 433 refers to one of Laws; frs. 434 and 435 refer to one of miscellaneous works (cookbooks and the like); frs. 441 and 450 imply one of lyric poets, fr. 451, implies one of tragedians; frs. 439 and 440 imply one of comic poets; fr. 437 implies one of historians.

37. See Blum 1991: 154–155.

38. For the debate over whether Callimachus included biographical information, and if he did, how much information he included, see Daub 1880: 419–421; Schmidt 1922: 66; Blum 1991: 155–156. In Call. fr. 447 (=D.H. *Din.* 1), Dionysius of Halicarnassus, the historian and critic, complains that neither Callimachus nor the grammarians from Pergamum had given accurate information (οὐδὲν ἀκριβές) about Dinarchus. I suppose Blum 1991: 155 is referring to this fragment when he says, "[f]rom a remark by Dionysius of Hallikarnassos we learn that Kallimachos generally recorded biographical data on the authors listed by him." Blum's thinking is that Dionysius expected such data to be provided by Callimachus. Perhaps more certain evidence of biographical information in the *Pinakes* is Call. fr. 429 (=D.L. 8.86). In this fragment, Diogenes Laertius credits specific biographical information on Eudoxus to the *Pinakes*. Also see fr. 438 (= Athen. 6.252C) on Lysimachus, the teacher of King Attalus. In Athenaeus, we learn that Callimachus said that Lysimachus was the pupil of Theodorus.

39. For such see Call. fr. 429 (=D. L. 8.86 on Eudoxos), 430 (=Athen. 15.669 on Dionysius Chalchus), 438 (=Athen. 6.252 C on Lysimachus).

40. Frs. 433 and 434 are direct quotes of the *Pinakes*. These quotes, however, consist of titles (fr. 434) and the first line of the works (frs. 433 and 434).

41. For a discussion of titles, see "Introduction: The *Suda* on Simonides" at nn. 73–78 and "Chapter 1.3A: The Salamis Poem: The Evidence" at nn. 48–60. For the Alexandrian arrangement of author's works, see Harvey 1955: 157–174; Rutherford 1990: 201–206; Obbink 2001: 74–81.

42. For opening words and number of lines, see Call. frs. 433 and 434.

43. For such endeavors see Sandys 1906 and Pfeifer 1968.

44. Modern texts do not agree on what the phrase δι' ἐλεγείας modifies. It can be construed with both Ξέρξου ναυμαχία and ἡ ἐπ' Ἀρτεμισίῳ ναυμαχία, presumably poem titles, or with just the latter. For the first option, the text of Adler places a comma *before* the phrase, and so implies that it modifies both headings. The text

of Campbell 1991 follows Adler, but places ἡ Καμβύσου καὶ Δαρείου βασιλεία καὶ Ξέρξου ναυμαχία καὶ within obeli because of confusion in the text, to which we will return below. Bergk *PLG* 3⁴: 423 prints the text of the *Suda* as Σιμωνίδης . . . καὶ γέγραπται αὐτῷ Δωρίδι διαλέκτῳ ἡ Καμβύσου καὶ Δαρείου βασιλεία καὶ Ξέρξου ναυμαχία δι᾽ ἐλεγείας, ἡ δ᾽ ἐν Σαλαμῖνι μελικῶς; that is, Bergk shows that the text of the *Suda* omits the words ἡ ἐπ᾽ Ἀρτεμισίῳ ναυμαχία, which he says must be supplied from the better text found in the *Eudociae Violarium* 883 sv. Περὶ Σιμωνίδου τοῦ λυρικοῦ (Flach). For Eudocia, see Krumbacher 1897: 578 and Sandys 1906: 408. The text of the Simonides entry in Flach's edition of the *Violarium* includes the phrase ἡ ἐπ᾽ Ἀρτεμισίῳ ναυμαχία and places the comma *after* the phrase δι᾽ ἐλεγείας. The only references to the absence of the phrase ἡ ἐπ᾽ Ἀρτεμισίῳ ναυμαχία in the *Suda* that I can find are: 1) Daub 1880: 427, who is citing Bergk; 2) Boas 1905: 226, who encloses the phrase in angular brackets and attributes it to Eudocia; 3) a note in Adler's *app. crit.* s.v. Σ 439, where she notes that Gutschmid deleted this phrase. At this time, I am unable to identify Adler's reference to Herr Gutschmid nor have I been able to confirm Bergk's comments on the missing phrase in the *Suda*. Nevertheless, with the text as it is printed, the definite article in the heading ἡ ἐπ᾽ Ἀρτεμισίῳ ναυμαχία suggests that we should read δι᾽ ἐλεγείας only with this title; therefore the comma should be removed, as it is in the text printed at *IEG*² 2: 114. The text printed here follows *IEG*².

45.    Bergk *PLG* 3⁴: 423; Bernhardy 1853 v.2: 756; West 1993b: 2. On the other hand, Schneidewin 1835: 3–4 accepted *The Kingship of Cambyses and Darius* as a legitimate title. This view is no longer accepted.

46.    To support his interpretation, Bergk refers to the Ambrosian *vita Pindari* (= *post* fr. 4 W²), where reference to Simonides' poem on Salamis and a mention of the kingship of Cadmus (?) are used to indicate the ages of these poets in relation to each other. For a fuller discussion of this passage, see "Chapter 1.3A: The Salamis Poem: Evidence" at n. 47.

47.    Cambyses dies in 522 BCE. Darius rises to power in 521 BCE, after a period of revolt and control by the Magi (Hdt. 3.124–5, 3.61–88). Xerxes comes to the throne in 486 BCE. See Marincola 1996: xxxvix–xlvi and notes on the passages of Herodotus cited above.

48.    In particular, the verses on Plataea seem to have appeared shortly after the battle. See "Chapter 2.2D: Content of Fr. 11 W² and the Spartans: Epigrammatic Record" at n.105.

49.    For a consideration of the arrangement of Simonides' works on the Persian Wars in an Alexandrian edition of his works, see Obbink 2001: 78–80. Obbink compellingly shows that these poems are not differentiated in their titles by "addressee, recipient, or honorand" (79).

50.    Pickard-Cambridge 1968: 72.

51.    Novati 1879: 461–464. The text also appears as Koster 1975: 142 (=XXXa) and *PCG* 3.2 T2. The list is accompanied by a biography that contains the same details that we find in the *Suda* entry s.v. Aristophanes (A 3932 Adler).

52.    Wilamowitz 1879: 464–465.

53.    Blum 1991: 192–193.

54.    Obbink 2001: 76–77.

55.    Obbink 2001: 77.

56. Str. 15.3.2 = Simon. fr. 539 *PMG*.
57. Obbink 2001: 78.
58. For the text and a fuller discussion of this passage, see "Chapter 1.3A: The Salamis Poem: Evidence" at n. 47.
59. κατὰ δὲ ἐνίους ἐν τῷ εἰς τοὺς ἐν Μαραθῶνι τεθνηκότας ἐλεγείῳ ἡσσηθεὶς Σιμωνίδη (Page 1972: 332) ("but according to some [Aeschylus] was beaten in (a contest for) *elegiacs* by Simonides.")
60. For the term see West 1974: 3–4, Bowie 1986: 25–6, Boedeker-Sider 2001: 4 n. 4; Obbink 2001: 79. Also see "Chapter 3.2A: Form" n. 16.
61. See Schneidewin 1835: XVII, 80–82 (fr. 58); Barigazzi 1963: 74; Molyneux 1992: 148–155; Cameron 1995: 331.
62. See "Introduction: Background" n. 16.
63. For the problems of dating Simonides, see "Introduction: Background" at n.6.
64. See "Introduction: The *Suda* on Simonides" at n. 55.
65. Molyneux 1992: 117–138. See "Chapter 3.4D: New Considerations of Generic Features in the 'New Simonides:' Lament" at nn. 183–190.
66. For a fuller discussion of these texts, see "Chapter 1.2A: The Artemisium Poem: Evidence" nn. 3–6.
67. Bergk *PLG* 3$^4$: 424. Followed by Barigazzi 1963: 63, Podlecki 1968: 266–67, West 1972: 112, Molyneux 1992: 187–88.
68. See "Chapter 1.3A: The Salamis Poem: Evidence" at n. 47.
69. For example see *IEG* 2: 112.
70. Parsons 1992: 6 and 41; Followed by *IEG*$^2$ 2 and West 1993b: 3. For fuller discussion of this fragment, see "Chapter 1.2B: The Artemisium Poem: The "New Simonides": Fr. 3 W$^2$ (=POxy 3965 fr. 20)."
71. *IEG*$^2$ 2: 114.
72. Rutherford 2001a: 35–36.
73. Hdt. 2.117 (*Cypria*); 4.32 (*Epigone*). See Schmalzriedt 1970: 23–26. Schmalzriedt notes that Herodotus' reference to Arion, the inventor of the dithyramb, is exception to this practice. Hdt. 1.23 tells us that Arion named his dithyrambs.
74. For titles attached to Attic drama, see Pickard-Cambridge 1968: 72. The *Didaskalia,* a group of fragments of an inscription (=*IG* II$^2$ 2319–23), contains, among other things, titles of plays. While the list goes back to the fifth century BCE, Pickard-Cambridge suggests that it was probably compiled after 288BCE. Schmalzriedt 1970: 27 n. 11; Blum 1991: 147; Dover 1993: 56.
75. Consider the example of Attic comedy, where titles seem to arise from the chorus of the play. Dover 1993: 56.
76. Blum 1991: 146–148.
77. Blum 1991: 156.
78. Schmalzriedt 1970: *passim;* Obbink 1988: 433 n. 26.
79. ἡ δ' ἱστορία καὶ παρὰ Σιμωνίδη ἐν ταῖς Κατευχαῖς. ("The story is also (told) by Simonides in his *Prayers* (or *Curses*)." Also, 538 *PMG* (= Schol. Plu. *Ex Etymol. i* Luperci.), which cites verses from the work.
80. ὡς εἴρηκε Σιμωνίδης ἐν Μέμνονι διθυράμβῳ τῶν Δηλιακῶν. ("Thus Simonides said in a dithyramb, *Memnon,* in the *Deliaca.*"). The *Deliaca,* specifically means dithyrambs "composed for performance in Delos." See "Introduction: The *Suda* on Simonides" at nn. 56–57.

81.  1.763 (Wendel): ὥς φησι Σιμωνίδης ἐν Συμμίκτοις. ("Thus Simonides says in *Miscellany*"). The *Miscellany* could be the title of a roll which contained miscellaneous verses by Simonides or the title of a roll with the works of various authors, including Simonides.

82.  Bowie 1986: 27–35; see also Bowie 2001: 45–58.

83.  Bowie 1986: 27–34. It should be noted that Bowie 2001: 55–56 see some difference between the so-called "Plataea poem" and other poems that he puts into the category narrative elegy. "[The Plataea poem] seems, therefore, to fall in or near to the class of narrative elegy I have just discussed. In, or near? I am less confident than some scholars that this poem fell into the same class." He gives two reasons: 1) Length; it seems that the Plataea poem would be too short to constitute a narrative elegy. 2) Theme; the events depicted by Simonides are much more recent than the events found in other narrative elegy. He does suggest, however, a "festive and perhaps competitive performance" (58) for the "Plataea poem."

84.  Aloni 2001: 102–104. An earlier version appeared as Aloni 1997: 8–28, which poses a similar argument as is found in Italian at Aloni 1994a: 9–22.

85.  Schachter 1998: 29–30.

86.  Shaw 2001: 164–181.

87.  Boedeker 1995: 224–25.

88.  Bearzot 1997: 77–79. Cf. Rutherford 2001a: 39–41.Rutherford (41) also suggests a performance at Delphi during the dedication of the Serpent Column.

89.  Huxley 2001: 75.

90.  Rutherford 2001a: 50, Obbink 2001: 83–85, Sider 2001b: 285–286.

91.  Boedecker 2001a: 133–134; Hornblower 2001: 147. See also Bowie 2001: 45–66.

92.  Stehle 2001: 106–119; Clay 2001: 182–4. On Simonides and heroization see also Boedeker 2001b: 148–163.

93.  Obbink 2001: 73, 84–85.

94.  Rutherford 2001a: 50.

95.  Sider 2001b: 285–6.

96.  Rutherford 2001a: 33–36, for a list of possible ways to interpret these fragments in terms of the corpus of Simonides that is reconstructed from the Suda and other witnesses. For the suggestion that some epigrams may represent sections of elegies, see Raubitschek 1968: *passim;* also noted by Obbink 2001: 78 n. 53. For the related issue of the interaction between audience and epigram in a ritual context (i.e. a context in which we might find the performance of elegiac verses), see Day 2000: *passim.*

## NOTES TO CHAPTER ONE

1.  Lobel 1954: 67–76; Parsons 1992: 4–50; electronic images of POxy 3965, as well as parts of POxy 2327, are available at Obbink 1998: http://www.csad.ac.uk/POxy/ (cited June 29, 2002); images of POxy 2327 are found at Lobel 1954: plates 9–10; Images of POxy 2327 and 3965 are published at Boedeker-Sider 2001: 8–12.

2.  *IEG*² 2: 114–135; Sider 2001a: 13–27. G-P 2² rev.: 183–233. Boedeker-Sider 2001a. The texts of West and Sider differ in important ways. In West, the elegiac fragments of Simonides are the scraps of POxy 2327 and 3965 as well as previously published citations. These are grouped under the following headings: "1–4. ἡ ἐπ᾽ Ἀρτεμίσιωι

ναυμαχία;" "5 (+6–9?). ἡ ἐν Σαλαμῖνι ναυμαχία;" "10–17 (+18?). *De proelio Plataeaco;*" "19–33. *Convivalia;*" "34–85. *Incerti Contextus.*" Sider only prints the scraps of POxy 2327 and POxy 3965 as well as the citations of and *testimonia* for these elegies (=frs. 1–22 W²). That is, Sider prints only the fragments of the "new Simonides" that are perceived to pertain to the Persian War poems and the major sympotic fragments. He does not print any headings, but he does follow West's numeration. Sider also relegates some of West's supplements to his *apparatus criticus*. Unlike Sider, Rutherford's commentary (2001), which accompanies Sider's text, prints headings that follow the spirit of those in West. Rutherford uses three main headings, which he then divides into sub-groups. His first heading is "Military Fragments." This group is divided into the sub-headings, "The *Naumachia*" and "The Plataea Poem." He further classifies "The *Naumachia*" as "Fragments attributed to the Artemisium Poem by West" and "Fragments attributed to the Salamis Poem by West." He also further distinguishes the parts of "The Plataea Poem" according to content. The second main heading is "The Sympotic Fragments." This group is subdivided into "The Leaves (frs. 19–20 W²)" and "A Wish to Be Somewhere Else (21–22 W²)." The third main heading is "Other Fragments," under which he briefly comments on frs. 23–85 W², which Sider does not print. Most recently, the reprint of the second edition of G-P ii, augmented by the inclusion of the "new Simonides," prints its own text and numeration of these fragments. The new fragments are grouped as "ΕΙΣ ΤΗΝ ΕΠ' ΑΡΤΕΜΙΣΙΩΙ ΝΑΥΜΑΧΙΑΝ," "ΕΙΣ ΤΗΝ ΕΝ ΠΛΑΤΑΙΑΙΣ ΜΑΧΗΝ," "INCERTUM UTRUM AD PUGNAM ARTEMISIAM AN PLATAICAM REFERENDA," "CONVIVIALIA," and "INCERTIS SEDIS." No fragments are assigned to a "Salamis Poem." Another text of and comments on the "new Simonides" is Pavese 1995: 1–26, with *addenda et corrigenda* at 1996: 56–58. A text of and notes on fr. 11 W² can be found at Luppe 1993: 1–9 and Capra-Curti 1995: 27–32, with *addenda et corrigenda* at 1996: 248. Luppe 1994: 21–24 comments on frs. 15–16 W².

3. 533 *PMG* = Prisc. (ca. fifth/sixth century AD) *de metr. Terent.* 24 = *Gramm. Lat.* iii. Keil. The text cited here is that of Campbell 1991: 424–26. The lines following the citation of Simonides do not appear in *PMG*. The quotations scan; a) $\cup - - -\cup - X$ ; b) $\cup\cup\cup - \cup - X$.

4. 532 *PMG* = *IEG*² 2: 114 = T1 Campbell = *Suda* Σ 439 Adler.

5. For the ancient practice of titling works, see "Introduction: The *Suda* on Simonides" at nn. 73–78 and "Chapter 1.3A: The Salamis Poem: The Evidence" at nn. 48–60.

6. Before the publication of the "new Simonides" Lobel, with reservations, suggested that POxy 2327 fr. 27 ii (=fr. 13 W²) might refer to the battle of Plataea and POxy 2327 fr. 31 ii (=fr. 7 W²) might belong to either the Artemisium or Salamis poem (1954: 67). His reasons are: A) Simonides composed elegiac verses on the Persian Wars; B) POxy 2327 belongs to a larger collection of fragments gathered together because they are in the same hand. Within this larger collection there is another set of fragments, POxy 2430 (=519 *PMG*), that contains lyric verses likely to be by Simonides. See also Lobel 1981: 21–23. Parsons 1992: 6 suggests that POxy 2327 fr. 31 ii (=fr. 7 W²) belongs to the "Artemisium poem." West prints the fragment as part of the "Salamis poem," yet he later admits that such a poem may not exist as an elegy. See West 1993b: 2–3 n.7. This fragment will be discussed further at "Chapter 1.3D: The Salamis Poem: The 'New Simonides:' Frs. 6 and 7 W² (=POxy 2327 fr. 31 coll. i and ii)" after n. 68.

7. 534 *PMG* = West 1992: 116 = Schol. Ap. Rhod. 1.211–15c, "Ζήτης καὶ Κάλαϊς." West capitalizes Ναυμαχίᾳ. *PMG*, followed by Campbell 1991: 426, does not.

8. Podlecki 1968: 264 assumes the reference is to *The Sea-battle at Artemisium*. Parsons 1992: 41 finds such a suggestion attractive, especially in view of West's placement of POxy 3965 fr. 20 (=fr. 3 W²) in an "Artemisium elegy," for which see "Chapter 1.2B: The Artemisium Poem: 'The New Simonides:' Fr. 3 W² (=POxy 3965 fr. 20)" at n. 24ff. West 1993b: 3 explicitly reads the scholium as referring to an "Artemisium poem."

9. Hdt. 8.96.2; Plu. *Them.* 14.2; A. *Pers.* 481. See also the discussion of the Himerius passages at "Chapter 1.2A: The Salamis Poem: The Evidence," n. 13ff.

10. Schneidewin 1835: 8 assigns the fragment to *The Sea-battle at Artemisium*, as a lyric. Page 1962 does not include this fragment (635 *PMG*) with those he assigns to *The Sea-battle at Artemisium* (532–535 *PMG*). He does note Schneidewin's suggestion at 635 *PMG*. Podlecki 1968: 264 and Campbell 1993: 493 accept Schneidewin's placement. *IEG*² 2 : 114 assigns the fragment to an elegiac *The Sea-battle at Artemisium*. This fragment did not appear in the first edition of *IEG*.

11. Hdt. 7.176, 179; 8.7.

12. Rutherford 2001a: 36 suggests a possible Simonidean paean for a Skiathian theoria visiting Delphi. He refers to Sokolowski 1962, n. 16. It is not entirely clear what text in Sokolowski Rutherford has in mind here. Sokolowski 1962: 83–85 (number 41) is an inscription from the sixth century BCE, which may refer to a Skiathian involvement in a Delphic Theoxenia (lines 29–31).

13. *PMG* 535 = *Orat.* 47.14; 12.32–33. The text printed here is, for the most part, that of Campbell 1991: 426–428.

14. Bowra 1967: 344 suggests that Simonides' poem was a *prosodion* in the Panathenaia.

15. Rutherford 2001a: 37.

16. In fr. 543 *PMG*, the blasting wind (ἄνεμος . . . πνέων) appears in line 3. Although the wind in Himerius (*Orat.* 12.32) presumably is gentle (ἀπαλός), it is probable that Simonides described a calmer wind later in the poem.

17. Molyneux 1992: 159 and 161–162 discusses these passages. The textual problems are discussed at 159 nn. 56–60. For the most part, these problems cannot be solved.

18. Wilamowitz 1913: 208 suggests "nach dem Meere, also nachdem er (Boreas) auf dem Meere seine Gnade beweisen hatte." Edmonds 1931: 280 emends to μετὰ τὴν ⟨κατα⟩ θάλατταν ⟨μάχην⟩. Podlecki 1968: 264 n. 33 suggests θάλαττ⟨ιαν ναυμαχί⟩αν. Molyneux 1992: 161 translates "after the events at sea."

19. Wilamowitz 1913: 206–209; Schneidewin 1835: 49, simply mentions the suggestion, "nisi ad Naumachiam Artemisium pertinebat." Molyneux 1992: 156–166 follows Wilamowitz.

20. Bowra 1967: 343–44. Bowra assigns the reference to *The Sea-battle at Salamis* because ἀπαλός is unsuitable for Boreas. Podlecki 1968: 265 demonstrates the flaws of Bowra's connection and connects the reference to *The Sea-battle at Artemisium*. It should be kept in mind, as Professor Sider points out to me, that "gentle" would be suitable in a prayer to a god for calm breezes. Even so, such a prayer was made at both Artemisium and Salamis. For Artemisium, see Hdt. 7.189; for Salamis, although not explicitly to the winds, see Hdt. 8.64.

21. Podlecki 1968: 365. Him. *Orat.* 12.33, οὐ γὰρ ἀτασθάλους μαστεύων ἔρωτας τὴν σὴν πλεῦσαι σπουδάζει θάλλασσαν. ("For not craving arrogant desires is he

(Flavianus) eagar to sail your sea"). Himerius is referring to a journey by the consul Nichomachus Flavianus (382 CE). See Völker 2003: 179 n. 1 and 184 n. 64.

22. For the lacuna, see Him. *Orat.* 12.33 [Colonna, p. 99].

23. Parsons 1992: 6; West 1993b: 2; Rutherford 2001a: 35–36. All are following Bergk *PLG* 3⁴: 423–24 (Simon. fr. 83). Each rejects the suggestion in the light of the "new Simonides."

24. Parsons 1992: 41; West 1993b: 3.

25. For the reconstruction see Parsons 1992: 18.

26. Parsons 1992: 41.

27. West 1992: 115; Parsons 1992: 41 accepts the reconstruction.

28. Parsons 1992: 41; West 1993b: 3.

29. West 1993b: 3. West bases his conclusion largely on a comparison with the epic adjective ἀτρύγετος. Concerning this adjective, he says, "many of the ancients understood [it] to mean bottomless, i.e. having no τρύξ (sediment at the bottom)." West does not specify which ancients defined this adjective as bottomless. *LSJ* defines the word as "barren, unharvested," when it is applied to the sea. Parsons 1992: 41 cites Schol. AbT *Il.* 15.27 as an ancient etymology: "ἀτρύγετον· ἄβυσσον, τρύγα μὴ ἔχοντα." *LSJ* s.v. τρύξ cites no example of this word referring to sediment other than that found in wine. An unattested metaphoric usage remains possible, if the reading is accepted.

30. Parsons 1992: 18. The join occurs in line 3 after ν·[.

31. Rutherford 2001a: 33 and Parsons 2001: 59 express the general consensus that POxy 3965 appears to contain all elegiacs. This conclusion is not certain. POxy 3965 overlaps POxy 2327 in two places (frs. 11 and 22 W²) and these papyri may represent the same collection of poems. The contents of POxy 2327, however, are not clear. Lobel 1981: 21–23 finds that POxy 2327 is written in the same hand as POxy 2430, which contains paeans of Simonides. If POxy 2430 represents not only a papyrus written by the same hand, but also the same scroll as POxy 2327, it must be concluded that POxy 2327 represents a papyrus that held both elegies and lyric poems. It is also known that POxy 2327 contained at least two separate poems because a *coronis,* a sign marking a division between poems, appears at POxy 2327 fr. 7.2. If POxy 2327 and POxy 3965 represent the same group of poems, the possibility exists that POxy 3965 contained more than one poem and that it represents a papyrus with both lyric poems and elegies.

32. Simon. frs. 21 and 22 W². Cf. Archil. fr. 4 W², ἄγρει δ' οἶνον ἐρυθρὸν ἀπὸ τρύγος ("Take the red wine from the lees."). ἀπό cannot be read at fr. 3.12 W², as Parsons 1992: 41 notes.

33. Note that West's text does not place sub-linear dots under these letters, while Parsons prints only sub-linear dots to indicate the uncertainty of the lettering on the papyrus.

34. Parsons 1992: 18, "5 ˌ [, lower part of an upright, ink above to left (stroke, or left-hand dot of diaeresis?)."

35. West 1993b: 2.

36. Parsons 1992: 14.

37. *IEG²* 2 : 115; West 1993b: 3–4.

38. A form of χείμων appears at 7.188.2, 3 (twice) and 189.2.

39. There seem to be larger difficulties with the line that may further add doubt to West's supplement. The first letter is read by Parsons and West as an unambiguous *epsilon.*

Inspection of the image of the fragment, however, suggests that there is room for some doubt. If the letter is an *epsilon*, it appears to be incomplete with only the top loop and possibly part of the bottom stroke visible. Other readings for these marks are available. In fact, other fragments that have similar markings are read as either *sigma* (POxy 3965 fr. 1.1, 2, 10) or an *omicron* (POxy 3965 fr. 1.2). At POxy 3965 fr. 1.2, part of a *mu* appears under the *omicron*. A similar reading is possible for the lower mark in the line under discussion here.

40.  Parsons 1992: 10, 18, 39 and 41. West 1992: 116 expresses no doubt that these fragments come from the same column, but does not mention his reasons or the sheet-join. Sider 2001a: 15 follows West. Rutherford 2001a: 36 mentions nothing about the relation of these fragments.

41.  This suggestion comes in Parsons 1992: 39.

42.  West 1993b: 2 n. 6. Rutherford 2001a: 36 lists this possibility and mentions (n. 13) *FGE* 24, possibly by Simonides, as another elegiac treatment of Artemisium. The epigram accompanies a dedicatory inscription on a stele in a temple to Artemis Προσηώιας at Artemisium. See *FGE*: 236–237.

43.  Hutchinson 2001: 289–29. Rutherford 2001a: 36. Rutherford is more cautious: "'The publication of the new papyrus has increased the probability that the Artemisium poem was in elegiacs, but there is still room for doubt.'"

44.  The possibility that Plu. *Them.* 15.4 (=fr. 5 W²) contains the words of Simonides will be considered below. See "Chapter 1.3A: The Salamis Poem: Evidence" at n.61ff.

45.  *IEG*² 2 includes other fragments in an elegy on Salamis, although West later renounces this placement and explicitly calls the Salamis poem a lyric poem (1993b: 2–3 n. 7). These fragments are fr. 8 W² (= 625 *PMG* = *Et. Gen.* p. 256 Miller; *Et. Mag.* p. 692. 25; Zonaras p. 1581) and fr. 9 W² (= Schol. Hom. *Il.* 7.76 in P.Oxy 1087. 22 ff. "ἐπὶ μάρυτρος ἔστω"). Fr. 8 W² is a grammatical citation of the word κυανοπρώϊραν, which is said to occur also in Homer as κυανοπρώιρους. The word is not in our Homer. *Il.* 15.693 has κυανοπρώιοιο and *Od.* 3.229 has κυανοπρωρείους, both of which would fit the final position of the hexameter. Bergk *PLG* 3⁴ (Simon. fr. 241) emends the citation to read κυανοπρώειραν, which would provide a closer parallel to *Od.* 3.229 and would create a word that fits the elegiac meter. West does not emend the word. As it stands, how κυανοπρώϊραν is to be placed in an elegiac couplet is not clear. κυανοπρώϊραν scans ∪ ∪ – – ∪ ∪, which could not fit a hexameter line. It could fit the pentameter, but it would bridge the two cola and would not allow a caesura. This phenomenon would be unusual because the "caesura in the pentameter is invariable, though it may depend on elision." (West 1982: 44). The fragment, then, represents a lyric poem. Furthermore, not only could the word belong in a poem about any sea battle, but it also need not come from a composition on a sea-battle, as Rutherford rightly points out (2001a: 37). Fr. 9 W² is a citation by a scholiast on Homer. The citation, ξύλα καὶ λάους ἐπιβάλλων (∪ ∪ – – – ∪ ∪ – –), could metrically fit in an elegiac couplet. There is no reason, however, to assign this fragment to *The Sea-battle at Artemisium* or any other poem.

46.  Bergk *PLG* 3⁴: 423; West 1972: 112; Barigazzi 1963: 67–68; Podlecki 1968: 267–71; Molyneux 1992: 187–192. Schneidewin 1835: 9 suggests that what later became 571 *PMG* (= Plu. *de exil.* 8 (iii 519 Pohlenz-Sieveking)) belonged to a "Salamis poem;" therefore, he seems to have believed the poem to be a lyric. Rutherford 2001a: 38 is non-committal, but points to Schneidewin's suggestion. Bowra 1967: 343–44

hypothesizes that the "Salamis poem" was a lyric *prosodion* in the context of the Panathenaia. Harrison 2001: 264, 266, 267–68 believes that the "new Simonides" confirms a lyric on Salamis which is echoed by Horace.

47. Specifically, the *vita* says that Simonides wrote about Salamis and Pindar mentions the reign of Cadmus, the fifth-century companion of Gelon (Hdt. 7.163–4). Rutherford 2001a: 37 n.18 doubts τῆς Κάδμου βασιλείας in the text of the life of Pindar and considers the emmendation of Boekh 1819: 657–658 (fr. 195), τῆς Καμβύσου βασιλείας. In the *apparatus criticus* of Drachmann 1903: 3, the suggestions of J. G. Schneider (Δαρείου) and C. Schneider (Ξέρξου) are found. These suggestions are attractive because they appear to make the comparison with Simonides more obvious. The manuscript, however, appears to have Κάδμου. Any of these readings provides a curious similarity between the wording used to describe Pindar's subject, τῆς Κάδμου βασιλείας (or τῆς Καμβύσου βασιλείας), and the work, ἡ Καμβύσου καὶ Δαρείου Βασιλεία, attributed to Simonides by the *Suda*. It is this similarity that Bergk *PLG* 3[4]: 423 uses to suggest that the *Suda* is indicating the time of Simonides' life.

48. See above, "Introduction: The *Suda* and Its Predecessors."

49. The translation of the *vita* in T 7 Campbell treats τὴν ἐν Σαλαμῖνι ναυμαχίαν as a title by analogy with the list is the *Suda*. Sider 2001a: 15 does not translate it as a title. Sider also does not include the *Suda* entry as one of his texts. Rutherford 2001a: 38, in his note on fr. 8 W², does not appear to understand the *vita* as containing a title *The Sea-battle at Salamis*. On the *Suda*, Rutherford 2001a: 35–36 is also cautious. He treats the references the *Suda* as the subjects of poems. It should be noted that the *Suda* uses the same verb (γέγραπται) in reference to the works of Simonides as is found in the *vita* (γέγραφε). All three scholars agree that the *vita* records the subject of Pindar's work, not the title.

50. Gomme 1956: 89; Hornblower 1997: 4–5. Both commentaries clearly understand Thucydides as referring to his subject matter.

51. This comparison was suggested to me by D. Sider. The text is the Loeb text of Hort 1926: 390 (= Theophr. fr. 6 Wimmer 1866: 386). For problems with the ascription of this text to either Theophrastus or Aristotle see Sharples 1998: 19, 144–152.

52. Cronin 1992: 307–345; Sharples 1998: 144.

53. Cf. Schmalzriedt 1970: 64–72; Blum 1991: 151.

54. For prose titles and the difficulties with the use of the title *peri phuseos*, see Schmalzriedt 1970: 83–119 and *passim*.

55. See Schmalzriedt 1970: 28, 30; Dover 1993: 56. For the ancient practice of titling see, "Introduction: The *Suda* on Simonides" at nn. 73–78 and "Chapter 1.3A: The Salamis Poem: The Evidence" at nn. 48–60.

56. Aristophanes refers to titles of comedies (Eupolis' *Marikas* and his own *Knights* at *Nu.* 553–54) and tragedies (E. *Palamedes* at *Th.* 770, 848, E. *Hel.* at *Th.* 850, and the E. *Andr.* at *Ra.* 52–4).

57. Obbink 2001: 74–81, a reconstruction of the Alexandrian collections of Simonides' work and the titles of these collections, assumes that the attestations of the Salamis and Artemisium poems provide titles for these poems.

58. See "Introduction: The *Suda* and Its Predecessors" at n. 20.

59. Compare the "Novati Index" of Aristophanes' works which also contains a *vita* similar in detail to the entry in the *Suda*. See "Introduction: The *Suda* on Simonides" at nn. 51–53.

60. For the assignment of a title by Callimachus, see Blum 1991: 156.
61. Bergk *PLG* 3⁴: 423 (=Simon. 83); Page 1967: 278 (= note on 536 *PMG*); *IEG*² 2: 116 (=fr. 15 W²). Molyneux 1992: 188–189 and nn. 55–61 provide a survey of others' opinions. Molyneux, following Edmonds 1931: 334 (Simon. fr. 91) and Bowra 1967: 344 n.1, takes μέχρι δείλης ἀντισχόντας as either a direct quote or close approximation of Simonides' words. As a direct quote, these words could represent an elegy. Bowra, however, argues for a lyric poem. Boas 1905: 52–3 takes the quote from this point until περιβόητον ἀράμενοι νίκην or ἔργον εἴργασται λαμπρότερον. Podlecki 1968: 271–3 extends the quote beyond the fragment as it is printed in West. Podlecki continues with ἀνδρεία μὲν καὶ προθυμία κοινῇ τῶν ναυμαχησάντων, γνώμῃ δὲ καὶ δεινότητι τῇ Θεμιστοκλέους ("by the shared manliness and courage of those who fought in the sea battle, and by the judgment and shrewdness of Themistocles").
62. For the adjective as lyric, see Poltera 1997: 93.
63. *LSJ* s.v. περιβόητος. A search of TLG E word list reveals that in fact the word is common in Plutarch. In the nominative, it appears in *Pel.* 30.2; *Cat. Mai.* 4.1; *Cat. Mi.* 2.8 and 30.7; *TG* 4.1; *Dem.* 24.2; *Demetr.* 16.5; *Brut.* 5.4, 48.4; *Galba* 19.2, *de defectu oraculorum* 436 A; *de fraterno amore* 489 D.
64. Various scholars suggest other evidence for a "Salamis poem." First, Wilamowitz 1913: 144 n. 2 suggests that "The Democritus Epigram" (= Simon. *FGE* XIX = Plu. *de Herod. malign.* 869c) belongs in an elegiac poem and is not an epigram. Barigazzi 1963: 67–68 and Podlecki 1968: 268 assign this epigram to the "Salamis poem" mentioned by the *Suda* and the *vita*. Page 1981 (*FGE* XIX) proposes that the epigram is a short elegiac poem composed by a Naxian. The problem is that the reference to Democritus' being third suggests an elegiac poem and the mention of Salamis suggests an epigram. For these points, see Molyneux 1992: 190 and Rutherford 2001a: 37. For the possibility that epigrams could be excerpted elegies, see Raubitschek 1968. Second, Podlecki 1968: 268, 270–71 puts forward Ar. *Pax* 736 sq. + Schol. (V) παρὰ τὰ Σιμωνίδου ἐκ τῶν ἐλεγείων· = 86 W² as the opening of the "Salamis poem." Barigazzi 1968: 74 and Molyneux 1992: 150 suggest that this passage refers to Marathon. On this fragment, see also Rutherford 2001a: 38. Third, West 1993a: 3 n. 7 suggests that 629 *PMG* (=Schol. Theoc. 12.27–33bc (Wendel)) might come from a lyric poem on Salamis or Artemisium. Here, the scholiast notes that Simonides praised the Megarians for their seamanship. Finally, Molyneux 1992: 192–196 lists epigrams for the Corinthians (*FGE* XI–XIV) as pertaining to Salamis. He also lists *FGE* X, an epigram for Adeimantus, who fought at Salamis, but died later. This epigram is not relevant to a discussion on the "Salamis poem." The relation of these epigrams to the "Salamis poem" is dubious as well is their authenticity. None of this additional material can be securely assigned to a "Salamis poem" or used as a witness for the existence of such a poem.
65. In the first edition of *IEG,* these fragments are *Adespota Elegiaca* frs. 59 and 60 W.
66. West 1992: 2–3: "In the first edition of *IEG,* accepting Bergk's reasoning, I included the two (extra Sudam) references to a Salamis poem, which Page quotes under 536 and tentatively associated them with two small elegiac fragments that looked as if they could have to do with a naval battle. In the second edition I retained this arrangement, adding P.Oxy. 2327 fr. 31, now that this papyrus was known to be Simonides. I probably ought to have discarded the heading ἡ ἐν Σαλαμῖνι and the testimonia

to it; the other fragments (6–9) may equally well have come from the Artemisium poem or some other."

67. Cf. Simon. frs. 21–22 W², which are from adjacent columns and may, but need not be, from the same poem. See Rutherford 2001a: 53.

68. Lobel 1954: 67 with a similar suggestion for POxy 2327 fr. 27 col. ii, which is now fr. 13 W².

69. Lobel 1954: 76 suggests πεζοβόας (*LSJ:* "one who responds to the battle cry on foot.") in Pindar *N.* 9.34 as a parallel.

70. Barigazzi 1963: 64 argues for this connection. It is accepted by Podlecki 1968: 268 and it is mentioned sympathetically by Molyneux 1992: 189. Bowra 1967: 344 n.4 points to the possibility that this fragment is from a "Salamis poem" by Simonides. Bowra cites the fragment as part of "*Ox. Pap.* XXXII 2137." I believe he means POxy 2327, which belongs in *The Oxyrhynchus Papyri* XXII. The war-trumpet does not appear in Herodotus' account of Salamis.

71. West prints Φρυξίτ[ε at fr. 7.6 W²(= POxy 2327 fr. 31 col. ii line 9) apparently because Lobel 1954: 75 notes the presence of ξιτ[ in line 9 on the papyrus in an "earlier copy." Lobel's *editio princeps* does not print the letters after ξ because they could no longer be read at the time of his publication. West's inclusion of these letters, however, is unaccompanied by a note. Sider 2001a: 16, follows West. These letters are not visible on the images at Boedeker-Sider 2001: 8. They should be removed from the text, marked as spurious, or noted as no longer visible.

72. Barigazzi 1963: 64 and Podlecki 1968: 268 print παισὶν Μη[δων. Barigazzi 1963: 64–65 cites a number of fifth-century parallels for a phrase such as "children of the Medes," i.e. the Persians. Significant among these parallels is παῖδες Ἑλλήνων at A. *Pers.* 402, a verse in close proximity to the mention of the war-trumpet (392). West more cautiously prints παισὶν μη[ and suggests the supplements Μη[δείων or Μη[δείης in his *apparatus criticus*.

73. Rutherford 2001a: 36–37.

74. Hdt 7.96.1.

75. Hdt. 7.89.1–2, 8.85–90. See also Lazenby 1993: 28, 187–94.

76. Hdt. 7.73.

77. Hdt. 9.32.1.

78. Parsons 1992: 6.

79. *IEG²* 2: 118–122. Parsons 1992: 6 gives a synopsis of the fragments that are pertinent to the battle of Plataea. Sider 2001a:17–24, for the most part, follows the text of West, but he omits West's headings that group the fragments according to battles. See above "Chapter 1.1: Introduction" n. 2. Sider also publishes two separate versions of fr. 11 W². The first is his text with supplements. The second is West's more generous restoration of the fragment. Rutherford 2001a: 38 uses the heading "*The Plataea Poem* (10 W²–18 W²)."

80. Epigrams on Plataea are ascribed to Simonides: Simon. XVI *FGE,* to the Megarians; Simon. XVII(a) *FGE,* dedicated at Delphi by Pausanias, the Spartan leader; Simon. VIII and IX *FGE* might be the epigrams at Plataea mentioned by Pausanias, the periegete, at 9.2.4. See Page 1981: 197–199; Simon. LIII *FGE,* to those who fell defending Tegea. See Page 1981: 278–79.

81. The verses, quoted as a single unit by Plutarch, are generally divided into two (or more) groups. Wilamowitz 1913: 144 n. 2, *IEG²* 2: 121–122, and Sider 2001a: 22

divide the citation into two groups of three lines because the first foot in line four lacks one long or two short syllables required by the meter. Pavese 1995: 5, 18–19, also divides the citation into two groups, but assigns two verses to fr. 15 W² and four verses to fr. 16 W². Luppe 1994: 21–24 separates the citation into four units. For suggestions that attempt to preserve the citation as a single unit, see Sider 2001a: 22 (app. crit.).

82. It is not clear which words the genitives χρυσοῦ τιμήεντος limit. I follow the translation of Campbell 1991: 515, which makes them an attribute of μάρτυν. This translation also accompanies Sider's text and is implicit in the comments of Rutherford 2001a: 49. Sider, however, makes something else besides the Corinthians the subject of the verb. He translates "[who] served as the finest witness of their toils, the precious gold in the sky." Luppe 1994: 23–24 attributes the genitives to something actually made of gold. Pavese 1994: 19 suggests that the phrase is a genitive of material and denotes an attribute of the sun. Further comments, showing a connection between the Corinthians and Helios, are at Pavese 1995: 57.

83. Bergk *PLG* 3⁴ (Simon. 84), Edmonds 1933 (Simon. 92) and Diehl (Simon. 64) place these verses under the heading "εἰς τὴν ἐν Πλαταίας μάχην." Wilamowitz 1913: 144 allows that Simonides mentioned Plataea in elegiac verses, but is not more specific. Lobel 1954: 67 mentions a "poem about Plataea" and refers to Plutarch. Molyneux 1992: 198 mentions "the elegy in which the Corinthian's part at Plataea is praised." These headings and references to a "Plataea elegy" are modern inventions. It must be noted that ancient witnesses for this poem as a separate elegy on Plataea have not survived.

84. *IEG:* 115–116.

85. West 1974: 3–4 defines ἐλεγεῖα: "frequently used from fifth century onwards in referring to stretches of elegiac verse . . . It is used of a poet's whole elegiac *oeuvre* . . . and often later, in the same sense as ἐν ταῖς ἐλεγείαις (i.e. "in a book of elegies") . . . But ἐλεγεῖα could also be applied to tomb inscriptions . . . even to a dedicatory inscription in a single couplet."

86. This overlap is a primary reason for assigning POxy 3965 to Simonides. The overlap of POxy 3965 fr. 26 and fr. 20 W² (=Stobaeus 4.34.28) is the other piece of evidence.

87. Fr. 11.9–13W² contain an overlap between POxy 3965 fr. 1.1–5 and POxy 2327 fr. 6.5–9. Fr. 22 W² contains an overlap between POxy 3965 fr. 27 and POxy 2327 fr. 3 +2(a) col. ii +(b) + 4. Parsons 1992: 29 argues persuasively for connection between POxy 3965 fr. 1+2 (= 11.9–41 W²) and POxy 2327 fr. 27 col. i. This connection is accepted and provides the text of West edition. See "Chapter 1.4B: The Plataea Poem: The 'New Simonides:' Fr. 11 W² (=POxy 2327 frs. 5+6+27 col. i + 3965 fr. 1+2) at nn. 90–91.

88. Strong affirmation of the appearance of the figures other than Pausanias is reserved because in each case the papyrus is incomplete.

89. Parsons 1992: 33. My numbering of the verses here only takes into account POxy 3965 frs. 1 and 2 and not the overlap between POxy 3965 fr. 1 and POxy 2327 fr. 6, which adds four lines to the start of the fragment. See immediately below for this connection. Parsons' numbering of the POxy 3965 fr. 1 throughout takes this overlap into account. So, for example, what I am citing here as POxy 3965 fr. 1.14 Parsons numbers as fr. 1.18. Parsons explains his numbering at 1992: 28.

90. Parsons 1992: 29–34 *passim;* Luppe 1993: 1–9; Capra-Curti 1995: 27–32.
91. Lobel originally noted this overlap. See Parsons 1992: 5, 28.
92. Parsons 1992: 28. West 1992: 118; Lloyd-Jones 1994: 1.
93. West 1993b: 5–6; Barchiesi 2001: 255–60, especially 257 n. 6. Barchiesi supports West's placement by showing that Hor. *Carm.* 4.6.9–12 refers to the death of Achilles with a similar image. Although Barchiesi's argument is persuasive, the fragment should still be kept separate from fr. 11 $W^2$ because the image could also come later in the poem, as we will see. For the imagery of heroes who fall like trees in Homer, see Schein 1984: 73–76, 96–97.
94. For the suggestion that fr. 11.7–8 $W^2$ refer to Apollo as the killer of the hero read in 11.1–4 $W^2$ see Parsons 1992: 28, West 1993b: 5, and Rutherford 2001a: 43. For the suggestion that fr. 11.5–6 $W^2$ refer to a burial see West 1993b: 5–6 and Rutherford 2001a: 43.
95. Parsons 1992: 28.
96. Parsons 1992: 25 followed by Lloyd-Jones 1994: 1. Compare, however, Barchiesi 2001: 255–260 and n. 84 above.
97. For a similar suggestion concerning fr. 10 $W^2$, see Rutherford 2001a: 43.
98. Any interpretation of the "new Simonides" should take this point into consideration given our knowledge of the "Plataea poem." The length of this poem is unknown. It will also be generally accepted that the specific details of what is not preserved are shadowy at best. The *Persae* of Timotheus provides an excellent parallel. It is stressed by Janssen 1989: 14 n.10 that to assume that Timotheus composed a poem on the battle of Salamis without a focus on Athens is methodologically flawed because approximately two-thirds of this poem is lost. A similar methodological error is possible with the "new Simonides." It cannot be assumed that the Spartan prominence in fr. 11 $W^2$ ensures this prominence throughout the poem.
99. Parsons 1992: 37 suggests the supplement. West 1992: 120, Pavese 1995: 2, and Sider 2001a: 18 print this text. The final sigma is faint on the papyrus and should have an underscore dot to indicate that the text is uncertain.
100. *LSJ* s.v. ἐξελαύνω 2(transitive), 2b (intransitive). Rutherford 2001a: 47 succinctly presents the problems with this supplement.
101. Hdt. 9.19.2.
102. Parsons: 1992: 37; Schachter 1998: 27; Rutherford 2001a: 47.
103. Parsons 1992: 37.
104. Rutherford 2001a: 47. See Hdt. 9.19.2.
105. West 1993b: 7 implies such an interpretation. The translations of West found at West 1993a: 168–169 and Sider 2001a: 28–29 make this interpretation explicit.
106. Schachter 1998: 27. Rutherford 47: 2001 seems to favor West's interpretation, but notes the discrepancies it creates between Simonides and Herodotus. See Hdt. 9.12–13.
107. Schachter 1998: 27–28; Huxley 2001: 76 makes the same observation.
108. Schachter 1998: 28.
109. Schachter 1998: 27, 30.
110. West and Parsons agree that Pandion is the Athenian hero.
111. For a fuller discussion of the Megarians in fr. 11 $W^2$, see "Chapter 2.2D: Content of Fr. 11 $W^2$ and the Spartans: The 'New Simonides'" at n. 141 ff. and "Chapter 2.2E: Content of Fr. 11 $W^2$ and Plataea" after n.169.

112. Note the more cautious statement at Huxley 2001: 76, "The alleged presence of the archer-Medes near Pagai may also be relevant—Pausanias 1.44.4."
113. Parsons 1992: 37–38.
114. *IEG*² 2: 120 and 1993b: 7.
115. Teisamenos appears in Hdt. 9.33.
116. Schachter 1998: 25–30 argues for a Peloponnesian focus. Aloni 2001: 86–105 argues for a Spartan emphasis.
117. Rutherford 2001a: 47.
118. Obbink 2001: 74. Obbink 1998 at http://www.csad.ox.ac.uk/POxy/ provides the digital images.
119. Parsons 1992: 38.
120. Huxley 2001: 76.
121. *SIG*³ 31; *SEG* 14.412; *GHI* I² 19; *LSAG2* ² 104 no. 15; M-L 27. The column now stands in the Hippodrome in Istanbul.
122. The thank-offering at the Isthmus that is mentioned by Herodotus is lost. A similar inscription that pertains to the Persian Wars and lists the Lacedaemonians, the Athenians, and the Corinthians is the problematic Decree of Themistocles of 480 BCE (M-L 23 = *SEG* 18.153 = EM 13330). In lines 12–18, the decree states that the Athenians will fight with the Lacedaemonians, Corinthians and the Aeginetans (μετὰ Λακεδαιμονίων καὶ Κο- /ριν[θιων καὶ Αἰγινητῶν]). The date and text of this inscription are the subject of much debate. See discussion in Habicht 1961: 1–35, Hignett 1963: 458–68, Burn 1984: 364–66, and Meiggs-Lewis 1988: 49–52.
123. It should be noted that a Spartan commission or simply an emphasis on the Spartans is not incompatible with a panhellenic scope in the poem represented by fr. 11 W². I shall return in more detail to the question of why a Spartan focus does not do justice to the interpretation of this fragment. See "Chapter 2.2D: Content of Fr. 11 W² and the Spartans."
124. On Achilles as the hero of the panhellenic *Iliad,* see Nagy 1999: 9–11 and *passim.*
125. West 1993b: 5.
126. See Parsons 1992: 31. Lobel suggested that ]αλίου could be supplemented in various ways and that it might refer to Thetis or Achilles. Lobel also suggested that POxy 2327 fr. 30 contained the line beginnings of POxy fr. 27 col. i lines 8–10, which would correspond to our fr. 11.20–22 W². This placement would alter West's reconstruction. Parsons rejects this placement.
127. Parsons 1992: 42.
128. Barchiesi 2001: 259 makes a good literary argument for linking frs. 10 and 11 W². For Barchiesi, Hor. Carm. 4.6.6 (filius . . . Thetidis marinae) parallels both fr. 11.19–20 W² (θεᾶς ἐρικυ[δέος υἱέ / κούρης εἰν]αλίου Νηρέος) and fr. 10.5 W² (κούρης εἰν]αλίης ἀγλαόφη[με πάϊ). The parallel exists, however, only if the supplements are accepted. It might be conceded that Horace confirms the spirit of the supplement; however, Horace does not confirm the arrangement or the interpretation that these fragments belong in a "Plataea poem."
129. Rutherford 2001a: 43.
130. Simon. fr. 558 *PMG* (= Ibyc. 291 *PMG* = Schol. A. R. 4.814–15a (Wendel))
131. Lobel 1954: 72.

132. Lobel 1954: 74; *IEG²* 2: 12. The same connection between POxy 2327 fr. 18+30 and fr. 27 col. ii was noted in the first edition of West, where these fragments are *adesp. el.* frs. 57–58 W.

133. Parsons 1992: 29, 33–34 makes this discovery. POxy 2327 fr. 27 col. i runs from fr. 11.12–30 W², but the line ends are only provided for frs. 11.13, 15, 17, 21, 23, 25 and 27 W². Marginal notes appear on the papyrus at fr. 11.18, 22, 28 W². POxy 2327 fr. 27 col. ii contains two more lines than col. i.

134. Parsons 1992: 29, 31. The allusion to Homer is to *Il.* 1.19, ἐκπέρσαι Πριάμοιο πόλιν, εὖ δ᾽ οἴκαδ᾽ ἱκέσθαι (cf. fr. 11.13 W²) The allusion in Theocritus is at *Id.* 16.42–47. Hutchinson (*apud* Parsons) suggested the allusion and made the supplement ὁπ[λοτέρ]οισιν. Parsons' placement of POxy 2327 fr. 27 col. i confirms the suggestion. Finally, the pronoun σ᾽ in POxy 3965 fr. 1.13(= fr. 11.20 W²) confirms the vocative Μοῦσα at the end of the same line.

135. Parsons 1992:33. Note the occurrence of ἀν]θρώπων at fr. 11.22 W² (+POxy 3965 fr. 2.1).

136. Lobel 1954: 67.

137. West 1993b: 7–8. The decent into the Asopus plain is narrated at Hdt. 9.19.3. West cites Simon. XVI.7 *FGE,* an inscription at Megara for the Persian Wars, (τοὶ δὲ καὶ ἐν πεδίωι Βοιωτίωι) as a parallel for the reference to the Asopus plain at fr. 13.11 W² (δ᾽ ἐπεὶ ἐς πεδίον). Lobel 1954: 67 appears to have had the same episode in mind, since he notes that the Asopus cannot be found in the traces at POxy 2327 fr. 27.17 (= POxy 2327 col. ii line 12 = fr. 13.12 W²).

138. Cf. Rutherford 2001a: 47.

139. Barigazzi 1963: 74. See "Introduction: The *Suda* on Simonides" at n. 59ff.

140. Simonides mentioned Thermopylae in a lyric (531 *PMG*). If fr. 13 W² contains verses relevant to Thermopylae, it would have to be conceded that Simonides mentioned the battle in both a lyric and an elegiac poem.

141. Parsons 1992: 19, 41. "A sheet join touches the end of 7, and runs through δ at the end of 9" (19).

142. Parsons 1992: 10, 41. "Sheet-join to the far right of 8–10, cutting through ν of λιπουτ[" (10).

143. Parsons 1992: 41. The battle above the Asopus is recounted at Hdt. 9.20.

144. West 1993b: 8. Rutherford 2001a: 48 accepts West's suggestion that the verse contains a prophecy, but not the details. He suggests that the speaker may not have been Teisamenos.

145. The Γ on the fragment is difficult to read. Parsons 1992: 19 remarks that the top of the upright exists with an abnormal hook to the left. The ink for the E is also incomplete.

146. Parsons 1992: 42.

147. Parsons 1992: 41–42; West 1993b: 8. Parsons 1992: 42 at his note on line 4 also suggests "β[ι]η[σάμενοι or the like."

148. Parsons 1992: 42 also suggests ἀμαι]μάκετον or ἀμαι]μακέτην ("irresistible") for the initial letters.

149. It needs to be noted that West is highly cautious in his presentation of this reading.

150.   The letters are in line 17. Parsons 1992: 40 records ]˳ακου, ]˳αβου, or ]κ̣ακου as possible readings. He suggests that these letters might continue the note at POxy 3965 fr. 18.8, but does not find a physical link between the fragments.

151.   Lobel originally saw two lines after line 24: 25, ]θυ ˳ α[, and 26, ]ασ[. These are no longer visible. See Parsons 1992: 17 and West 1992: 122 (app. crit.) and Sider 2001a: 23 (app. crit.).

152.   West 1993b: 9.

153.   Rutherford 2001a: 49. Rutherford considers the fragment as part of the "Plataea poem," but places it (and fr. 18 W²) under the heading "Unassigned."

154.   Rutherford 2001a: 49. Rutherford remarks that "dramatic speech in the description of a battle is illustrated in the *Persai* of Timotheus." The papyrus, however, is not clear at either place. Parsons 1992: 17, 40–41.

155.   Parsons 1992: 41 on line 8 simply records the possible repetition. Line reads 9 ˳ αιμ[. By analogy with line 8, which reads actually κάιμ[, Parson suggests κάιμ[ε for both lines. However, an accent above the α (seen in line 8) is difficult to discern in line 9. Parsons (1992: 17) indicates a "high point of ink to the right" of this letter. The images published by Obbink do not easily reveal this mark to me. It should be noted that Sider prints καὶ μ[ in both lines. For the second line, the text of G-P has: . αιμ[.

156.   Rutherford 2001a: 49.

157.   Parsons 1992: 40, "δημητ[ possible." This reading is also printed by Sider and Gentili-Prato.

158.   For other possible instances of direct speech in the "new Simonides," see West 1993b: 4. West suggests that Nereus speaks in the "Artemisium poem."

159.   Note the heading in *IEG*² 2, "10–17(+18?). De Proelio Plataiaco."

160.   Parsons 1992: 39.

161.   Parsons 1992: 39.

162.   Pavese 1995:1–26 does not include this fragment as part of his text.

163.   See Obbink 2001: 67–73.

164.   For the estimated dimensions of columns see Parsons 1992: 5.

165.   POxy 2327 fr. 6.9 represents the same line as POxy 2327 fr. 27 col. i line 1.

166.   Parsons 1992: 33 remarks that a column on POxy 2327 is known to have contained at least 24 lines. His reason is that POxy 2327 fr. 1 is a column top and belonged to the same column as fr. 27 col. i. I do not understand Parsons here. POxy 2327 fr. 1 (= fr. 21 W²) is certainly a column-top, but it belongs to a sympotic fragment. If this fragment is the column top of fr. 27 col. i, then the sympotic poem needs to come to an end soon after the verses which survive (POxy 2327 fr. 1) to allow for the opening lines of the poem represented by fr. 11 W², which is lost, as well as fr. 11.5–30 W² in the same column. From this evidence, it would seem that the column length according to Parsons' estimate should be at least 31 (= 13 lines from fr. 21 W² (=POxy 2327 fr. 1) + 18 lines from fr. 11 W² (=POxy 3965 fr. 1)). So, Parsons must mean POxy fr. 6, which is also a column top and was certainly in the same column as fr. 27 col. i. This change however, would seem to give a column length of at least 26 lines. I am unable to solve the difficulty in Parsons' estimation.

167.   This estimation is only possible if POxy 3965 frs. 1 and 2 belong to the same column. See the discussion above for the certainty of this arrangement.

168.   Rutherford 2001a: 47.

169. If frs. 14–17 W² are considered as part of the same poem as fr. 11 W², this poem would have contained more than 84 lines. If frs. 10 W² and 11.1–4 W² are included, this poem would have been over 94 lines long.
170. Rutherford 2001a: 36.
171. Obbink 2001: 81–82. Sider 2001b: 285–286 also proposes the placement of some of the sympotic fragments in the "Plataea poem."
172. Obbink 2001: 82 The suggestion arises from the reading at 34.2 W²: c·αλ[ . The sigma is a partial letter. It is proposed by Obbink that this sigma is the last letter of the title: [Σαλαμί]ς. The supplement is far from certain and the only reason for connecting the lines before the coronis with the Plataea poem is the inability to determine a title for the "Plataea poem" that ends in a sigma.
173. Other suppositions can be imagined. If the letter at fr. 34.2 W² is a final sigma in a title of a poem or a section of a book, one might also suggest [παιᾶνε]ς. This would create a book with both elegies and lyric poems. On this possibility see Lobel 1981: 21–23.
174. Podlecki 1968: 267 has a similar suggestion concerning the Salamis poem.
175. Cameron 1993: 1–2.

## NOTES TO CHAPTER TWO

1. Rutherford 2001a: 38.
2. Lloyd-Jones 1994: 3; Capra-Curti 1995: 30; Poltera 1997: 354–55; Fantuzzi 2001: 235 at n. 11.
3. West 1993b: 5 also reads fr. 10 W² as an address to Achilles. So too Rutherford 2001a: 43, but Rutherford brings forward the difficulty in placing this fragment in relation to fr. 11 W².
4. Schein 1984: 129–142.
5. West 1993b: 5–6; Rutherford 2001a: 43. For the link between Patroklos and Achilles in burial see Schein 1984: 129–132.
6. See "Chapter 1.4B: 'New Simonides': Fr. 11 W² (=POxy 2327 frs. 5+6+27 col. 1 + POxy 3965 fr. 1+2)" at n. 93ff. Fr. 11.1–4 W² (=POxy 2327 fr. 5) is a column bottom and fr. 11.5–13 W² (=POxy 2327 fr. 6) is a column top, thereby allowing a potential, but not certain, physical link.
7. Schein 1984: 73–76; Barchiesi 2001: 258.
8. Barchiesi 2001: 255–60. Barchiesi 2001: 257 at n. 6 does admit that the felling of a tree is an apt simile for the death of any hero in Homer. For the reference to heroes as trees when they die in the *Iliad,* an image used only of Trojans and Achilles, see Schein 1984: 73–76, 96–97.
9. Parsons 1992: 28 and Lloyd-Jones 1994: 1 suggest that the death of Masistius or Mardonius found in Herodotus' depiction of the battle of Plataea may be read in this fragment. Even if the simile is applied to Achilles, a return to the hero at the end of the poem is conceivable. See Rutherford 2001a: 43 on fr. 10 W². Compare Theoc. *Id.* 22, where the Dioscouri are addressed as the subject of the hymn at the outset and returned to at the hymn's conclusion. This conclusion happens to be a depiction of the destruction of Troy that is reminiscent of the Simonidean passage under discussion here.

10. Gentili-Prato judiciously prints these lines (fr. 11.1–4 W²) as a separate fragment (=fr. 3g).

11. For the idea that the Muse is evoked as the poet's helper, see O'Hara 1998: 69–74; Stehle 2001:108–114; Rutherford 2001a: 46–47. Cf. Obbink 2001: 71. For the interesting aspect of these verses in terms of poetic form, see Obbink 2001: 69–73.

12. The line, spread over three separate papyrus fragments, is read by Parsons as:

    ] . . καιτονδ[         ] . φρονακ[         ] . δης

    It is printed by West and Sider as:

    ἔντυνο]ν καὶ τόνδε[ μελ]ίφρονα κ[όσμον ἀο]ιδῆς

    While it seems clear in theory that Simonides is asking for help with his song, the letters are simply not there. For other supplements, Capra-Curti 1995: 31 who read ] . δης as ]ρδης, suggest –κε]ρδης (-gain) or χο]ρδῆς (note).

13. All texts print Σπάρτ[ηι. One might also conjecture Σπάρτηνδε, which is Homeric. It occurs at the *Od.* 2.326 and 4.10. In both passages, the word bridges the second half of the 2nd foot and the first half of the 3rd foot, as is likely the case in the Simonidean passage here. Other poetic uses appear at A.R. 1.148, Nonn. 34.120, Q. S. 2.55, Coluth. 314. Σπάρτηθεν would also work, which appears at *Od.*1.285. See *LSJ* s.v. Σπάρτη.

14. West 1993b: 14 suggests a reference to the Isthmus here by comparing Bacchylides 1.13, which apostrophizes the Isthmus as the gates to the Peloponnesus: ὦ Πέλοπος λιπαρᾶς νάσου θεόδατοι πύλαι ("O god-built gates of shiny island of Pelops").

15. See Rutherford 2001a: 47 at n. 67 and "Chapter 1.4B: 'New Simonides': Fr. 11 W² (=POxy 2327 frs. 5+6+27 col. 1 + POxy 3965 fr. 1+2)" after n. 111.

16. For the evidence, Obbink 1998: http://www.csad.ox.ac.uk/POxy/ must be consulted. For the liberation of Attica at this point in the narrative see West 1993b: 7. West's translation is found at West 1993a: 168–169 and Sider 2001a: 28–29. Consider also Schachter 1998: 27 and Rutherford 2001a: 47. For the arrival of the Athenians at this point in the narrative, see Parsons 1992: 37–38 and Obbink 2001: 74. Cf. Huxley 2001: 76.

17. Bowie 1986: 13–35.

18. West 1974: 10–13.

19. West 1974: 18.

20. West 1974: 14.

21. Bowie 1986: 15–21.

22. For elegy at symposia see Thgn. 237–54; West 1974: 11–12; Bowie 1986: 15–21 and 1990: 221–29; Rösler 1990: 230–32.

23. The case for performance at *komoi* is less explicitly made by Bowie. At 1986: 15, he remarks, "Allusions also show such songs (i.e. elegies) continuing during the *komos* that could follow a banquet." He refers the reader to West 1974: 12 for the evidence (Thgn. 1045, 1065, 1207, 1351; *eleg. adesp.* 26; Hermesianax fr. 7.35–40).

24. The case for performance of elegy at public festivals is made at Bowie 1986: 27–34.

25. A note on terminology is necessary. Bowie used the descriptive heading "narrative elegy" to refer to publicly performed elegiac poems in which historical narratives were a primary feature. This term is paraphrased variously: "epic elegy" (Obbink 2001: 65), "historical narrative elegy" (Aloni 2001: 93), "encomiastic narrative elegy that

celebrates historical events" (Boedeker 2001a: 120), "historical elegy" (Stehle 2001: 106, but cf. 106 n. 2 where "historical narrative elegy" is used). Recently, Sider (unpublished) addresses the validity of the category "historical elegy" by which, he means Bowie's category of "narrative elegy." Throughout I will use (and have used) Bowie's term, "narrative elegy," with all of its implications. That is, by "narrative elegy," I mean an elegy with a narrative of both past and contemporary events as its focus.

26. Bowie 1986: 33.

27. Bowie 1986: 28–29, 34.

28. Bowie 1986: 29, 30–31.

29. Bowie 1986: 30, 33. On narative elegy and historiography see Bowie 2001: 45–56.

30. Bowie 1986: 27–34. Bowie allows two contexts for the performance of elegy: symposia (and *komoi*) and public festivals.

31. Sider unpublished: 13–14. Sider points to a scholiast on Pl. *R.* 368A as a possible description of elegiac sub-genres. ᾠδαὶ τὰ ἐλεγεῖα, ἢ θρῆνοι, ἢ μῦθοι· ἔνθεν καὶ τὰ ἐπιτάφια ποιήματα ἐλεγεῖα καλοῦνται ("elegies are songs, either laments or narratives (?); hence poetic epitaphs are called elegies."). Sider's point is to show that the ancients did not define a sub-type of elegy as "historical elegy," i.e. Bowie's narrative elegy. That the scholiast refers to elegies as μῦθοι need not lead to the conclusion that ancient commentators identified "narrative elegy," historical or otherwise, as a sub-genre. Certainly, as Sider points out, the scholium does not get us any closer to historical narratives in elegy. I take the scholiast to mean that elegies could contain narrative or lament, not that they were defined by it. Yet, the possibility remains that the scholiast can be understood as defining two types of elegy.

32. ἐπε[ὶ ῥ'] ἐ[ν]εδέξατο μῦθον ("since, as it turns out, they were ordered.") The direct speech is implied by μῦθον. See West 1974: 74; Allen 1993: 23, 112.

33. Bowie 1986: 29.

34. Bowie 2001: 48.

35. Bowie 1986: 29–30 and 2001: 48–49.

36. For the reconstruction of Mimnermus' works, and the *Smyrneis* in particular, see West 1974: 74–76; Bowie 1986: 28–30; Allen 1993: 20–26; Cameron 1995: 310–314; Bowie 2001: 47–49. While Allen allows that the *Smyrneis* may have contained narrative, he does not believe that it was narrative for its own sake. Allen also does not believe that it was performed in a competition.

37. Bowie 2001: 49.

38. Bowie 1986: 29 and 2001: 48.

39. Εὐνομία: Aris. *Pol.* 5.6.2(1306b36) (= fr. 1W²) and Str. 8.4.10 (= fr. 2 W²); πολιτεία Λακεδαιμονίοις: the *Suda* T 1205 Adler (= *IEG*² 2: 169). Bowie 1986: 30 reasonably equates the two. For the ancient practice of giving titles to poetic works, see "Introduction: The *Suda* on Simonides" at nn. 73–78 and "Chapter 1.3A: The Salamis Poem: Evidence" at nn. 48–60.

40. Bowie 1986: 29–31.

41. Bowie 1986: 30–31.

42. Bowie 2001: 47.

43. See Bowie 1986: 31, specifically n. 31.

44. Stehle 1996: 221 n. 59 notes that it is not certain that Semonides' composition was in elegiacs. This doubt, however, does not appear in the revised version of this article, Stehle 2001.

45.  Bowie 1986: 32–33.

46.  *LSJ* s.v. ἔπος IV.

47.  Evidence in West 1974: 7. The point was suggested already by Bowra 1970: 121. See also Bowie 1986: 32 n. 100.

48.  Bowie 1986: 32 argues that all of the hexameters of Xenophanes are philosophical and, therefore, the verses mentioned by Diogenes on historical matters should be elegiacs. This reasoning, however, does not seem to be solid enough to establish the poem by Xenophanes as an example of narrative elegy. To be sure, there are elegiac fragments by Xenophanes that have historical content (frs. 3, 7a (on Pythagoras), 8 W²). Yet, an important feature of Bowie's category of narrative elegy is that it is to be performed in a public setting. It is not entirely certain that these elegiac fragments of Xenophanes that pertain to historical subjects are unsuitable for sympotic performance. Stehle 1996: 221 n. 59 expresses doubts about the meter of Xenophanes composition. These doubts, however, do not appear in the revised version of this article, Stehle 2001. Bowie 2001: 49 accepts this criticism as correct.

49.  Matthews 1974: 26–27; Bowie 1986: 32; Rösler 1990: 235, who classifies the poem as a "historical elegy."

50.  Matthew 1974 assigns Fr 24 K, 25 K, and 29 K to this poem. Only 29 K is a possible direct quote. The hexameter, however, is a reconstruction.

51.  Bowie 1986: 32. The reason for seeing Panyassis as an example of the established tradition of narrative elegy is that the *Suda* also records a hexameter poem by Panyassis on Heracles in 14 Books, totaling 9,000 lines. Bowie concludes that hexameters would have been the appropriate choice for mythographic works on panhellenic heroes, while elegiacs would have been the meter for local histories such as the Ἰωνικά. The distinction between hexameters and elegiacs in terms of content is elaborated at Bowie 2001: 50–51.

52.  For similar difficulties concerning meter in the *Suda*, consider the entry on Simonides (Σ 439 Adler). See above, "Introduction: The *Suda* on Simonides" at n. 66 ff.

53.  See "Chapter 1.3: The Salamis Poem." *The Sea-battle at Artemisium* and the "Plataea poem" are not mentioned here because Bowie's article predates the publication of the "new Simonides." Bowie 1986: 32 also refers to Solon's *Salamis* (fr. 1–3 W²), but separates it from narrative elegy. Bowie believes that this poem was performed in a symposium (1986: 19–21) and, for this reason, that it would not have been a narrative elegy, which is closely associated with performance at public festivals. Yet, the first person address in frs. 1–3 W² and the implied action would seem to meet at some of the features shared by other poems of this category, that is, *oratio recta*. Is it possible that these addresses belong to speeches within a poetic historical narrative, like those implied in Mimnermus *Smyrneis* (fr. 13a W²)? The subject of Solon's *Salamis* also was certainly historical events, another criterion shared by the other narrative elegies. If we must have a category of narrative elegy, it would seem that this poem should be considered part of it. It seems to have been excluded by Bowie because it is too short, although he does not say so explicitly. Plutarch reports that the poem was only one hundred lines long, but he also adds that it was performed publicly. The exclusion of Solon's *Salamis,* however, reveals that the definition of this group of poems is difficult.

54.  Bowie 1986: 32–33 n. 104, which suggests that the quote may be a verse that has been corrupted.

55. Bowie 2001: 50 n. 18.
56. Bowie 2001: 51–53 adds two more bits of evidence for the appearance of narrative in early elegiac poetry. First, he mentions a poem in which Archilochus told of Heracles' murder of the centaur Nessus (frs. 286–289 W²). Dio Chrysostom tells us that in this composition Deianeira is said to have told a long story while she was raped by the centaur (D. Chr. 60.1 = Archil. fr. 286 W²). Bowie links these *testimonia* with the words of Longinus (33.4–5), where a poem of Archilochus is compared with the *Erigone* of Eratosthenes. Bowie posits that since the *Erigone* was an elegiac mythical narrative, Longinus is comparing a mythical narrative in the same meter by Archilochus. He proposes that the composition on Heracles is the one Longinus has in mind because of the wording of criticism in both Dio Chrysostom and Longinus. Bowie rightly is cautious and goes no further than to use Archilochus as an example of narrative in elegy. Cf. Bowie 1986: 34. The second example of narrative in elegy is *The Sack of Troy* by Sacadas, the sixth/seventh-century poet from Argos, mentioned by Athenaeus (13.610 C). There are textual difficulties in the passage and the name of Sacadas appears only through an emendation that is not universally accepted. West does not include the passage in *IEG*² and Gentili-Prato consider the fragment dubious in *PEG*. Bowie notes these problems, but he hazards two conclusions. First, that this poem may have been an elegy. Second, if so, it may explain why Euripides' *Andromache,* which may have been performed in Argos, contains an elegiac song, our only example of this meter in fifth-century tragedy. Even if these guesses are correct, Bowie does not elaborate on how Sacadas' poem helps to make the case for a category of narrative elegy as he defines it. Rather, it would seem the Sacadas' work, if it were an elegy, would be an example of a mythographic narration of a panhellenic story, a type of content Bowie 2001: 50 reserves for hexameters. It is possible that Sacadas' poem represents an early point in the tradition of narrative elegy in which the distinctions set out by Bowie are not firmly established, but Bowie does not make this point. For the distinction between hexameter and elegiacs see Bowie 1986: 32 and 2001: 50–51. To this evidence, we perhaps should add Callinus T 1 Gerber (on an account of the Magnesians), T 4 Gerber (on an account of the Teucrians), and T 5 Gerber and fr. 5 W² (on Cimmerians and the capture of Sardis). See Sider unpublished: 7.
57. Bowie 1986: 3, "If both the existence of this genre (i.e. narrative elegy) and of elegiac competitions at festivals are admitted, then they surely go together."
58. It is right to remember, as was stated above, that Bowie later admits that it is doubtful that the works of Xenophanes and Ion were poetic. Bowie 2001: 49 n. 15 and 50 n. 18.
59. Bowie 1986: 33.
60. Rösler 1990: 236.
61. For the ancient practice of titling see "Introduction: The *Suda* on Simonides" at nn. 73–78 and "Chapter 1.3A: The Salamis Poem: Evidence" at nn. 48–60.
62. Sider unpublished: *passim,* but conclusions are drawn on 19–20. Dougherty 1994: 35–46 reaches similar conclusions about *ktisis* poetry. Dougherty, however, accepts narrative elegy as one genre which could have contained a *ktisis*. Her reason for accepting this sub-genre is Bowie's argument that these verses were sung at public festivals, that is, they have an occasion that defines their genre.
63. Bowie 2001: 55–58. For a succinct statement of the importance of Bowie's article as well as its prophetic status see Sider unpublished: 6.

64.     Boedeker-Sider 2001: 4 n. 5 exemplifies the *communis opinio:* "Bowie's important article will be cited many times in this volume for the ways its arguments on the nature of historical elegy (i.e. narrative elegy) are borne out or refined by the evidence of the new Simonides."

65.     For a prooimion in a narrative elegy, see Mimn. fr. 13 W$^2$. For references to events that are in the recent past, see Mimn. fr. 13, 13a and 14 W$^2$, Tyrt. fr. 4 W$^2$. For references to a mythical past or mythical exempla, see Tyrt. fr. 2 W$^2$ and Panyas. T 1 *PEG.*

66.     For an initial approach to fr. 11 W$^2$, and in fact most of the "new Simonides," as a narrative elegy see the comments of Parsons 1992: 6 and West: 1993b: 4–9. For the most part, other scholars follow the general idea set down by these scholars, namely that the "new Simonides" contains a narrative of Plataea. West does not cite Bowie.

67.     West 1993b: 5–7. For Herodotus and Simonides see Boedeker 2001a: 120–134 and Hornblower 2001: 135–147.

68.     At fr. 11.33–34 W$^2$, the texts of West and Sider are reconstructed to have Pausanias, son of Cleombrotus, leading out the army ἔξ[α]γ'. Parsons' *editio princeps,* however, records [ ], [ ]γ'. Inspection of the images of the fragment reveals a large hole in the fragment to the left of the Γ' . In fact, it might be suggested that Γ' may be T'. The left cross bar of the T may be cut by the hole in the papyrus. The reading printed by West and Sider, then, remains conjectural. At fr. 11.41 W$^2$, some action is introduced by the letters εξε[ ]ντε , [, but the text is too incomplete to find the sense of it. No supplement has gained universal acceptance. See "Chapter 1.4B: 'New Simonides:' Fr. 11 W$^2$ (=POxy 2327 frs. 5+6+27 col. 1 + POxy 3965 frs. 1+2)" at nn. 100–113. Finally at fr. 11.47 W$^2$, the letters δαμασαντ[ suggest that someone is conquering; but again, how the action pertains to the content of the poem is a mystery.

69.     Sider unpublished: 1–21 argues that narrative elegy—his term is historical elegy—was not a legitimate poetic category of early Greek elegy and shows that historical narrative would have been at home in various other types of early verses where it would not have been the sole focus of the poem. Consider also Bowie's new conclusions that the *Eunomia/Politeia* of Tyrtaeus may have contained only bits of narrative in a larger exhortatory elegy found at Bowie 2001: 47.

70.     See Flower 2000: *passim,* especially 65–69.

71.     Aloni 2001: 102–104. This article is a later version of Aloni 1997: 8–28, which has the same argument as Aloni 1994a: 9–22. See Bowie 1986: 33 for a competitive performance context for "narrative elegy" in general and Boedeker 1995: 223–225 for such a context for the so-called "Plataea poem." For a similar assumption that the poem focused on the Spartans at Plataea, see Stehle 2001: 106–119; Shaw 2001: 180–181. Rutherford 2001a: 38–39 also favors an emphasis on Spartans, but admits that they were not the sole focus.

72.     Aloni 2001: 98. Cf. Lloyd-Jones 1994: 1; Shaw 2001: 79; Pavese 1995: 24–25.

73.     Aloni 2001: 98.

74.     Aloni 2001: 100.

75.     For the term "poly-hellenic" see Boedeker 1995: 220, 222. Also, Boedeker 2001b: 158. Boedeker 1995: 223–225 is a point by point consideration of Aloni 1994a: 9–22.

76.     Boedeker 2001b: 158.

77.     Boedeker 2001a: 127. Cf. Boedeker 1995: 225.

78. Boedeker 2001b: 163 and 2001a: 125–127.
79. Cf. Hdt. 9.71–72, where the Spartans are given their due as the leaders at Plataea.
80. Boedeker 1998b: 166–167 discusses the association of these figures with Laconia.
81. Bowie 2001: 55–56 suggests that the upper limit for the length of the longer poems represented by the "new Simonides" would be 900 lines and that they may not have exceeded 600 lines.
82. For epigrams on the Persian Wars see Appendix 1.
83. Aloni 2001: 98–101.
84. Simon. *FGE* XV = Plu. *Arist.* 19.6 F and *de Herod. malign.* 42, 873 B. The second line only appears in *AP* 6.50.
85. Page 1981: 212. For the Serpent column, see "Chapter 1.4B: 'New Simonides:' Fr. 11 W$^2$ (=POxy 2327 frs. 5+6+27 col. 1 + POxy 3965 frs. 1+2)" at n. 122ff.
86. Simon. VIII *FGE* = *AP* 7.253.
87. Simon. IX *FGE* = *AP* 7.251.
88. For the arrangement of these epigrams in *AP*, see Bergk *PLG* 3$^4$: 456–457 and Page 1981: 197–199. For the arrangement of the *AP* in general, see Cameron 1993: 98–120.
89. For the Thermopylae inscriptions, see Hdt. 7.228 and Str. 9.4.2. Strabo says that five stelae were inscribed at Thermopylae, including one for the Locrians, which he quotes (Simon. XXIII *FGE*). Herodotus quotes three: Simon. XXII (a) *FGE,* for the Peloponnesians who died with Leonidas; Simon. XXII (b) *FGE,* for the Lacedaemonians specifically; and Simon. VI *FGE* for the Spartan seer Megistias. See Page 1981: 231–234. Page 1981: 78 records the *communis opinio* that one of these five inscriptions was for the Thespians (Philiadas I *FGE*). Cf. Molyneux 1992: 180–85, who expresses more uncertainty than Page about which inscriptions are to be placed at Thermopylae. For the epigrams quoted above, see specifically, Molyneux 1992: 184–185, 197.
90. Bergk *PLG* 3$^4$: 456–458, followed by Page 1981: 198–9. Simon. VIII and IX *FGE* = Simon. 99–100 Bergk *PLG* 3$^4$. Cf. Aloni 2001: 98–99 who accepts this association and Boedeker 1995: 225 n. 31 who does not.
91. Cf. Peek 28 *GVI* (= Simon. VIII *FGE*) which suggests 338/337 BCE as the date of the inscription; therefore, he links the verses with the Battle of Chaeronea.
92. For similar sentiments in inscriptions concerning the Persian Wars, consider Simon. XVI *FGE,* on a memorial for Megarians who fell in the Persian Wars. This epigram is discussed at "Chapter 2.2E: Content of Fr. 11 W$^2$ and Plataea" following n. 169. Also consider, Simon. XIX (a) and (b) *FGE,* the fragmentary epigrams for the Athenians who fell in the Persian Wars. For these epigrams, see "Appendix: Persian War Epigrams."
93. Page 1981: 198.
94. Page 1981: 189–190 discusses the practice of identifying the dead and the battlefield on *polyandria*.
95. [D.] lix 97, *In Neaeram,* which also records the inscription, reports that the Serpent column commemorated Salamis and Plataea. I follow M-L who suggest that the Serpent Column refers "to the whole of the Great Persian Wars down to Plataea."
96. Simon. XVIIa *FGE*= Thuc. 1.132.2. Page reports, "There is said to be no trace of erasure on the snake column." Thucydides places the inscription on the tripod (ἐπὶ τὸν τρίποδα). The verses may have been inscribed on the steps of the pedestal. Page 1981: 216.

97.     Cf. Simon. XXXI *FGE*, an inscription that supposedly accompanied a dedication
        of a bronze bowl at Exampaeus by Pausanias. Here Pausanias is designated ἄρχων
        Ἑλλάδος εὐχόρου. On "assertive personal dedications," see Hornblower 1997: 218.
        Hornblower 1982: 281–85 provides a brief historical survey of the Greek attitude
        toward personal dedications on temples as a comparison for the practices of the Heca-
        tomnids, the Hellenistic Carian dynasts of the fourth century BCE.
98.     Hornblower 1997: 218. Huxley 2001: 76: "The original wording [of this epigram]
        may have been less boastful: ἐπεὶ στρατὸς ὤλετο Μήδων."
99.     Thucydides says the Spartans erased the inscription; however, see Hornblower 1991:
        218–219 for the involvement of the Delphic amphictiony, omitted by Thucydides
        but reported in [D.] lix. 97–98, *In Neaeram*. It may be possible that the "panhellenic"
        presentation of the victory at Delphi was imposed on the Greek cities.
100.    Simon. XVIIb *FGE* = D. S. 11.33.
101.    Gomme 1956: 434 observes the unusual lapse in the reliability of Diodorus.
102.    There are epigrams on the Persian Wars that do emphasize individuals and cities:
        Simon. XXII (b) *FGE* (on Thermopylae) and Simon. XXI *FGE* (on Marathon) are
        examples. It should be noted, however, that Thermopylae and Marathon were battles
        fought largely by individual cities. Simon. XII *FGE* (on a monument at the Isthmus
        that commemorates Corinthian dead in the Persian Wars) explicitly states that the
        Corinthians saved all of Greece. A similar sentiment is expressed by the Corinthians
        on an epitaph set up at Salamis (Simon. XI *FGE*). Likewise Simon. XXIV *FGE* (a
        dedication to Artemis) is an Athenian claim to have subdued the Persians at Arte-
        misium without reference to any allies. A similar claim in terms of the Persian Wars
        is made at Simon. XVIII, generally thought to be a later literary exercise; however,
        Page argues that the epigram is possibly inscriptional (1981: 229–30). The Megarians
        also set up an inscribed memorial in their city. The inscription, Simon. XVI *FGE*,
        claims that those who died "increased the day of freedom for Greece and Megara." See
        "Chapter 2.2F: Content of Fr. 11 W² and Plataea: The 'New Simonides'" following
        n. 169.
103.    Aloni 2001: 100.
104.    *CAH* 5²: 100; Rhodes 1985: 5–11.
105.    See Boedeker 1995: 225. For Pausanias' troubles following Plataea see Hdt. 5.32,
        Th. 1.128.4–130. On the difficulties of exact dating of the final condemnation of
        Pausanias see *CAH* 5²: 100–101. Huxley 2001: 75 suggests more precise parameters.
        In raising the possibility of a Thessalian context for Simonides' poem, he suggest a
        composition at a time before Pausanias is disgraced but after the failure of Spartan
        attempt to expel the Thessalians from the Delphic amphictiony (Plu. *Them.* 20.3–4)
        and Leotychidas' failure in his campaign to punish the Thessalians for siding with
        the Persians (Hdt. 6.72.1–2). Firm dating of Leotychidas' Thessalian campaign is
        debated. He is believed to be in exile in 476 BCE. See *CAH* 5²: 97–100, 499. So, fol-
        lowing Huxley's thinking, Simonides' composition would have had to appear before
        this date.
106.    This is not to say that Aeschylus provides an accurate account of Salamis, or that
        his purpose was to present history *per se*. Here, I distinguish between drama that
        has contemporary or near contemporary history as its subject and drama that took
        myth or what may have been distant history to an ancient mind as its subject. For

the considerations of what it means to be "historical" tragedy as a class of drama see Hall 1996: 5–10, especially 7–9, and Harrison 2000: 25–31.

107. Echoed in the words of Artemisia at Hdt. 8.68γ: δειμαίνω μὴ ναυτικὸς στρατὸς κακωθεὶς τὸν πεζὸν προσδηλήσηται ("I fear that the injuring of the fleet will utterly destroy the army"). Herodotus expresses a similar thought in the prelude to the battle of Artemisium where he equates the absence of the fleet with defeat on land for the Greeks (7.139).

108. Cf. the messenger's words at 285, φεῦ, τῶν Ἀθηνῶν ὡς στένω μεμνημένος ("Alas, how I groan, when I remember Athens.") and the phrase that Darius commands his servant to repeat to him at Hdt. 5.105 δέσποτα, μέμνεο τῶν Ἀθηναίων ("Master, Remember the Athenians").

109. For the Delian League, see Thuc. 1.95–97 and Rhodes 1985: 5–11.

110. Broadhead 1960: 76–77; Hall: 1996: 123.

111. Schol. in Ar. *Ach.* 106 (Wilson): πάντας τοὺς Ἕλληνας Ἰάονας ἐκάλουν οἱ βάρβαροι ("The barbarians used to call all of the Greeks Ionians"). Cf. scholium on 104: Ἴαον δὲ ἀντὶ τοῦ Ἀθηναῖε Ἴωνες γὰρ Ἀθηναῖοι ἀπὸ Ἴωνος τοῦ Ξούθου ("Ionian instead of Athenian, for Ionians are Athenians from Ion, son of Xuthus"). Sommerstein 1980: 162 remarks, "it is noticeable that except here, Ar. uses the terms "Ionian" only of non-Athenians and usually in a disparaging context." Also Olson 2002: 106 who emphasizes "the strong overtones of cowardice, effeminacy, and the like" in the Aristophanic use of "Ionian." Aristophanes here shows that the term can refer specifically to the Athenians.

112. Hdt. 7.9.1: Ἴωνας τοὺς ἐν τῇ Εὐρώπῃ κατοικημένους.

113. Hdt 1.143.3: οἱ μέν νυν ἄλλοι Ἴωνες καὶ οἱ Ἀθηναῖοι ἔφυγον τὸ οὔνομα, οὐ βουλόμενοι Ἴωνες κεκλῆσθαι, ἀλλὰ καὶ νῦν φαίνονταί μοι οἱ πολλοὶ αὐτῶν ἐπαισχύνεσθαι ("Now the other Ionians and the Athenians avoided the name, not wanting to be called Ionians, and furthermore now many of them seem to be ashamed of the name").

114. Also at 563, 898, 950–951, 1011, 1025.

115. 182–3: ἡ μὲν πέπλοισι Περσικοῖς ἠσκημένη / ἡ δ᾿ αὖτε Δωρικοῖσιν ("One woman was dressed in a Persian cloak, the other was dressed in a Doric one"). Broadhead 1960: 183; Hall 1996: 124. Both refer to Hdt. 5.88 which claims that in ancient times all Greeks wore Doric chitons.

116. 816–17: τόσος γὰρ ἔσται πέλανος αἱματοσφαγὴς / πρὸς γῇ Πλαταιῶν Δωρίδος λόγχης ὕπο· ("So much bloody gore will there be at the land of Plataea from the Dorian spear").

117. Broadhead 1960: 204; Hall 1996: 817. For the Spartan victory, Hdt. 9.71.

118. This catalogue contains the only Homeric reference to the Ionians. See Janko 1992: 132–33.

119. For Cleisthenes and the Ionian tribes, see Hdt. 5.66.2 and 5.69.2. For the continuation of the political validity of Ionian tribes, see Sokolowski 1962: 27–31 (no. 10). Sokolowski prints two inscriptions which are Athenian religious calendars from the agora dating to the late 5th and early fourth century BCE. In the first there is a reference to the Ionian tribe the Gelontes (Γ(ε)λεόντων φυλῆι in lines 35 and 47). This inscription was first published and discussed at Oliver 1935: 5–32. See Huxley 1966: 31–33.

120.   Although it is not certain exactly when the distinction between Ionian (i.e. Athenians)
       and Dorian (i.e. Spartans) began to play a significant role in political propaganda in
       Athens or elsewhere, Ionian-Dorian tensions were relevant during the Peloponnesian
       War. Hornblower 1992: 169–197 argues for a noticeable religious significance to the
       dichotomy Ionian-Dorian during the Peloponnesian War; see specifically 173–75,
       196–97. The importance of Ion in Athenian mythology is addressed by Parker 1987:
       205–207. It may also be significant that Doros appears in Simon. fr. 14.9 $W^2$, pre-
       sumably, although not certainly, in reference to the Spartans.
121.   Broadhead 1960: 204.
122.   For the idea that this historical drama would have presented a view that was sympa-
       thetic to the Athenians, compare the fate of Phrynichus after the performance of his
       *Sack of Miletus* told at Hdt. 6.21.2. No such fine was imposed on Aeschylus and it is
       reasonable to conclude that the Athenians found the view of the wars in the *Persae* to
       be agreeable to them.
123.   Rhodes 1985: 5–11, 22–29. On p. 11, Rhodes concludes that "The origins of the
       Delian League are to be sought in the naval campaigns of 479–478, not in the events
       surrounding Plataea." Podlecki 1970: 7–8 sees the victory of Salamis as not only an
       Athenian victory, but a victory of Themistocles. He explains the emphasis on Salamis
       as being related to the waning political fortunes of Themistocles in the decade fol-
       lowing the Persian Wars. The play, then, would serve as a reminder of Themistocles'
       service to Athens.
124.   Marincola 1996: xix–xx. For the overall structure of Herodotus see the bibliography
       found at xx n. 34 as a starting point.
125.   Specifically, Hdt. 7.139.5: νῦν δὲ Ἀθηναίους ἄν τις λέγων σωτῆρας γενέσθαι
       τῆς Ἑλλάδος οὐκ ἂν ἁμαρτάνοι τἀληθέος. ("Now, anyone saying that the
       Athenians are the saviors of Greece would not miss the mark of the truth"). Earlier,
       Herodotus states that Athens was the stated object of Xerxes' attack, while the actual
       goal was the conquest of Greece: ἡ δὲ στρατηλασίη ἡ βασιλέος οὔνομα μὲν
       εἶχε ὡς ἐπ' Ἀθήνας ἐλαύνει, κατίετο δὲ ἐς πᾶσαν τὴν Ἑλλάδα. (7.138.1:
       "The campaign of the king was in name that he drove against the Athenians, but the
       campaign was set in motion against all Greece").
126.   This is not to say that Herodotus did not view the Persian Wars as a panhellenic
       effort. The difficulties of pinning down the biases of the historian suggest that he
       viewed the wars as panhellenic in scope. It would help to know whom the historian
       conceived of as his audience, a problem that has not been solved by modern schol-
       arship. For considerations of Herodotus' audience see Flory 1980: 18–22, 26–28;
       Evans 1991: 94–101, and Marincola 1996: xi–xii. Herodotus' presentation of the
       Persian Wars as battles won by individual cities may reflect a developed tradition
       of patriotism on the parts of the cities to which he assigns the victories at specific
       battles.
127.   For the publication date of Herodotus' work see Evans 1982: 15–18 and 1991: 89–
       90; Fornara 1981: 149–56. The specifics of the date are not important here. It need
       only be noted that the work comes sometime in the second half of the fifth century
       BCE, by which time the panhellenism that I am claiming for the aftermath of the
       Persian Wars had certainly disintegrated.
128.   For the Serpent Column, see "Chapter 1.4B: 'New Simonides:' Fr. 11 $W^2$ (=POxy
       2327 frs. 5+6+27 col. 1 + POxy 3965 frs. 1+2)" at n. 122.

129. Plu. *Them.* 17 suggests that this visit was on the invitation of the Spartans. D. S. 11.27 says that the honors given to Themistocles by the Spartans were diplomatic efforts to calm the Athenians after Salamis.

130. Cf. Th. 1.95.7. Thucydides' mention of the Athenians' control of the fleet following the removal of Pausanias can be read as offering a view of these wars as being a panhellenic effort. This passage is discussed at "Chapter 2.2D: Content of Fr. 11 W² and the Spartans; The Epigrammatic Record" at n. 104.

131. See Obbink 2001: 69–73 for a discussion of the prooimial features of fr. 11 W². Contrast Aloni 1994a: 20–21.

132. For text and translation, see "Chapter 1.4A: The Plataea Poem: Evidence" at nn. 82–83.

133. Luppe 1994: 21–22. Luppe reads μέσσοι for μέσσοισι of the manuscript. Also in Aloni 2002: 198. Cf. Campbell 1991: 515; West 1992: 121; Sider 2001a: 22; Catenacci 2001: 120 and 126.

134. Boedeker 1995: 224–25; see also, Boedeker 2001a: 127, 129. Concerning the catalog, Obbink 2001: 69 n. 11 rightly points out, "[i]t is unclear whether this is meant to be a static catalogue or a narration of an action."

135. Luppe 1994: 24–25; Catenacci 2001: 120.

136. It should be noted that Luppe's estimate would allow the Corinthians to have only two lines less than those which are believed to pertain to the Spartans in what survives of fr. 11 W².

137. Boedeker 1995: 225 and 2001a: 127.

138. The link is fairly certain. All three fragments pertain to Plataea and all three are part of POxy 3965, the papyrus scraps that constitute the bulk of the "new Simonides." See "Chapter 1.4: The 'New Simonides:' Fr. 11 W² and Frs. 15 and 16 W²."

139. See Parsons 1992: 36–38; West 1993b: 7, 14.

140. Boedeker 2001a: 125, "It is unlikely that Simonides would mention them [Corinth, Megara, and Athens] in this context if they were merely serving as geographical markers without any relevance to their role in the forthcoming battle."

141. Parsons 1992: 36–37.

142. See "Chapter 2.2E: Content of Fr. 11 W² and Plataea" following n. 169.

143. Simon. XVI *FGE* = *IG* VII 53. Rutherford 2001a: 47 n. 67 points to this connection.

144. Theocr. 12.27 Νισαῖοι Μεγαρῆες ἀριστεύοντες ἐρετμοῖς. Gow 1950 v. 2: 226 remarks that the adjective is used to define the Megarians of the Isthmus.

145. Schol. Theocr. 12.27–33 (b) and (c) (Wendel) = 629 *PMG:* (b) ναυτικοὶ γάρ εἰσι. μαρτυρεῖ δὲ αυτοῖς ⟨καὶ⟩ Σιμωνίδης ⟨τὴν⟩ ναυτικήν. (c) καὶ Σιμωνίδης ἐπαινεῖ τοὺς Μεγαρεῖς. ("(b) For (the Megarians) are sailors. Simonides also is a witness to their seafaring capability. (c) Simonides also praises the Megarians.")

146. Schneidewin 1835: 160 suggests that the scholiast refers to the Megarian inscription on the Persian Wars ascribed to Simonides (Simon. XVI *FGE*), for which, see below, "Chapter 2.2E: Content of Fr. 11 W² and Plataea" following n. 169. Bergk *PLG* 3⁴: 523 first suggested that the scholiast refers to a context other than this inscription. He is followed by Boas 1905: 79 n. 3. Molyneux 1992: 200 suggests that the reference is to a poem on Salamis or the Persian Wars in general. Campbell 1991: 491 also proposes the Salamis poem as a possibility.

147. See "Chapter 1.4B: 'New Simonides:' Fr. 11 W² (=POxy 2327 frs. 5+6+27 col. i + POxy 3965 frs. 1+2" at n. 100 ff.

148. Parsons 1992: 37–38.
149. Cf. fr. 11.36 W² with the possible periphrastic reference to the Peloponnesus or the Isthmus, fr. 11.37 W² with the possible periphrastic reference to Megara as the city of Nisus, and fr. 15.3 W² with the periphrastic reference to Corinth as the city of Glaukos.
150. Parsons 1992: 37 also suggests the passive ἐξε[λαθέ]ντες. Rutherford 2001a: 47 objects to the passive verb because he views the participle as referring either to the Athenians' movement from Salamis or to the Lacedaemonians' "driving out" the Persians.
151. West 1992: 120 (app. crit.).
152. In West's interpretation of the poem Teisamenos returns in fr. 14 W².
153. Obbink 1998.
154. Huxley 2001: 76.
155. West 1993b: 8–9.
156. Flower 2001: 67–68 accepts West's interpretation and sees Simonides' fragment as early evidence of the panhellenism that would develop later in the fourth century BCE. A large part of the basis for this interpretation comes from the reading of fr. 14.7 W². In this verse West supplements the letters ] ̣ ̣ [ ]ϲελαϲ[ ] as ἐξ ᾿Α]σί[η]ϲ ἐλάσει and so reads the lines as a reference to someone's driving the Medes out of Asia. Huxley 2001: 75, however, rightly points out that ἐξ ᾿Υ]σίηϲ would also work for the ink (] ̣ ̣ [ ]ϲ)that appears in this line. Hdt. 9.15 and 25 mention Hysiae as a point of reference in the arrangement of the Persian and Greek forces at Plataea. For the singular toponymn, Huxley refers to Steph. Byz. *s.v.* ᾿Υσία (653.6 Meineke). For the meter of the toponymn, he refers to E. *Ba.* 751. It should be noted that Huxley's reading also assumes that the fragments are to be reconstructed in the manner of a narrative on the battle of Plataea.
157. Parsons 1992: 41–42.
158. The text of the oath, in nearly identical wording is found at Lycurg. *Leoc.* 81, D.S. 11.29.3, and *GHI* ii: 204.
159. For the historicity of the oath see Hignett 1963: 460–61, who views the oath as a fabrication; Meiggs 1975: 155–156, 504–507 accepts the historicity of an oath, but allows for doubt on the versions that have survived.
160. See "Chapter 1.4B: The 'New Simonides:' Fr. 14 W² (= POxy 3965 fr. 21)."
161. The text is that of Snell-Maehler. For text and commentary, see van der Weiden 1991: 208–213. Van der Weiden also collects the various passages where this fragment is found. The phrase, ᾿Ελλάδος ἔρεισμα, which Plutarch justifies with fr. 77, is part of Pindar fr. 76; therefore, it seems likely that the fragments are from the same poem. A scholiast on Ar. *Ach.* 637 quotes fr. 76 as being from a dithyramb.
162. Plu. *de glor. Ath.* 7 = 350A–B ταῦτα τὴν πόλιν ἦρεν εἰς δόξαν, ταῦτ᾿ εἰς μέγεθος· ἐπὶ τούτοις Πίνδαρος ἔρεισμα τῆς ᾿Ελλάδος προσεῖπε τὰς ᾿Αθήνας, οὐχ ὅτι ταῖς Φρυνίχου τραγῳδίαις καὶ Θέσπιδος ὤρθουν τοὺς ῞Ελληνας, ἀλλ᾿ ὅτι πρῶτον, ὥς φησιν αὐτός, ἐπ᾿ ᾿Αρτεμισίῳ ... (fr. 76) ... ἐπίτε Σαλαμῖνι καὶ Μυκάλῃ καὶ Πλαταεαῖς ὥσπερ ἀδαμαντίνως στηρίξαντες τὴν ἐλευθερίαν τῆς ᾿Ελλάδος παρέδοσαν τοῖς ἄλλοις ἀνθρώποις. (These things have lifted the city (i.e. Athens) to a good reputation and to greatness; for these things, Pindar addressed the Athenians as "the mainstay of Greece," not because she honored Greece

     with the tragedies of Phrynichus or Thespis, but because, as he himself says, at Artemisium . . . fr. 76 . . . and as soon as they established at Salamis, Mycale and Plataea the freedom of Greece, hard as adamant, they handed it over to other men").

163.   A slightly different image appears on the recently discovered pieces (*Lapis* c) of the Athenian inscriptions on the fallen in the Persian Wars (*IG* I³ 503/504). In this inscription, someone or something is referred to as ἕρκος ("fence or wall"). If the reference is to those who died, then the image is similar to the one evoked by Pindar fr. 76, where the Athenians are the ἔρεισμα ("mainstay"). The Athenians may have been commemorated in several places and various mediums with imagery of an entity that stands against or keeps something out in reference to the Persian Wars.

164.   The text is that of West 1990 (Teubner). The problems lie in κρηπὶς ὕπεστιν and ἐκπιδύεται. For an analysis of the problems and possible emendations, see Broadhead 1960: 202–204. Most find the reference to a foundation that is "not yet set under" odd in a play that emphasizes the importance of Salamis in the destruction of the Persians. ἐκπιδύεται is an emendation for ἐκπαιδεύεται ("(the troubles) are reared from their infancy"), which is also difficult to make sense of in these verses. To solve these difficulties, Housman emended the line to read κρηνὶς ἀπέσβηκ' ("the fountain of troubles has not yet been extinguished). Broadhead prints this emendation. Hall 1996: 164 follows West's text and suggests that κρηπίς might mean "military boot" in this context. *LSJ s.v.* κρηπίς, however, lists this meaning for the plural κρηπῖδες. Another possibility could be "the walled edge of a river, a quay" (*LSJ s.v.* κρηπίς II 2).

165.   This interpretation was suggested to me by D. Sider in his comments on an earlier draft of this study. Cf. *LSJ s.v.* κρηπίς II, which translates this passage as "not yet got to the *bottom* of misery."

166.   See "Chapter 2.2D: The Content of Fr. 11 W²: The 'New Simonides'" at n. 141 ff.

167.   The multi-battle aspect of the Persian Wars is certainly present in the *Persae*, which mentions both Salamis and Plataea, as well as in Herodotus, which is a narrative of the Wars in general. Cf. P. P. 1.75–80, composed in 470 BCE for Hieron's victory in the chariot race. The ode commemorates the founding of Aetna six years earlier. Here Pindar depicts the Persian Wars with reference to two battles: Salamis, an Athenian victory, and Plataea, a Spartan victory. Pindar's division of the credit for these battles perhaps reflects an atmosphere of discord concerning the victory over the Persians; however, in this discord, Pindar emphasizes the multi-battle aspect of the Persian Wars. For the text, see Snell-Maehler. For circumstances surrounding this ode, see Lefkowitz 1976: 104–105 and Race 1997: 210–211 (followed by text and translation). An emphasis on the Persian Wars as a series of battles is evident in later sources as well as in ones that emphasize the efforts of one city or one battle.

168.   Cf. the Thermopylae epigram for the Peloponnesians (Simon. XXII (a) *FGE*). For the Thermopylae inscriptions, see "Chapter 2.2D: Content of fr. 11 W² and The Spartans: Epigrammatic Record" n. 89. Surely, this epigram, quoted by Herodotus (7.228), commemorates the larger force at Thermopylae, including the Lacedaemonians, who also receive a specific epigram (Simon. XXII (b)). At Thermopylae, then, there was one inscription commemorating the larger effort which was accompanied by other inscriptions commemorating the individual contributions to the battle. A similar emphasis on the larger effort is found in Simon. VII *FGE* on the same battle

which Page deems "plainly a literary composition, probably from the later Hellenistic age" (197). Cf. Boas 1905: 219–31. In this epigram, there appears to be an attempt at some level to emphasize the larger effort.

169. There are several Persian war epigrams that explicitly focus on individual battles: on Marathon: Simon. XXI *FGE;* on Thermopylae, Simon. XXII (a) and (b), Simon. VI *FGE,* Simon. XXIII *FGE,* Piliadas I *FGE;* on Artemisium, Simon. XXIV *FGE;* on Salamis, Simon. XI *FGE* (=*IG* 1³ 1143 = EM22 = M-L 24), Simon. XII *FGE,* although the lines that contain the specific reference to the Corinthians are of doubtful authenticity (See Page 1981: 205); on Eurymedon, Simon. XLVI *FGE;* on Eion, Simon. XL *FGE.* Simon. X *FGE* and XIX (a) are epigrams on specific individuals. It should be noted that epigrams are usually so short that a focus on a single event or individual is normal. The point being emphasized here is that epigrams that present a panhellenic perspective, especially those concerning the victory at Plataea, also appear to focus on the multi-battle perspective of the Persian Wars.

170. Simon. XVI *FGE = IG* VII 53.

171. Preface: τὸ ἐπίγραμμα τῶν ἐν τῶι Περσικῶι πολέμωι ἀποθανόντων καὶ κειμένων ἐνταῦθα ἡρώων, ἀπολόμενον δὲ τῶι χρόνωι, Ἑλλάδιος ὁ ἀρχιερεὺς ἐπιγραφῆναι ἐποίησεν εἰς τιμὴν τῶν κειμένων καὶ τῆς πόλεως. Σιμωνίδης ἐποίει ("Since the epigram for those who died in the Persian Wars and the heroes who lie here had been destroyed by time, Helladios, the high-priest, had it inscribed for the honor of those lying here and the city. Simonides composed it.") Closing: μέχρις ἐφ' ἡμῶν δὲ ἡ πόλις ταῦρον ἐνάγιζεν ("Up until our time, the city has sacrificed a bull to the dead.") For the evidence this inscription provides for hero cults for those who fell in the Persian Wars, see Huxley 2001: 77.

172. Page 1981: 213–214.

173. Page 1981: 215.

174. Huxley 2001: 76. See "Chapter 1.4B: 'New Simonides:' Fr. 11 W² (=POxy 2327 frs. 5+6+27 col. i + POxy 3965 frs. 1+2)" at nn. 108–111.

175. For the link between fr. 11.1–4 W² and the death of Achilles, see "Chapter 2.2A: Elements of Content in Fr. 11 W²" at nn. 6–10.

176. Parsons 1992: 32. Also, Lloyd Jones 1994: 1, "Surely the poet addresses Achilles . . . because he is aiming to do for Pausanias and the other heroes of Plataea what Homer did for Achilles and the heroes of the Trojan War."

177. Shaw 2001: 181. The italics are hers.

178. Pavese 1995: 24. Also, Burzacchini 1995: 24–25.

179. West 1993b: 6 at n. 15. West 1993b: 5, suggests, "Possibly, the poem happened to be composed at the time of some festival or ritual in Achilles' honor, and Simonides took his cue from that." This statement, certainly relevant to the poem's genre, would seem to imply little relationship between Achilles and the content of the poem.

180. Aloni 2001: 98; likewise, Rutherford 2001a: 38 and Stehle 2001: 112.

181. Aloni 2001: 102–104.

182. Boedeker 2001b: 158.

183. For the poly-hellenic content of Plataea, see Boedeker 1995: 220–225.

184. Schein 1984: 92. On prominence of Achilles' death throughout the *Iliad,* see Schein 1984: 129–163.

185. Schein 1984: 130–31, 155–56.

186. Schein 1984: 129.

187.   Text and *testimonia* at *PEG:* 65–71. Also, Davies 1988: 45–48. For translation, summary, and comments, see Davies 2001: 51–59.

188.   Details concerning the death of Achilles appear in early poetry at P. *P* 3.101, where reference is made to Achilles' death by an arrow and his subsequent funeral; Also see P. *Pae.* 6.75–86. The paean survives as a long fragment containing parts of 180 verses of a poem presumably performed at a Delphic *Theoxenia*. The poem consists of three triads. The second triad mentions the death of Achilles at the hand of Apollo, the destruction of Troy and slaughter of Priam by Neoptolemus, and the subsequent death of Neoptolemus at Delphi, also through the agency of Apollo. The emphasis in this context is on the story of Neoptolemus, which provides a mythical precedent for the ritual of the Delphic *Theoxenia*. For the text of and commentary on this paean in general see Rutherford 2001b. The *Posthomerica* of Quintus Smyrnaeus (probably third century CE) is a later work that provides a full account of the death and funeral games of Achilles in Books 3–4.

189.   This account largely corresponds to Proclus' epitome of the *Aithiopis*. For a brief discussion of the objections to the authenticity of *Od.* 24.1–209, with bibliography, see Russo, Fernandez-Galiano and Heubeck 1992: 356–358. Here, Heubeck makes a compelling case for the integrity of these verses as part of the *Odyssey*. Nevertheless, the point here is that these verses represent a poetic tradition, echoed elsewhere, concerning the death of Achilles. It is as part of such a tradition that they are valuable for this discussion.

190.   On the structural features of the *deuteronekuia* see Russo, Ferndandez-Galiano, and Heubeck 1992: 363–364. The section is a formal unit that consists of two pairs of speeches, the first by Achilles and Agamemnon (24–97), and the second by Agamemnon and the suitor, Amphimedon (106–190). As an epilogue, Agamemnon concludes the section with a speech in praise of Odysseus (192–202).

191.   Schein 1984: 90–91, 163.

192.   For the link between κλέος and epic poetry see Nagy 1974: 244–255.

193.   See "Chapter 2.2A: Elements of Content in fr. 11 W²" at n. 3.

194.   The meaning of ἐπώνυμον is not certain. The allusion to this verse in Theoc. *Idyll* 16.46, ὀνομαστούς / ὁπλοτέροις, (noted by Hutchinson, see Parsons 1992: 31) suggested to Parsons that Theocritus understood it to be equivalent to ὀνομαστός (*LSJ* s.v. ὀνομαστός: I. "named" or "to be named"; II, "of name or note" or "famous"). Yet, Parsons admits this meaning of ἐπώνυμος is not paralleled elsewhere. (*LSJ* s.v. ἐπώνυμος 1. "given as a significant name;" 2. "surnamed;" 3. "named after;" or II. "giving one's name to a thing or person.") Lloyd-Jones 1994: 2, suggests that a parallel is to be found in Quintus of Smyrna (8.452). The parallel, however, is itself a conjecture. Furthermore, Lloyd-Jones hypothesizes that his conjecture, found nowhere else, would have been a word invented by Quintus. The circularity of Lloyd-Jones' argument makes caution necessary. Poltera 1997: 344 suggests that Simonides might use ἐπώνυμον as the opposite of the hypothetical word ἀνώνυμος. The word is discussed at Capra 2001: 43–47, which develops the argument set out at Capra-Curti 1995: 29–31 and directly addresses objections raised by Burzacchini 1995: 31. Capra suggests that the word refers to Homer actually giving a name to the race of heroes, that is, the *hemitheoi:* "Simonde direbbe dunque che Omero <<rese eponima>> la caduca stripe de semidei, ossia le attribuì il nome che porta" (2001: 45).

195. At *Odyssey* 24.84–85, the reason for building Achilles' tomb on a headland of the Hellespont is given: ὥς κεν τηλεφανὴς ἐκ ποντόφιν ἀνδράσιν εἴη / τοῖς οἳ νῦν γεγάασι καὶ οἳ μετόπισθεν ἔσονται ("so it would be visible from the sea at a distance to men, both those who live now and to those who will be hereafter").
196. Boedeker 2001b: 158.
197. See "Chapter 1.2B: The 'New Simonides:' Fr. 3 W$^2$ (POxy 3965 fr. 20)."
198. West 1993a: 3; Rutherford 2001a: 36.
199. See "Chapter 2.2F: Content of Fr. 11 W$^2$ and Achilles: Homer" after n. 189.
200. West 1993a: 168.
201. Μνημοσύνης καὶ Ζηνὸς ἐριγδούποιο θύγατρες,
Μοῦσαι Πιερίδες, μεγαλώνυμοι, ἀγλαόφημοι,
71.1–2
["The daughters of Mnemosyne and thundering Zeus, Pierian Muses, with great names and shining fame."]
202. Admittedly, there is need for caution in accepting this conjecture outright because the fragment is incomplete and the adjective is rare. To be sure, it cannot be said that this adjective is used exclusively of the Muses in archaic poetry. Elsewhere it is applied to other figures: Of the Kouretes, Orph. *H.* 31.4; As the name of one of the Sirens, *Scholia in Odysseum (scholia vetera)* Book 12.39, lines 4 and 10 (Dindorf), Lyd. *Mag. incert.* 4.7, and Eust. vol. 2, p. 5, line 7. 'Αγλαοφάμω is the name of a Thracian mystic in Iam. *VP* 28.146.18 and Proc. *In Ti.* v. 1, p. 25, line 27 and v.3, p. 168, line 11.
203. At fr. 10.5 W$^2$ West conjectures κούρης εἰν]ạλίης ἀγλαόφη̣[με πάϊ (Parsons=] ̣ λιηcαγλαο ̣ ̣ [ ). Despite the disagreement over the arrangement of this fragment in relation to fr. 11 W$^2$, the *communis opinio* is that fr. 10 W$^2$ is part of a hymn to Achilles largely because of West's conjecture. See also Rutherford 2001a: 43.
204. See West 1993a: 5; Obbink 2001: 71–72; Boedeker 2001b: 155–161.
205. Shaw 2001 *passim.* The conclusions are drawn at 170. An important question to raise is, if Achilles is associated with sites near the sea, why was he not associated with Thetis, another prominent sea-deity and his own mother? Huxley 2001: 75 suggests a Pharsalian context for the performance of this poem, noting "[t]here was a Thetideion in Pharsalian territory" and "[i]n post-Homeric legend Pharsalus was regarded as the homeland of Achilles (Tzet. *On Lycophr.* 1268 [2.360 Scheer] embodying *Ilias Parva* fr. 20 Davies)." On the sparse evidence for Thessalian cults to Achilles, see Shaw 2001: 167.
206. Shaw 2001: 179.
207. Shaw 2001: 165, 178, 181. At *Il.* 2.684, the Hellenes are part of the contingent that followed Achilles to Troy. In Simon. XVII (b), the epigram placed on the "Serpent Column" by Pausanias but removed by the Spartans, Pausanias claims to be "leader of the Hellenes" (Ἑλλήνων ἀρχηγὸς). Both passages are noted by Shaw.
208. Shaw 2001: 181.
209. For surveys of Achilles' hero cult, see Farnell 1921: 285–289; Fortenrose 1960: 256; Nagy 1999: 59–65, 119–127 and 317–347.
210. See "Chapter 2.2F: Content of Fr. 11 W$^2$ and Achilles: Homer" n. 188.
211. Fortenrose 1960: 207–210 links Achilles and Neoptolemus as the same hero. See also Nagy 1999: 124–25, 284–88.

212. For Achilles in Athenian drama, see Michelakis 2002: 8–21.
213. Shaw 2001: 180–81.
214. Nagy 1999: 7–9 and 1996: 39–42.
215. For the emphasis on Achilles' death in the *Iliad*, see Schein 1984: 129–163. See also "Chapter 2.2F: Content of Fr. 11 W² and Achilles: Homer" at nn. 185–186.
216. For a synopsis of Achilles' various associations in fifth century Greece, see Michelakis 2002: 1–8.
217. 894 *PMG* = Athen. 695 B.
218. For Achilles, married to Medea, on the Island of the Blest, see Ibyc. fr. 291 *PMG* = Simon. fr. 558 *PMG*. Perhaps also one should consider in this context the new elegiac fragments Simon. frs. 20–22 W².
219. Pl. *Ap.* 28B9–D5. Achilles is an example elsewhere in Plato: *Smp.*221c2–d6. He also appears as an example in *Hi. Mi.* as one who is involuntarily false. At *R.* 390E–391C, Homer's Achilles is a poor example for one to follow. See Michelakis 2002: 9.
220. Achilles was the subject of a lost trilogy by Aeschylus, which dramatized episodes from the *Iliad* surrounding Achilles' revenge for the death of Patroklos. The trilogy most likely dates to the early fifth century. See Michelakis 2002: 22 n. 1. For a survey of Achilles in Athenian tragedy, see Michelakis 2002: 8–21.
221. The presence of Achilles in a painting depicting the *Nekyia* (i.e. in the underworld) and his connection to Patroklos suggests that it is Achilles' death that has some paradigmatic value. "Chapter 2.2F: Content of Fr. 11 W² and Achilles: Homer" at n. 185 ff.
222. For an overview of the discussions about these paintings see Kebric 1983: 16–24.
223. This date for the battle argued for by Meiggs 1972: 80–81.
224. Kebric 1983: 37. See also 24–32 for the Athenian and specifically Cimonian bias of both paintings.
225. Stansbury-O'Donnell 1990: 213–230 for the entire reconstruction; for centrality of Achilles, 226, 230–232.
226. Stansbury-O'Donnell 1990: 231.
227. Stansbury-O'Donnell 1990: 232.
228. The conclusions of Kebric and Stansbury-O'Donnell, in fact, may not be mutually exclusive. Michael Flower has recently argued that Cimon may have been an early proponent of panhellenism, defined as the belief that all of Greece could and should unite to destroy the Persians. Flower suggests that this perspective is evident in the Cimonian monuments (2001: 71–89).
229. "Eion poem" = Simon. XL *FGE* = Aeschin. *In Ctes.* 183. See Page 1981: 255–57; in terms of the "new Simonides," see Boedeker 2001a: 125–126, and 2001b: 154; also, Rutherford 2001a: 42.
230. For the "Stoa Poikile," see Paus. 1.15.1–4. According to Pausanias, Miltiades, the father of Cimon, figures prominently in the images of Marathon. The Trojan episodes described by Pausanias as being depicted on the *Stoa Poikile* pertain to the aftermath of the destruction of Troy and the outrages of Ajax against Cassandra.
231. The date of the dedication of the Lesche is unknown. Kebric 1983: 3–13 places it in the first half of the fifth century and hazards a guess at the more specific date 469 BCE. Cf. Stansbury-O'Donnell 1990: 231.
232. Cf. Flower 2000: 71–89.

# NOTES TO CHAPTER THREE

1. Nagy 1990: 362 at n. 127. He continues, "the very concept of genre becomes necessary only when the *occasion* for a given speech-act, that is, for a given poem or song, is lost." Cf. Bartol 1993: 7, "[A] genre in the archaic sense is first of all a means of identifying and interpreting a poem by its recipients, and the process of classification is only a consequence." Consider also, Depew-Obbink 2000: 6, "genre is a conceptual orienting device that suggests to a hearer the sort of receptional conditions in which a fictive discourse might have been delivered."

2. For an introduction to such an approach to genre as well as an application of it in terms of various classes of early poetry, see Day 2000, Depew 2000 and Boedeker 2000. The notes in these articles contain much useful bibliography.

3. Day 2000: 37–38.

4. Day 2000: 39–41. In terms of archaic hymns and prayer, Depew 2000: 62 remarks that "in a poetic performance, context is not something that is applied to preexisting formal elements, but it is negotiated between a performer (or a poet) and those present at the performance."

5. Depew 2000: 59–61; Day 2001: 38–42.

6. Bowie 1986: 27–35 and 2001: 45–61.

7. Bowie 1986: 33–35.

8. See "Chapter 2.2 C: Content of Bowie's Narrative Elegy and fr. 11 $W^2$" at n.65ff.

9. Cf. Huxley 2001: 78, "It is needless to force Simonides into one particular genre in a poem composed for a special, unique occasion. Archaic poets were not the slaves of Alexandrian literary taxonomies. Simonides is pre-eminent in range, versatility, and combinatory skills." Huxley is commenting on Mace 2001. While his point is made in reference to the so-called sympotic fragments of the "new Simonides," it is equally valid for the verses on the Persian Wars.

10. Obbink 2001: 66.

11. Sider unpublished: 13–14.

12. Cameron 1993: 1–3.

13. See below, "Chapter 3.2A: Elegy as Genre: Form" at nn. 18–20.

14. The major comprehensive attempts to consider elegy as a genre are found in West 1974; Bowie 1986; Bartol 1993. See also Gentili 1968; Raubitscheck 1968; Gerber 1997.

15. West 1982: 44–46. A hemiep in form equals one half of a hexameter.

16. There is no agreement on the meaning of these terms. Bartol 1993: 28 argues that they are synonyms in that they refer in some way to elegiac meter, but they differ in that they refer to poems of different lengths. On the other hand, West 1974: 3–10 suggests a difference in the meanings of these terms: ἔλεγος means "sung lament," ἐλεγεῖον refers to the class of poetry, that is elegy as a genre, and ἐλεγεία refers to all verses in the elegiac meter. In this debate, Bowie 1986: 27 argues that, ἔλεγος must mean either "what we mean by elegy," "a song sung to an *aulos* (in general)" or "the sort of song usually accompanied by the *aulos*." I am following Bartol (explicitly) and Bowie (implicitly), who allow that to some extent the terminology refers to form, at least by the end of the fifth century BCE. It must be remembered, however, that none of these terms appears in the Archaic or early Classical ages to refer to what we understand as the genre of elegy (West 1974: 7, Bowie 1986: 26–27, Bartol 1993:

7). The only possible exception is the early dedicatory epigram for Echembrotus' victory in aulodic competitions at the Pythian games of 586 BCE (Paus. 10.7.5–6 = Echembrotus in *IEG²* 2). The type of poetry described in the inscription is not clear. Pausanias, who quotes the inscription, equates ἔλεγος with ἐλεγεῖα. Pausanias, however, only reflects what he, in the second century CE, understands as an ἔλεγος. For this inscription, see "Chapter 3.2C: Elegy as Genre: Content: Threnodic Elegy" at nn. 41–42. ἐλεγεῖον appears first at the end of the fifth century (Critias fr. 4.3 W², Pherecrates fr. 153.7 *CAF*) in a fragment that refers to Thgn. 467 and, by chance, mentions Simonides; ἐλεγεία is first in *Ath. Pol.* 5.2 and 3. As generic terminology, these words appear in literature much later than the poetry which they describe. The ancient sources for this terminology are usefully collected in Bartol 1993. There are some omissions in Bartol (i.e. Plu. *de Herod. malign.* 872 D = Simon. fr. 16 W²).

17. West: 1974: 2, "I have thus excluded an element (i.e. epigrams) for the inclusion of which Bergk was criticized by Ahrens and Diehl by Pfeiffer, and I believe that by so doing I shall have helped the reader to form a clearer and truer picture of what classical Greek elegy was."

18. Frielander-Hoffleit 1948: 66–70.

19. Cameron 1993: 1–3; Gutzwiller 1998 *passim*.

20. For the uncertain relation between epigrams and elegies, see Raubitschek 1968; Obbink 2001: 78. A good example of the difficulty of distinguishing between epigram and elegy is Simon. XIX *FGE*. Plu. *de malign. Herod.* 36 (869C) quotes these verses on Democritus, a Naxian, who fought in the battle of Salamis, as an ἐπίγραμμα. Yet, as Page 1981: 219 points out, "This is not an ordinary epigram." The style and content of these verses are suitable to an epigram, but the verses open with a reference to Democritus as the third to begin battle; therefore, the verses seem to be part of a longer poem. Page solves the problem by suggesting that these verses are "probably a *skolion*, a short piece designed for recitation at symposia." Still, these verses highlight the difficulty of determining what makes a set of verses in the elegiac meter an elegy proper or an epigram.

21. See "Chapter 2.2B: Content of Bowie's Narrative Elegy Before the 'New Simonides.'"

22. West 1974: 10–13. "Chapter 2.2B: Content of Bowie's Narrative Elegy Before the 'New Simonides'" at nn.18–20.

23. See "Chapter 2.2B: Content of Bowie's Narrative Elegy Before the 'New Simonides'" at n. 22ff.

24. For the evidence and some skepticism, see Gerber 1997: 96–98.

25. West 1974: 18, "Elegiac poetry, then, has a wide range. Not an unlimited one: it was not used, so far as we can tell, for the straight-forward telling of myths and legends, physical philosophy, for didactic poetry of a technical or factual kind, for sexual narratives and fantasies; but otherwise more or less any theme that can be treated in poetry at all can be treated in elegiacs." The "new Simonides" allows us to broaden West's pronouncement. These fragments provides examples of "straight-forward telling of myths and legends" (i.e. frs. 3 W² (?) and 11 W²) and "sexual narratives or fantasies" (i.e. fr. 22 W²). The "new Simonides," then, highlights our incomplete knowledge of archaic elegy. It also reveals that this lack of knowledge masks the true scope of content found in elegiac poetry. See also, Sider unpublished: 2–3, 12–15 for a discussion of the range of content that is found in elegy.

26. Bowie 1986: 15–27; Bowie 1990: 221–29; Rösler 1990: 230–37. For an example of the inexact delineation of so-called public and sympotic elegy, see Rutherford 2001a: 40, where the possibility of a performance in both a public and a sympotic setting is suggested for Simonides' "Plataea poem," and 50.

27. See "Chapter 2.2C: Content of Bowie's Narrative Elegy and Fr. 11 W$^2$."

28. Bowie 1986: 3.

29. For this play, see Hdt. 6.21.2 and "Chapter 2.2D: Content of Fr. 11 W$^2$: Aeschylus *Persae*" n. 123.

30. See "Chapter 2.2D: Content of Fr. 11 W$^2$: Aeschylus *Persae*."

31. See "Chapter 1.4B: The Plataea Poem: The 'New Simonides:' Fr. 11 W$^2$ (=POxy 2327 frs. 5+6+27col. i +POxy 3965 frs. 1+2" at n. 99.

32. See "Chapter 1.3: The Salamis Poem."

33. See *P.* 1.75–80 and frs. 76–77. See also the discussion at "Chapter 2.2D: Content of Fr. 11 W$^2$ and the Spartans: The 'New Simonides'" at n. 161ff.

34. Sider unpublished: *passim*, and in particular 14–15, especially n. 40, and 19–20. Dougherty 1994: 35–46 reaches similar conclusions about *ktisis* poetry. Dougherty, however, accepts narrative elegy as one genre which could have contained a *ktisis*. Her reason for accepting this sub-genre is Bowie's argument that these verses were sung at public festivals; that is, they have an occasion that defines their genre.

35. Bowie 2001: 47. See also, Bowie 1990: 221–29. Cf. Rösler 1990: 234–35.

36. For example, Page 1936 and West 1974. Contrast Bowie 1986.

37. Singular: Critias fr. 4.3 W$^2$; Th. 1.132.2–3 (the dedicatory inscription of Pausanias, the Spartan leader, on the Serpent column); Ion of Samos = M-L 95 (c) line 5. Plural: Pherecrates fr. 153.7 *CAF* in reference to Thgn. 467. See Chantraine s.v. ἔλεγος; Dover 1964: 187–89; West 1974: 6; Bowie 1986: 24–26; Bartol 1993: 26.

38. As a lament, E. *Tr.* 119, *IT* 146, 1091, *Hel.* 185, *Hyps.* fr. 1iii line 9 (Bond); Ar. *Av.* 218.

39. Bowie 1986: 25 suggests that at the end of the fifth century the relation derives from an attempt to etymologize the word ἔλεγος and explain the link between the elegiac meter and sepulchral inscriptions.

40. Chantraine s.v. ἔλεγος.

41. Paus. 10.7.6 =*IEG$^2$* 2: 62.

42. θρῆνος appears in the text but is usually considered a gloss of ἐλεγεῖα. See West 1974: 5 n. 5.

43. Page 1936: 206–230. For this tradition, see specifically 210–217. The dates are taken from *IEG$^2$* 2.

44. West 1974: 13. See also West 1974: 7, "[h]owever this (i.e. the explanation of lament in elegy) may be, the *elegos*-lament is at best no more than one type of composition for which the 'elegiac' metre was used. There is no reason to seek the origin of elegiac poetry generally in this one type, just because the metre was named after it." Cf. Dover 1964: 189 "there were ἔλεγοι, of which some were threnodic and aulodic, of which some, again, were in the elegiac metre; and that is how and why the elegiac distich acquired the name by which it was known universally from the fifth century B. C. onwards."

45. Bartol 1993: 27–28 argues that the distinction must be metrical.

46. Bowie 1986: 23 n. 52. Cf. West 1974: 7, which also admits that Pausanias offers little evidence that the ἔλεγοι of Echembrotus were mournful.

47. Bowie 1986: 24, where the evidence reduces to the elegiac lament in Euripides *Andromache,* which is the very passage Page is attempting to explain.
48. West 1974: 13.
49. Bowie 1986 22–23, 26.
50. Threnody was a lyric genre that was distinguished from elegy. See Simon. 528 *PMG* (= Aristid. *Or.* 31.2) in which Simonides and Pindar are praised for their lamentations. Also, Simon. 521, 523, 529 *PMG* which are references to and excerpts from the *threnodies* of Simonides.
51. Lewis 1987: 188 discusses the first three of these inscriptions in response to Bowie's pronouncement "little or no early Greek elegy was lamentory" (1986: 22).
52. Matthaiou 1986: 31–4 = *SEG* 36.51. The inscription is one of two grave stelae. The first is too fragmentary for comment. Lewis 1987: 188 dates the inscription.
53. For the cretic in Αὐτοκλείδο see Lewis 1987: 188.
54. Cf. Page 1936: 211 "They (i.e. funerary epigrams) are rarely if ever the voices of the men and women weeping over the dead." It should be noted, however, that Page is writing well before the publication of any of these inscriptions with the exception of Simon. LXXV *FGE.* For Page, this inscription is not a funerary epigram because of its inclusion of the first person perspective.
55. Schneidewin 1835: 166 suggests that the verses are part of an elegy. Bergk *PLG* 3⁴: 466 (= Simon. fr. 113) attempts to identify other verses that may be joined to these in order to create an elegy. Frielӓnder-Hoffleit 1948: 69 understands the verses as part of threnody. Page 1981: 295 identifies the verses as part of an elegy and states, "one may look through a couple thousand of epitaphs of all periods without finding anything comparable with this anonymous first-person address to the bereaved, combined with the curious phrase '*whenever I see his tomb.*'"
56. Bowie 1986: 22 would class this epigram as consolatory.
57. Gentili 1968: 62.
58. I have translated ἔλπ' as ἐλπίδ'. Comments from A. Dyke have suggested to me that what we appear to have is a form from *ἔλψ, an otherwise unattested by-form of ἔλπις.
59. Dated to ca. 510? in *CEG.*
60. Willemsen 1963: 118–22, followed in *CEG* 51. Cf. Peek 1976: 93 n. 1.
61. The text printed here is that found at *SEG* 41.540A, where it is accompanied by an *apparatus criticus.*
62. Or ἀλκινόεντα ("mighty"?), suggested by Matthaiou 1990–1991: 271–77, after inspection of stone.
63. Or Ναυσίστρατο⟨ν⟩ αὐτὰ παθόντε. See *SEG* 41.540A.
64. See *LSJ* s.v. αἰκίζω, supplement.
65. Andreou 1988: 109–113. See *SEG* 45.661.
66. Page 1936: 210–214 does not allow that funerary epigrams are the immediate "literary ancestor" of the elegiac lament in E. *Andr.* "Such hints of sorrow (i.e. in funerary epigrams) are not the seeds of elegiac threnody; they are its rudiments and relics" (214). Page is correct. As Bowie rightly points out, the elegiac meter does not become the standard in inscriptional epigrams until the mid-sixth century (1986: 26). For one searching for threnodic verses in the early stages of elegy, something funereal must have been associated with the elegiac meter for it to usurp hexameter as the inscriptional meter; that is, elegy perhaps transferred its connection with lament to

funerary epigrams. Yet, for one looking simply for elements of lament in the content of early elegy, I hope to have shown that funerary inscriptions provide a good source of evidence. It should be remembered that the distinction between epigram and elegy in the terminology of the fifth century is tenuous. See Gentili 1968: 39–40. In the sixth century BCE, it is imaginable that the distinction was less clear.

67. For the Plataea poem, various occasions have been suggested: the funeral for the dead at Plataea (Aloni 2001), the *Eleutheria* at Plataea (Boedeker 2001b), the Isthmian games (Shaw 2001), the Achilleion near Sigeum (Schachter 1998), Pharsalus in Thessaly (Huxley 2001) or a public performance in general (Boedeker 1995). For *The Sea-battle at Artemisium,* Wilamowitz 1913: 206–8 suggests the founding of a temple to Boreas by the Athenians on the Ilissus as a suitable performance context. See also Molyneux 1992: 159–61.

68. There are also a large number of fragments too incomplete to determine content; therefore, their context remains uncertain. These fragments are listed in *IEG*² 2 as *Incerti contextus* (frs. 34–85 W²) or *Incertum an ex epigrammatis* (frs. 86–92 W²). In the latter group, none of which are from the new fragments, there are two fragments that may belong in narrative poems: fr. 86 W² (= fr. 9 W) is assigned by Barigazzi 1964: 74 and Molyneux 1992: 150 to a Marathon elegy, possibly composed by Simonides in competition with Aeschylus. See 15 T Campbell (= *vita Aeschyli*). Cf. Rutherford 2001a: 35. Podlecki 1968: 269 assigns this fragment to a Salamis poem. Fr. 87 W² is another reference to the sun as witness, which should be compared with fr. 16 W² assigned to the "Plataea poem." Fr. 92 W² invokes the Muse, which may belong either in a poem with historical content (fr. 11 W²) or with sympotic content (cf. Thgn. 15–18). The rest would be suitable for performance at symposia: fr. 88 W² (= Simon. LXXXIX *FGE*) reflects on the effects of time; fr. 89 W² pertains to the memory of Simonides and his age; fr. 90 W² claims that a city teaches a man. Fr. 91 W² is the funerary epigram for Megakles discussed in this chapter at "Chapter 3.2A: Content: Threnodic Elegy" at nn. 55–57.

69. It is difficult to see why frs. 28, 29, 30, 31 and 32 W² are assigned to a sympotic context. In no instance is the text complete enough for such an assignment.

70. For suggestions that some of the new sympotic and narrative fragments go together, see Rutherford 2001a: 50; Obbink 2001: 81–85; Sider 2001b: 285–86 and unpublished: 1, 18.

71. See "Chapter 3.3: The Current Status of the Genre of the 'New Simonides'" at n. 69.

72. Aloni 2001: 102 suggests that this burial ceremony would have been a suitable occasion for the performance of an elegy.

73. The ceremony: Th. 2.71.2. The inscription: Simon. XV *FGE* = Plu. *Arist.* 19.7 = *AP* 6.50.

74. Th. 3.58.4 mentions an annual offering at Plataea to the *Plataiomachoi;* Plu. *Arist.* 21 assigns the creation of the *Eleutheria* to Aristides immediately after the battle. He adds that every fourth year festival games are held as well as a description of the festival. The festival is also mentioned at D. S. 11.291–2, Str. 9.2.31, where it is said that the victor in athletic games wins a crown, and Paus. 9.2.5, where competitions in running are emphasized. It is not certain, however, that this festival can be dated as early as the fifth century. For a discussion of this problem and the relevant bibliography, see Rutherford 2001a: 40–41 and Boedeker 2001b: 151–152. Both come to

the conclusion, that even if a fifth century *Eleutheria* cannot be proven, it still remains plausible that a primitive festival existed earlier.

75. Obbink 2001: 73, *passim*.
76. Stehle 2001: 106–119. Cf. Clay 2001: 182–184.
77. Obbink 2001: 65, "I argue that the new fragment confirms Bowie's suspicions with a new twist: the epic elegy turns out to be introduced by a proemial hymn to a divinity." Stehle 2001: 106 "Recovery of the fragments of Simonides' elegy on the battle of Plataea gives us an example of a genre, historical elegy, that we had not had." Stehle continues by noting that Simonides' poem is an "anomaly" within this category. Throughout her argument, Stehle understands that the poem is narrative in the vein of Homeric epic.
78. West: 1993a: 157 translates the line, "so that attention is attuned to good." Cf. West 1974: 189. For the difficulties in the passage see Gerber 1970: 246, who follows the emendation of Schneidewin (οἱ for ἢ or η and τόνος for τὸν ὅς). Gerber translates the line, "as his memory and striving for excellence (or virtue) enable him." For Rösler 1990: 230–237 the very point is that the emphasis is on memory being the subject, rather than the means, of the performance. See "Chapter 3.4A: New Considerations of Generic Features in the 'New Simonides:' Xenophanes fr. B1 W$^2$" at nn. 82–83. Cf. Bowie 2001: 60–61. For my argument, however, either interpretation would work because I am concerned more with what Xenophanes excludes. I follow the text and interpretation of West.
79. For example, see Campbell 1982: 330.
80. For the *Theognidea* and symposia see Gerber 1997: 92–93, 96–98.
81. For Archilochus and Solon, see Bowie 1986: 15–21. For Callinus, see Bowie 1990: 221–229. For Tyrtaeus, see Bowie 1990: 221–229; Bowie 2001: 46–47, 61; Rösler 1990: 234–235. For Theognis and elegy at symposium in general, see Gerber 1997: 92–93, 96–98.
82. Rösler 1990: 231. Rösler points to Attic skolia to show that Xenophanes and Anacreon are being prescriptive rather than descriptive.
83. Cf. Bowie 1986: 33, 1990: 221–229, and 2001: 60–61.
84. For the suggestion that Simonides' "Plataea poem" might have been performed originally in a public setting, but also might have been reperformed at symposia, see Rutherford 2001a: 40.
85. See "Chapter 2.2A: Elements of Content in fr. 11W$^2$" before n. 2 and "Chapter 2.2F: Content of fr.11W$^2$: The Homeric Tradition and the 'New Simonides'."
86. Stehle 2001: 106–119 on the invocation of a mortal and the reference to a Muse as an ἐπίκουρος (military auxiliary); Clay 2001: 182–84 on the word ἡμίθεοι.
87. One point of differentiation may be pointed out here. Stehle notes that one point of divergence from Homer in Simonides is the invocation of a mortal rather than a divinity. It is certainly not standard that a mortal is the addressee and the subject of a prooimial hymn. Yet, it also should be noted that it is in the very moment depicted here, the death of Achilles and the fall of Troy, that the hero receives κλέος. In this moment, the line between his mortality as a human figure and immortality as a hero celebrated in song is blurred. Furthermore, other figures of dubious status as mortals received Homeric Hymns: Heracles (*hh* 15) and the Dioscouri (*hh* 17, 33). Of course, these figures are the sons of Zeus and are so called in these hymns. The *Hymn to the Dioscouri* (*hh* 33) is interesting here. Allen-Halliday-Sikes 1936: 436–437 suggest

that this hymn was probably known no later than the sixth century BCE. This hymn, then, may be the earliest tradition of these deities being depicted as the sons of Zeus (Dioscouri) (1, 9). In this hymn, the Dioscouri, are bidden farewell to as Τυνδαρίδαι (33.18); that is, their mortal heritage is emphasized. In this way, the hymn provides an archaic parallel for a hymn devoted to mortals with divine heritage. Moreover, it is significant that this hymn is the model for the prooimion of Theoc. *Id.* 22. See Sens 1997: 75–76. It should be noted that Theocritus also seems to have had the Simonidean prooimion in fr. 11 $W^2$ in mind at the conclusion to the *Idyll* (214–223). Here, Theocritus mentions the Greeks who followed Menelaus to Troy, the destruction of the city, Chian Homer as provider of renown, and a programmatic comparison between the current composer and Homer which includes a reference to Achilles. Sens 1997: 217 points to this parallel. It seems, however, that we might be able to read an elaborate allusion to Simonides in this passage. So, to return to the prooimion of fr. 11 $W^2$, it may not be quite so stark a differentiation from the Homeric tradition that this prooimion is addressed to Achilles and not a divinity.

88.   See "Chapter 2.2F: Content of fr.11$W^2$: The Homeric Tradition and the 'New Simonides.'"

89.   Simonides quotes and Mimnermus refers to Homer's simile (*Il.* 6.146) in which generations are likened to leaves. For the suggestion that Simonides is also referring to Mimnermus, see Sider 2001b: 282.

90.   A reworking of *Il.* 13.130–3 = *Il.* 16.215–17. The situation in the fragment of Tyrtaeus is the engagement of opposing armies, while in Homer the situation is the advancement of one army. See Campbell 1982: 175.

91.   See Parsons 1992: 44.

92.   Zetes and Calias (?) in fr. 3.5 $W^2$ and Boreas (?) in fr. 4.8 $W^2$ (cf. Schol. A.R. 1.211–15C Wendel); in fr. 11 $W^2$, the Tyndarids (29–30), Menelaus (30), Pelops, son of Tantalus (36), Pandion (41); in fr. 13 $W^2$, Doros (9) and Heracles (10); in fr. 15 $W^2$, Glaucus (3); in fr. 17 $W^2$, Demeter? (1); in fr. 24 $W^2$, Dionysus; in fr. 25 $W^2$, Boreas (2); in fr. 30 $W^2$, Dionysus? (5); in fr. 33 $W^2$, Kypris? (14); in fr. 70 $W^2$, the Tyndarids? (2); in fr. 92 $W^2$, Heracles, son of Alcmene (1–2).

93.   *Il.* 21.15; *Od.* 1.170, 7.238, 10.325, 14.187, 15.264, 19.105, 24.298.

94.   *Il.* 3.123, 15.247, 24.387; *Od.* 1.405, 7.269.

95.   In the form that has survived from antiquity, the *Theognidea* appears to be a collection of verses which opens with a set of four hymns. Each of these hymns approximates a prooimion. They appear to be arranged at the opening of this collection for this reason. On the history of the text of the *Theognidea*, see West 1974: 40–64. On the arrangement of the *Theognidea* as a collection of fragments, see Bowie 1997b: 61–66.

96.   For hymnic association, see *hh.* XXI.4. Van Groningen 1966: 9 demonstrates that to sing "first and last" of a subject is a common formula in a hymn. Similar expressions are in *hh.* IX and XXIX. The second example is not an expression of intent.

97.   This phrase, or a variation of it, occurs five times in Homer. *Il.* 5.703 and 11.299 contain the phrase printed above. *Il.* 16.692 has the verb in the second person. *Il.* 8.273 has the first half of the line. A variation occurs at *Od.* 9.14. Odysseus asks Alkinoos, τί πρῶτόν τοι ἔπειτα, τίδ' ὑστάτιον καταλέξω; ("What shall I recount to you first and what shall I recount to you later?"). The parallel is not exact, but it does reinforce the pattern noted above.

98. Obbink 2001: 73.
99. Obbink 2001: 81.
100. Obbink 2001: 81–85; See also Rutherford 2001a: 50, who suggests that fr.11 W² might have contained a sphragis in which these so-called sympotic fragments may have been found; Sider 2001b: 284–85 suggests the inclusion of at least frs. 19–20 W² in the same poem as fr. 11 W². For Sider, fr. 19–20 W² might represent Simonides' blame of other poets who failed to do what he does.
101. For Homeric Hymns as prooimion see Nagy 1990: 359; Obbink 2001: 69; Aloni 2001: 93. χαῖρε appears as a marker of transition in the following: *hh* 1.495, *hh* 6.21; αὐτὰρ εγώ appears in the following as a marker of transition: *hh* 3.177–78 and 545–46, *hh*. 4.579–80, *hh*. 9.7–9, *hh*. 10.4–6, *hh*. 19.48–49, *hh* 25.6–7, *hh*. 27.21–22, *hh* 29.17–18, *hh* 30.17–19, *hh* 29.13–14 *hh* 31.18–19.
102. For the invocation of the Muse (fr. 11.21 W²) as a second invocation, see Parsons 1992: 32 and Obbink 2001: 169. Both see a mixing of closing and opening formulae here in the farewell to Achilles and the invocation of the Muse. Obbink 2001: 69–71 demonstrates that the double invocation (first of Achilles or Thetis in the lost part of the fragment and then of the Muse in 21) is not unique.
103. For ritual significance of χαῖρε and related forms, see Day 2000: 37–57 (in epigrams) and Depew 2000: 59–79 (in hymns).
104. Athen. 694 A–C; cf. Xenophan. Fr. B1.13–17 W².
105. 885 *PMG* = Athen. 15.694C.
106. For the "seal" of Theognis and *sphrageis* in Greek literature, see Edmunds 1997: 30–40.
107. For an argument that Simonides' poetry on the Persian Wars emphasized "consolation and lamentation" more than verses on the same topic by later writers, see Mac-Farlane 2002: 23–25, 56–92.
108. Alexiou 2002: 108.
109. Alexiou 2002: 102–103.
110. Alexiou 2002: 104–108.
111. Alexiou 2002: 133. The primary examples are the laments for Hector at *Il.* 24.725–45, 748–59, 762–75. See also Derderian 2001: 35–38. At pages 32–33, Derderian lists eight examples of ritual laments in Homeric epic that are quoted in direct speech.
112. Alexiou 2002: 137–139; Derderian 2001: 63–113.
113. Alexiou 2002: 161.
114. Alexiou 2002: 165–166.
115. Alexiou 2002: 171.
116. Alexiou 2002: 178.
117. Alexiou 2002: 182.
118. Alexiou 2002: 133 and thereafter.
119. Derderian 2001:15, 63–76, 102–113, 114–117. For Derderian, this development in expressions of lamentation arises from the use of writing in the form of epigrams at gravesites. A similar development, although without the emphasis on writing, is implied in Alexiou's classification quoted above.
120. For the example of epigrams and continuing the use of thematic and formal characteristics of expressions of lamentation, see Derderian 2001: 64–68.
121. See "Chapter 3.2C: Elegy as Genre: Threnodic Elegy."
122. For praise in expressions of lament, see Day 1989: 16–19.

123.  For the emphasis on commemoration and praise in lament, see Alexiou 2002: 55; for link between elegy, mournful content, commemoration and praise, see Alexiou 2002: 104–105. It is suggested, here, that the shift away from mournful content, which is evident in our remains of elegy, is not a change in elegy. Rather, this shift is the extension of certain themes that would have been found in mournful elegy which is entirely lost to us. See also Derderian 2001:102–113.

124.  See "Chapter 2.2D: Content of fr. 11W² and the Spartans: Epigrammatic Record" and "Chapter 2.2D: Content of fr. 11W² and the Spartans: The 'New Simonides.'"

125.  For epigrams and the function of commemoration see Day 1989: 16–28. See also Day 2000.

126.  *IG* VII 53 = Simon. XVI *FGE*. See "Chapter 2.2E: Content of Fr. 11 W² and Plataea" at n. 168ff.

127.  This inscription shows us that perhaps such commemoration for the victors in the Persian Wars went beyond simply setting up the monument in Megara. As Huxley 2001: 77 points out, this inscription refers to a hero cult for the Megarians who fell in the Persian Wars. A prose explanation that follows the verses of the inscription tells that "Up until our time (fourth century CE), the city has sacrificed a bull to the dead." See "Chapter 2.2E: Content of Fr. 11 W² and Plataea" at n. 171. If the sacrifice of a bull to the Megarian War dead dates to the time when the inscription was set up, the verses not only commemorate the war dead, but function as part of a larger commemorative effort. Namely, the inscription marks the introduction of a hero cult. In this way, the commemorative function of the verses is reinforced. See also Boedeker 2001b: 160–61. For laments in Homer as γέρας θανόντων see *Od.* 24.188–190 and Derderian 2001: 34.

128.  Simon. VIII and IX *FGE*. See "Chapter 2.2D: Content of fr. 11 W² and the Spartans: Epigrammatic Record" at nn. 86–93.

129.  See "Chapter 3.4D: New Considerations of Generic Features in the 'New Simonides:' Lament" at n. 122–123.

130.  See "Chapter 3.2C: Elegy as Genre: Threnodic Elegy."

131.  For the certainty of this supplement, see Parsons 1992: 31.

132.  For the relationship to Homeric poetry Boedeker 2001b: 153–163, Stehle 2001 and Clay 2001.

133.  For the emphasis in Simonides' verses on those who had died in the Persian Wars, see Boedeker 2001b. On the deemphasizing of death and mourning in the epigrams on the Persian Wars, see Derderian 2001: 103, 109.

134.  See "Introduction: The 'New Simonides:' The Problem in Modern Scholarship" at nn. 83–90, "Chapter 2.2D: Content of fr. 11 W² and the Spartans" at n. 71ff., and "Chapter 3.4: New Considerations of Generic Features in the 'New Simonides'" at nn. 72 ff.

135.  Catul. 38.7–8 (= T37 Campbell); Hor. *Carm.* 2.1.37–8 (= T38 Campbell); D. H. 2.240 *Imit.* (= T40 Campbell); Quint. *Inst.* 10.1.64 (= T41 Campbell); Ael. Arist. *Or.* 31.2 (= 528 *PMG*). See "Introduction: Background" at n. 16.

136.  The *Suda* Σ 439 Adler (= 532, 536 PMG = *IEG*² 2, p. 114 = T1 Campbell) records that Simonides composed *threnoi*. The fragments believed to represent such poems are collected as 520–531 *PMG*. Stobaeus quotes fragments from Simonides' *threnoi* (Σιμωνίδου θρήνων) and he also quotes passages assigned to this category simply with the heading Σιμωνίδου (521, 523 *PMG*). Schol. Theoc. 16.32 and 44 (Wendel) (= T 13 Campbell) refers to the *threnoi* of Simonides for Scopads of Thessaly.

137. On the gnomic character of Simonides' *threnoi,* see Alexiou 2002: 104.

138. For a discussion of the relation between elegy and lament in terms of a contrast between lamentation in epigrams and the τέρψις of elegy performed in symposia, see Derderian 2001: 66–71.

139. See Sider 2001b: 272–280.

140. I have only translated the complete verses.

141. Fr. 21 W² is composed of POxy 2327 frs. 1 and 2 (a) col. i. The link between the fragments derives from the possibility that a marginal note in POxy 2327 fr. 2 (a) col. i (ἐλἐφαντίνεον) refers to letters (ελεφαντι|) in POxy 2327 fr. 1.5. This link provides the verse beginnings and ending that currently make up the fragment. See Lobel 1954: 69 and 75. Fr. 22 W² is composed of POxy 2327 frs. 3. 2(a) col. ii, 2 (b) and 4 and POxy 3965 fr. 27. POxy 3965 fr. 27 overlaps POxy 2327 frs. 3.7–8 and 4. POxy 2327 fr. 2 (a) col. ii is linked to these fragments by its perceived relation to POxy 2327 fr. 4 and the resulting sense obtained by placing it (fr. 2 (a) col. ii) as the line beginnings of fr. 4. See Parsons 1992: 45–49.

142. For the erotic elements, see West 1974: 167–68; more cautiously, Parsons 1992: 49; Bartol 1999: 26–28.

143. The text given is that of West. The translation follows this text.

144. For the vocative, see Obbink 2001: 84 n. 78. West 1993b: 11 suggests the dative, but he prints the vocative in *IEG²* 2; Bartol 1999: 26–28, following a suggestion of Danielewicz, prefers the accusative.

145. Alexiou 2002: 161–162.

146. See "Chapter 3.2C: Elegy as Genre: Threnodic Elegy."

147. *Il.* 24.725–45, 748–59, 762–75. Alexiou 2002: 132.

148. Alexiou 2002: 171. Cf. *Od.* 20.18, where Odysseus addresses himself by calling on his heart (κραδίη) and reflects on his situation. While not a lament, Odysseus' words to himself provide a parallel for addressing the self by talking to one's inner parts in a context that involves reflection. For a similar reflective context see E. *Med.* 1056. For other such addresses, see Page 1952: 149 and Russo, Fernández-Galiano, and Heubeck 1992: 109. A closer parallel to Simonides' verses is Thgn. 695–96. Here, the heart (θυμέ) is also addressed in a context where the speaker admits an inability to do something. While none of these examples is a lament, they provide a parallel for addressing the heart as a way of introduce some inward reflection. It is possible that Simonides takes this manner of being reflective and employs it in a context that involves lamentation.

149. Lobel 1954: 75, "The context does not appear to admit 'from which first.' But the ξ itself is somewhat uncertain and a noun in the genitive is not to be ruled out."

150. Alexiou 2002: 165–166, 171–173; Derderian 2001: 36.

151. For a succinct explication of the various possibilities of interpreting the journey in these verses, see Rutherford 2001a: 52–53.

152. Mace 2001. See also West 1993b: 12–14; Hunter 1993 and 2001.

153. Yatromanolakis 2001. For Simonides' threnody for one of the Echecratidae, see 528 *PMG* (= Arist. *Or.* 31.2 and Schol. Theoc. 16.34) and T 13 Campbell (= Theoc. 16.42–47). For the poet's relationship to Dyseris and the Thessalian Echecratidae, see Molyneux 1992: 127–129 and Huxley 2001: 75–76.

154. See "Chapter 3.4D: New Considerations of Generic Features in the 'New Simonides:' Lament" at nn. 108–120.

155. Parsons 1992: 45 in his note on POxy 3965 fr. 27.8. Hunter 1993: 13 suggests
     ἵκο[ιτο by comparison with Theoc. *Id.* 7.61–71.
156. Parsons 1992: 45, 47.
157. Lobel 1954: 68.
158. Parsons 1992: 48. Printed by Mace 2001: 186 as ἐγ[ω (ν)].
159. Yatromanolakis 2001: 215.
160. West in *IEG*² 2, emends λείβει of the papyrus in line 12 to λείβοι. This text is
     also printed by Sider 2001a. There is also a—π—written above the—β—on the
     papyrus.
161. Parsons 1992: 48 notes "in Homer normally optative, once subjunctive (*Il.* 24.655),
     once future (*Od.* 16.257), past contrafactual (*Il.* 5.898, *Od.* 20.222)." A *TLG* search
     for κεν in elegiac poets reveals similar features: Optative (potential): Thgn. 57, 103,
     125, 747 W²; Xenoph. fr. B1.17, 5.1 W². Optative (future less vivid): Thgn. 1109
     W² (mixed condition); Xenoph. fr. 2.8 W². Subjunctive (relative): Tyrt. fr. 10.7–8
     W²; Thgn. 807 W²; Subjunctive (temporal): Callin. Fr. 1.7 W².
162. Yatromanolakis 2001: 214.
163. Yatromanolakis cites Kühner-Gerth I, 235. See also Smyth 1832.
164. Alexiou 2002: 161–62.
165. Alexiou 2002: 178–80.
166. Mace 2001: 195, 201–203.
167. Alexiou 2002: 132–134.
168. On emphasis on the future in ritual laments, see Derderian 2001: 36–37.
169. Parsons 1992: 49.
170. West 1993b: 12;
171. Hunter 1993; Mace 2001; Yatromanolakis 2001.
172. Hunter 2001.
173. See "Chapter 3.2B: Elegy as Genre: Context: Symposia and Public Festival" at nn.
     21ff. Rutherford 2001a: 50 observes "Several passages of poetry to which the two
     papryi [POxy 2327 and 3965] contribute seem to have been sympotic in character.
     The sympotic poems from which these come are generally regarded as distinct from
     the military/historical elegies and different in character; but these distinctions may
     be in part bogus, especially if any of the military/historical elegies were performed at
     *sumposia.*"
174. Cf. Hunter 2001.
175. See "Chapter 2.2D: Content of fr. 11 W² and the Spartans: Epigrammatic Record."
176. Aloni 2001: 104–105 argues a similar point. He concludes his argument, "[w]hat we
     have here is a narrative elegy on a historical subject, destined to serve as a threnody
     for public performance." In my argument, however, I want to put less emphasis on
     the narrative elegy. I focus on linking fr. 11 W² and the other Persian War poems
     with other elegies and not separating the fragment as part of a supposed sub-genre,
     narrative elegy.
177. For the link between hymn and lament, see Alexiou 2002: 131–139.
178. Rutherford 2001a: 50; Obbink 2001: 82–84; Sider 2001b: 285–286; Hunter
     2001: 243.
179. Yatromanolakis 2001: 208–225. Specific arguments against this reading are found at
     Mace 2001: 203–207.
180. 529 *PMG.*

181. 528 *PMG* (= Aristid. *Or.* 31.2). Cf. Mace 2001: 204 for a different interpretation of Aelius Aristides' words.
182. Parsons 1992: 47; see also 24 and 46.
183. On Simonides and the Thessalian rulers, see Molyneux 1992: 117–145.
184. See Molyneux 1992: 127.
185. Th. 1.111.1.
186. Molyneux 1992: 127. Cf. Yatromanolakis 2001: 210 n13, which remarks, "this link is not confirmed by any evidence." See also, Mace 2001: 206 which notes that "it makes little sense to ignore the fact that Orestes' father has the same name, place of origin, status, and conjectural date as the Echecratidas whose existence is suggested by the internal logic of Simon. 22 $W^2$."
187. Yatromanolakis 2001: 211–212, 223.
188. Mace 2001: 200–201, 206.
189. Huxley 2001: 76.
190. Huxley 2001: 75. This person would be Mace's hypothetical Echecratidas.
191. For an alternative suggestion that the Muses may be addressed here, see "Chapter 2.2F: The Content of fr. 11 $W^2$ and Achilles: The Homeric tradition and the 'New Simonides'" at nn. 202–203.
192. *Iliad* 24.725–45, 748–59, 762–75. Alexiou 2002: 133.
193. The address is reminiscent also of Tyrtaeus fr. 5.6 $W^2$ (αἰχματαὶ πατέρων ἡμετέρων πατέρες) which refers to a past time, and implicitly draws a contrast with the present.
194. West actually prints ποταμô, but the final *upsilon* is clear on the papyrus. See also West 1993b: 8–9.
195. Parsons 1992: 42.
196. Inspection of images of the papyrus for this line reveals a further possible first person reference. In the sequence ]εγωποτάμουϲ, the α is unclear on the papyrus. It is possible to read ε instead. We, then, may have the pronoun ἐμοῦ in this line.
197. Parsons 1992: 42, "ἐλάϲει might be read for want of anything better."
198. See "Chapter 3.3D: New Considerations of Generic Features in the 'New Simonides:' Lament" at n. 190.
199. Rutherford 2001a: 49.
200. Alexiou 2002: 134–36.
201. The link is provided by POxy 3965 fr. 27 (fr. 22.6–15 $W^2$).
202. Lobel 1954: 70.
203. For the details of this reconstruction see Parsons 1992: 49. For the relation between POxy 2327 frs. 5 and 6, see Parson 1992: 28 and "Chapter 1.4D: The 'New Simonides:' Fr. 11 $W^2$ (=POxy 2327 frs. 5+6+27 col. i + POxy 3965 frs. 1+2)" at nn. 93–98.
204. Aloni 2001: 91.

## NOTES TO APPENDIX

1. All headings are from either *FGE* or M-L or both.
2. All texts are those of *FGE,* except where otherwise noted.
3. Text of M-L.

4. Text of M-L.
5. πειθόμενοι νομίμοις Lycurg., D.S., Strabo: ῥήμασι πειθόμενοι Hdt. *A.P, Suda.*
6. For the arrangement, see Beckby 7.344b and *FGE:* 298–99.
7. Text of M-L:

> [Ὁ ξένε, εὔh̄υδρ]όν ποκ' ἐναίομες ἄστυ Ϙορίνθο,
>    [νῦν δ' h̄αμὲ Αἴα]ν̄τος [νᾶσος ἔχει Σαλαμίς].
> [ἐνθάδε Φοινίσσας νᾶας καὶ Πέρσας h̄ελόντες]
>    [καὶ Μέδους h̄ιαρὰν h̄ελλάδα ῥυσάμεθα.]

8. While not specifically concerned with Plataea, this epigram is a commemoration by Pausanias, the Spartan leader at Plataea; therefore, the epigram should be associated with this battle despite its larger claims. Similarly, Simon. XVII(a), quoted below as 21, is relevant to the battle at Plataea. It is quoted below because of its association with the "Serpent Column."
9. See Simon. XXXIX *FGE,* quoted above as 19 above.
10. The text is that of *IG* I³ 503/504.

# Bibliography

Adler, Ada, ed. 1928–1938. *Suidae Lexicon.* 5 vol. Stuttgart: Teubner.

Alexiou, Margaret. 2002. *The Ritual Lament in Greek Tradition.* 2d ed. Rev. by D. Yatromanolakis and P. Roilos. Lanham: Rowan and Littlefield.

Allen, Archibald, ed. 1993. *The Fragments of Mimnermus: Text and Commentary.* Stuttgart: Franz Steiner.

Allen, T. W., W. R. Halliday and E. E. Sikes, eds. 1936. *The Homeric Hymns.* Oxford: Oxford University Press.

Aloni, Antonio. 1994a. "L'Elegia di Simonide dedicata alla battaglia di Platea." *ZPE* 102: 9–22.

———., ed. 1994b. "Appendice: Simonide, *Elegia per la battaglia di Platea.*" In Lirici Greci: Alcmani e Stesichoro, 101–142. Milan: Mondadori.

———. 1997. "The Proem of Simonides Elegy on the Battle of Plataea (Sim. Frs. 10–18 W²) and the Circumstances of Its Performance." In *Poet, Public and Performance in Ancient Greece,* ed. Lowell Edmunds and Robert W. Wallace, 8–28. Baltimore: The Johns Hopkins University Press.

———. 2001. "The Proem of Simonides' Plataea Elegy and the Circumstances of Its Performance." In *The New Simonides: Contexts of Praise and Desire,* ed. Deborah Boedeker and David Sider, 86–105. Oxford: Oxford University Press.

Andreou, I. 1988. "Τα επιγράμματα της Αμβρακίας και τα απαράδεκτα ερμηνείας." *AD* 43: 109–113.

Barbantani, Silvia. 2001. "Introduzione: L'elegia storico-encomiastica in età ellenistica: uno sguardo diacronico." In Φάτις νικηφόρος: Frammenti di elegia encomiastica nell' età delle Guerre Galatiche: *Supplementum Hellenisticum* 958 e 696, 3–61. Milan: Università Cattolica.

Barchiesi, Alessandro. 2001. "Simonides and Horace on the Death of Achilles." In *The New Simonides: Contexts of Praise and Desire,* ed. Deborah Boedeker and David Sider, 255–260. Oxford: Oxford University Press.

Barigazzi, A. 1963. "Nuovi framenti delle elegie di Simonide (Ox. Pap. 2327)." *MH* 20:61–76.

Bartol, Krystyna. 1993. *Greek Elegy and Iambus: Studies in Ancient Literary Sources.* Poznań: Uniwersytet im. Adama Mickiewicza.

———. 1999. "Between Loyalty and Treachery: P.Oxy. 2327fr. 1 +2 (a) col. I = Simonides 21 West 2—Some Reconsiderations." *ZPE* 126: 26–28.

Bearzot, Cinzia. 1997. "P.Oxy 3965: Considerazioni sulla data e sull'ispirazione dell'elegia di Simonide per la battaglia di Platea." *APF* 3: 71–79.

Beckby, Hermann, ed. 1957–1958. *Anthologia Graeca.* 4 vol. Munich: Heimeran.

Bekker, I., ed. 1824–1825. *Photii Bibliotheca.* 2 vol. Berlin: Reimer.

Bergk, Theodor, ed. 1882. *Poetae Lyrici Graeci.* 4th ed. Vol. 3. Leipzig: Teubner.

Bernabé, Albert, ed. 1987. *Poetarum Epicorum Graecorum: Testimonia et Fragmenta.* Leipzig: Teubner.

Bernhardy, G. 1853. *Suidae Lexicon.* 2 vol. Halis: Schwetschkiorum.

Bernsdorf, Hans. 1996. "Zu Simonides fr. 22 West." *ZPE* 114: 24–26.

Blum, Rudolf. 1991. *Kallimachos: The Alexandrian Library and the Origins of Bibliography.* Trans. Hans H. Wellisch. Wisconsin Studies in Classics. Madison: University of Wisconsin Press.

Boas, Marcus. 1905. *De Epigrammatis Simonideis. Pars Prior: Commentatio Critica de Epigrammatum Traditione.* Groningen: J. B. Wolters.

Boedeker, Deborah. 1995. "Simonides on Plataea: Narrative Elegy, Mythodic History." *ZPE* 107: 217–29.

——. 1998a. "The New Simonides and Heroization at Plataia." In *Archaic Greece: New Approaches and New Evidence,* ed. Nick Fisher and Hans van Wees, 231–49. London: Duckworth. (Earlier version of Boedeker 2001b)

——. 1998b. "Hero Cult and Politics in Herodotus: The Bones of Orestes." In *Cultural Poetics in Archaic Greece,* ed. Carol Dougherty and Leslie Kurke, 164–77. Oxford: Oxford University Press.

——. 2000. "Herodotus's Genre(s)." In *Matrices of Genre: Authors, Canons and Society,* ed. M. Depew and D. Obbink, 97–114. Cambridge: Cambridge University Press.

——. 2001a. "Heroic Historiography: Simonides and Herodotus on Plataea." In *The New Simonides: Contexts of Praise and Desire,* ed. Deborah Boedeker and David Sider, 120–134. Oxford: Oxford University Press.

——. 2001b. "Paths to Heroization at Plataea." In *The New Simonides: Contexts of Praise and Desire,* ed. Deborah Boedeker and David Sider, 148–163. Oxford: Oxford University Press. (Later version of Boedeker 1998a)

Boedeker, Deborah and David Sider, ed. 2001. *The New Simonides: Contexts of Praise and Desire.* Oxford: Oxford University Press.

Boekh, A. 1819. *Pindari opera quae supersunt.* Vol. 2. Leipzig: Gottlob Weigel.

Bond, G. W., ed. 1963. *Euripides: Hypsipyle.* Oxford: Oxford University Press.

Bowie, E. L. 1986. "Early Greek Elegy, Symposium and Public Festival." *JHS* 106: 13–35.

——. 1990. "*Miles Ludens?* The Problem of Martial Exhortation in Early Greek Elegy." In *Sympotica: A Symposium on the Symposion,* ed. Oswyn Murray, 221–29. Oxford: Clarendon Press.

——. 1997a. "Plutarch's Citation of Early Elegiac and Iambic Poetry." In *Plutarco y la Historia: Actas del V Simposio Español sobre Plutarco, Zaragoza, 20–22 de Junio de 1996,* ed. C. Schrader, V. Ramón, and J. Vela, 99–108.

——. 1997b. "The *Theognidea:* a step towards a collection of fragments?" In *Collecting Fragments.* Aporemata 1, ed. Glenn W. Most, 53–66. Göttingen: Vandenhoeck and Ruprecht.

——. 2000. "Athenaeus' Knowledge of Early Greek Elegiac and Iambic Poetry." In *Athenaeus and His World: Reading Greek Culture in the Roman Empire,* ed. D. Braund and John Wilkins. Exeter: University of Exeter Press.

——. 2001. "Ancestors of Historiography in Early Greek Elegiac an Iambic Poetry." In *The Historian's Craft in the Age of Herodotus,* ed. N. Luraghi, 45–66. Oxford: Oxford University Press.

Bowra, C. M. 1935. *Early Greek Elegists*. Cambridge, Mass.: Harvard University Press.

———. 1967. *Greek Lyric Poetry: From Alcman to Simonides*. 2d ed., corr. Oxford: Clarendon Press.

———. 1970. "Xenophanes on the Luxury of Colophon." In *On Greek Margins*, 109–133. Oxford: Clarendon Press. Slightly altered from original publication "Xenophanes, fragment 3" *CQ* 35 (1941): 119–26.

Brillante, Carlo. 2000. "Simonide, fr. eleg. 22 West². " *QUCC* 64: 29–38.

Broadhead, H. D., ed. 1960. *The Persae of Aeschylus*. Cambridge: Cambridge University Press.

Burn, A. R. 1984. *Persia and the Greeks: The Defense of the Waest, c. 546–478 BC*. 2d ed. Stanford: Stanford University Press.

Burnett, Anne Pippin, trans., 1970. " Introduction." In *Ion by Euripides*. Prentice-Hall Greek Drama Series, 1–15. Englewood Cliffs, NJ: Prentice-Hall.

Burzacchini, Gabriele. 1995. "Note al nuovo Simonide." *Eikasmos* 6: 21–38.

———. 1997. Review of *IEG²*. *Gnomon* 69: 193–98.

Cameron, A. 1993. *The Greek Anthology from Meleager to Planudes*. Oxford: Clarendon Press.

———. 1995. *Callimachus and his Critics*. Princeton: Princeton University Press.

Campbell, David A., ed. 1982. *Greek Lyric Poetry: A Selection of Early Greek Lyric, Elegiac, and Iambic Poetry*, 1967. London: MacMillan. Reprint, with corrections, additional bibliography, and new appendix London: Bristol Classical Press.

———, ed. 1991. *Greek Lyric*. Vol. 3. Loeb Classical Library. Cambridge, Mass.: Harvard University Press.

Capra, Andrea, and Matteo Curti. 1995. "Semedei Simonidei: Note sull'elegia di Simonide per la battaglia di Platea." *ZPE* 107: 27–32.

———. 1996. "Corrigenda." *ZPE* 113: 248.

Capra, Andrea. 2001. "<<Addio Achille>>, o il commiato dall'*epos* (Simon. fr. 11, 13 21W.²)." *Eikasmos* 12: 43–54.

Catenacci, Carmine. 2000. "L'eros impossible e ruoli omoerotici (Simonide fr. 21 West²)." *QUCC* 66: 57–67.

———. 2001. "Simonide e i Corinzi nella battaglia di Platea (Plut. *De Herodt. malign.* 872 D–E = Simon., frr. 15–16 West²)." *QUCC* 67: 117–131.

Chantraine, Pierre. 1968–1980. *Dictionnaire étymologique de la langue grecque*. 4 vol. Paris: Klinksieck.

Christ, Georg. 1941. *Simonidesstudien*. Freiburg: Paulsdruckerei.

Clay, Jenny Strauss. 2001. "The New Simonides and Homer's *Hemitheoi*." In *The New Simonides: Contexts of Praise and Desire*, ed. Deborah Boedeker and David Sider, 182–184. Oxford: Oxford University Press.

Colonna, Aristides, ed. 1957. *Himerii Declamationes et Orationes cum deperditarum fragmentis*. Rome: Typis Publicae Officiniae Polygraphicae.

Cronin, Patrick. 1992. "The Authorship and Sources of the *Peri semeion* Ascribed to Theophrastus." In *Theophrastus: His Psychological, Doxographical, and Scientific Writings*, ed. William W. Fortenbaugh and Dimitri Gutas, 307–345. New Brunswick, NJ: Transaction Books.

Daub, A. 1880. "De Suidae Biographicorum Origine et Fide." *Jahrbücher für classische Philologie*, Supplement 11: 402–490.

Davies, Malcolm, ed. 1988. *Epicorum Graecorum Fragmenta*. Göttingen: Vandenhoeck and Ruprecht.

———, trans. 2001. *The Greek Epic Cycle*. 2d ed. London: Bristol Classical Press.

Day, Joseph. 1989. "Rituals in Stone." *JHS* 109: 16–28.

———. 2000. "Epigram and Reader: Generic Forces as (Re-)Activation of Ritual." In *Matrices of Genre: Authors, Canons and Society,* ed. M. Depew and D. Obbink, 37–58. Cambridge: Cambridge University Press.

Depew, M. and D. Obbink, eds. 2000. *Matrices of Genre: Authors, Canons, and Society.* Cambridge. Cambridge University Press.

Depew, Mary. 2000. "Enacted and Represented Dedications: Genre and Greek Hymn." In *Matrices of Genre: Authors, Canons and Society,* ed. M. Depew and D. Obbink, 37–58. Cambridge: Cambridge University Press.

Derderian, Katharine. 2001. *Leaving Words to Remember: Greek Mourning and the Advent of Literacy.* Mnemosyne Supplement, 209. Leiden: Brill.

Diehl, E., ed. 1949–1952. *Anthologia Lyrici Graeci.* 3d ed. Vol. 1. Leipzig: Teubner.

Dindorf, Wilhelm, ed. 1829. *Aristides.* 3 vol. Leipzig: Weidmann.

Dittenberger, Wilhelm. 1915–1924. *Sylloge Inscriptionum Graecarum.* 3d ed. 4 vol. Ed. by Hiller von Gaertringen *et al.* Leipzig: Hirzelium.

Dögler, Franz. 1936. "Der Titel des sog. Suidaslexikons." *Sitzungsberichte der der philisophisch-historischen Abteilung der Bayerischen Akademie der Wissenschaften,* 6. Munich: C. H. Beck.

Dougherty, Carol. 1994. "Archaic Greek Foundation Poetry: Questions of Genre and Occasion." *JHS* 114: 35–46.

Dover, Kenneth. 1964. "The Poetry of Archilochus." In *Archiloque.* Entriens sur l'antiquité classique, 10, 183–222. Geneva: Foundation Hardt.

———. 1993. "Introduction." In *Aristophanes: Frogs,* ed. K. Dover, 1–106. Oxford: Clarendon Press.

Drachmann, A. B., ed. 1903. *Scholia vetera in Pindari Carmina.* Vol. 1. Leipzig: Teubner.

Edmonds, J. M., ed. 1931. *Lyra Graeca.* Vol. 2. Loeb Classical Library. London: William Heinemann Ltd.

Edmunds, Lowell. 1997. "The Seal of Theognis." In *Poet, Public and Performance in Ancient Greece,* ed. L. Edmunds and R. Wallace, 29–48. Baltimore: The Johns Hopkins University Press.

Edmunds, Lowell, and Robert Wallace, eds. 1997. *Poet, Public and Performance in Ancient Greece.* Baltimore: The Johns Hopkins University Press.

Evans, J.A.S. 1982. *Herodotus.* Boston: Twayne.

———. 1991. *Herodotus: Explorer of the Past.* Princeton: Princeton University Press.

Fantuzzi, Marco. 1998. "Il proemio di Theocr. 17 e Simon. *IEG²* Fr. 11 W.: eroi, discendenti di semidei." *Prometheus* 24: 97–110.

———. 2001. Heroes, Descendants of *Hemitheoi:* The Proemium of Theocritus 17 and Simonides 11 W². In *The New Simonides: Contexts of Praise and Desire,* ed. by Deborah Boedeker and David Sider, 232–241. Oxford: Oxford University Press.

Farnell, Lewis Richard. 1921. *Greek Hero Cults and Ideas of Immortality.* Oxford: Clarendon Press.

Flach, Ioannes, ed. 1880. *Eudociae Violarium.* Leipzig: Teubner.

———., ed. 1882. *Hesychii Melisii Onomatologos quae Supersunt.* Leipzig: Teubner.

Flory, S. 1980. "Who Read Herodotus' *Histories.*" *AJP* 101: 12–28.

Flower, Michael. 2000. "From Simonides to Isocrates: The Fifth-Century Origins of Fourth-Century Panhellenism." *ClAnt.* 19: 65–101.

Fornara, C. 1981. "Herodotus' Knowledge of the Archidamian War." *Hermes* 109: 149–56.

Fortenbaugh, W. W. 1998. "Theophrastean Titles and Book Numbers: Some Reflections on Titles Relating to Rhetoric and Poetics." In *Fragmentsammlungen philosophischer Texte der Antike,* ed. Walter Burkert, *et al.,* 182–200. Göttingen: Vandenhoeck and Ruprecht.

Fortenrose, Joseph. 1960. "The Cult and Myth of Pyrros at Delphi." *University of California Publications in Classical Archaeology,* 4: 191–266.

Friedländer, Paul and Herbert Hoffleit. 1948. *Epigrammata: Greek Inscriptions in Verse From the Beginning to the Persian Wars.* Berkeley: University of California Press.

Frommel, Wilhem, ed. 1826. *Scholia in Aelii Aristidis sophistae Orationes Panathenaicum et Platonicas.* Frankfort: Broenner.

Gentili, Bruno. 1968. "Epigramma ed elegia." In *L'épigramme grecque.* Entretiens sur l'antiquité classique 14, 39–90. Genève: Foundation Hardt.

Gentili, Bruno, and Carlo Prato, ed. 1988–2002. *Poetarum Elegiacorum: Testimonia et Fragmenta.* 2 vols., 2nd ed. Vol. 1, Leipzig: Teubner; Vol. 2 Munich: Saur.

Gerber, Douglas E., ed. 1970. *Euterpe: An Anthology of Early Greek Lyric, Elegiac, and Iambic Poetry.* Amsterdam: Hakkert.

———, ed. 1997. *A Companion to the Greek Lyric Poets.* Mnemosyne Suppl. 173. Leiden: Brill.

———, ed. 1999. *Greek Elegiac Poetry: From the Seventh to the Fifth Centuries B.C.* Loeb Classical Library. Cambridge, Mass.: Harvard University Press.

Gomme, A. W. 1956. *A Historical Commentary on Thucydides.* Vol. 1. Oxford: Clarendon Press.

Gow, A. S. F., ed. 1953. *Theocritus.* 2 vol., 2d ed. Cambridge: Cambridge University Press.

Groningen, B. A. van, ed. 1966. *Theognis: Le premier livre.* Verhandelingen der Koninklijke Nederlandse Akademie van Wetenschapen, Afd. Letterkunde, 72.1. Amsterdam: N. V. Noord-Hollandsche Uitgevers Maatschappij.

Gutzwiller, Kathryn. 1998. *Poetic Garlands: Hellenistic Epigrams in Context.* Berkeley: University of California Press.

Habicht, Christian. 1961. "Falsche Urkunden zur Geschichte Athens im Zeitalter der Perserkriege." *Hermes* 39: 1–35.

Hall, Edith. 1989. *Inventing the Barbarian: Greek Self-Definition through Tragedy.* Oxford Classical Monographs. Oxford: Clarendon Press.

———, ed. 1996. *Aeschylus: Persians.* Warminster: Aris and Phillips, Ltd.

Hansen, Peter Allan, ed. 1983–1989. *Carmina Epigraphica Graeca.* 2 Vols. Berlin: Walter de Gruyter.

Harrison, Stephen. 2001. "Simonides and Horace." In *The New Simonides: Contexts of Praise and Desire,* ed. by Deborah Boedeker and David Sider, 261–271. Oxford: Oxford University Press.

Harrison, Thomas. 2000. *The Emptiness of Asia: Aeschylus' Persians and the History of the Fifth Century.* London: Duckworth.

Harvey, A. E. 1955. "The Classification of Greek Lyric Poetry." *CQ* 49: 157–174.

Haslam, Michael W. 1993. Review of M. L. West, *Iambi et Elegi Graeci ante Alexandrum Cantati,* v. 2 editio altera. *BMCR* 04.02.14.

Hauvette-Besnault, Amedee. 1896. *De l'authenticite des epigrames de Simonidee.* Paris: Alcan.

Hense, Otto and Curtis Wachsmth, eds. 1985. *Ioannis Stobaei Antholgium.* 2nd ed. 2 vol. Berlin: Weidman.

Hignett, C. 1963. *Xerxes' Invasion of Greece.* Oxford: Clarendon Press.

Hodern, J. H., ed. 2002. *The Fragments of Timotheus of Miletus*. Oxford: Oxford University Press.

Hommel, Hildebrecht. 1980. *Der Gott Achilleus*. Sitzungsberichte der Heidelberger Akademie der Wissenschaften, 1980.1. Heidelburg: Carl Winter.

Hornblower, Simon. 1982. *Mausolus*. Oxford: Clarendon Press.

———. 1992. "The Religious Dimension of the Peloponnesian War, or, What Thucydides Does Not Tell Us." *HSCP* 94: 170–97.

———. 1997. *A Commentary on Thucydides*. Vol. 1: Books 1–3. Oxford: Clarendon Press.

———. 2001. "Epic and Epiphanies: Herodotus and the "New Simonides." In *The New Simonides: Contexts of Praise and Desire*, ed. Deborah Boedeker and David Sider, 135–47 Oxford: Oxford University Press.

Hort, Arthur, trans. 1926. *Theophrastus: Enquiry into Plants and Minor Works on Odours and Weather Signs*. Vol. 2. Loeb Classical Library. Cambridge Mass.: Harvard University Press.

How, W. W. and J. Wells. 1928. *A Commentary on Herodotus*. Vol. 2. Oxford: Clarendon Press, 1912. Reprint, Oxford: Clarendon Press.

Hubbard, Thomas K. 2001. "'New Simonides' or Old Semonides? Second Thoughts on POxy 3965 fr. 26." In *The New Simonides: Contexts of Praise and Desire*, ed. Deborah Boedeker and David Sider, 226–231. Oxford: Oxford University Press.

Hudson-Williams, T. 1926. *Early Greek Elegy: The Elegiac Fragments of Callinus, Archilochus, Mimnermus, Tyrtaeus, Solon, Xenophanes and Others*. Cardiff: The University of Wales Press.

Hunter, Richard. 1993. "One Party or Two?: Simonides 22 West$^2$." *ZPE* 99: 11–14.

———. 2001. "The Poet Unleaved: Simonides and Callimachus." In *The New Simonides: Contexts of Praise and Desire*, ed. Deborah Boedeker and David Sider, 242–254. Oxford: Oxford University Press.

Hutchinson, G. O. 2001. *Greek Lyric Poetry: A Commentary on Selected Larger Pieces*. Oxford: Oxford University Press.

Huxley, G. L. 1966. *The Early Ionians*. London: Faber and Faber.

———. 2001. Review of *The New Simonides: Contexts of Praise and Desire*, ed. by D. Boedeker and D. Sider. *Hermathena* 171: 69–78.

Jacoby, F. et al., eds. 1923–. *Die Fragmente der griecheschen Historiker*. Berlin and Leiden: Weidmann and Brill.

Janko, Richard. 1992. *The Iliad: A Commentary, Books 13–16*. Vol. 4 of *The Iliad: A Commentary*, ed. G.S. Kirk. Cambridge: Cambridge University Press.

Janssen, T. H., ed. 1989. *Timotheus: Persae, A Commentary*. Amsterdam: Hakkert.

Jeffery, L. H. 1990. *The Local Scripts of Archaic Greece: A Study of the Origin of the Greek Alphabet and Its Development from the Eight to the Fifth Centuries B.C.* Rev. ed., with supplement by J. W. Johnston. Oxford: Clarendon Press.

Johnstone, Hugh. 1997. "A Fragment of Simonides?" *CQ* 47: 293–295.

Junghahn, Emil August. 1869. *De Simonidis Cei epigrammatis quaestiones*. Berlin: F. Krüger.

Kaibel, G., ed. 1961–2. *Athenaei Naucratitae Dipnosophistae libri XV.* 3 vol., 1897–1890. Reprint, Stuttgart: Teubner.

Kassel, R and C. Austin. 1983–. *Poetae Comici Graeci*. Berlin: De Gruyter.

Kebric, Robert B. 1983. *The Paintings in the Cnidian Lesche at Delphi and Their Historical Context*. Mnemosyne Supplement, 68. Leiden: E. J. Brill.

Kegel, Willem Johannis Hendrik Fredrik. 1962. *Simonides*. Groningen: J. B. Wolters.

Kock, Theodor. 1880–1888. *Comicorum Atticorum Fragmenta.* 3 vol. Leipzig: Teubner.

Koster, W.J.W., ed. 1960–. *Scholia in Aristophanem.* Groningen: Bouma.

———. 1975. *Prolegomena de Comoedia.* Scholia In Aristophanem, 1.1A. Groningen: Bouma.

Krumbacher, Karl. 1897. *Geschichte der byzantinischen Literatur von Justinian bis zum ende des Oströmischen Reiches.* 2d ed. Handbuch der klassischen Altertums wissenschaft, 9.1. Munich: C.H. Beck.

Lazenby, J. F. 1993. *The Defense of Greece: 490–479 BCE.* Warminster: Aris and Phillps.

Lauriola, Rosanna. 1998. "Ricerche sul nuovo Simonide." *SCO* 46.3: 1111–1164.

Lefkowitz, Mary R. 1976. *The Victory Ode: An Introduction.* Park Ridge, NJ: Noyes Press.

Lemerle, Paul. 1986. *Byzantine Humanism: The First Phase.* Trans. Helen Lindsay and Ann Moffatt. Byzantina Australiensia, 3. Canbera: Australian Association for Byzantine Studies.

Lewis, D. M. 1987. "Bowie on Elegy: A Footnote." *JHS* 107: 188.

Lloyd-Jones, Hugh. 1994. "Notes on the New Simonides." *ZPE* 101: 1–3.

Lobel, E. 1954. "2327: Early Elegiacs." *The Oxyrhynchus Papyri* 22: 67–76.

———. 1981. "Simonides." In *Papyri Greek and Egyptian, Edited by Various Hands in Honour of Eric Gardner Turner.* Graeco-Roman Memoirs, 68. London: Egypt Exploration Society.

Luppe, W. 1993. "Zum neuesten Simonides. P.Oxy 3965 fr. 1 / 2327 fr. 6." *ZPE* 99: 1–9.

———. 1994. "Die Korinther in der Schlacht von Plataiai bei Simonides nach Plutarch (Simon. Fr. 15 und 16 W²; P.Oxy 3965 fr. 5)." *APF* 40: 21–24.

MacFarlane, Kelly Anne. 2002. "'To lay a Shining Foundation . . .': The Theme of the Persian Wars in Classical Greek Poetry. Ph.D. diss., University of Alberta, Edmonton.

MacLachlan, Bonnie. 2002. Review of *The New Simonides: Contexts of Praise and Desire,* ed. by D. Boedeker and D. Sider. *AJP* 123: 516–521.

Mace, Sarah. 2001. "Utopian and Erotic Fusion in a New Elegy by Simonides." In *The New Simonides: Contexts of Praise and Desire,* ed. Deborah Boedeker and David Sider, 185–207. Oxford: Oxford University Press.

Maehler, H. 1987–1989. *Pindari Carmina cum Fragmentis.* post B. Snell. 2 Vol. Leipzig: Teubner.

Marincola, John. 1996. "Introduction." In *Herodotus: The Histories,* trans. by Aubrey de Sélincourt. London: Penguin Books, ix–xxviii.

Matthaiou, A. P. 1986. "Δύο ἀρχαϊκές ἀττικές ἐπιτύμβιες στῆλες." *HOROS* 4: 31–34.

———. 1990–1991. "'Αμβρακίας ἐλεγεῖον." *HOROS* 8–9: 271–277.

Matthews, Victor J., ed. 1974. *Panyassis of Halikarnassos: Text and Commentary.* Leiden: Brill.

Meiggs, Russell. 1975. *The Athenian Empire.* corr. ed. Oxford: Clarendon Press.

Meiggs, Russell and David Lewis, eds. 1988. *A Selection of Greek Historical Inscriptions to the End of the Fifth Century B.C.* Oxford: Clarendon Press, 1975. Reprint, Oxford: Clarendon Press.

Meineke, A., ed. 1839–1857. *Fragmenta Comicorum Graecorum.* 5 vol. Berlin: Reimer.

Michelakis, Pantelis. 2002. *Achilles in Greek Tragedy.* Cambridge Classical Studies. Cambridge: Cambridge University Press.

Migne, J.-P., ed. 1896–1900. *Patrologiae Cursus Completus.* Vols. 101–104, *Photii Constantinopolitani Patriarchae Opera Omnia.* Paris: Garnier.

Molyneux, John H. 1992. *Simonides: A Historical Study.* Wauconda: Bolchazy-Carducci.

Murray, G., ed. 1955. *Aeschyli septem quae supersunt tragoediae.* 2d ed. Oxford: Clarendon Press.

Nagy, Gregory. 1974. *Comparative Studies in Greek and Indic Meter.* Harvard Studies in Comparative Literature, 33. Cambridge. Mass.: Harvard University Press.

―――. 1990. *Pindar's Homer.* Baltimore: The Johns Hopkins University Press.

―――. 1996. *Homeric Questions.* Austin: University of Texas Press.

―――. 1999. *Best of the Achaeans.* rev. ed. Baltimore: The Johns Hopkins University Press.

Nietzsche, Friedrich. 1867. "Zur Geschischte der Theognideischen Spruchsammlung." *RhM* 22: 161–200.

Novati, F. 1879. "Index Fabularum Aristophanis ex Codice Ambrosiano L 39 Sup." *Hermes* 14: 461–464.

Obbink, Dirk. 1988. "Hermarchus, *Against Empedocles.*" *CQ* 38: 428–435.

―――. 1998. Images of POxy vol. 59. At http://www.csad.ac.uk/POxy/ (cited June 29, 2002).

―――. 2001. "The Genre of Plataea: Generic Unity in the New Simonides." In *The New Simonides: Contexts of Praise and Desire,* ed. Deborah Boedeker and David Sider, 65–85. Oxford: Oxford University Press.

O'Hara, James J. 1998. " Venus or the Muse as 'Ally' (Lucr. 1.24, Simon. Frag. Eleg. 11.20–22 W)." *CP* 93: 69–74.

Oliver, J. H. 1935. "Greek Inscriptions" *Hesperia* 4.1: 5–90.

Olson, S. Douglas, ed. 2002. *Aristophanes: Acharnians.* Oxford: Oxford University Press.

Owen, A. S., ed. 1939. *Euripides: Ion.* Oxford: Clarendon Press.

Page, D. L. 1936. "The Elegiacs in Euripides' *Andromache.*" In *Greek Poetry and Life: Essays Presented to Gilbert Murray on his Seventieth Birthday,* 206–230. Oxford: Clarendon Press.

―――. 1951. "Simonidea." *JHS* 71: 133–142.

―――., ed. 1952. *Euripides: Medea.* Oxford: Clarendon Press.

―――., ed. 1967. *Poetae Melici Graeci.* Oxford: Clarendon Press.

―――, ed. 1972. *Aeschyli septem quae supersunt tragoedias.* Oxord: Clarendon Press.

―――, ed. 1974. *Supplementum Lyricis Graecis.* Oxford: Clarendon Press.

―――, ed. 1981. *Further Greek Epigrams.* Cambridge: Cambridge University Press.

Parker, Robert. 1987. "Myths of Athens." In *Interpretations of Greek Mythology,* ed. Jan Bremmer, 187–214. London: Croom Helm.

Parsons, P. J. 1992. "3965: Simonides, *Elegies.*" *The Oxyrhynchus Papyri* 59: 4–50.

―――. 2001. "'These Fragments We Have Shored against Our Ruin.'" In *The New Simonides: Contexts of Praise and Desire,* ed. Deborah Boedeker and David Sider, 55–64. Oxford: Oxford University Press.

Pavese, Carlo Odo. 1995. "Elegia di Simonide agli Spartiati per Platea." *ZPE* 107: 1–26.

―――. 1996. "Addenda et Corrigenda a 'Elegia di Simonide per gli Spartiati a Platea, *ZPE* 107 (1995) 1–26.'" *ZPE* 112:56–58.

Peek, Werner, ed. 1955. *Greek Verse Inscriptions.* Vol. 1. Berlin, 1988 Reprint, Chicago: Ares.

―――. 1976. "Grabepigramm aus Selinus." *ZPE* 22: 93–94.

Petrovic, Andrej. 2004. Kommentar zu den simonideischen Versinschriften. Ph.D. diss., Ruprecht-Karls-Universität, Heidelberg.

Pfeiffer, R., ed. 1949–1953. *Callimachus.* 2 vol. Oxford: Clarendon Press.

―――. 1968. *History of Classical Scholarship from the Beginnings to the End of the Hellenistic Age.* Oxford: Clarendon Press.

Pickard-Cambridge, Arthur. 1968. *The Dramatic Festivals of Athens.* 2d ed. rev. by J. Gould and D.M. Lewis. Oxford: Clarendon Press.

Podlecki, A. J. 1968. " Simonides: 480." *Historia* 17: 257–275.

————, trans. 1970. *The Persians by Aeschylus.* Englewood Cliffs, N.J.: Prentice-Hall.

————. 1984. *The Early Greek Poets and Their Times.* Vancouver: University of British Columbia Press.

Poltera, Orlando. 1997. *Le langage de Simonide.* Bern: Lang.

Race, W. H., trans. 1997. *Pindar.* 2 vol. Loeb Classical Library. Cambridge, Mass.: Harvard University Press.

Raubitschek, A. E. 1968. "Das Denkmal-Epigramm." In *L'épigramme grecque.* Entretiens sur l'antiquité classique 14, (Genève: Foundation Hardt, 1968): 3–36. Reprinted in *The School of Hellas,* ed. D. Obbink and P. A. Vander Waerdt, 245–65. New York: Oxford University Press.

Reitzenstein, R. 1893. *Epigramm und Skolion.* Geisen: J. Ricker'Sche Buchandlung.

Rhodes, P. J. 1985. *The Athenian Empire.* Greece and Rome, New Surveys in Classics, 17. Oxford: Clarendon Press.

Roberts, W. Rhys. 1920. *Eleven Words on Simonides: An Address Given to the Branch at an Opening Meeting in the University of Leeds on 21 October 1919.* Cambridge: Cambridge University Press.

Rosenmeyer, T. G. 1968. "Elegiac and Elegos" In *California Studies in Classical Antiquity.* Vol. 1, 217–31. Berkeley: University of California Press.

Rösler, Wolfgang. 1990. "Mnemosyne in the Symposion." In *Sympotica: A Symposium on the Symposion,* ed. Oswyn Murray, 230–37. Oxford: Clarendon Press.

Russo, Joseph, Manuel Fernández-Galiano and Alfred Heubeck. 1992. *A Commentary on Homer's Odyssey.* Vol. 3. Books XVII–XXIV. Oxford: Clarendon Press.

Rutherford, Ian. 1990. "*Paeans* by Simonides." *HSCP* 93:169–209.

————. 2001a. "The New Simonides: Toward a Commentary." In *The New Simonides: Contexts of Praise and Desire,* ed. Deborah Boedeker and David Sider, 33–54. Oxford: Oxford University Press.

————. 2001b. *Pindar's Paeans: A Reading of the Fragments with a Survey of the Genre.* Oxford: Oxford University Press.

Salvato, Ester. 1998. "Simonide, l'elegia per Platea." *A&R* 43: 110–126.

Sandys, John Edwin. 1906. *A History of Classical Scholarship from the Sixth Century B.C. to the End of the Middles Ages.* 2d ed. Cambridge: Cambridge University Press.

Sbardella, Livio. 2000. "Achille gli eroi di Platea: Simonide, frr. 10–11 W²." *ZPE* 129: 1–11.

Schachter, Albert. 1998. " Simonides' Elegy on Plataia: The Occasion of Its Performance." *ZPE* 123: 25–30.

Schalmzriedt, E. 1970. *Peri physeos: Zur Frühgeschichte der Buchtitel.* Munich: Fink.

Schneider, Otto. 1870–1873. *Callimachea.* 2 vol. Leipzig: Teubner.

Schneidewin, F. G., ed. 1835. *Simonidis Cei Carminum Reliquiae.* Brunswick: Friderick Viewig et filius.

Schein, Seth. 1984. *The Mortal Hero: An Introduction to Homer's Iliad.* Berkeley: University of California Press.

Scherer, Karl. 1886. *De Aelio Dionysio musico qui vocatur.* Ph.D. diss., Universitas Fridericia Guilelmia Rhenana.

Schmidt, Freidrich. 1922. *Die Pinakes des Callimachos.* Klassisch-Philologische Studien, 1. Berlin: Ebering.

Schroeter, Wilhelm. 1906. *De Simonidis Cei melici sermone quaestiones.* Leipzig: Robert Noske.

Sens, Alexander, ed. 1997. *Theocritus: Dioscuri ('Idyll 22'): Introduction, Text, and Commentary.* Göttingen: Vandenhoeck and Ruprecht.

Sharples, R. W. 1998. *Theophrastus of Eresus: Sources for his Life, Writings, Thought and Influence: Commentary Volume 3.1, Sources on Physics (Texts 137–223)*. Leiden: Brill.

Shaw, P.-J. 2001. "Lords of Hellas, Old Men of the Sea: The Occasion of Simonides' Elegy on Plataea." In *The New Simonides: Contexts of Praise and Desire*, ed. Deborah Boedeker and David Sider, 164–182. Oxford: Oxford University Press.

Sider, David, ed. 2001a. "Fragments 1–22 W²: Text, Apparatus Criticus, and Translation." In *The New Simonides: Contexts of Praise and Desire*, ed. Deborah Boedeker and David Sider, 13–29. Oxford: Oxford University Press.

———. 2001b. "'As is the Generation of Leaves' in Homer, Simonides, Horace, and Stobaios." In *The New Simonides: Contexts of Praise and Desire*, ed. Deborah Boedeker and David Sider, 272–288. Oxford: Oxford University Press.

———. Unpublished. "The New Simonides and the Question of Historical Elegy." 1–25.

Smyth, H. W. 1956. *Greek Grammar*. Rev. by Gordon M. Messing. Cambridge, Mass.: Harvard University Press.

———., ed. 1963. *Greek Melic Poets*. New York. Biblo and Tannen.

Sokolowski, Franciszek, ed. 1962. *Lois sacrées des cites grecques*. Supplément. Paris: De Boccard.

Sommerstein, Allan., ed. 1980. *Aristophanes Acharnians*. The Comedies of Aristophanes, 1. Warminster: Aris and Phillips.

Stansbury-O'Donnell, Mark D. 1990. "Polygnotus' *Nekyia*: A Reconstruction and Analysis." *AJA* 94: 213–235.

Stehle, Eva M. 1996. "Help me to Sing, Muse, of Plataea." *Arethusa* 29: 205–222.

———. 2001. "A Bard of the Iron Age and His Auxiliary Muse." In *The New Simonides: Contexts of Praise and Desire*, ed. Deborah Boedeker and David Sider, 106–119. Oxford: Oxford University Press.

Stella, L. A. 1946. "Studi Simonidei." *RFIC* 24: 1–24.

Suárez de la Torre, Emilio. 1998. "El adjetivo ἐπώνυμος en la elegía por la batalla de Platea de Simónides (fr. 11.17 West²)." *Lexis* 16: 29–32.

Ternavasio, Daniela. 1998. "Contesto di esecuzione e committenza del De Proelio Plataico di Simonide: una nuova proposta." In *Quaderni di filologia, linguistica e tradizione (Università degli Studi di Torino)*, 17–30. Bologna: Pàton.

Tod, Marcus, ed. 1948. *A Selection of Greek Historical Inscriptions*. Vol. 2. Oxford: Clarendon Press.

———., ed. 1951. *A Selection of Greek Historical Inscriptions*. Vol. 1. 2d ed. Oxford: Clarendon Press.

Vetta, M. 1983. "Introduzione: Poesia simposiale nella Grecia arcaica e classica." In *Poesia e simposia nella Grecia antica*, Universale Laterza, 621, xi–lx. Rome: Laterza.

Völker, Herald. 2003. *Himerios: Reden und Fragmente: Einführung, Übersetzung und Kommentar*. Serta Graeca, Beiträge zur Erforschung griechischer Text, 17. Wiesbaden: Ludwig Reichert.

Wachsmuth, C. 1867. "De Fontibus ex quibus Suidas in Scriptorum Graecorum Observationes per Saturam Factae." In *Symbola Philologorum Bonnensium in Honorem Friderici Ritschelii*, 135–152.

Weiden, M. J. H. van der, ed. 1991. *The Dithyrambs of Pindar*. Amsterdam: J. C. Gieben.

Wendel, Carl, ed. 1914. *Scholia in Theocritum Vetera*. Leipzig: Teubner.

———, ed. 1958. *Scholia in Apollonium Rhodium Vetera*. 2d ed. Berlin: Weidmann.

West, M. L., ed. 1969. *Hesiod: Theogony*. Oxford: Clarendon Press.

————, ed. 1971–1972. *Iambi et Elegi Graeci.* 2 Vols. Oxford: Oxford University Press.

————. 1974. *Studies in Greek Elegy and Iambus.* Berlin: Walter de Gruyter.

————. 1982. *Greek Metre.* Oxford: Clarendon Press.

————, ed. 1989–1992. *Iambi et Elegi Graeci.* 2d ed. 2 Vols. Oxford: Oxford University Press.

————, ed. 1990. *Aeschyli Tragoediae cum Incerti Poetae Prometheo,* Stuttgart: Teubner.

————, trans. 1993a. *Greek Lyric Poetry: The poems and fragments of the Greek iambic, elegiac, and melic poets (excluding Pindar and Bacchylides) down to 450.* Oxford: Oxford University Press.

————. 1993b. "Simonides Redivivus." *ZPE* 98: 1–14.

Wilamowitz-Moellendorf, Ulrich von. 1879. "Index Fabularum Aristophanis ex Codice Ambrosiano L 39 Sup." *Hermes* 14: 463–464.

————, ed. 1903. *Timotheos: Die Perser aus einem Papyrus von Abusir.* Leipzig: J. C. Hinrichs.

————. 1913. *Sappho und Simonides.* Berlin, 1966 Reprint, Berlin: Weidmann.

————, ed. 1914. *Aeschyli Tragoediae.* Berlin: Weidmann.

Willemsen, H. 1963. "Archaische Grabmalbasen aus der Athener Stadtmauer." *AM* 78: 104–153.

Wilson, N. G. 1996. *Scholars of Byzantium.* Rev. ed. London: Duckworth.

Yatromanolakis, Dimitrios. 2001. "To Sing or to Mourn? A Reappraisal of Simonides 22 W$^2$." In *The New Simonides: Contexts of Praise and Desire,* ed. Deborah Boedeker and David Sider, 208–225. Oxford: Oxford University Press.

# Index to Appendix

# Index to Figures

# General Index

# Index Locorum

Numbers in italics refer to ancient sources; numbers in Roman font indicate pages in this volume. Ancient texts included in the appendix under the heading "sources" have not been catalogued here unless they are mentioned elsewhere in the text.

## A

Aelian
 *Varia Historia 9.41,* 162 n. 11
Aelius Aristides
 *Orationes 32.2 see* Simonides 528 *PMG*
 *scholium on III 154–5 Dindorf, see* Simonides
  VIII *FGE*
Aeschylus
 *Persae 178,* 81, 82; *182–83,* 82 n. 115;
  *226–245,* 81; *285,* 189 n. 108;
  *353–432,* 81; *395,* 38; *447–479,* 81;
  *472–479,* 81; *473–6,* 82–3; *481,* 26,
  170 n. 9; *496,* 31; *563,* 189 n. 114;
  *728,* 81; *807,* 83; *816–17,* 82 n.
  116, 83; *824,* 81; *898,* 189 n. 114;
  *950–1,* 189 n. 114; *1011,* 189 n.
  114; *1025,* 189 n. 114;
 *vita Aeschyli* 3 n. 15, 12–13, 52, 164 n. 33,
  202 n. 68
 *I FGE,* 160
Anacreon
 *eleg. fr. 2 W²,* 122
*Anthologia Palatina*
 *4.1.8, see* Simonides T 36
 *6.50, see* Simonides XV *FGE*
 *7.251, see* Simonides IX *FGE*
 *7.253, see* Simonides VII FGE
 *9.184.5, see* Simonides T 42
 *9.571, see* Simonides T 43
Apollonius Rhodius
 *1.148,* 182 n.13
 *scholium on 1.211–15c (Wendel),* 23–24, 204
  n. 92, *see also* Simonides 534 *PMG*

 *scholium on 1.583–4a (Wendel), see* Simonides
  fr. 1 W² and 635 *PMG*
 *scholium on 1.763 (Wendel),* 168 n. 181, *see
  also* Simonides 540 *PMG*
 *scholium on 4.814–15a (Wendel), see* Simonides 558 *PMG*
Archilochus
 *fr. 1 W²,* 122
 *fr. 2 W²,* 122
 *fr. 3 W²,* 122
 *fr. 4 W²,* 122, 171 n. 32
 *fr. 5 W²,* 122
 *frs. 286–9 W²,* 185 n. 56
Aristophanes
 *Aves 218,* 200 n. 38
 *Nubes 553–4,* 173 n. 56
 *Pax 695–701,* 174 n. 64, *see also* Simonides
  T 22
 *scholium on Acharnians 104,* 81, 189
  n. 111; *106,* 189 n. 111; *637,*
  192 n. 64
 *scholium on Pax 825, see* Ion of Chios *IEG²*
  2: 79
Aristotle
 *Nichomachaean Ethics 4.1.27,* 161 n. 7
 *Politics 1306b36–1307a2,* 70, *see also* Tyrtaeus
  fr. 1 W²
 *Rhetoric 1391A, see* Simonides T 47d
Athenaeus
 *6.252C,* 165 n. 38–9
 *12.536A, see* Simonides XXXIX *FGE*
 *13.610C,* 185 n. 56
 *14.656D–E, see* Simonides T23

# Index of Greek Words and Phrases